The Atomic Human

The Atomic Human

Understanding Ourselves in the Age of AI

NEIL D. LAWRENCE

ALLEN LANE
an imprint of
PENGUIN BOOKS

ALLEN LANE

UK | USA | Canada | Ireland | Australia
India | New Zealand | South Africa

Penguin Books is part of the Penguin Random House group of companies
whose addresses can be found at global.penguinrandomhouse.com.

Penguin
Random House
UK

First published by Allen Lane 2024

003

Copyright © Neil D. Lawrence, 2024

The moral right of the author has been asserted

Set in 12/14.75pt Dante MT Std
Typeset by Jouve (UK), Milton Keynes
Printed and bound in Great Britain by Clays Ltd, Elcograf S.p.A.

The authorized representative in the EEA is Penguin Random House Ireland,
Morrison Chambers, 32 Nassau Street, Dublin D02 YH68

A CIP catalogue record for this book is available from the British Library

ISBN: 978-0-241-62524-8

To Valerie, Mark and Garth

Contents

Prologue

December 8th, 2013: Penthouse Suite, Harrah's Casino, Stateline, Nevada. This was the moment at which I became an artificial intelligence researcher. Or, at least, the moment when the research field I work in started calling itself 'artificial intelligence'.

I was at the casino for a scientific meeting called Neural Information Processing Systems, the main international machine-learning conference. I'd attended every year for sixteen years, and I'd just been asked to chair it the following year. But the community I was leading was about to take a major turn.

A handful of global experts had been invited to Mark Zuckerberg's penthouse suite. Corporate events were not uncommon at the conference: after all, Stateline, on the south-eastern shore of Lake Tahoe, is where Nevada borders California and is only a four-hour drive from Silicon Valley. But this Facebook gathering had a different feel. Twelve months earlier, a breakthrough study had been published, a step-change in the computer's capability to digest information. Computers were now able to discern objects in images – finally, computers could see. You could present them with a picture, and they might (correctly) tell you it contained, for instance, a container ship, or a leopard, or some mushrooms. The key advance emerged from an approach known as 'deep learning'. This works in the opposite way to how an artist paints. Artists compose pictures from brushstrokes; deep learning decomposes images into mathematical signatures that give the *essence* of an object. The team that delivered the result quickly formed a company. It was bought by Google in a multimillion-dollar deal.

Our new millennium's medium of communication is images, videos, text messages and likes, and deep learning now gave us the ability to read the images being shared by Facebook's users, potentially allowing the company to *understand* what its users were sharing without having to manually view the hundreds of millions of photographs on the site. The knock-on effects, not only in terms of advertising and moderation but in many other aspects, could be enormous.

Facebook's rival, Google, had stolen a march on it by buying up the talent that made this breakthrough. Facebook was about to make its response. It was a gamble, a major investment in a new direction. That was why we were in the penthouse suite: Facebook was going all in on machine learning, all in on deep learning. To show the company was serious, the small group assembled at the top of Harrah's Casino included Facebook's Chief Technology Officer, Mike Schroepfer, and their 29-year-old CEO, Mark Zuckerberg.

The plan was simple. Recruit one of the principal researchers driving the revolution in machine learning. Unveil them as the head of Facebook's new research lab, then develop and monetize this new technology which could radically change the platform. They chose Yann LeCun, a professor from New York University with twenty-five years' experience in the field. Yann's early career had been spent working at Bell Labs, developing the ideas that would deliver deep learning's success. He would go on to win the 2018 Turing Award, the 'Nobel Prize of Computer Science', for this work, but five years earlier in Harrah's, the attention was not from his academic peers but from industry. Having known Yann for fifteen years, the words that came out of his mouth when he launched the lab surprised me. He was quite specific: 'The new lab will be focused on advancing AI.'

AI – artificial intelligence. This wasn't to be a machine-learning research lab, or a deep-learning research lab. It chose to call itself 'Facebook AI Research', and at that moment the die was cast.

The term 'artificial intelligence' has a chequered history. Classical AI techniques relied on logical reasoning about the world, like a silicon version of Sherlock Holmes. Outcomes were deduced through weighing evidence according to the strict rules of mathematical

logic. But while Sherlock Holmes's deductions may make an entertaining read in a detective novel, they prove to be very brittle when
deployed on real-world problems. The world we live in is more
complex and nuanced than a simplistic logical representation can
accommodate. Back in 2013, my community, the machine learners,
associated the term 'AI' with a group of researchers that had heavily over-promised and considerably under-delivered. Despite these
failings, AI had maintained a strong hold on the popular imagination. Perhaps Yann wanted to capitalize on that, but the term
comes loaded with cultural baggage. Past promises have led to representations on film and in literature that, like Sherlock Holmes,
entertain but mislead us about the nature of intelligence. So what is
intelligence – and what is artificial intelligence? One of the major
challenges when writing about intelligence is that 'intelligent'
means different things to different people in different contexts.
In this book, I will look at how this shapes – and sometimes
distorts – our perceptions of what artificial intelligence is, and what
it can be. That's why sometimes I refer to machine intelligence
instead of artificial intelligence. I am hoping that a fresh term will
bring fresh understanding.

Henry Ford built his eponymous car company around the principles of mass production, creating the first widely affordable car,
the Model T. When designing it, the story goes that if he had asked
his customers what they wanted, they would have asked for 'a faster
horse'. If Henry Ford were selling us machine intelligence today,
would the customer call for 'a smarter human'? On that evening in
Nevada, Mark Zuckerberg was the customer: he was buying an AI
lab, so just what did he think he was getting for his money?

Zuckerberg spent the event glad-handing potential recruits and
outlining his vision for Facebook. At one point I stood listening to
him, standing alongside two friends and colleagues, both long-time
academics in the machine-learning world. Max Welling was a professor at the University of Amsterdam and Zoubin Ghahramani a
professor at the University of Cambridge. Zuckerberg laid out his
vision to the three of us, one of an interconnected world. A pure,

single-minded vision. I was reminded of listening to a very bright graduate student, one who was flexing the new-found intellectual freedoms offered at university, imagining the changes their ideas would bring to the world. I had to resist my conditioned response. Normally, I enthuse about my students' dreams but warn of the reality of the challenges they are likely to face. Encouragement and guidance. That evening, I was listening to a billionaire who had already connected a fifth of the world's population to one another. His dream had already been realized, and artificial intelligence was a new frontier for him to assimilate within his ambitions.

And it wasn't only Facebook that was turning its focus to AI. Within a month there was another announcement, in London. Google had built on its initial investment by spending a further $500 million on a London-based start-up, DeepMind. This ambitious venture had the stated aim to first solve intelligence, then use it to solve everything else. But what does this tag line even mean? Can intelligence be 'solved'? Is it like a crossword puzzle, where the words just need to be slotted into place? I'm uncomfortable with that idea. I prefer to think of it as a riddle, where the wording of the riddle itself might be misleading you.

In retrospect, for me, that December day in Nevada was the start of a journey. Since then, my research field has transformed into something unrecognizable from its beginnings. That conference in 2013 attracted a record 2,000 delegates. Six years later, there were 13,000 attendees, and a long waiting list. As the meeting has changed, our community has also had to change: machine learning has become more important within society. Algorithms we develop are now widely deployed. Not only on social networks but in robotic systems and driverless cars. These algorithms have a direct effect on our lives and on our deaths. Most recently, the techniques we have developed have been able to pass the Turing Test, a long-time flagship challenge in AI. Zoubin went on to be Uber's first Chief Scientist and now leads Google's AI division. Max became Vice President of Machine Learning at Qualcomm and is now a

Distinguished Scientist at Microsoft. I spent three years heading up an Amazon machine-learning division. Facebook's wooing of us would, as it turned out, presage a movement across the tech industries and the wider world: one that we're still just at the beginning of.

I.

Gods and Robots

At the centre of the Sistine Chapel's ceiling, far above your head, is probably the most famous image of God and Adam. It depicts the creation story from Genesis: in the Bible, man is described as being formed of the dust from the ground, with God blowing the breath of life into his nostrils. The great Renaissance artist Michelangelo represented God in classical form on the chapel's ceiling. A white man with a large white beard and a flowing robe, God reaches out to touch the finger of a languid Adam, who reclines on a hillside.

Today, society is focused on a different form of creation – the realization of machine intelligence – and for *this* creation we form our own modern images. There was a time when the lead image of just about every article on artificial intelligence was a red-eyed android. While God breathed life into Adam, James Cameron's Terminator was created to snuff out life from humanity.[1]

These two images are separated by five centuries, and they are opposites: God is creator; the Terminator is created. God is our patron; the robot our nemesis. But the images have a thread of commonality to them, one that is intrinsically linked to a key characteristic of human intelligence.

Machines automate human labour, and we can trace the history of automation to the period when Michelangelo was finishing the Sistine Chapel ceiling. In his time, any image that was created had to be manually rendered: the Sistine Chapel ceiling was painted in fresco by the artist lying on his back. The Terminator, by contrast, was rendered by machine-augmented special effects and a film camera. It can be reproduced almost instantaneously wherever it is required.

Yet the efficient reproduction of images and text dates back to Michelangelo's lifetime. When he was painting the ceiling the printing press was already becoming popular. Initially it was used for the reproduction of biblical texts, but it was soon employed to automate the work of writing indulgences – promissory notes granted by the Catholic Church intended to provide relief in Purgatory for earthly sin. The printing press allowed for widespread sale of indulgences, which no longer had to be laboriously copied. The proceeds were used to fund one of Michelangelo's later commissions: the dome of St Peter's Basilica in Rome.

The printing press automated the copying of writing and so facilitated the rapid exchange of information. The high-pressure tactics used to promote the sale of indulgences led, both directly and indirectly, to the Protestant Reformation. But the printing press also enabled classical works on mathematics, logic and science to be widely shared. The printed word propelled Europe from the Renaissance to the Enlightenment. Literacy increased, and, from da Vinci to Kepler to Newton, innovation transferred across generations.

Printing removed a blockage on our ideas, allowing them to flow more freely across time and distance, and leading eventually to our modern, technology-driven society. Photography and film cameras automated the creation of images, removing obstacles to the labour of creation. The printing press automated the sharing of the written word, releasing our ideas. Artificial intelligence is the automation of decision-making, and it is unblocking the bottleneck of human choices.

In this book I will explain how artificial intelligence does this, and what it means for the human left behind. More specifically, the book is about *human* intelligence, through the lens of the artificial – and whether there is an essence of the human that can't be replaced by the machine.

To better understand human intelligence, I will look closer at the perils, pitfalls and potential of a future that is already here: the future of AI. To understand that future I will look at stories from the past, using them to develop our understanding of what artificial intelligence is and how it differs from our human intelligence.

In 1995, when he was Editor-in-Chief of *Elle* magazine in France, Jean-Dominique Bauby suffered a stroke that destroyed his brain-stem. He became almost totally paralysed, but he remained mentally active, suffering from what is known as locked-in syndrome. The only movement he could voluntarily make was to wink with his left eyelid. From his hospital bed, incredibly *after* he became paralysed, Bauby wrote a memoir, *Le Scaphandre et le papillon* (*The Diving Bell and the Butterfly*).

It took Michelangelo four years, lying on his back, to paint the Sistine Chapel ceiling. Bauby's book was written in the same supine position from his sanatorium bed. Over ten months, in sessions that lasted four hours a day, Bauby winked to indicate a letter on an alphabet grid to spell out the words.

His ability to communicate was severely curtailed. He could think as freely as each of us, but he couldn't share his ideas. A diving suit[2] is a claustrophobic space where communication with fellow humans is limited. For Bauby, the diving suit represented how it felt to be restricted in this way. The butterfly represented the freedom of his internal thoughts, his ability to retreat into memories and dreams. *The Diving Bell and the Butterfly* gives us an insight into a state of isolation, physically constrained but mentally free.

Stories of locked-in syndrome seem to have a fascination for us. I think this reflects our fears of being in a similar state. So, it may surprise you to learn that we are all already in that state. Our intelligence, too, is heavily constrained in its ability to communicate. Each of us is, in a sense, a butterfly within a diving suit.

Today, written words are spread not just by the printing press but by a network of electronic machines that communicate almost instantaneously across the globe. This network allows us to view Michelangelo's ceiling, or James Cameron's Terminator, wherever we are. To share these images, we have built an international infra-structure that carries information through the heavens, across the sky, under the seas and over land. Whether through satellites, mobile phones, undersea cables or copper telephone lines, our images and words are converted into digital streams and propagated around the planet.

Early communication networks were built by the Bell Telephone Company, and laying the cables was expensive. Telephone companies needed to estimate how much information was moving between cities so they could plan how many cables to lay, so they needed a way of quantifying the information to be carried. Claude Shannon, an American engineer who worked at Bell Labs, where Yann LeCun would find himself many years later, came up with a mathematical representation of information to help quantify the content the telecommunications cables were to convey. We call it *information theory*. He suggested information should be separated from its original context: it should be rendered not as a word or a sound but as a 1 or a 0. He called each 1 or 0 a *bit* of information.

In the moment I share the result of a coin toss, where 1 represents heads and 0 tails, you gain a single bit of information. This holds for any result from any two equally probable outcomes. If the odds of a tennis player winning a match are even, then learning that they've won gives you one bit of information. The quantity of information doesn't depend on whether you're a fan of the particular player, how you feel about the match, or even whether you're interested in tennis. Shannon's idea was to quantify information in a *universal* manner, in a way that doesn't depend on circumstance.

Shannon was interested in maximizing the amount of information we can share across the telephone network, but he also quantified the amount of information we share in our language. He estimated that the average word in English contains twelve bits of information. That's the same as we find in twelve coin tosses.

Jean-Dominique Bauby wrote his autobiography at an average pace of two minutes per word. This means that he was sharing information at a rate of six bits a minute. In computing, the technical term for this rate of communication is *bandwidth*. If Bauby had been able to dictate his biography, he would have communicated with a higher bandwidth. Speech rates vary between 100 and 200 words per minute, so we can speak words 300 times faster than Bauby could communicate them through winking. We can share around 2,000 bits of information per minute. Bauby is around 300 times more 'locked in' than we are.

But the bandwidth comparison I'm more interested in is not between Bauby and us, but between us and the interloping machine. Although machines use different methods – Wi-Fi or cables – we can measure the machine's communication rate in the same terms. Machines can communicate with each other at a rate of 60 *billion* bits per minute. They are 30 *million* times faster than we are.

These numbers can be hard to digest. To give a sense of scale, think of these information budgets in terms of money. Let's map these communication bandwidths on to monthly salaries. Bauby's salary would be $6 a month, an amount even stingy parents would be ashamed to be giving in pocket money. Your information bandwidth translates to around $2,000 a month. By European or North American standards, that would be a relatively low salary, but one many families across the world live on today. In comparison, the computer has a stratospheric salary. The machine earns the net worth of the world's richest person every few months. The computer's salary is closer to the UK government's total annual national budget than to any individual's salary. It could fund the entire UK social and healthcare service, national defence, the national science budget, and still have change left for constructing and maintaining assorted airports, railway lines and national road networks.

Our information budget is impressive in comparison to Bauby's, but it pales in comparison to the machine's. However, being locked in also implies that there are thoughts to be shared. To Bauby these thoughts are the butterfly – his ability to think and to dream, to let his mind roam beyond the confines of his physical body. If he thinks nothing, there is nothing to share. So, to understand how locked in we are, we must compare our ability to *think* with the machine's ability to *compute*.

Thoughts are ill-defined concepts, so the comparison is challenging.

But our thoughts stem from the operation of our brains, from the interconnection of billions of neurons that fire in tandem to represent and respond to the world around us. We can estimate how large a computer we would need to simulate all that activity. Our best guess is that for a machine to simulate all the computations occurring in our brain, it would require the computational capacity of the UK's Met Office supercomputer in Exeter in south-west England. When it was built in 2016 this machine was the eleventh fastest in the world. It spends its mornings computing the weather across that world and its afternoons simulating our future climates. A machine this vast is required to simulate our brains: a typical computer is many thousands of times slower.

So, when it comes to our cognitive capabilities, we can think of our brains as analogous to a Formula One racing-car engine: immense power in a small package. But when it comes to our ability to share our thoughts, to distribute information – our ability to deploy our intelligence in practice – we should think of a Formula One car but one mounted on spindly bicycle wheels which force it to choose carefully how and when it deploys its power. The computer is lower-powered, with a small go-kart engine, but its ability to distribute that power is well matched to its engine. It can deploy its cognitive power directly on to the track.

The art to our human intelligence is controlling and wielding our immense cognitive power, given the limit on our ability to communicate – the fundamental constraint on human intelligence that defines who we are. Our intelligence is locked in; the computer's is not. Modern machine-intelligence systems are exploiting the machine's large bandwidth to examine datasets that are beyond any individual human's ability to absorb.

It is this constraint that leads to the power of those two images of God and the Terminator. One is rendered in paint on wet plaster, the other on 35mm film, but both reflect a fundamental aspect of our intelligence that cannot be emulated by a machine. It is an aspect that comes from our locked-in state, one that emerges from a particular human weakness. In both of those images we are *embodying* intelligence. The painting of God embodies the supernatural intelligence described in the Bible. The image of the Terminator embodies artificial intelligence. When we imagine these unfamiliar intelligences, supernatural and artificial, we envisage them as originating from bodily forms.

I call the ratio of computational to communication ability the *embodiment factor*; it represents how isolated our individual intelligences are from those of our fellow humans. It represents how embodied we all are in our physical persona. The embodiment factor is fundamental to understanding the nature of our intelligence. In the original Hebrew, the breath of life that came from God also has a connotation as *spirit*. Although not a believer, I have sympathy with the idea that there is a spirit within us that cannot be replaced by a machine. Machines already have the capacity to displace us physically – we have invented combine harvesters, mechanical looms, robots that build cars – and with the development of artificial intelligence machines are now able to displace us in our mental work. Modern computers absorb information about humans at an unimaginable scale. Their capacity to consume and process that information renders the printing press, so vital to our development, a laughable anachronism. The latest machine-learning models, such as ChatGPT, are known as large-language models. They have absorbed an internet of human written knowledge and can converse like a human. This leads to a question: is there a part of us, a piece of being human, that is specific to us and cannot be emulated by the machine?

In the fifth century BCE, the Greek philosopher Democritus posed a similar question about our physical universe. He imagined cutting physical matter into pieces in a repeated process: cutting a piece, then taking one of the cut pieces and cutting it again so that each time it becomes smaller and smaller. Democritus believed this process had to stop somewhere, that we would be left with an indivisible piece. The Greek word for indivisible is *atom*, and so this theory was called *atomism*. This book considers this question, but in a different domain, asking: As the machine slices away portions of human capabilities, are we left with a kernel of humanity, an indivisible piece that can no longer be divided into parts? Or does the human disappear altogether? If we are left with something, then that uncuttable piece, a form of atomic human, would tell us something about our human spirit.

Where, exactly, does the atomic human lie?

That is the question I will examine in this book. We can better understand ourselves by dividing away tasks that can be done by the computer. We can search for our atomic core by understanding other intelligences. We have already introduced the first major difference between us and the machine: our (in)ability to communicate. We've seen that our intelligence is *embodied*, and that we like to represent other intelligences as embodied. But this embodied representation is misleading, and it's not the only misleading aspect of the term 'intelligence'.

Rightly, society has started paying much more attention to what artificial intelligence is and what it does. Other academic fields, members of the wider public, companies and governments all now take a keen interest in developments in machine learning. It's become impossible for me to escape my work; even sitting in the sun in my garden reading a book I can overhear my neighbours talking about AI.

To better understand this riddle, I began giving public talks about AI. I worked out ways of explaining what machine intelligence can and cannot do. I doubled down on my efforts to work with real-world applications of machine intelligence. I knew that, just like classical AI approaches, our modern methods would exhibit some brittleness when deployed. How would the limitations of this new wave of AI manifest themselves? The journey has taken me from my academic position as Professor of Machine Learning in Sheffield, through three years building AI solutions for Amazon, then back to academia. One indicator of the scale of the change is that my current academic position is funded by a benefaction from the start-up that Google bought: I'm the inaugural DeepMind Professor of Machine Learning at the University of Cambridge.

I'm an optimist about AI, but I'm aware that we face decisions today about how we use these new tools. When we get decisions wrong, there are long-term consequences. Today our social media communications take place in echo chambers. The posts and adverts we see are the outcome of the algorithms Facebook and Google have deployed. Fake news has become the feedstock of these algorithms, fanning the flames of societal divisions. Only by learning from our errors and considering the harm that AI can do will we achieve the benefits we desire. On the positive side, modern technology has made smartphones that cost only $60. In Uganda, the AI lab at Makerere University is using these phones to develop solutions for health monitoring across the country which enable efficient distribution of medicines before outbreaks of disease can take hold. The lab is also developing approaches to crop surveillance that empower farmers to check their smallholdings for disease, improving food security. In one of my favourite projects, the lab works with the UN to have small AI devices listening to rural radio phone-in shows. The devices detect words like 'flood' or 'famine', alerting UN staff to emerging problems before they become humanitarian disasters.

Regardless of whether it's Google or Uganda, these artificial systems are closely integrated with our personal and social activities. This means that they are intertwining with our intelligence. To make good decisions about their design, we need to have a better understanding of who we are, what our intelligence is and what we value about ourselves. Only by understanding ourselves can we decide whether, when and where we wish artificial intelligence to be intervening.

My interest in machine learning was triggered not by a desire to solve intelligence but by my background as an engineer. I was working alongside expert geologists on oil rigs measuring the properties of the Earth. Intrigued by how they translated the information in my measurements into a vivid picture of the rock formations below our feet, I started studying machine learning because I wanted to understand how the geologists' expertise might be encoded in a machine. For me, the motivation was problem-solving, machine learning as a means to an end, to achieving our aims. But after that night in 2013 in Harrah's Casino I realized that many of my colleagues viewed intelligence itself as the goal.

Henry Ford was able to produce the Model T by optimizing a production line, decomposing a complex problem like building a car into a set of simpler tasks that can be performed by specialized labour or machines. Ford decomposed car manufacturing in order to improve the speed of production. Can we decompose intelligence in a similar way? Can it be reduced to a set of separate processes? The answer depends on what you mean by intelligence.

When considering human intelligence, we focus on our brains and our consciousness. The brain is the main hub of our central nervous system, the signalling apparatus in our body that first evolved when we began to move. But that form of intelligence is just one example. Even within our own bodies, another intelligence coexists and interacts with this centralized intelligence. Our immune systems are highly sophisticated detection and decision-making systems that constantly patrol our bodies to identify pathogens. Unlike our brain, our immune system is a *distributed* intelligence: its capabilities are honed in several organs across our bodies. It mostly operates below our conscious awareness – it is only when we fall ill, when our immune system is struggling, that we become aware of its presence. Our brains communicate by means of fast electrical signals. Within our bodies, our nervous system's communication bandwidth is high due to the rapid transmission of neural signals. The immune system uses biochemical signalling to communicate. Various messaging molecules are used, one of which is the cytokine. These protein-based molecules help cells to communicate with each other and to move towards infected or inflamed areas of the body. Our brain and our immune system operate within our bodies in tandem, but the nature of their decision-making is very different.

Another form of distributed intelligence is found in colonies of social insects. Ants, bees and termites operate from nests, foraging independently but towards a shared goal. Social insects often have different roles, for example there are worker ants and soldier ants. As in a production line, they decompose the challenge they face into different tasks. Our human intelligence is also a social intelligence: since 2007, the majority of the world's population has lived in cities.[3] Organizationally, cities operate as large 'nests', just like large groups of social insects. A beehive or an ants' nest doesn't have all the local resources it needs to sustain its population. These nests rely on infrastructure to transport goods from regions of production to regions of consumption. In ant populations, this process of communal intelligence involves forager ants who go exploring for new resources and share their location with worker ants. Chains of movement are formed to bring the resource back to the nest,[4] where it is stored or consumed. Honeybees also form colonies, and they forage at distances of over 9 kilometres away from their hives,[5] sharing the location of food discoveries through 'waggle dances'.

The human equivalent of these processes is known as a supply chain. In the three years I spent at Amazon, I was Director of Machine Learning in the supply-chain-optimization team. Amazon's supply chain is one of the most automated in the world, balancing demand for goods with the ability of manufacturers to produce them. It does this through transporting goods to warehouses that can redistribute them when they are ordered. The movement or storage of goods costs money, and the objective of the supply chain is to deliver the goods while minimizing costs.

The challenge of a supply chain is to decide *what* to buy, *whom* to buy it from and *where* to store it. The illusion of an efficient supply chain is to persuade the consumer that these goods are instantly and always available at low cost. To achieve this, the supply chain needs to estimate what the consumer's needs are, i.e., what they are likely to buy and when they are likely to buy it. The scale of Amazon's supply chain, with hundreds of millions of dollars of automated purchase decisions being made every week, makes it the world's largest machine intelligence.

All the functions of a social insect colony can be found within Amazon's system. Just as with social insects and our immune

17

systems, the intelligence is not restricted to any one entity but is associated with an ecosystem of decision-making. The objective of the supply chain is to estimate what human needs are going to be and ensure that the products are available to fulfil those needs, but it does this in two stages. There is a gap between the original promise to deliver and the execution of the delivery by the machine. It is in this gap that a supply-chain intelligence must second-guess itself. This process of second-guessing yourself, or itself, is critical to intelligence. Although the basic idea of a supply chain is quite simple, efficiently realizing the idea becomes complex. The key challenge is that you are trying to achieve your goal with limited resources. If the ant colony had unlimited ants, or the beehive had unlimited worker bees, then the problem would become trivial, but those ants and bees all need feeding. They have a cost for the colony. The same is true of human supply chains: decisions need to be made about what resource to deploy at which location.

Let's go back to Amazon and consider the problem of how to deliver products. When you click on the website and view an item the website gives you a message in the form 'Order within 12 hours to receive delivery by tomorrow.' For Amazon, this is known as *the promise*. It is a promise to customers about how long it will take to deliver the item. From a business perspective, it's important to get this promise right. Demand for products goes up when items are likely to arrive sooner. Just imagine the choice between two websites, both selling Bauby's book. All else being equal, most people will choose the site that can deliver the book more quickly. However, if Amazon makes that promise and fails to deliver, that's a bad experience for the customer, and Amazon prides itself on providing good customer experiences.

Speed of delivery for Amazon is dependent on *how* it delivers. When you click on a product on a page, computers decide how to deliver that product. That decision must be made *while* the webpage is loading. A slow-loading web page is a bad customer experience, and Amazon wants to avoid that. So the computers make that decision very quickly.

If you do then choose to order the product, then the computers have more time to decide how to fulfil your order. They can revisit their original decision at their leisure. But they revisit the decision having already made a promise about when the product will arrive. The computer, in its slower decision-making, becomes constrained by a judgement it made in a faster-reacting decision-making mode. The final decision about the *delivery* is constrained by the earlier decision about the promise.

That is one example, but this happens across supply-chain decision-making. The placement of products in the warehouses is also driven by anticipating where the customers are likely to be, so even before you click on the website the computer has made plans about where it believes the demand for the product will come from. The same prediction is made multiple times with different levels of knowledge and across different timescales. The computer can keep revisiting the plan until the moment the product arrives at the customer's doorstep. The system is constantly second-guessing itself.

The tension between fast solutions (the initial promise) and slower solutions (the final delivery plan) emerges in real-world decision-making because time horizons become an important factor in planning. You might think the optimal solution would be to have an overall 'grand plan' for how the product will be delivered. Then everything could be kept consistent by revisiting this 'grand plan'. For product catalogues containing hundreds of millions of items and a customer base consisting of hundreds of millions of people, the grand plan would consist of 10 quadrillion possible deliveries, almost all of which would never occur. When you consider the possibility that any customer might buy multiple items that could be in different warehouses, then the number of possible deliveries is even greater. So following a 'grand plan' is totally impractical. Despite the computer's massive information budget, it still needs to plan on the hoof, and as a result it has to second-guess itself. It has to abstract and simplify circumstances and build an initial plan in the absence of all the facts.

Behavioural psychologist Daniel Kahneman explores the rationality of human decision-making in his book *Thinking, Fast and Slow*. He uses a dual-process model to explain cognition, suggesting that we have two systems in our brains: System 1, which is fast-thinking and responsive; and System 2, which is slow-thinking and more reflective. To go back to Amazon, the promise would be a System 1 decision and the delivery a System 2 decision.

If I were to write a book on the rationality of machine decision-making in the Amazon supply chain, I might call it *Reacting, Fast and Slow*. When I worked there, I saw that all the decisions were being driven by events in the outside world and the timeframes over which answers were needed. The computer *reacts* to the circumstances. The dual-process model does not cover this. For me, the ideal intelligence would not have two systems but a spectrum of answers that could be given according to the best currently accessible information and the timescale over which the response is required.

The supply-chain example gives some insight into the practical challenges of an artificial intelligence system. But there is also an emotive aspect to the term 'artificial intelligence', which I think arises from the fact that we humans see intelligence as something very specific to us. We seem to take a particular, and very natural, interest in this aspect of ourselves. The ancient Greeks had a story about a young hunter who was so beautiful that when he caught sight of his face in a pool he became transfixed by it. He neglected everything else in life, eventually dying by the water. The young man was called Narcissus, and from his story we have gained the English word 'narcissist'. It feels like there's a connection between Narcissus' fascination with his beauty and our interest in our intelligence.

There are other parallels between this story and our interest in AI: there are aspects to beauty that make it hard to define. It isn't as simple as facial symmetry, or secondary sexual characteristics being heightened in some way. As anyone considering the relative beauty of Beyoncé and Tom Hiddleston could tell you, beauty is obvious to you when it is there, but enormously difficult to pin down. Similarly, there are aspects to intelligence that make it hard to define. In a 1964 US Supreme Court case, Justice Potter Stewart was asked to judge whether Louis Malle's *The Lovers* was an obscene film. Attempting to characterize obscenity, he wrote, 'I know it when I see it.' His judgement was fundamentally *subjective*. What is true of obscenity is also true of beauty and intelligence. For many people, when thinking of intelligence or beauty, they say that they know it when they see it.

Our literature and mythology hold up a mirror to humanity's fascination with our own intelligence. From Prometheus to the Golem, from Frankenstein's monster to the Terminator, our stories represent the dangers of creating intelligence, and the implication is that this creation should be the preserve of the gods, something that is prohibited to mortal humans. One common narrative in these stories begins with the wonder of creation and the idealism of the creator. It ends with the created failing to be grateful for what their creator has done for them. The created are independent of mind and spirit and keen to break away from servile bondage. Anyone would think that whoever wrote these myths had a lot of experience of bringing children into the world.

These are cautionary tales of the perils of hubris, so it's unsurprising that the creation of artificial intelligence is often viewed with trepidation. But these stories were written at a time when the only other intelligences we engaged with were either human, animal or supernatural. Through the lens of artificial intelligence, we can see our intelligence from a different perspective. That perspective has already shown us one of our limitations: our restricted communication bandwidth. How we overcome the locked-in nature of our intelligence is at the core of the idea of the atomic human.

Human intelligence is a social intelligence: it is isolated, but it doesn't exist in isolation. It sits instead within a broader culture. The term 'culture' originates from the Roman orator Cicero, who wrote of *cultura animi*, the cultivation of our minds. He drew an analogy with agriculture: human knowledge is cultivated similarly to the way crops are raised from the land: our minds grow and respond to their intellectual environment.

It is impossible to understand humans without understanding our context, and human culture is a key part of that context, but the culture that sustains our minds is also evolving. Over time, how we see ourselves within the universe has changed. The world looks different to us today than it did to Michelangelo. Many of these changes have improved our ability to understand the world around us.

For me, resolving the riddle of intelligence has become a personal journey: as I fell into a maelstrom of increased public interest in my research, I started to look for landmarks by which I could orient and stabilize myself. If the aim of my field was to create 'artificial intelligence', just what was intelligence, and what should we be doing with it? Not only did I ask myself that question; other people asked me it too. Overnight, I had become an expert in AI. I hadn't changed my thinking, but the context had shifted around me. When I explained to people at social gatherings that I was working on machine learning, they would nod and look blankly at me. But when I clarified that it was the 'principal technology underpinning the current revolution in artificial intelligence', their faces would light up. Eventually, I'd just tell people I worked on AI . . . concise is not always precise. I went from being the person people most wanted to avoid at parties to the one people most wanted to talk to. People were both curious and afraid – curious about how you make a computer intelligent, and afraid of what it meant for them personally and for their livelihoods.

Back then one book that was influencing the wider conversation was *Superintelligence*. Written by Oxford professor Nick Bostrom, it warned of the dangers of creating an intelligence that is beyond our understanding and control. Bostrom finesses the problem of defining intelligence by focusing on 'superintelligence':

We can tentatively define a superintelligence as *any intellect that greatly exceeds the cognitive performance of humans in virtually all domains of interest.*[6]

It is not a new idea. It goes back to the 1960s and a scientist called Jack Good, who called it *ultraintelligence.*[7] Good was the child of

Polish-Jewish immigrants living in London. His father was a watch-maker, but Jack studied Mathematics at Cambridge University, and in 1941 started working closely with Alan Turing, one of the fathers of the field of computer science. Turing had a different trick for assessing intelligence. He suggested an imitation game. Turing's idea was that if the computer can fool a human into believing it is human, then the computer can be thought of as intelligent. This game became known, famously, as the Turing Test. Variations of this test have been run as an annual competition with, until recently, computers only occasionally fooling participants into believing they are human. Now, however, machine-learning chatbots have become so good that computers regularly fool entrants.

Bostrom's idea of superintelligence allowed him to explore the capabilities of imagined intelligent machines in a range of scenarios. A major focus of his book was the harms such machines may do and how we should look to control them. *Superintelligence* was influential, triggering global figures such as Elon Musk, Bill Gates and Stephen Hawking to warn of the dangers of creating such extraordinary power. More recently, tools like ChatGPT that can pass the Turing Test have sparked international conversations around controlling superintelligent machines.

Now that I'm an artificial intelligence expert, I am invited to important meetings called things like 'International Cooperation on AI' or the 'Global Forum on AI for Humanity'. I am asked to comment on articles for *Nature* such as 'How artificial intelligence is being used to prevent blindness'. But the artificial intelligence we are peddling, the techniques we are using, simply combine very large datasets and computers. It is a mix of advanced computation and statistics. One of my favourite tricks is to mentally correct these headlines, and so to wonder if a meeting on 'International Cooperation on Computers and Statistics' would attract such interest, or whether we would convene a 'Global Forum on Computers and Statistics for Humanity'. I ask myself whether *Nature* would be interested in a piece on 'How computers and statistics are being used to prevent blindness'. Very often, my conclusion is that they would not.

Having said that, public obsession with intelligence is offering an opportunity: perhaps there *should* be international meetings on cooperation for computers and statistics. Perhaps *Nature should* be more interested in how computers and statistics are being used to prevent blindness. These are new technologies, and we should welcome public participation in what we have created and input into how it is being deployed.

Whether or not we have created anything that should be called intelligence, what we can say is that the techniques we have developed are allowing computers to make decisions that in the past may have been taken by humans. The use of computers to make decisions is not a new idea. But what *is* new is the power of the computers available. Accompanying this technological leap, there has been a massive increase in the raw materials required for computation and statistics. Whether it's crop surveillance in Uganda, Facebook's adoption of machine learning, or the new generation of large-language models like ChatGPT, it's the increase in the availability of data for computation that is driving widespread adoption of the techniques we are calling AI. This is triggering a new wave in automation: the large-scale automation of decision-making, such as in the Amazon supply chain.

Tracing the history of automation, going back to the printing press, the steam engine or the combine harvester, we see that, on average, population wealth has improved with increasing automation. However, averages do not capture the full picture. Even if they go up, when we look across the whole population we find that there are winners and losers. The benefits of automation are often unevenly distributed, and commonly it is those on the margins of society who are most negatively affected. Automation can, and often does, increase societal inequalities. Perhaps, by thinking about computers and statistics carefully, we can ensure that we compensate for this tendency. Perhaps we can go further and use these new technologies to narrow opportunity gaps and create a more equitable society.

Unfortunately, our fascination with intelligence can also be an obstacle. We can become distracted by fictional narratives around the creation of intelligences rather than focusing on what we've actually built. Our tendency to embody intelligence means that for many people the notion of creating AI implies creating an intelligent entity: an artificial being that is intelligent. However, we have to be careful to separate the notion of intelligence as a property from that of an intelligence as an entity. We can probably all agree that we would like our decisions to become more intelligent, but we might disagree on whether we would like to create *an* intelligence.

However, regardless of what we as a society may want, some companies are keen to create an intelligence anyway. In 2017, I was on the working group of the Royal Society Machine Learning review. We surveyed the UK public on what they wanted from machine learning. The public could see how it could help across a range of different areas – health, transport, better cities, social care; they could even see possibilities in more controversial areas like policing. The one area where the public was not keen on advances was human creativity. The public could not see the point in machines that created paintings or poetry; these were seen as fundamentally human endeavours. And yet what is the one domain where we have made unquestionable progress since 2017? We now have computer programs such as ChatGPT that can write poems and image-generating programs like DALL-E which can imitate human painting.

I started on my journey in machine learning as an engineer. A problem-solver. But when I became an AI expert I was accused of being a problem-generator. Confusion between intelligence as an entity and intelligence as a property is not restricted to the general public. Eminent scientists also make this error. In 2017, Stephen Hawking was quoted as saying that the emergence of artificial intelligence could be 'the worst event in the history of our civilization'.[8] Wow, kinda makes you feel bad about what you do!

Our modern encounters with artificial intelligence have led to the emergence of a transhumanism movement proposing that our reaction to the rise of machine intelligence should be to build on our cognitive capabilities by combining them with those of the machine. One of its proponents, Ray Kurzweil, has popularized the notion of the *technological singularity*. This is the idea that there's a moment when machines become clever enough to design themselves. At this point, the reasoning is, each new generation of machines becomes more intelligent, resulting in runaway ultraintelligence that operates beyond our control.

I think this is hooey. Both Bostrom's definition of superintelligence and the notion of the technological singularity are flawed. They misrepresent intelligence as a unidimensional quality and this doesn't reflect the diversity of intelligences we experience.

The real nature of intelligence reminds me more of the children's card game Top Trumps. In different versions of the game, the cards represent different entities, for example superheroes or fictional monsters. The idea of the game is to win your opponent's cards by comparing the capabilities or properties of the superhero or monster. But let's imagine, for a moment, we're playing with the automobile set. When it is your turn, you nominate one category, perhaps acceleration or top speed. The player who holds the card with the dominant characteristic trumps the others, wins their cards and takes the next turn.

At school, my friends and I were so keen on this game we created our own sets of Top Trumps. We invented categories and cards and played them against one another. Making our home-made cards was a lot of fun, but playing them was less interesting than the originals. Ours lacked the essence that makes the game interesting. In Top Trumps, strong cards that dominate across several characteristics are called supertrumps. In a vehicles set, for example, the Ferrari F40 sports car is strong in speed, acceleration and monetary value. Much of the game is about winning these supertrumps. When we created our sets, we spent a lot of time creating supertrumps. But the game is easy to win and quite boring if one card dominates the others in all characteristics. In well-designed versions of the game, even supertrumps can be vanquished by a humbler card.

Let's consider a hypothetical example. In the vehicles set, one of the characteristics might be carrying capacity – so the mighty

F40 can be brought crashing to the ground by the humble Ford
Transit. This was the essence of the game, an essence that my
friends and I failed to re-create with our own Top Trumps. We
created ultratrumps that could surpass all other cards in all
characteristics – but in the real world the choice of the better vehicle depends on the context. Ferraris are good for racing, but less
good at carrying bathroom tiles.

Intelligence is similar. There are different natures to different
intelligences. As a result, the notion of a superintelligence is a distraction. It is not relevant to the intelligent systems we build in the
real world. And as far as the technological singularity goes, to the
extent it will happen, it already has happened. In many domains,
machines already wildly surpass us. They can communicate much
more quickly than us, and they perform basic mathematical operations far faster than we do. This has happened because we used the
previous generation of machines to build the next generation. We
are already in a world where the machine can store a vast quantity
of information about each of us individually. Indeed, we have been
in this world for over fifty years.

In 1971, Harvard law professor Arthur Miller warned in *The Assault
on Privacy* of a world where 'Today's laser technology already makes
it feasible to store a twenty-page dossier on every American on a
piece of tape that is less than 5000 feet long.'[9] Fifty years later, those
dossiers fit easily into the palm of your hand and could contain a lot
more than twenty pages of text. Miller writes that the major issue is
the individual's loss of control over who has access to their information profile. This is the world we live in today, and it's problematic
precisely because of the nature of our locked-in *human* intelligence.
Part of how we control who we are is through choosing what to
reveal about ourselves. By giving the machine access to so much
information about us, we are undermining our ability to exercise
that control and making ourselves vulnerable to the machine.

Far more important than a notion of superintelligence is the
question: what is particular about *our* intelligence? And, therefore,
what is *precious* about our intelligence? If something as simple as a

motor vehicle can exhibit different aspects, some of which are strengths in a given situation but may be weaknesses in a different situation, what does that mean for intelligence? Top Trumps shows us that the Henry Ford notion of a 'faster horse' needs clarification. We need to know the horse's job before we understand what characteristics it needs to complete it more quickly. Is it carrying a message or is it delivering bulky goods? Naturally, when we're thinking about a *smarter human*, the different aspects of intelligence also need to be contextualized.

The technical term for this concept is the *competitive intransitivity of intelligence*. Intransitivity is a type of non-linearity, one in which the world is no longer quite as simple as we might expect. A transitive relationship is where when A is better than B, and B is better than C, then A is better than C. In an intransitive relationship, this is no longer the case. Another playground game, Rock, Paper, Scissors, displays this intransitivity. Scissors beats paper but loses out to rock. If the relationships were transitive, we would expect rock to beat paper, because it beats scissors and scissors has already vanquished paper, but, in the game, paper wins.

These intransitive relations are what make these games interesting. The non-linear quality emerges because the ranking of these items is not one-dimensional. The same is true in Top Trumps: the Transit van is not transitive. Just as the vehicles are multifaceted, intelligence is multifaceted, and the relationship between intelligent entities is also multifaceted, so we should be very wary of any argument that characterizes the relationship between intelligent entities as one-dimensional.

The mistake that Kurzweil and Bostrom make is to conflate the intelligence of a decision with the notion of an intelligent entity. It is conceivable that the quality of an individual decision can be measured: I can imagine a way of ranking different decisions if I know the context in which they are being taken. However, when I separate out the decision-maker from the context and simply look at the entity that makes decisions without knowing the task the decision is meant to facilitate, I see no easy way of ranking them.

I think Zuckerberg was also conflating different forms of intelligence when he imagined what his investment in Yann's new lab was buying him that day in Harrah's. I think he really believed that his investment would, in time, buy him a smarter human.

It may be that this conflation is common because of our tendency to embody intelligences. I first introduced the embodiment factor in a TEDx talk I gave in Exeter, to help explain how a computer's intelligence is different from ours. Afterwards, a follow-up thought occurred to me: given how constrained we are in communication bandwidth, why are we so wasteful of what we have? When I meet with my research group, we may have only half an hour together, so why do we waste time on small talk? Why do we choose to check in on how each of us is in our personal lives? Why do we discuss the weather, or what we did at the weekend? We are so information-constrained, why do we spend our time talking about frivolities? The answer is that these conversations help others understand who we are, and it is this understanding of each other that helps us when we try to communicate with each other.

We have an evolved intelligence, one that has emerged across thousands of millennia of survival in an oftentimes inhospitable environment. To get where we are today, our species has survived floods, earthquakes, ice ages, volcanoes, tornadoes, droughts and predation. But on a daily basis the most complex and challenging entity we continually encounter is an adversary of enormous capability but also familiarity: our fellow human beings. Regardless of whether they are friend or foe, we are always dealing with a highly intelligent entity – one that has its own goals, which may or may not be aligned with ours. As a further challenge, we are limited in our ability to communicate with this other entity. We carry a powerful cognitive capability, but we cannot share all the subtleties and complexities of our objectives and as a result we dedicate a large portion of our brain's activity to understanding our fellow human beings. Their thoughts, and ours, are clouded by the locked-in nature of our intelligence. In the absence of direct access to their thoughts, we dedicate much of our own cognitive capacity to *second-guessing* our human companions. Just as the Amazon supply-chain intelligence has to second-guess how a delivery will be carried out, we need to make predictions about each other and how we are likely to behave.

To be able to write the prologue to this book, and this chapter, and convey the ideas that are inside my head, I need a sense of who you are. I need to understand what stories you may know, and which of them will resonate with you. I can then use this knowledge to choose words that can build on your lived experience. I can use our shared contextual understanding of the world and the human condition to communicate the notions in my head. So far, I have used a little over 8,000 words. Shannon's theory tells us that I've shared about 100,000 bits of information. But I have also relied on your knowledge of Michelangelo, the *Terminator* films, motor cars, daydreaming, being bed-bound, deep-sea diving, games like Top Trumps and Rock, Paper, Scissors, and Amazon deliveries.

According to Shannon's information theory, the ideas I have shared could have been exchanged between two computers in under a tenth of a millisecond. In contrast, it will have taken a typical reader perhaps twenty minutes to get through these thirty pages. Shannon defined information as being separated from its context, but I have relied *utterly* on context to communicate my message. This is why those social niceties in my research group meetings are not frivolities: they are a vital piece in our communication puzzle. To communicate well with another human being, we need to understand who they are and where they come from. We need the cultural context as well as the details of the situation. The form of this communication is a fundamental difference between human intelligence and machine intelligence.

Our human communication relies on a shared experience that comes from a shared perception of the world. But that perception is a consequence of our limitations. Our intelligence is so biased towards understanding and communicating with other humans that when we experience other phenomena in our world we impose our human perspective upon them. We anthropomorphize the world around us. We imbue our pets, our vehicles, our plants with human personas.

Our perspective on ourselves, our view as a butterfly trapped in a diving suit, gives us a distorted perspective on intelligence. When considering intelligence, we focus on our brains and our consciousness. The brain is the main hub of our central nervous system, the signalling apparatus in our body that first evolved when we began to move. But that form of intelligence is just one type of intelligence. The atomic human has a brain locked into her body. She is restricted in the bandwidth she has to communicate with the outside world, and this limits her understanding of the complexities around her.

Our brains scramble to grab an intellectual foothold on the world to lever ourselves up. In religion, we embody the notion of a pervasive intelligence in a robed figure of God painted by Michelangelo on the ceiling of the Sistine Chapel. In artificial intelligence, it's the red-eyed Terminator that has been projected on our cinema screens. But this foothold is a poor one to rely on for attaining the intellectual vista we need to understand the nature of the artificial intelligence systems we've created.

We need better insights to understand artificial intelligence so that we can bridge the gap between our intelligence and the intelligence which we are creating. Bridging this gap is vital if we are to work collaboratively with this new intelligence. By developing a better understanding of ourselves, we can be better prepared to accommodate this new intelligence. The potential for good is enormous, but to make the right choices we must also understand the considerable potential for harm.

What are the things I've been doing with AI? I've built systems for understanding the causes of diseases, algorithms that helped Formula One teams design cars, mathematical models which made more realistic digital character animation, techniques which assisted with the design of drones that could take off vertically and fly horizontally. In Amazon's supply chain, our algorithms helped to deliver people's Christmas parcels on time. So far, none of these systems has expressed any ill will towards me. They haven't really expressed themselves at all.

The notion of an intelligence as an entity and the nature of the AI we have created have become conflated not just in the minds of Bostrom and Kurzweil but in the wider public debate. There is a large gap between what I have been building and what I am asked about. *The Atomic Human* aims to disentangle this confusion. Our obsession with machine intelligence is a fascination about who we are, but we can convert this narcissism into introspection by wielding machine intelligence as a mirror to our own cognition. This will give us a deeper understanding of who we are, what our needs are and how we might achieve them. In this way we can substitute the hype around machine intelligence with the hope that we can close the gap between our perception of who we are and the reality. By using the machine as a mirror to reflect who we are, we can better understand what we want, and this understanding should enable us to decide how we want our societies to function in this new age of AI, and how individuals in those societies can carry out their roles in a way that balances their personal liberty with the social need for coherence and security. *The Atomic Human* is my attempt to address the riddle of intelligence.

2.

Automatons

My grandfather, Fred Lawrence, was a military engineer, a sapper. He wasn't a sapper by choice, but by circumstance. Before the Second World War he was a carpenter and a gardener, but he was conscripted into the UK's military to build bridges, clear mines and dig trenches.

In early June 1944 he was stationed in the garrison town of Alder- shot, in the county of Hampshire in southern England. Troops were being amassed for the planned invasion of France and the engineers had been called in to build the infrastructure to transport the army and ensure that the servicemen were fed. Fred liked to be fed. He spent his idle hours finding ways to supplement his meagre meal rations. He was committed to his country, but he was also committed to his family, and he took any opportunity to go home to his wife, daughter and infant son, my father.

The troops were not told when the invasion would be launched, the German defenders, led by Field Marshal Rommel, didn't know when it was due to be launched and, with less than a week to go, even the Supreme Commander of the Allied forces, General Dwight Eisenhower, didn't know. Eisenhower had a million troops waiting in Hampshire. Rommel had troops and tank divisions waiting to defend against the invaders. What was missing for everyone was *information*.

A combined army, navy and air force invasion is a vast logistical exercise, and an amazing example of how humans work together despite the limitations on their ability to communicate. The Allies under Eisenhower had to decide what troops and materials needed to be where and when. The task is similar to the one I faced when I was working on Amazon's supply chain. The supply chain needs to understand what employees and materials need to be where and when to fulfil customer demand. Eisenhower commanded the Allies, and when I was at Amazon Jeff Bezos was the CEO. Both had ultimate responsibility for decision-making, but how much control did Eisenhower and Bezos really have? Eisenhower's title of Supreme Commander implies that power was absolute, that collaboration would occur through command and control. Jeff's title of Chief Executive Officer implies similar capabilities, but at Amazon I was able to see first-hand the limitations on that power.

I once built a survival shelter with Jeff Bezos. We were in the desert wilderness near Palm Springs in California. Jeff is very hands-on. He spent the summers of his childhood at his grandfather's ranch in Texas. Building a shelter with him mainly involved not getting in his way. When it was done it looked great, but Eisenhower and Bezos can't build a shelter for every person in their organization. They sat at the top of a command hierarchy that was too vast for them to be involved in every decision. When my grandfather arrived in France, he and the other troops dug their own shelters in areas chosen by their immediate commanders.

If we were to use logical relations to describe where the power was in Amazon, it would imply that Bezos could directly order anyone in the organization what to do. But in practice Bezos's and Eisenhower's communication bandwidth was limited. As a result, their power was indirect. The information they received was filtered for them and their capacity to decide was dependent on the decisions the hierarchy chose to place in front of them. Every organization has a strategy for how it propagates information through its decision-making systems. I call the structure that comes from this strategy the *information topography*.

In geography, the topography is the configuration of natural and man-made features in the landscape. It is the lie of the land, an arrangement of physical features that designate different uses we can make of our environment. How easy is it to irrigate? How easy is it to excavate? How easy is it to navigate? How easy is it to invade?

These questions are framed by the topography. An information topography is similar, but instead of the movement of goods, water and people, it dictates the movement of information. Britain is an island, and this makes it difficult to invade but also difficult to launch invasions from. The embodiment factor shows us that, in information terms, humans are also islands. Britain's physical topography means we must cross the sea in a boat; the atomic human's information topography dictates how we share our ideas.

The Allies built their own information hub to filter and interpret information for Eisenhower, based in a country estate north-west of London called Bletchley Park. This was where the ideas behind our modern information topography were developed. Bletchley Park is roughly halfway between Oxford and Cambridge, and in 1939 a train line connected the two university cities. It passed through the town of Bletchley, and this ease of access was why the estate was chosen as the home for the UK government's communication headquarters.

It's difficult to hide a million hungry men. The Allies' plan for the invasion of France centred on an ambitious amphibious landing on the beaches of Normandy. These beaches were best attacked from Hampshire, and both the Germans and the Allies knew this. A large build-up of troops in the county could give away the location selected for the landings. If the Germans guessed the target, then Rommel's tank divisions could be put in position to prevent the Allies from consolidating their position.

The Second World War arrived at a time when the information topography had been disrupted. In the Blitzkrieg, radio was used to coordinate the German tanks with air support as they thundered across Europe. Radio was also used to spread news and propaganda: political leaders could talk directly to people in their homes. Radios were made possible by an electronic innovation, the *thermionic valve*.

A thermionic valve is an electrical switch, but it operates by bending a beam of electrons instead of moving a metal contact. This means it has no mechanical parts, which allows it to switch much faster than earlier devices could. These valves sat inside portable radio sets, and the radio sets were used by commanders to pass orders to the troops. But radio waves are easy to eavesdrop on, so the location of the troops, and their communications, were difficult to hide. Eisenhower's Bletchley Park was listening in to German radio messages.

The Germans also had mobile units from their intercept service listening to the Allies. Hiding the build-up of troops would be like hiding a house party from a neighbouring apartment. A radio-based information topography leaks like sound throbbing through a flimsy wall. The party in Hampshire was going to be hard to muffle.

Keeping the party quiet was going to be impractical. So rather than doing that, the Allies arranged for a bigger party to take place in another apartment. They invented a new army group and positioned it in the south-eastern county of Kent. This group was poised to attack across the narrowest part of the English Channel, from Dover to Calais. It was the US First Army Group, commanded by General George S. Patton. But this was a party without any guests. It was deployed across Kent in rubber tanks, plywood planes and canvas trucks. The force was also provided with a flotilla of canvas ships in Dover Harbour. The Allies had planned a feint. They were trying to mislead the enemy with false information. They tried to hide the Hampshire house party by playing louder music from the far eastern side of the country. The Allies drove trucks broadcasting fake radio signals among this fake army, generating the radio chatter of an entire army group to confuse the German defence, which now had to make a decision about which party to break up.

In the armed forces, the information topography stretches from the Supreme Commander to the troops on the ground. In this network, Fred was as distant as you can be from General Eisenhower, and he was blissfully unaware of all these goings-on. He had his own objectives. Much of his focus was on stilling his growling stomach and getting home to cradle his gurgling baby. The Supreme Command sent out orders and, because of the impending invasion, all home leave was cancelled, so Fred was stuck in Hampshire. But he discovered that forty-eight-hour *local* leave passes were available. Had Fred known why home leave was cancelled, he wouldn't have done what he did next.

Fred obtained a pass for local leave but then made his way up from Hampshire to London. At Euston Station, he dodged the Military Police by ducking into a goods elevator and caught the train to Coventry. He was going home. He lived about five miles outside the city, in the town of Kenilworth. Fred was abusing his local leave to snatch a night with his family.

Like many households, Fred's family owned a domestic radio set. It would have stood in his sitting room, a large wooden box with a mesh-covered speaker in its centre. Fred and his family could relax in chairs around it and listen to Churchill's broadcasts. By 1944, the thermionic valve was being mass-produced, and radio sets were common. The morning after he'd travelled home, Fred woke up, headed down to his sitting room and turned on the radio. At 10 a.m. normal programming was interrupted by a special bulletin:

'D' Day has come. Early this morning the Allies began the assault on the north-western face of Hitler's European Fortress. The first official news came just after half past 9 when Supreme Headquarters of the Allied Expeditionary force – usually called SHAEF from its initials – issued Communiqué no. 1.
This said:
    'Under the Command of General Eisenhower, Allied Naval Forces supported by strong Air Forces, began landing Allied Armies this morning on the Northern coast of France.'

This was how Fred found out that his unit was shipping out to France, while he was 80 miles away at home in Kenilworth.

Fred's story highlights one of the challenges for the information topography. He was ordered to stay in Hampshire, but he didn't know the motivation for the order. He was balancing his obligation to his family against his wider obligation to his army unit. Fred had made his own decision about what to do, but now the context had changed. He left Kenilworth immediately and spent the next two years fighting in France and Germany. When he did eventually get back to Kenilworth, his son, my father, didn't know who Fred was. He kept asking my grandma, 'When is that man going to leave?'

According to the logic of command, Eisenhower was in charge of Fred, but the devolution of authority meant that Fred could operate outside Eisenhower's orders. Limited information bandwidth didn't just undermine Fred's understanding, it also restricted Eisenhower's ability to control his men. You might think the answer is simple – servicemen like Fred should just obey orders – but it's not quite that easy. Troops on the ground have information that their commander doesn't have. Sometimes they need to follow their instinct rather than their orders. By devolving authority to troops rather than micromanaging their activities the military can be more flexible.

I often think of this devolutionary step as being akin to riding a bicycle with no hands. A simple logical model for a bike would suggest that it is steered through the actions of the rider's hands on the handlebars, but the reality is more nuanced. A professional cyclist steers not just with her hands but through her body's position on the bicycle. She steers with her posture, using the weight of her body to guide the bicycle. If the distribution of weight is correct, the bicycle begins to steer itself.

A bicycle is more stable when the rider's weight is towards the rear wheel. So, somewhat counterintuitively, it is easier to ride leaning back with no hands on the bars. Devolving responsibility is analogous. People become more confident when you empower and entrust them, but just like a rider leaning back on a bicycle, this empowerment can feel to the leader like a loss of control. Leaning back makes the bicycle more stable, but it makes any necessary interventions – braking or negotiating a tricky corner – harder because the rider's hands are further from the controls than she would like. Devolution of power has similar challenges: it implies a different form of exercising authority.

*

When not building survival shelters in the Palm Springs desert, one of Jeff Bezos's interests was machine learning. I met Jeff in Palm Springs when I was still a professor in Sheffield. The survival shelter construction was part of the MARS conference: a thought-space event focusing on space, robotics and machine learning with team-building activities like the shelter construction.

I had given a talk there about the challenges of data and artificial intelligence. Machine learning is programming a computer by providing it with examples. But the really big breakthroughs in machine learning that triggered international interest in artificial intelligence were achieved only when we acquired a *lot* of examples – many more examples than humans require to do the same job. The success of machine learning was driven by an internet-enabled information topography. With the internet, data was easier to acquire, but raw internet data is not always sufficient to teach the machine. Each example needed to be refined before the machine could consume it, and the new breakthroughs were coming only when the machine was shown millions of these refined examples.

This meant that large tech companies had a significant edge over their smaller rivals when using this new technology. My team at Sheffield had started a small company. It focused on how to do machine learning when examples are scarce. Either the talk went down well, or maybe Jeff was impressed by my ability to stay out of his way when he was building survival shelters, because within a year Amazon had acquired my team and Jeff had become my supreme commander.

It was seeing how Amazon operated to devolve authority that drew my attention to the challenges of leading a large company. When I joined, in 2016, it had a quarter of a million employees. By the time I left, in 2019, it had close to a million. Eisenhower had commanded over a million troops, many of whom were, like my grandfather Fred, waiting in English fields under their own canvas shelters for the invasion to start.

Jeff may have been hands-on when building shelters, but his approach to running his company was largely hands-off. Amazon has a corporate culture that teaches its employees how Jeff sees the company and its role and empowers them to make decisions in the light of that knowledge. I used to joke that it's as if Amazon surgically implants a little Jeff Bezos inside your head. Whatever the circumstances you find yourself in, you have been trained to think how Jeff thinks. The hope is that you act as Jeff would act. Of course, Jeff does intervene in the company, but his interventions are calculated and strategic. They are the equivalent of putting the brakes on the corporate bicycle or steering around a tricky obstacle. The day-to-day management is devolved to the employees through their understanding of the company's culture: mostly, the bicycle has been trained to steer itself. Amazon is managed like this because it's run on too large a scale for Jeff to be involved in every important decision. It focuses on building a culture and training its employees in it. Then it trusts its employees to try and make the decision that Jeff would have made, had he been there. Like Cicero's notion of art, music and literature cultivating our minds, Amazon cultivates its employees through training them in the company's priorities.

In any large organization there is a tension between an individual's autonomy and the advantages that come through wider coordination of their activities. The human's locked-in condition provides bottlenecks: information cannot propagate instantaneously through an organization. When Bezos was still in charge at Amazon, he mostly steered the company through posture, enabling it to run itself, and much of the communication within the company was through the sharing of culture.

We have an expression in English: 'It goes without saying'. We use it to suggest that the next piece of information to be exchanged is superfluous. For example: 'It goes without saying that, after listening to the morning radio bulletin, Fred hightailed it back to Aldershot on the next available train.' The use of 'it goes without saying' is reflecting the fact that Fred's next actions are predictable. They are a direct result of his understanding of a wider common purpose. It is a purpose you can instinctively recognize, even though you know very little about Fred, other than knowing that he is a human living in a society with certain obligations. So, it goes without saying that's what he did. Of course, I'm saying it anyway, because his actions are important in the context of the wider narrative we're building.

So, Fred boarded the next train and headed off to war. As an isolated decision, this might not seem like rational behaviour, but when you know his obligations to his unit and to the wider society, the decision makes sense. Perhaps the only thing missing for you to be able to predict Fred's actions is an understanding of his personal values. Well, now you know him a little better, because Fred got on a train to go to war.

Imagine you own a small shop and I come in and tell you what a lovely window display it has. Then, if I say how terrible it would be if someone threw a brick through the window, you may perceive what I'm saying as a threat and think I represent some form of protection racket. Although I have vocalized my hope that your window display will not suffer any damage, you may feel intimidated.

Why is that? It's perfectly reasonable for me to hope silently that your shop window won't be smashed: it goes without saying it would be a terrible shame if it was. By choosing to say it, by using our precious bandwidth to communicate information that should be obvious, then I'm implying that the opposite may happen. This sophisticated form of communication relies on a shared understanding of common purpose and context. We expect each other to come to our own conclusions about appropriate actions given this context, we can second-guess what those actions should be, and we can allow for individuals to operate autonomously given our shared purpose. This is how we deal with our very limited bandwidth, and it's also why it's difficult to capture the nuance of human communication and actions without accounting for this context.

The common purpose in war is the defence of a nation or a people: having an adversary brings alignment among the people. But in peace we can also coordinate around common ideals. Recent advances in our AI capabilities have been developed by building neural networks which have read all digitally available human written knowledge. These networks, known as transformers, have consumed billions of documents and given the machine an ability to converse. This ability is built on an awareness of our context gathered from consuming our written works. The different roles we each play in society are intertwined in this context. In modern society, some of that context is given by our working life: we have defined a set of professions just as the ants and the bees have evolved to carry out different roles in their colonies. As an academic, my profession conforms to a common set of ideals that informs my work. I started my academic career at Aston University in Birmingham, moved across to Cambridge, then north to Sheffield, on to Manchester, then returned to Sheffield and most recently to Cambridge. This range of universities share a common feature: a sense of academic culture. Academics have their own mythology. We view ourselves as fiercely independent, objective truth-seekers. Our research is curiosity-driven and its impact is measured through the respect of our esteemed peers. We combine this with the education of the next generation, ensuring a ready supply of fertile minds to carry the baton forward. In practice, academic reality often departs from our mythology, because academics are also humans. We have individual autonomy and are subject to human weaknesses such as egotism. Our academic ideals are often sacrificed to our desire for recognition, funding and promotion. Despite this, the academic ideal still serves as a cultural regularizer. Even if very few of us fulfil it, it represents something to strive for. We know what we should do, even if we don't always do it. Just like in Top Trumps, individual academics may be better at certain aspects of the role than others. Some may be better lecturers, others may be better researchers and still others may be better mentors.

After two decades steeped in academic culture, when I left Sheffield to join Amazon in 2016 I had some adapting to do. While my caricature of Amazon's corporate culture is that it places a little Jeff in your head, you won't be surprised to hear that that's not how the culture is presented to new recruits. What you are taught is a set of values that capture the essence of how the company wants you to behave. The core component is known as the 'leadership principles', and they are like the ten commandments of the company. But there are a couple of differences. First, there were fourteen of them at the time, and, secondly, they can change over time. For example, since I left Amazon, they have added two more, so now there are sixteen. One of the most important is 'customer obsession'. The company likes to view the customer's interests as being at the heart of all the decisions it makes. Another is 'earn trust', which describes how you build relationships with other employees and different teams and reflects the importance of trust in any system of devolved autonomy. Trust between individuals and groups is one way we overcome our bandwidth limitations. There are also other, more complex principles like 'right a lot', about how you assimilate information to make decisions.

The leadership principles give Amazon a set of common values, but the company recognizes that specific projects may need a different set of more focused ones. Teams are encouraged to come up with a list of 'tenets' for their projects. In Amazon parlance, tenets are values that individual teams design, a set of mini-commandments to represent how that team addresses problems. This allows for some adaptation of the corporate common purpose to better suit the needs of individual teams, so the values can be contextualized according to the circumstances the team finds itself in. The system of shared corporate values creates a culture that gives the context for individuals to make decisions. By teaching values, the company can devolve decision-making, trusting that individuals are capable of the nuance required to judge a particular situation. This topography helps Amazon deal with the communication barriers associated with locked-in intelligence. It gives Jeff a set of cultural levers through which he can steer his company.

Let's contrast human communication with two machines engaged in similar conversations. Machines don't have access to context or an understanding of common purpose, but they do have a great deal of bandwidth. So if a customerbot walked into a shop and suggested to a shopkeeperbot that it would be a shame if the shopkeeperbot's window was broken, then the shopkeeperbot will not find it unusual that this information has been shared, because it would only be a small part of the myriad facts and figures the two machines are capable of exchanging in milliseconds.

When the Allies were about to invade France, the Eisenbot, on finding the Fredbot was out of position on the day of the planned invasion, could use its enormous bandwidth to send direct orders about exactly what the Fredbot should do to get back to its unit. The Eisenbot could directly order the Fredbot to report to a particular place while simultaneously giving the 160,000 troopbots crossing the Channel that morning their specific landing orders. Further, the Eisenbot could have compelled the Fredbot to remain in Aldershot. In a machine-dominated topography, a mechanistic topography, the Eisenbot would control everything, and the Fredbot and the other troopbots would not be autonomous but automatons.

As embodied humans, we cannot handle the quantity of communication this mechanistic topography would require. Instead, imbued with a sense of common purpose, we short-circuit our embodiment. We view the circumstances we are faced with, we understand our common purpose, we understand our fellow humans, we second-guess their behaviours and we choose how to act. Humans do not coordinate as directed automatons; we coordinate through devolved autonomy. Or at least that's how it *used* to be.

I decided to start my career in neural networks when I was working on oil rigs in Liverpool Bay. It was 1996 and the internet was still in its infancy. I didn't have a network of tech-world contacts I could ask for advice, so I headed to Foyles, a bookshop on Charing Cross Road in London, once the world's largest. I found my way through the maze of shelves to the neural-network books. A fellow browser had a professorial look about him, so I asked him which book I should buy.

In the information topography, Foyles was providing an information hub where I could meet like-minded people and exchange understanding and opportunities, a place where information could be exchanged and redistributed. A bookshop becomes a hub because it stores information in the form of books and those books attract interested readers to congregate around its shelves. The internet has radically altered this information landscape, but twenty-five years ago, when I had to physically travel to Foyles, the information topography was closely tied to our physical topography.

Today we have networks of interconnected machines that can coordinate decision-making between them. This is the tectonic shift in the information topography we are faced with, and the early tremblings of this shift originate in the moment when Eisenhower decided the invasion of Europe should be launched.

On 5 June, Eisenhower was in conference with his staff. Tidal patterns were dictating that a landing in France would have to be on the 6th or 7th June. Allied forces had an information topography that shared orders and plans. The military has a culture around how orders are followed. But plans were shared only on a need-to-know basis, which is why soldiers like Fred were not told when the invasion was due to begin, but that afternoon even Eisenhower didn't know the invasion was about to begin.

The problem was the weather: storms would make an amphibious assault across the Channel difficult and prevent air forces from supporting the naval troops. The UK Met Office had predicted a possible break in the weather on 6 June, but this window was short and uncertain. Eisenhower was faced with a difficult decision. At a key moment during the conference he was handed a slip of paper, and he turned to the attendees and announced: 'We go tomorrow.'

Later that day, Eisenhower reflected in a letter: 'My decision to attack at this time and place was based upon the best information available.' It certainly was, because that slip of paper contained Rommel's direct orders from Adolf Hitler, his Supreme Commander in Berlin. Those orders told Rommel to hold back the German tank divisions from Normandy, as an attack was anticipated at Calais. The attack was expected five days after the one on the Normandy coast.[1] Creating the phantom army in Kent had worked. Eisenhower had a window of opportunity to establish his forces in France.

How did Eisenhower come to know Rommel's orders? The information was from the hub at the heart of the Allied information topography: Bletchley Park.

Eisenhower's decision had millions of downstream effects. He didn't have the capacity to follow up with each of his subordinates, but he had the confidence to know the organization around him would do the right thing. He could 'lean back on the bicycle', knowing it would respond to his posture as he willed it in this new direction. And so it was that Fred, who until that moment had represented a bent spoke up in Kenilworth, could respond to Eisenhower's command and straighten himself out.

Much of the Supreme Commander's control is through posture, but there are still major decisions, like the launch date for the invasion to be made. To ensure those decisions are well informed the command structure assimilates, sifts and summarizes information, bringing it to the attention of the leaders. This distillation process led to the secrets that were unpicked at Bletchley Park being presented to Eisenhower at the conference.

Even with the information from Bletchley Park, Eisenhower's decision required judgement. Despite the positive news, Eisenhower would still have had doubts. There were many things that could go wrong: lives were at stake, and nobody would want that decision to be made automatically. Even in today's information-rich era we would expect such a consequential decision to be made by a human; we would not want this degree of responsibility to be devolved to the machine. But other decisions are totally clear-cut. A decision so clear-cut it becomes a logical consequence of the facts could be devolved – if it doesn't require judgement, then the decision is an interesting candidate for automation.

Artificial intelligence is a technology for automating decisions. In Amazon's supply chain, many decisions are automated: the purchasing of goods to sell, where to store and source them from. The information these decisions require is automatically gathered: Amazon monitors the clicks on its website to estimate demand and gathers data on suppliers to estimate the time it will take to deliver the goods. The supply chain is a physical infrastructure – warehouses, vans and workers – which matches the demand for goods with their availability. My job was to use machine-learning techniques to automate this decision-making. Alongside our physical infrastructure, we had an information topography that allowed us to aggregate the data about supply and demand automatically, and we used computational and mathematical tools to automate the ordering process. These decisions were fully devolved to the machine. We can trace the origins of this automated decision-making to Bletchley Park and the efforts made to understand German radio signals. The Germans were listening to British radio messages to work out where an invasion would be launched from, but the British were also listening to the Germans, and not just to the chatter of their noisy neighbours; they were also straining to pick out specific conversations in the crowd.

Eisenhower made his decision on the back of the information he had, but the timing of his decision was forced by events. His final decision to invade was made at the last minute, less than twenty-four hours before troops arrived in Normandy.

In 1940, very few automated decision-making systems were available. Most of the information Eisenhower needed had to be gathered and processed by humans. I say *most* of the information was processed by humans because by 1944 the house and grounds of Bletchley Park were home to an array of machines designed to automatically process information. Alan Turing was based at the estate, as was the originator of the idea of ultraintelligence, Jack Good. Less famously but just as importantly, Bletchley Park was home to 12,000 other staff, including thousands of women who processed despatches delivered by motorcycle couriers from listening stations across the country.

In *The Debs of Bletchley Park*, Michael Smith describes the lives and work of many of these young women. One of the first to arrive was Diana Russell-Clarke, who joined in August 1939, before the outbreak of war. Diana told Michael about the nature of the work: '. . . it was very, very boring, just subtracting one row of figures from another'.² She was working as a *human* computer, engaged in the laborious task of manually processing German messages. A task that could be completed through logic alone, so one that was ripe for automation. Diana was at the hub of a vast network of information processors that digested the torrent of radio signals arriving from the enemy and prepared reports for Eisenhower and the rest of the Allied Command.

Amazon's decision-making is fed by historical data from the behaviour of customers and suppliers. Clicks on a website give Amazon an understanding of the customer's intent, allowing the company to guess what they might do next. Eisenhower's information infrastructure was fed by military intelligence and espionage. Espionage is a route to understanding enemy intent, guessing what your adversary will do next. In both these scenarios the aim is to understand intent, whether on the part of the customer or of the enemy. Counterintelligence efforts, like the phantom army in Kent, attempt to ensure that the actual intent stays locked away in the command structure, invisible to the enemy.

Diana's father had worked with codebreakers in the First World War. That had been a static affair – the troops bogged down in trenches – but the Second World War was very different. It was a dynamic, shifting encounter. The changes in the nature of warfare were being driven by changes in communication technology: mass-production of thermionic valves had led to the introduction of portable radios for communication. This changed the information topography and gave rise to a new style of battle, the Blitzkrieg: swift, coordinated and focused attacks by highly mobile units. From the start of the war, there was a radio in every German tank. Radio communication allowed joint attacks between armoured units with air support. Communication meant coordination. This new, dynamic warfare pushed back defending armies across Europe. By the end of 1941 most of Europe and half of the Soviet Union had submitted.

In the 1940s, radio was a mature technology. Guglielmo Marconi had sent the first transatlantic radio signal in 1901, and in 1919 the Radio Corporation of America (RCA) was founded. In 1920 the

British Broadcasting Corporation (BBC) followed. By the outbreak of war in 1939 radio had become well established as a broadcasting and communications tool. At the battlefront it was used to coordinate the troops and on the home front popular opinion. On that morning of 6 June 1944 my grandfather found out about the invasion at the same moment as millions of others listening to their sets. But, as well as informing populations, any system that connects people instantly is also an excellent tool for propaganda – for fake news. In Germany, Joseph Goebbels used radio to spread propaganda and build a base of popular support for the war.

The phantom army in Kent had been used to deal with the main weakness of radio. When coordinating troops, the ability of radio to connect populations is a problem: it makes the job of spies easy. By listening to enemy messages, you can read your enemy's mind. To prevent this, military orders need to be hidden, through cryptography: hiding the messages in a secret code.

You can think of hiding a message in code as like using a combination lock to secure a message in a box. If you share the PIN code with the intended recipient, then you can send them the box and, when they receive it, they can unlock it using the PIN and read the message. But anyone trying to intercept the box can't unlock it without the PIN code. The same is true of an encrypted message. An adversary listening to your radio transmissions doesn't know the code and can't unlock the message.

We use physical combination locks to lock our bicycles to lamp posts or to secure our clothes in a locker at the gym. The digits of the combination form the key to the lock. If someone else knows the key to our lock, then they can also open it; if a thief can guess the combination, they can steal your bicycle. Radio messages in the war were locked with mathematical combination locks that, like these physical locks, had PIN codes called keys. But just like the physical combination lock, there is a weakness to this approach – if the enemy can guess or discover your key, then they can pick your lock and read your messages.

The history of the Second World War can't be told without

unravelling the information war. The surging battles across North Africa, the German defeat on the Eastern Front, the lifting of the Siege of the Atlantic, the Battle for France – each of these campaigns can only be fully understood through the lens of the information war. Who was picking whose mathematical locks? Who was reading whose codes? Who was reading whose mind?

Amazon's main objective is to understand its customers. The company analyses what parts of the website are interesting for their customers, and from this decodes what the customer demand for different products is. Eisenhower's objective was to understand his enemy. In the information war, the aim is to collect the enemy's messages and decode what their intent is.

Humans are embodied, our intelligence is locked in, and so the information we can access is precious to us. Compared to the computer, our low rate of information communication means we hoard details we believe may help us decide what to do next. Our actions are often driven by our understanding of others' intent. Just like Amazon attempts to study its customers and armies attempt to understand their enemy.

When Rommel arrived in France to take charge of the Atlantic Wall, he already had a reputation. The British press called him the Desert Fox. He had led the Afrika Korps and outwitted the British 8th Army across North Africa in daring raids. But he met his match in the wiry 'Spartan' General Bernard Montgomery. The story goes that he was forced out of Africa with his foxtail between his legs.

The reality is somewhat different. When Rommel arrived in North Africa, the British had broken the German codes and could unlock the mathematical combination the Germans used to send messages. They knew the details of Rommel's North Africa orders from Hitler. Rommel had been told to 'hold the line'. Unfortunately for the British, Rommel took advantage of his devolved autonomy. He saw the situation on the ground, understood his country's common purpose and decided to attack. The British, having read Rommel's instructions from Hitler, were surprised by his actions and were not ready for his assault.

Rommel also knew the plans of the British. The US military attaché in Cairo was reporting back to Washington with a compromised code, exposing their plans to the Germans. The attaché changed the code on 29 June 1942. Montgomery arrived a few weeks later, just at the point that the balance in the intelligence war shifted. Rommel's efforts were now stymied because he'd lost access to Allied plans, and the Allies had detailed knowledge of Rommel's extended supply chain through their own efforts at codebreaking. Rommel relied on naval transport for fuel, food and equipment. The Allies knew when and where these deliveries were due and destroyed 70 per cent of the supplies, damaging the Afrika Korps' ability to manoeuvre and forcing them to withdraw to Southern Italy.

Rommel and Montgomery were both high-achieving commanders doing a demanding job, but in retrospect we know their achievements in the field were less because of their own intelligence and more as a result of their military intelligence. Their successes came when they broke their enemy's codes. Their failures were a result of their own plans being known to the enemy.

North Africa was a relatively small theatre of operations, but the same story played out across the war. The Battle of the Atlantic, Hitler's plan to starve Britain into submission, was derailed by the breaking of German naval codes. The movement of every German U-boat pack was known and the Atlantic convoys simply sailed around them.

In the Soviet Union, Hitler's plan for launching the German offensive of 1943 was known three months before the attack began. Hitler planned a pincer movement on the Russian city of Kursk. The number and types of tanks and the timing and locations of the attack were known in advance by the Red Army. It deployed its tanks and defensive lines in full knowledge of the German strategy. The battle involved over 2 million combat troops and is the largest tank battle the world has ever seen. It was a major Soviet victory that triggered Germany's retreat from Russia and turned the tide of the war.

These plans were being decoded by Diana Russell-Clarke and her colleagues in Bletchley Park. Failures of cryptography had a major effect on the direction and outcome of the war. The ability to understand your enemy's intent is a major advantage on the battlefield. The use of radio to control troops allowed for coordinated attacks that led to some stunning successes, but the failure to protect communications left troops vulnerable to devastating counterattacks. Information is power.

What is true for armies is also true for humans. Choosing what information we share and for what purpose is one of the ways that we maintain control over who we are. In a world where information is precious, where it can be used to either collaborate or compete with us, it's understandable that we choose to be circumspect about who we share our personal information with.

Mathematical locks share the need for a key with physical combination locks. To break a physical combination lock there are three principal approaches. First, I could try all possible keys. Many combination locks have four-digit codes. I could try all 10,000 possible keys to unlock the box. Second, I might be able to discover the key by carefully feeling the lock as I change the combination. Flaws in the lock's design or usage might allow me to feel when I touch part or all of the right key. Third, I might try to guess the key – and if I know who closed the lock, I might guess that they use their birthday or another special date for their key.

Mathematical combination locks are similar: each of these three attacks can be tried. Trying every different combination is known as a *brute-force attack*. Flaws in the mathematical lock's design and usage are attacked with an approach known as *statistical attack*. These two attacks were the reason for so much of the tedious work of Diana Russell-Clarke and her friends. Both attacks could require considerable computation, much of it very repetitive. The third attack is also useful: I might be able to guess what sort of PIN code my enemy used, a birthday perhaps, or the initials of a loved one. The Bletchley Park codebreakers called these guesses *cribs*, a word that in British slang refers to information that can be used for passing an exam.

One way of thinking about how a brute-force attack works is to imagine an empty crossword with no clues. There are very many different possible words that could fit in the space. A brute-force attack would try all possible placements of letters in the squares in the hope that one combination is right. But for a large crossword, the number of possible letter placements is so huge a human can't go through them all. There just isn't enough time.

Now, I don't want to give too much away here, but you can see what we're building up to. We invented computers. Or, more precisely, we invented automatic computers. At the start of the war, Bletchley Park was staffed by thousands of women who performed the role of information processors. At this point, automatic computers didn't exist, so we called these *people* computers. What happened next was that the work of Diana Russell-Clarke and her colleagues was automated to the best extent we could manage, and that's the origin of the modern computer.

But let's pause for a moment to reflect and clarify. It suits my narrative to have Bletchley Park as the origin of all these innovations, but the need for the automatic computer was widespread. In Germany, Konrad Zuse built computation machines based around telephone switching relays for the German aviation research institute. In the United States, a machine called the ENIAC was designed for computing artillery tables. The need for machines to automate the process of calculation goes back even to the nineteenth century. The Cambridge mathematician and inventor Charles Babbage studied the efficiency of factories, introducing many of the ideas behind the production lines Henry Ford used for the Model T. Babbage also designed a mechanical computer for automatically creating mathematical tables. I could have chosen to go through any one of these stories and we would have seen the same pattern of automation of cognitive labour. But humans, unlike computers, share information via narratives, and it suits my narrative to focus on the events at Bletchley Park.

The original human computers, like Diana Russell-Clark, were performing tasks that relied on the application of relatively simple rules of arithmetic. Unlike Eisenhower's decision to invade France, which was a matter of judgement, answers *could* be arrived at through logical deduction, and automating this process was the moment we sliced away arithmetic from the atomic human and conceded it to the machine.

I've drawn an analogy between decrypting German codes and doing crosswords. Real crosswords are made more interesting by interconnecting clues. If the answer to 1 down is the word debut, then you know that the answer to 1 across must also start with a 'D'. Once you've guessed one answer, constraints are placed on what the other answers can be. Any correct word reduces the number of possibilities a brute-force attack needs to explore.

It's these guesses, or cribs, that provide a very human aspect to the art of codebreaking. In Bletchley Park, the Allies made use of humans to imagine the sort of things German soldiers might be writing. If one German unit was responsible for weather reports, you might guess that one of the words in their message was *Wetter*. If you guessed right, then you've reduced the search space for your brute-force attacks. Once you'd found a correct crib, the codes were easier to break. The similarity between codebreaking and crosswords was not lost on the cryptographers: among the many recruits at Bletchley Park were a number of regular completers of the famously fiendish *Times* cryptic crossword.

The brute-force approach to solving a crossword feels like a good candidate for automation. It involves a repetitive set of actions: the testing of plausible words in different combinations. The inputs to this process are the structure of the puzzle. The output is the completed puzzle. Designing a machine that can repeat these actions saves a lot of human effort. In Bletchley Park these machines were called *bombes*, and they were designed by Alan Turing. Given a crib, the bombe could explore different settings of the key to see if they broke the code.

However, imagining plausible cribs seems quite a lot harder for a machine. A good crib would require an understanding of the human context: how might the radio operator behave in different circumstances, for example. It is a task that requires empathy. Today, we are just on the cusp of building machines that understand some of our human context. These large-language models have read all the text they can find, and through our writings they are beginning to understand something about us. This is a very recent development and it has required massive amounts of data to achieve, but it is far beyond anything a machine could have done in the 1940s. But let's be careful: we have stumbled across a trap for machine intelligence. While it *is* true that empathy is a very difficult problem for machines, it turns out we *can* automate the process of guessing cribs.

The trap we have fallen into is to assume that a machine-intelligence solution should copy the human approach to the problem. It triggers a form of introspection that misleads about the way a machine could complete the task. We make the mistake of assuming that the machine's solution should be human-like. We like to share information through narratives, but computers are much more comfortable sharing information through statistics. This means the machine has shortcuts which are not available to us. These shortcuts go to the heart of how machine learning works.

Radio operators have habits, and it turns out many of these habits are shared across different radio operators. We can make predictions about what radio operators are likely to do based on knowledge of what they have done in the past. We use past examples to teach the machine. The machine doesn't need to understand humans to discern patterns in human behaviour. It can just use the statistics about how a human has behaved in the past to predict how they will behave in the future.

Bletchley Park didn't have the technology to use machines to automate the process of producing cribs, but the codebreakers did systematize the process of crib production, and their system can help us understand the techniques Amazon and Facebook use today in their machine-learning algorithms.

Bletchley Park codebreakers used the historic behaviour of different radio operators in different units to predict what their future behaviour might be. They kept paper files which contained words commonly used by these operators. The foibles of the different operators were stored in the filing system, and when a prediction for a new crib was required codebreakers could look up these previous behaviours to get an idea of suitable cribs. In machine learning we would call this approach a *bag-of-words model*, because the system stores the individual words the different operators use. Bag-of-words models are a simple form of machine learning; early spam filters for email used them. In Bletchley Park these words were stored in filing cabinets; in machine learning we store the words in the computer.

Much of the automatable cognitive labour at Bletchley Park was performed by human operators, whether it was filing or computing, but the overall organization was also structured in a way that made information processing more efficient. Complex problems were decomposed into simpler tasks. Those tasks were completed by humans like Diana or machines like the bombes. Henry Ford mass-produced an affordable car by constructing an assembly line – this involves decomposing the different processes that are needed to produce the car into repeatable activities, each of which is performed at a different place in the line. By decomposing the decryption problem, Bletchley Park created an assembly line for information. Modern artificial intelligence systems work in much the same way. In computer science, this strategy is known as *divide and conquer*, but the strategy was well known across the Industrial Revolution. Charles Babbage's work *On the Economy of Machinery and Manufactures* was published in 1832. So even in the 1940s these ideas were not new, but the big difference between the 1940s and today is the availability of data and the power and flexibility of modern computing machines.

The story of Bletchley Park is the story of decryption on an industrial scale. The machines that were built there, for specific tasks, were much faster than humans. Authority was devolved to machines to complete these jobs, but these were *not* tasks where there was any room for judgement or interpretation. These tasks were 'information complete' – the answer could be deduced given the information available without resorting to judgement. Autonomy was not devolved in the way it was by Eisenhower and Bezos in running the Allied armies and Amazon. Bletchley Park had a very rigid information topography; it was organized into different huts that worked on different German codes. Across the whole process, just as the storage of cribs was systemized, the processing of information was systemized. As in many factories, this production line was operated by a combination of humans and machines: machines were used to automate the highly repetitive tasks, and humans filled in as necessary to set up the machines or pass the information between the different processes. This pattern is common in automation. The machine rigidly performs repetitive tasks and humans' flexible capabilities are used to bridge the gaps.

The secret messages that were being processed at Bletchley Park were also constructed using machines: the Germans based most of their military codes on a machine called the Enigma. Reports and orders were sent via radio Morse code, one letter at a time. To encrypt the messages, the Enigma mapped each letter from each word in the original message to different letters in a coded message. In cryptography, the original message is called the *plaintext* and the coded message the *ciphertext*.

At Bletchley Park we can already see three components to an information assembly line: first develop an insight that gives you a clue that reduces the search space for the puzzle; at Bletchley these were the cribs. They used their contextual knowledge for this. The second step is to translate that insight into terms the machine can understand and compute with. This second job was given to the female operators, and today we would call it 'programming'. It involved setting up the machine to handle the information in the crib. Finally, the machine was used to exhaustively search through the different settings to solve the puzzle. These three steps remain similar for information-processing systems today. The change since the 1940s is the extent to which we have been able to devolve authority to the machine.

This process of breaking down a task into parts is called

decomposition. It's second nature to computer scientists to take any complex process and decompose it. Once decomposed, each part can be independently automated. The ideas came to computer science from manufacturing. Production lines process objects; computers process information. In both cases, humans are integrated in the processing. This brings us into a relationship with the machine. In a physical production line, humans set up the machines and accommodate any irregular circumstances, such as a manufacturing defect or any repairs for the machine. In an information assembly line we translate the ideas we have into terms the machine can understand. We program the machine according to that understanding. Across history, this has been our relationship with automation. Mechanical production lines require flexible and adaptable humans to service them, and until recently our information-processing pipelines have also required flexible human cognition to interpret and translate the ideas for processing. In the past, the machine could not adapt to us because it had no sense of who we are and how to communicate with us. Until recently, all the intelligences we created were designed for specific goals. In this sense, they are *directed* intelligences – they solve a particular task that is part of a larger whole. They are given the context of the task: the inputs and the necessary outputs. The performance of the solution they provide can then be measured, for example by how quickly the problem is solved. Automatic decryption gives us the background to how these intelligences came about: in brute-force decryption the goal is clear, but for our own intelligence there is often more ambiguity about what the goal should be. For a brute-force solution such as exhaustively exploring possible combination keys we can definitively say that the machine performs better than the human. This was urgent work – the phases of the Battle of the Atlantic shifted with the changes in the codebreakers' abilities to read the messages. Tons of shipping and thousands of lives depended on the ability of the people and machines at Bletchley Park to read the Enigma.

*

The Enigma machine hid plaintext messages in the form of a *substitution cipher*. Each letter from the original message in this cipher is mapped to a different letter in the locked ciphertext. So 'A' might be mapped to 'G', 'B' might be mapped to 'N', and so on. The statistical attack that is used to break a substitution cipher is known as *frequency analysis*. Frequency analysis works by noticing, for example, that 'E' is the most common letter in German. If 'E' is the most common letter in the plaintext, then if we substitute all the 'E's for a different letter, for example 'X', then 'X' will be the most common letter in the ciphertext. This attack is not guaranteed to work because it may be an unusual message without the letter 'E' in it, but it's likely to work, which is why it's called a statistical attack.

The Enigma machine had a keyboard with the twenty-six letters of the alphabet printed on the keys, and every time you pressed a key the machine would change the substitution letter. From a mathematical perspective, it was implementing a *function*. In mathematics, a function maps one set of values to another set of values. Like a machine, a function has inputs and it has outputs. But in a function those inputs and outputs are in the form of symbols or, more usually, *numbers*.

Sorry for the maths – you don't have to follow it in detail, but just get the sense that machines can be real-world implementations of mathematics. Sometimes it's obvious when this is happening, like with a calculator. But sometimes it's not so obvious, like with the Enigma machine.

What is an example of a simple function? Well, we can think about the simplest machine: one that does nothing.[3] In mathematics that function is known as the *identity function*. It takes numbers as inputs and gives the same numbers as outputs, meaning 1→1, 2→2. Another relatively simple function is one that turns numbers upside down. This is called the *reciprocal function*, in which 2→½, 3→⅓, and so on.

The idea of using machines to implement mathematical functions is at the core of machine learning. Perhaps that now gives you some more insight into the term '*machine* learning'. At one level, it is quite misleading: machine-learning engineers don't get covered in oil and wear overalls, they work with mathematics and computation – because it's not really machines that do the learning, it's mathematical functions implemented on computers that do the learning.

In the Enigma machine the input values are the original letters of the message, and the output values are the substituted letters of the secret message. The Enigma machine implements the mathematical function through electrical wires going from the keyboard letters to a set of light bulbs.

The Enigma machine provides a function that takes in a message and outputs an encrypted message. Modern machine-learning methods allow us to create machines which have mathematical functions that can 'see'. By that I mean they can detect faces or other objects in images. To allow machines to detect faces and objects, we have to decide what numbers represent which faces and objects. We call these numbers *labels*, then we create a mathematical function that takes in images and outputs labels for the objects. Even large-language models like ChatGPT have a function that takes words and phrases as input, then gives new words and phrases as the output. If the input is a question or a comment, and the output is a response, then you have a chatbot. We can even do this across languages to automatically translate them – the words or letters in a sentence are converted into a set of numbers, then we learn a mathematical function that converts those numbers from the original language to the right numbers for French, Swahili, German, Mandarin or a range of other languages. A big difference is the complexity of the machine. The mathematical functions we use today would be difficult to write down; they are implemented in modern digital computers. The Enigma machine also translated letters from the plaintext to the ciphertext (and back), but the functions it used to do this were simple enough that they could be packaged a in portable box using a combination of electrical and mechanical technologies already available in the 1920s.

The Enigma machine had a set of rotors. When the rotors were in a fixed position, the machine performed a substitution cipher, but if that's all it did, it would have made the machine vulnerable to frequency analysis, a statistical attack for breaking the code. To prevent this, the substitution changed with every key press. The rotors would turn every time the operator pressed a key, changing the wiring and substituting the letters differently. By using three rotors together, the Enigma machine could cycle through 18,000 different substitution ciphers.

To complicate the code further, the three rotors were interchangeable: they could be placed in any order. The machine also came with two spare rotors: there were five possible rotors in total. Different rotors would be used on different days. Setting the machine up involved picking the rotors, selecting their position and connecting the keyboard through a set of plugs. All these settings together are the equivalent of the combination key setting for the mechanical lock. The combination of different settings meant that instead of the 10,000 different key settings of a mechanical combination lock, the three-rotor military Enigma had over 150 billion billion possible keys.

The cribs gave clues to the codebreakers which reduced the number of keys that needed to be searched, but even with this reduction the number of keys was more than Diana Russell-Clarke and the other human computers could explore on their own. So Alan Turing designed the bombes to do this repetitive work – large machines that could automatically test different settings of the Enigma.

The social network of the 1930s was the telephone. In the 1940s Claude Shannon developed his theory of information in response to the demand for telephone lines and exchanges. When telephone exchanges were first built, human operators switched the lines to connect your call. But by the late 1930s many telephone exchanges had been automated. Switches called *relays* were automatically opened and closed by magnets to direct calls to the correct destination, automating the operation. These operations *could* be accurately modelled with logic. The relays operated as automatons; there was no space for devolved autonomy or interpretation. No risk of relays going off track to visit families when they were supposed to be waiting in Hampshire. This wave of automation relied on complete information.

The same relays were used by Turing in the bombes to automatically test different combinations of keys to decode messages. Turing had designed a machine that used these relays to automate the brute-force attack. It provided a simple automation of what had been human labour. The instructions for these machines became known as the program, and that's why today we still talk about programming computers.

The Bletchley Park operation was an information factory. But in devolving cognitive labour to the machine, there was no room for innovation, no tolerance for disobedience; there was no autonomy or judgement associated with these machines.

The Bletchley Park information topography fed a much larger ecosystem of decision-making, and on 5 June 1944 Eisenhower was at the hub of that system. But unlike the automatons that ran the brute-force calculations in Bletchley, Eisenhower didn't have complete information, he only had 'the best information available'. His decision required judgement: at the time he made it he knew he could be wrong, and being wrong would have dreadful consequences for thousands of soldiers and the long-term course of the war. Judgements of this form remained firmly the preserve of the human.

3.

Intent

My first job after university was as a field engineer working on oil rigs for a company called Schlumberger. The graduate-recruitment brochure for the company spoke of high salaries, large bonuses and exotic locations. The role also promised a form of 'supreme power'. I would be managing a small team, as well as expensive equipment. Having read the brochure, I imagined myself wandering in Egyptian deserts, floating on Nigerian oceans and sweating in Colombian jungles. I would stride the planet and measure the earth. In practice, my experience was more mundane. I was deployed to two faded English seaside resorts: Morecambe and Great Yarmouth. I worked on oil rigs in Liverpool Bay, gas rigs off Humberside and a series of land-based wells across England. The only common feature of each of these locations seemed to be that they each required a six-hour cross-country drive from wherever I was based.

The job was tiring, but it also involved a lot of waiting. The centre of activity on an oil rig is the drill floor. From there the driller threads long lengths of pipe into the earth to excavate the borehole and access the oil. My work required me to have full access to make my measurements. When I worked, the rig waited. Conversely, when the driller and his crew worked, I waited. These idle times combined with cross-country drives left time for thought and reading. My job was to measure the rock formations below the rig. The power delegated to me was responsibility for a large computer, a winch, an explosives store, a set of radioactive sources, the measurement tools to run into the well, and my team of two operators who helped to set everything up. Once I had access to the drill floor, I worked closely with my operators to prepare my tools and then with a geologist to identify formation types and the location of any oil or gas. The geologist would analyse my measurements and declare the results in a report.

The geologist was a representative of the oil company, and, while I had power over my team, the oil company was our customer, so the geologist had power over me. But just as things worked better in my team if I worked collaboratively with my operators, so things worked better with the geologist if we worked in collaboration. To help with this, I learned aspects of the geologist's role. Specifically, I began to understand how the rock formations were identified. Sometimes the rules seemed very simple, so I began to wonder why the computer I was using couldn't do this work for us.

Our tools measured properties of the rocks: their density, their porosity, their electrical conductivity. These properties revealed whether the formation was formed from limestone, sandstone or mudstone. But just as I thought I'd understood one of the geologist's rules, an exception would emerge. The rules were never hard and fast – there was always some nuance or context the geologist was considering. It reminded me of my attempts to learn languages at school. I would be taught a set of rules, and then when I tried to speak or write the language I would encounter a set of exceptions. This nuance came naturally to the geologist, just like the vagaries of language come naturally to a native speaker, but, like in my struggles with French at school, I stumbled as I struggled to formalize my understanding.

Arthur Conan Doyle's detective, Sherlock Holmes, was the master of deduction. In the novel *A Study in Scarlet*,[1] Holmes's assistant, Dr Watson, has a challenge facing him. He wants to understand how the detective can unerringly solve a variety of crimes through apparently unconnected observations. In a chapter titled 'The Science of Deduction', Watson describes Holmes as being ignorant on issues such as literature, philosophy and politics but having a deep knowledge of areas such as 'practical geology'. Specifically, Holmes knows the colours of the different muds that may be found around

London. This allows him to deduce where someone has been by the colour of the mud on their clothing. Watson explains that Holmes uses information like this, and logic, to solve crimes.

Logic represents the world as discrete objects: each category has particular properties. By defining relationships between these categories we can make logical *deductions*. It is not just Dr Watson and Conan Doyle's readers that have been seduced by this formalization of reasoning. In the 1980s the focus of artificial intelligence researchers was firmly on logic: defining objects and their properties to answer questions. Just as I tried to represent the geologist's expertise with a logical understanding of which measurements indicated limestone and which sandstone, computer programs were written that used logic to diagnose diseases in patients. Programs were even written to deduce the conclusions from a set of facts around a legal case, just like in the Sherlock Holmes stories.[2] These computer programs were called *expert systems*.

When we read about Holmes we are seduced by his deductions, partially because logic seems to give us a *model* for his decision-making skills. We use the word 'model' to describe an abstraction of reality, one that captures some salient aspects but is lacking in some or much of the detail. The statistician George Box once wrote, 'All models are wrong, but some are useful.'[3] This quote captures the challenge in creating a model. For a model to be useful, a balance must be found between which aspects of reality to capture and which to ignore.

Logic is a model for decision-making. It captures some of its characteristics, such as the idea that there are some inputs and a conclusion, but it is lacking in other respects. One big problem is that for logical deduction to work we must have *complete* information. It is not enough to know only about the presence of a particular colour of mud in the local area, we must know the locations of all such types of mud and all possible ways it can transfer on to clothing in order to draw a logical conclusion. In practice, this full knowledge is rarely available, and this would be a particular problem for humans if we relied only on logic. Our limited bandwidth means that we rarely know the full picture and our intelligence is usually dealing with an *absence* of information. You might think that the machine can escape these problems because its high bandwidth gives it access to so much more data, but deriving rules from large datasets can be difficult and, despite the machine's much greater bandwidth, the amount of data it can access is still only a tiny fraction of all possible data.

Logic provides a mathematical model, but models can also have physical forms. In Formula One, small-scale models of the racing cars are used in wind-tunnel tests. This allows the wind tunnels to be smaller and reduces the manufacturing cost of the model.

These physical models are also based on an abstraction of the problem: not only are the Formula One car models smaller, they don't have engines either. The engine is removed in the abstraction because it is not relevant to the aerodynamics.[4]

A logic model forms part of a class of models where we don't have to build a physical form. The model can be manipulated through calculation alone. These models are known as mathematical or computational models. These non-physical models are the foundation of how we automate decision-making: expert systems are mathematical models based on logic. But, like all models, they capture *some* salient aspects of reality and ignore others.

Expert systems became popular in the 1980s, but, just like my efforts to classify rock formations, expert systems find it easy to capture the rules but difficult to capture the nuance. The real world is more complex than simple logical models can represent. We need to handle ambiguity and conflict between rules. We need to assimilate the context and pass judgement as to when the rules might reasonably be broken, and a logic-based expert system cannot do this.

In *A Study in Scarlet*, Holmes can deduce where someone has been by the colour of the mud on their clothes, but in the real world there could be many explanations for how that mud got there. The key achievement of a gifted linguist, a good doctor, the geologist from the oil company or Sherlock Holmes is *not* the application of the rules of logic but the decision about what other important factors apply in a given context. When a geologist explained to me why they believed a layer of rock was limestone or sandstone, they would give me a logical explanation, but when I tried to imagine how I would program a computer to replicate their assessment, it appeared mysterious to me, because the real skill they were displaying was the distillation of information into the salient facts. Those facts were then presented as simple ideas. This is important, because both the geologist and I are locked in: the ideas the geologist shared needed to be simple so they could be communicated to me through our limited bandwidth.

A similar challenge applies to expert systems for medical data. It might seem reasonable to surmise that a patient with a runny nose and a headache has a cold. But if the pollen count is high and the patient is a student who's just finished her exams, then an alternative explanation is that the patient is dealing with mild alcohol poisoning and a case of hay fever. Context is important. Introducing context means creating a set of rules that is often too complex for a human to specify. When building expert systems it proved very hard to extract the domain experts' understanding into a set of consistent rules that could be fed into the computer.

Unlike Holmes, on the oil rig I couldn't see the colour of the rocks we measured. But I did have a tool that used gamma rays to measure formation density, another that used a neutron source to measure formation porosity, and a third that measured the formation's electrical resistivity. I would share these measurements with the geologist, who would give me logical reasons for an assessment of the formation. But the geologists were working with a lot more than the measurements I had just given them. They had an understanding of the local geology and how the formations in the UK differed from those elsewhere in the world. They used this understanding to judge how the measurements I shared were relevant to their deductions. This ability was associated with years of academic study followed by further refinement of their geological intuition through years of putting it into practice.

By the 1990s the challenges with expert systems meant that AI had failed to deliver on early promises. Others had also found the same problems I was experiencing. My downtime on the rig was spent reading popular-science magazines, and I began to read articles about a *new* way of automating decision-making. The articles claimed that, instead of building expert systems, we should be inspired to make decisions in the same way the brain does. Instead of directly programming the computer with the logical rules, we should provide it with examples and encourage it to learn rules from those examples. Instead of having me work out what the salient factors were and then program the computer, the computer should just work it out by itself. This is how I found out about the approach we now call *machine learning*. The brain-inspired ideas the magazine articles were talking about were mathematical models known as *artificial neural networks*.

Given my struggles to capture the geologist's thinking in a set of logical rules, the machine-learning approach appeared promising. So I swallowed my disappointment at the lack of international adventure in my day job and focused on the intellectual adventure these questions triggered. As I waited for the drill floor to be ready for my team, I taught myself how to build these neural-network models. Later, I decided that what had started as my hobby should become my new job and I left the oil rigs to study for a Ph.D. and learn more about these new methods.

After graduating, I joined Microsoft Research. At the time, Microsoft was the world's most valuable company, and its software was everywhere. I was keen to deploy my new knowledge of machine learning. The Bletchley Park information production line gives us a good idea about how we process information, but in the sixty years that had passed since then things had moved on. The team at Bletchley Park had set up the programs for their machine by hand-wiring relays together. In modern computers that wiring is stored in software: instead of a physical plugboard, the instructions are stored electronically. This made programs easier to create, store and share, like the printing press did for the written word. But it also made the programs incredibly complicated. When I joined

Microsoft, its most important products, like Office, were so complicated they took *two years* to finish. If I wanted my ideas to appear in the product, then they would need to be considered right at the beginning of the design process. With a lot of work and luck, they would make it into the released software two years later. Somewhat disillusioned, I left Microsoft and began a career as an academic at the University of Sheffield.

Mark Zuckerberg's interest in AI was driven by the extent to which his company, Facebook, needed to process information. Over a decade since I'd left Microsoft, and just over a year before Zuckerberg launched Facebook's AI lab, I was invited to Hacker Way in Silicon Valley's Menlo Park for Facebook's first ever academic summit. It started with a tour of the campus, and then Greg, a Vice President of Engineering, gave us a tour of Facebook's information systems. Facebook had begun to use machine learning to increase the engagement of its users and, flushed with its initial success, the company was looking to engage the academic community. Greg also expanded on Facebook's 'hacker culture'. The walls were covered with their mottoes, among them, 'Move fast and break things'; 'Done is better than perfect'. Facebook was building a corporate culture of agility, unlike Microsoft, and prominent in its principles was an emphasis on speed of deployment.

As we walked around the Facebook campus, Greg explained to us that Facebook deployed its software *every week*. The software engineers were writing code on a Wednesday, integrating it into their systems on a Friday, and the code was running with customers by the following Tuesday. This process is known as *continuous deployment*, and it reduced the time needed for code to go from conception to customer from Microsoft's two years to only six days.

The approach Microsoft used for software design required a centralized design process, and those ideas were implemented by teams of engineers according to a grand plan. But just like in a supply chain, grand plans can get complex very quickly. Making changes to the grand plan to accommodate unforeseen problems can require a lot of communication.

Facebook's approach of continuous deployment involved much less centralized design. It devolved autonomy to the software engineers, empowering them to bring their ideas to the customer. This allows for more innovation, but this innovation comes at a cost. Improvements tend to be tactical rather than strategic. Small changes are quick to deploy, but major changes that would require coordination across many engineers become harder, because they are difficult to coordinate. You can think of the Microsoft approach as like a group of artists creating a very large woven tapestry. The vision of what the tapestry should contain is controlled centrally. Individual weavers may have some latitude in how to interpret the central instructions, but it is limited. Everyone works to a grand plan. The continuous-deployment approach is more like a patchwork quilt. Innovation occurs in small patches but doesn't necessarily conform to an overall pattern. The patchwork quilt can be quicker to produce than the tapestry, because it doesn't require the same degree of centralized control, but the result may be less coherent than the story a tapestry can represent.

I wasn't the only ex-Microsoft employee at Facebook's academic summit. A close friend from Cambridge, Joaquin, had just made the move across the Atlantic to start working there. Joaquin and I had written papers, edited books and organized workshops together. He was born in Valencia in Spain but moved to Morocco when he was three years old. He'd studied in Denmark and had worked in Germany, relocated to the UK and had now arrived in California. His diversity of experience had left him with a natural ability to assimilate and work within different cultural contexts. There was no great fanfare about Joaquin's arrival at Facebook – there was no penthouse launch like there would be for Yann when he arrived – but what Joaquin was about to build for Facebook was far more significant than anything that Yann's AI team would later do.

As part of Facebook's agile culture, the company had devolved power to its software engineers. There was an intense interview process to select the best people, and once they arrived they completed a course on Facebook systems and culture known as the bootcamp. Joaquin had been managing a team for Microsoft's search engine, Bing. He knew the value of good engineering infrastructure, and he could see the challenges fast movement was bringing for Facebook's machine-learning systems. But he had also just completed the Facebook bootcamp, and he understood and was thrilled by the autonomy and power Facebook was about to devolve to him.

Joaquin's mixed background has given him extraordinary cultural agility. He can will himself to become the person he's expected to be. Whether it was in his role as an academic, his time at Microsoft or what was to become his leadership of Facebook's applied machine-learning team, Joaquin could adapt his approach to assimilate and operate the cultural levers at his disposal.

Bletchley Park was a large-scale information-processing pipeline performing specific tasks at scale. In Facebook's devolved approach engineers were trusted to make any improvements themselves and add them to the Facebook site. Each improvement was aiming to increase the site's appeal, so Facebook designed a way of measuring which improvements were better. It kept the changes that caused people to stay on their platform for longer periods of time: more interaction with the site meant more time for ads, which led to more revenue.

Joaquin's role was to augment the Facebook site with more machine intelligence. He was introducing the modern equivalent of Turing's bombes into the information-processing pipeline. Facebook engineers had already experimented with machine-learning algorithms. These algorithms worked in a similar way to Bletchley Park's systems for suggesting cribs. They looked at past user behaviour and used it to predict future behaviour. Just as particular German radio operators had foibles that would emerge in their pattern of message sending, each of Facebook's users has foibles around their personal interests, the posts they choose to like and the friends they choose to connect with.

Facebook's engineers had been designing algorithms that summarized previous user behaviour and used those algorithms to predict future user behaviour, but because of the company's agile infrastructure they were doing this in a piecemeal way. Their algorithms were being introduced as single patches in the wider quilt that made up the ecosystem. There wasn't a coherent strategy as to how this was being done. Joaquin was a machine-learning expert and knew that to do machine learning well you need to organize the information flow. Piecemeal approaches weren't appropriate. Instead of a patchwork quilt, you needed to weave a tapestry.

In 2005, a year before he joined Microsoft, Joaquin and I had organized an academic meeting at Bletchley Park. The focus of our meeting was on a missing piece of the logical puzzle – how to deal with the unknown. We were both interested in how to propagate *uncertainty* through information-processing pipelines.

Today the story of the Enigma machine is well known. Alan Turing's remarkable life has made him the subject of films and books. His achievements in cracking Enigma codes at Bletchley Park sit at the core of these stories, but back when we brought our colleagues together to talk about machine intelligence at the estate there was less understanding of this important work. The workshop organization was supported by volunteer local staff, many of them with connections to codebreakers. We were hosted by Margaret Sale. On the second day of the meeting she arranged for us to see a demonstration by her husband, Tony. He had spent his career at GCHQ, the UK's modern codebreaking centre, which emerged from Bletchley Park. Tony showed us a machine. It was reconstructed from his memory, rare photographs and a few snatched blueprints. He stood in front of his creation, a bank of switches and lights, and a long paper tape, that whirred noisily. The tape encoded a locked German message. Tony began to tell us the machine's story. A story Margaret and Tony had spent the best part of two decades striving to preserve. It's the story of how Eisenhower came to receive the note that launched the invasion of the beaches at Normandy.

Eisenhower's note contained vital information about enemy intent. But the note hadn't come from the bombe machines Turing had developed. They were for decoding the chatter between German troops. Tony Sale was showing us an utterly different machine. It was the source of the *most* secret intelligence to emerge from Bletchley Park. It was built to decode direct orders from Adolf Hitler.

The 2004 film *Downfall* depicts the last days of Hitler's regime. Bruno Ganz portrays the Nazi leader, his ravings and eventual suicide. The film is set in the command bunker he and his close confidants used in the final weeks of the war. It interleaves footage of the gathered generals with clips of incoming messages from the front. Each message reveals a new setback or an ignored order. Each message triggers an enraged outburst from the Führer. Those messages are received on a teleprinter: a large, automated typewriter. This teleprinter was part of a machine that was decoding the most important messages of the German military. This was coming from a machine with a far more sophisticated encryption mechanism than the Enigma – it was known as the *Lorenz cipher*.

A typical combination lock for securing a bicycle uses four rotors, each with ten digits. The Enigma machine had three wheels with twenty-six letters each, but the Lorenz cipher came from a machine with twelve wheels. This gave them 1.6 million billion more possible keys than the bicycle lock.

September 2019, I'm at my son's school in Cambridge, listening to his headmistress. My mind drifts and I look around the hall to the rolls of honour for former students. One name is everywhere: state scholarship, university scholarship, fellowship at Trinity College, fellowship of the Royal Society. Inscribed in gold letters: W. T. Tutte. These boards show a litany of achievements, but they only scratch the surface. There is no mention of Tutte's most important work, because he single-handedly reverse-engineered the Lorenz cipher. Even though he never saw a Lorenz machine until after the war, he was able to unpick this new lock.

In August 1941 a German operator made a major error: two almost identical messages were sent from the same cipher machine. Careful analysis unveiled both the plaintext form of the message and the encryption key used. Bill Tutte analysed the key, and in arguably the greatest single intellectual achievement of the Second

World War he was able to deduce the entire design of the Lorenz machine from patterns in the key.

Tutte's analysis identified weaknesses in the code. Just like the Enigma, the Lorenz cipher can be seen as a mathematical function. The Enigma was a substitution cipher, but the messages Hitler's machine sent were digitized, converted into a stream of electronic bits: 1s and 0s, like Shannon's representation of information. This bitstream was combined with a key of electronic bits to lock the message – the approach is known as a Vernam cipher.[5] Tutte's work enabled a statistical attack on the Lorenz cipher, but even with this statistical attack the follow-up brute-force work was too much for humans or even the electromechanical bombes. They needed a new machine, a new way of exploring the millions of combinations more quickly.

Jack Good, who coined the term 'ultraintelligence', was on the team asked to help. They were led by a mathematician called Max Newman, and they were also joined by Donald Michie, a nineteen-year-old wannabe linguist who had accidentally taken a cryptography course. The situation was becoming desperate. When the Germans first started using the Lorenz cipher, the operators were sloppy and made errors in their encryption. That made it easier to crack this new mathematical combination lock – the plans for the Battle of Kursk that turned the tide on the Eastern Front were unlocked in this way – but the operators' practices had improved and it was becoming harder to break the messages.

Newman's team built different machines, including one called the 'Heath Robinson'. Heath Robinson was a cartoonist who drew elaborate machines that performed simple tasks.[6] The machine was well named, because despite its spinning wheels and paper tapes it was performing a simple comparison-and-add task. Two paper tapes were used, one containing the ciphertext, the other containing part of the key, and comparing the tapes allowed the team to apply the statistical attack to decode the message.

Magnetic relays from telephone exchanges had enabled Turing to design the bombes for decoding Enigma. Tommy Flowers was a telecoms engineer who worked on those automated exchanges before the war. At Bletchley Park, experts like Flowers brought their knowledge of automated exchanges to help in building the bombes and other machines.

Flowers was called up to Bletchley Park from his office in London. Newman's team wanted him to design a counting system for comparing the two tapes in the Heath Robinson. Flowers realized that the counting system could work faster if they used thermionic valves instead of relays. Valves are the switches that radio sets, like my grandfather's, used. They switch faster than relays because they are switched by a beam of electrons instead of by a metal contact. With the valves the Heath Robinson could operate faster, but that caused its paper tapes to stretch, split and spread across the floor as they unspooled.

Flowers knew that the limitation of the machine was the spinning paper tapes and he believed that the solution was to replace the paper tape by storing the key electronically: by storing half the system as electrons, a much faster machine could be built. Flowers sketched out a plan. He would use thermionic valves to represent the Lorenz cipher key. He could use the valves to represent the 1s and 0s by having the voltage of the valve as either negative or positive. He sketched a design for the machine: it would need 1,600 valves.

For thousands of years, we have used paper to store and share ideas. In Michelangelo's time, the printing press sped up the copying of those ideas. Five hundred years after the printing press was developed, moving ideas from paper to electronics was the next step forward in the information revolution. What Flowers was proposing to build was the world's first electronic programmable computer. If it worked, it would enable near-real-time reading of Germany's most senior communications. It was massively ambitious.

In great expectation, Flowers shared the idea with Alan Turing, Jack Good and the rest of Newman's team. But to his disappointment, they pointed out a major flaw. Thermionic valves were known to be unreliable. As even my grandfather knew, they needed regular replacing: like an incandescent lightbulb, they could blow. Flowers was asking to use a colossal number of valves; failures would mean that, even if such a machine could be built, it would hardly ever be working. The idea was a non-starter. Flowers had just presented one of the most far-seeing ideas of the twentieth century to some of the world's most brilliant minds. Their disapproval must have been a severe setback. It could even have embarrassed him. How did he react? He built it anyway.

Flowers had worked on large-valve systems for automated telephone exchanges before the war and knew they could be reliable. Valve failure occurred due to heat cycling when the machine was switched on and off. The trick was, don't switch the machine off. Failure could not be eliminated, but it could be reduced to very manageable levels.

Flowers disobeyed his instructions and exercised his devolved autonomy. Turing, Newman, Michie and Good were some of the most intelligent people in Bletchley Park, but they didn't have Flowers's experience. That experience was locked into his mind: if he could have shared everything he knew, they would have backed him to the hilt, but, like all humans, he was bandwidth limited. He couldn't share both his intent and his full understanding with his allies. So they were sceptical. But Flowers had common purpose with Turing, Newman, Michie and Good. He was able to use that common purpose to support Bletchley Park by building the machine they thought wouldn't work.

People must have trusted Flowers, because not only did he decide to build the machine, he persuaded his boss to support him with staff, space and supplies. Supplies that included thousands of precious valves. Flowers inspired his team to work eighty-hour weeks, and they continued at this relentless pace for ten months. Only a few knew the true purpose of the machine, but all of them knew it was important for the war. By February 1944 it was complete. It was the largest machine yet at Bletchley Park. They called it Colossus.

Colossus was brought into operation, and Newman's team

waited for the inevitable valve failures. They didn't come. Flowers's instinct was right.

The machine we saw Tony Sale operating on that day at Bletchley Park in 2005 was a Mark II Colossus. I've worked with big computers and stood in the rooms where they used to operate. I also stood with my colleagues watching Tony's reconstruction of Colossus. The power requirements for heating thousands of valves are huge. Special electrical supplies are needed. The heat causes acrid smells to be emitted from the components. Tony slowly turned his creation on, powering it up gradually to avoid the heat cycling that would damage the valves. Today, we can visit these machines in museums; we can sample these smells from the past. But for Flowers, when he switched on Colossus, he was switching on the future – the electronic computer.

Turing and the team must have been astonished. In his pre-war mathematics work Turing had developed the *theoretical* idea of a 'computing machine'. He conceived of it to prove mathematical theorems. He invented an idea called *universal computation*, a machine that could simulate any other computing machine. He showed what properties such a machine would need to have. Until the day that Flowers switched on Colossus, Turing's machine had just been a notion, a concept for debate over a cup of tea. Flowers was demonstrating that universal computers could be built.

Colossus is the ancestor of all the computers we're working on today, including those at Facebook. It was Flowers's breakthrough that enabled the eventual vast assimilation of information that underpins the social network. Seven years after that demonstration, and seventy years after the Colossus was conceived, Joaquin joined Facebook. The company already had nearly a billion users and just under 5,000 employees. Facebook could track and store all conversations between those billion people. In 1943, Bletchley Park had 12,000 people to track and monitor the conversations of the German armed forces, which totalled 18 million men. Facebook can manage so much more information because it uses more automated decision-making. The information-processing pipelines pioneered at Bletchley Park could now be constructed by small groups of engineers using vast electronic databases. Processing information had moved from cottage industry to megafactory.

Still, on joining Facebook, Joaquin realized that even its information-processing pipelines were too piecemeal for the new approaches required for machine intelligence. He began working on a framework that would allow any engineer to quickly create and test new machine-learning algorithms. He automated the process of training those algorithms and testing how well they performed. The approach revolutionized how Facebook went about deploying machine learning. It was called *FBLearner*. By 2016 this new approach had become incredibly successful in the company:

> FBLearner Flow is used by more than 25 percent of Facebook's engineering team. Since its inception, more than a million models have been trained, and our prediction service has grown to make more than 6 million predictions per second.[7]

Joaquin had created an information infrastructure enabling software engineers at Facebook to deploy automated decision-makers at scale. Those 6 million predictions per second were decisions being made about over a billion people.

Back in Bletchley Park, they didn't have time to waste thinking about the broader implications of their new machine. Their aim was to crack the Lorenz cipher. Flowers had built a demonstrator system, but lessons had been learned. The team immediately commissioned him to build an updated version. His exhausted team redoubled their efforts to build the Colossus Mark II. Four months later, in the early hours of 1 June 1944, Flowers was wading ankle-deep in water from a broken pipe, making the final connections to bring the new machine online. Four days later, and Eisenhower was reading one of its first decrypts and ordering the invasion of Normandy. Eisenhower read his enemy's mind using the first electronic computer, and Fred woke up at his home in Kenilworth to hear that his unit was about to go and fight in France. Flowers's machine hadn't just launched an invasion, it had launched an intellectual revolution.

When looking to achieve their objective, the military intelligence services of the United Kingdom had one clear advantage over our brains. They knew who their enemies were. Human beings are placed in a different position. We are constantly faced with other humans who may be collaborating or competing with us. Our intelligence's high embodiment factor means that even if we want to openly share our knowledge and intent, we can't. At Bletchley Park there was a hybrid combination of human and machine working together in an information assembly line. The challenge they faced was decomposed into separate tasks and specially trained humans or machines were deployed to complete each task. This decomposition was possible because the objective was known: decode the German intercepts. In contrast, for human beings, the types of challenges we face vary, so our intelligence needs to be more adaptable.

Flowers surged ahead with developing Colossus despite the scepticism of the team. He couldn't share his deeper understanding of the thermionic valve. If he could have, they would have fully backed him. As it was, they had to trust him, but their trust was qualified. They didn't back him, but they didn't block him.

This notion of trust, a suspension of scepticism arising from faith in another's capability and motives, is critical to efficient human collaboration. It's a vital component of the system of devolved autonomy we use to collaborate. Operating within a network of trusted individuals towards a shared aim leaves us free to focus on our own tasks without concerning ourselves with the motives of others. It allows us to overcome our intelligence's high embodiment factor. However, imbued trust also comes with risk, because it leaves us vulnerable. Trust implies we are no longer sceptical of motives, because we believe we have alignment. When this is not true, we are exposed to manipulation.

On Thursday, 10 November 2016, two days after Donald Trump had been elected President of the United States, Mark Zuckerberg announced to assembled attendees at the Techonomy 16 meeting: '. . . the idea that fake news on Facebook . . . influenced the election in any way I think is a pretty crazy idea'.

Eleven months later, Zuckerberg was testifying in front of the US Senate. Facebook's own internal investigations had shown that a Russian company known as the Internet Research Agency (IRA) had engaged in systematic exploitation of the Facebook platform.

Facebook estimates that as many as 126 million Americans on the social media platform came into contact with content manufactured and disseminated by the IRA, via its Facebook pages, at some point between 2015 and 2017. Using contrived personas and organizations, IRA page administrators masqueraded as proponents and advocates for positions on an array of sensitive social issues. The IRA's Facebook effort countenanced the full spectrum of American politics, and included content and pages directed at politically right-leaning perspectives on immigration policy, the Second Amendment, and Southern culture, as well as content and pages directed at left-leaning perspectives on police brutality, race, and sexual identity.

So much for a pretty crazy idea. The IRA consisted of around 1,000 staff. By creating a few hundred pages they managed to coordinate a disinformation campaign which reached 126 million people. This small Russian entity could have such an outsize effect because it tailored the way it shared its posts to be sustained and spread by the artificial ecosystem Facebook had created. The IRA exploited Facebook's automated decision-making to propagate misinformation. As Facebook's supreme commander, Zuckerberg had lost control of his system.

In the Techonomy interview quoted above, Zuckerberg had explained how AI algorithms with thousands of parameters are used by Facebook to determine what content to share with which users. Zuckerberg's naive confidence in the algorithm is at the heart of the problem. The algorithm provides a single point of attack in a similar way to the German military's shared use of the Enigma code provided the Allies with a single point of attack. The IRA was able to identify weaknesses and exploit them. It leveraged its understanding of Facebook's information infrastructure to sow disruption across the social network.

Human intelligence evolved in social groups, and for coherence and trust those groups have depended on validation from their peers. This validation breeds the necessary trust between us. Given our limited communication bandwidth, it feels natural that we would seek out such validation. I sometimes think of our need for information as akin to our need for food. So we have a cognitive diet, just like we have an actual diet. Real-world social validation is like finding fresh fruit on a tree – a wonderful opportunity to eat. Our bodies have a particular response to fructose, the sugar we find in fruit. What the algorithms behind social media companies have been able to re-create is an artificial sense of social validation – they are feeding us with the cognitive equivalent of high-fructose corn syrup. It triggers our sense of validation, but it lacks the cognitive nutritional value that real social validation brings.

The algorithm that ranks your posts in Facebook is called the Newsfeed ranking, and the IRA managed to find the cognitive equivalent of catnip. The Russian agents flavoured their posts with sharp discord: tailored misinformation. The posts were widely shared by US citizens. The IRA found weaknesses in the Facebook algorithm in the same way the Bletchley Park codebreakers had found weaknesses within German codes. Once the algorithmic weakness was discovered it could be repeatedly exploited because decision-making had been devolved to automatons.

It wasn't only the Internet Research Agency that found Facebook's ecosystem to be a happy hunting ground for manipulation. The IRA operated in the shadows of Facebook, creating fake accounts to share fake news stories. The extent of the IRA's activities was revealed only after a ten-month investigation, but another would-be internet Svengali had no such qualms. This company was open about how it planned to influence elections and proud of its ability to deliver. Like a Bond supervillain, it boldly shared its plans for world domination while just on the cusp of success. Cambridge Analytica was a London-based company that sold services to political campaigns. It was interested in political advertising and its business idea was to tailor its adverts to the individual who was receiving them. The company could sell a different message to different voters. Adverts have always targeted different sectors of society, but the new proposal was to target the individual. The idea is known as *microtargeting*.

Just as the Bletchley Park codebreakers harvested information about individual radio operators and their foibles, Cambridge Analytica illegally harvested data about individual Facebook users. It used each individual's post-likes to assess their personality. The syrupy sweetness of Facebook's cognitive offering is the social validation given by receiving likes on a post. But, by sharing our preferences, we also share insight into our personalities. Our post-likes are a strong predictor of our *psychometric profile*. This profile is an advanced way of thinking about our individual personality, a deeper way of characterizing each one of us and what our susceptibilities are. The profile was then used to target specific political adverts at users.

This form of targeted advertising isn't new – for years, political campaigns have tailored their messages to different parts of society – but what was new was the scale of the targeting and the fine-grained manner in which Cambridge Analytica planned to do it. What was also new was that Cambridge Analytica's actions were illegal. The company had accessed large amounts of personal data without permission. This was the fulfilment of Arthur Miller's predictions in *The Assault on Privacy*. Individuals had ceded control of their personal data to Facebook, and Facebook's systems had failed to protect them. Eventually, Facebook was fined $5 billion for this breach.

So this was a crazy idea that was true. Perhaps the real crazy idea was that Zuckerberg didn't know that his information infrastructure was being manipulated by both the IRA and Cambridge Analytica. The vast number of decisions was too many for his company to track, and those individual decisions were being made by simple machine-learning algorithms: algorithms without a wider context, algorithms without a common sense of purpose, algorithms that had simplistic goals.

Joaquin's idea of a company-wide machine-learning platform had worked, but the scale at which it was deployed meant Facebook's information infrastructure was permeated by devolved decisions being taken by automatons. These models could exploit our interests, leverage our desire for validation and feed us with sensational information, but they couldn't decide whether doing this was damaging the wider interests of our community. They weren't empowered, like Fred or Tommy Flowers, to reflect on the situation, realize the threat and raise the alarm.

Efficient human collaboration is critically dependent on a shared understanding of who we are and a shared concept of what our objectives are. So much of the cracking of codes that took place at Bletchley Park depended on an understanding of the wider context.

Our intelligence has evolved in this environment, an environment of trust and scepticism, one of espionage and counterespionage, but between a shifting set of enemies and allies. It is to this landscape that today we have added the computer, a new cognitive entity. Facebook's systems had been thrust into this complex environment and given access to an inconceivable quantity of our personal data, but they were unaware of our human context and objectives. Today's new AI capabilities offer the potential to better understand human context through generative AI models that have absorbed our written works alongside artistic images, but they also offer new ways to manipulate us. Their ability to better emulate humans offers possibilities that can enhance us but also undermine us.

So, what are our objectives? Well, for this we must return to Fred: like him, we may individually long for the comforts of food, shelter and family, but our duty is also to a wider society. This society provides the security that enables us and our families to access those resources. Humans are a collaborative species that evolved in competition, and we remain in competition, therefore our environment is a dynamic world with evolving objectives that reflect different individuals' perspectives and their own outlooks. There is no singular goal for humanity.

The Bletchley Park team's ideas revolutionized computing. Those developments emerged across six years of honing skills against a capable adversary. The human brain has also evolved in competition, with other humans and with animals. But across the millions of years of our development as primates, we have never previously been exposed to an adversary that has such rich data about our behaviour. This is the assault on privacy Miller warned us about, and our sharing of this personal information leaves us vulnerable to manipulation.

Building on the technologies developed in Bletchley Park, Facebook is now part of a wider system of power I call the *digital oligarchy*. The computer is high bandwidth and can assimilate vast amounts of data to deliver decision-making in ways beyond the capabilities of individual humans. That power is controlled by a few large companies which have extensive access to our personal data, but those oligarchs are not in control of the systems they've created. This is clear from Zuckerberg's reaction to the infiltration of his systems by the IRA and Cambridge Analytica. Simultaneously, the complexity and inflexibility of Facebook's information infrastructure left it exposed to manipulation by adversaries. This exposure of Facebook also exposes us. Jonathan Zittrain, like Arthur Miller a Harvard law professor, has referred to this phenomenon where companies lose understanding of their own systems as *intellectual debt*. The debt he refers to is a debit on our understanding. The quilt of Facebook's information-processing infrastructure is composed of many different patches. Each individual patch can be understood by a particular engineer, but the overall quilt cannot. In software engineering this is called *separation of concerns*. It is an example of the divide-and-conquer strategy advocated by Charles Babbage and used by Henry Ford to build the Model T. Separation of concerns for information processing is the equivalent of division of labour for manufacturing. It enables the construction of systems that surpass any individual's understanding. But separation of concerns implies no one is concerned about the overall system. Having one individual who knew everything would introduce a bottleneck in the system management, akin to the challenges of micromanagement faced by Jeff Bezos and Dwight Eisenhower. But removing that bottleneck leads to intellectual debt. As a result, Facebook still doesn't understand how its overall system operates and it still doesn't know when its components are failing or being collectively manipulated. These ongoing challenges were revealed in detail by Frances Haugen, the Facebook whistleblower. Frances worked at the company as a Product Manager on the civic integrity team, and their objective was to stem the flow of misinformation. She has emphasized not just the scale of the problem of misinformation in the English language but also how hard it is to control in other languages, including the minority languages of Myanmar and Ethiopia, where the platform has been used by individuals and groups promoting extreme ethnic violence. The International Court of Justice in The Hague is proceeding with a case against the Myanmar government under the Genocide Convention.

Facebook moved fast to deliver new features and capabilities, but it constructed an interconnected system of decision-makers it didn't understand. It devolved power to automatons, leaving itself vulnerable to manipulation. This is the crazy idea that underlies the challenges the digital oligarchy presents us with: not even the oligarchs control it. If the oligarchs were wilfully harming society, then we could sanction them. Instead the challenge the oligarchs present is systemic. It emerges from naivety and clumsiness backed by significant funding from venture capitalists. Zuckerberg may have been naive and clumsy, but he isn't exceptional in that regard. There is a queue of other naive and clumsy individuals waiting to replace him.

A further irony is that Zuckerberg's naivety is also key to his success. It underpins his ability to give his company a common purpose, a vision his employees can align with. Facebook employees aligned around two things: the vision to connect the world he preached to us that evening in his penthouse suite in Stateline, and the hacker culture Greg described to us at that academic summit. And why wouldn't those employees align? Shouldn't connecting people be a good thing? It definitely can be, but the speed and scale at which computer technology can operate meant that those connections between people could be deployed before they could be understood. Moving fast does break things.

The Facebook website is updated every week. The website tailors its appearance to individual users based on their previous behaviour. Facebook's information infrastructure delegates almost all the decision-making involved in this system to automatons. These automatons were constructed and realized in software-engineering production lines enabled by Joaquin's FBLearner system. The FBLearner system validated that these automatons performed well only in a narrow sense: they increased engagement. The automatons could resolve the task set for them, but they lacked context and were missing the fail-safes that emerge from devolved autonomy.

Dave Eggers's novel *The Circle* depicts a dystopian future that emerges from a naive founder's plans to connect people. His co-founders bring technical capabilities and monetary nous. Eggers's description of how this fictional social media company operated was so apt that it was only once I'd finished his book and read the cover notes that I realized it was written as a dystopian parody rather than a reflection of reality.

Fortunately, Joaquin and Frances did have devolved autonomy. Joaquin's development of the FBLearner infrastructure was countercultural in Facebook. While everyone else was moving fast and breaking things, Joaquin was envisaging wider technical challenges and building solutions to address them. Unfortunately, that solution had enabled Facebook to move faster and break more. Reflecting on this led Joaquin to envisage the wider social challenges Facebook was triggering. I visited him at Facebook in March 2018. We went running together through a network of paths between his house and Facebook HQ. Those paths weave around the interstate highways and suburban houses where employees of Facebook, Google and Apple live. Joaquin's FBLearner system had given him enormous credibility within the company, and he took advantage of a reshuffling of the AI leadership designed to bring the algorithms under tighter control. He built a team that would focus on responsible AI – he launched the team that was going to build Facebook's conscience. Eventually he left Facebook, and today he continues to highlight these challenges in his talks and writings.

It wasn't despite Fred's disobedience to his orders that the Allies were able to coordinate the largest amphibious landings ever accomplished, it was because of it. Devolved autonomy alongside common purpose enabled Fred and Tommy Flowers to make their own decisions based on the information they had. Yes, Fred shouldn't have been in Kenilworth, but he understood the wider priorities and returned quickly to his unit in Aldershot. In Amazon, we sometimes jokingly called the devolved-autonomy structure 'organized chaos', and it is this dose of chaos that makes devolved autonomy robust. Tommy Flowers ignored his instructions, and because of his dedicated work the invasion of France proceeded on 6 June. As a result, Fred got caught out, but his sense of common purpose impelled him to get back to his camp and be shipped out to France as part of reinforcements for the landings six days later, on 12 June.

Contrast this organized chaos with the precise delegation of decision-making to automatons that underpins Facebook's information infrastructure. The use of thousands of Joaquinbots, Fredbots, Francesbots and Tommybots enables millions of decisions per second to be made about billions of different people, but the rigidity of the structure has meant that it is easily manipulated. In human decision-making structures, Joaquin, Fred, Frances and Tommy bring a dose of well-meaning chaos that increases the robustness of the system.

As humans, we coordinate our actions through the development of common purpose, and the need to do this comes from our high embodiment factor: our intelligence is locked in. But from the stories we tell and the visions we describe, from combining all of that with a little dose of chaos, emerges a key component of humanity. There is a tension between our individual freedom and the wider interests of our species. Culture guides us, while embodiment frees us. Is this tension particular to us? Is it an intrinsic part of the atomic human? Or is it another aspect that the computer will also eventually assimilate? To explore, we need to look further back and see the origin of that culture emerging from a journey we've been on together across many millennia.

4.

Persistence

My favourite building in Rome is the Pantheon. It has a classic Roman temple frontage, but it is topped by the largest unreinforced concrete dome in the world. It was masterfully built: it has stood for nearly two thousand years. But what does this tell us about the quality of a typical Roman building? This is a difficult question to answer because we can't see all the buildings the Romans constructed which have since fallen down.

Assuming that surviving buildings represent a typical building is a form of statistical error known as *selection bias*: buildings from the past that are still standing have a shared property of persistence. It's a quality that makes them different from other buildings, which have mostly fallen down. Persistence is also a quality of all current life on Earth. If something is alive today, unlike over 99.9 per cent of the species that have ever lived, it hasn't died out. We are observing surviving Pantheons from a panorama of lifeforms that, like the Romans' failed buildings, are buried in the fossil record.

Human intelligence has emerged from this selection bias. It has been subjected to a changing planet and it emerged as it persisted. Over billions of years, many billions of decisions have been made by evolving lifeforms. These decisions led to their survival as part of the broader ecosystem of animals, plants, fungi, bacteria and archaea that we coexist with today.

Charles Darwin called this emergent selection bias 'evolution'. The life we see today is created through selective destruction. Sometimes this process is summarized as 'survival of the fittest', but that gives the wrong impression. The Pantheon may be my favourite building, but we can't say the Pantheon is the best building that could be made; it's not in any sense the *fittest* building. It's just a building that works, one that's proven robust to the ravages of time. The same is true of human intelligence: it is like the Pantheon – it has been robust to selective processes over time – but that doesn't mean it is necessarily the best form of intelligence. As we've already argued, when it comes to intelligence, the notion of best, without context, is meaningless.

Humans are social animals and at the heart of our intelligence is a need to communicate with other humans, but we are bandwidth constrained, so we have to choose carefully what we communicate. Human intelligence is locked in, but it didn't become locked in in the sudden manner of Jean-Dominique Bauby's brainstem stroke. Our intelligence emerged in a locked-in form; it knows no other way.

Our limited bandwidth means that we need to second-guess one another. Our decisions have consequences for others. We accommodate for those consequences before we communicate: we use our brains to guess the needs of others; we decide what we should share within that broader context. By dedicating computational effort to understanding the motives of those we are communicating with, we come to know the most useful information to share. This second-guessing is second nature to us. It is so ingrained that even when we are interacting with non-human entities like cars, cats or computers, we attribute human-like motives to them.

We attribute our car's failure to start to grumpiness, we assume our cat's independence is haughtiness and we ascribe a computer's failings to intransigence. It's no surprise then, that when it comes to other intelligences, we also represent them in human form. Both Michelangelo's representation of God in a flowing robe and James Cameron's red-eyed representation of the ultraintelligent machine take forms of intelligence that are beyond our typical experiences and render them into more cognitively palatable humanoid forms. The word for this is 'anthropomorphization'. It's a particularly pernicious effect because it's very easy to do, but difficult to say. If I could invent one word, it would be a pithy way to say 'anthropomorphization'. Let's try calling it 'anthrox', where x = pomorphization.

The Romans designed and built the Pantheon, Michelangelo designed and painted the Sistine Chapel ceiling. Time has dictated that both these works persist. Life also emerged over time through persistence, but it wasn't designed like the Pantheon or the Sistine Chapel ceiling. Even so, when describing evolution, even the most anti-creationist scientist will slip into the language of *design* to explain life. This is another example of our tendency to anthrox.

Anthroxing can be a useful way to communicate. This book makes use of analogies to share ideas. These analogies overcome our limited bandwidth by relating a familiar concept to one that is unfamiliar. Perhaps anthroxing is another example of communicating by analogy. But like all analogies, it has its limitations. Evolved intelligences were not shaped by some hidden hand. They are just the current baton holders in the selective procession of their predecessors.

The lack of a designer is the principal difference between the natural systems we see around us and those we build ourselves. Tommy Flowers designed Colossus, Joaquin designed FBLearner, but Tommy and Joaquin's intelligences are not designed, they are emergent, and their emergent quality has some important consequences. In particular, emerged intelligences need to have been robust to changing circumstances.

At times we interfere with the processes of evolution. Selective breeding of animals and plants allows us to choose characteristics we want to enhance. In plants we interfere to select larger fruits or bigger seeds. Ten thousand years ago humans domesticated a wild grass called emmer, and the result is wheat seeds, a staple food for around 35 per cent of the world's population.[1] Selective breeding has produced wheat varieties with a larger yield. In animals we prefer faster-growing coats to produce more wool, larger muscles for more meat, bigger udders for more milk. In artificial selection we define what is best and we select which animals and plants reproduce. Artificial selection differs from natural selection in the same way that artificial intelligence differs from natural intelligence. In AI we choose the task and optimize the design, whereas natural intelligence is simply what has persisted from the past.

One problem with artificial selection is that our domesticated breeds tend to be *fragile*. Typically, they cannot persist without our interventions. They have difficulty giving birth, they suffer more often from disease, they are less able to deal with predators or pests. Artificial selection reduces resilience because it undermines the priority of persistence. Artificial intelligence systems are often similar. They are designed to perform particular tasks, but beyond the performance of those tasks they are fragile. If there are any circumstances that were unimagined by the designer, then artificial systems can fail.

Designing for the real world is difficult. The usual way we deploy automated systems is by controlling the environment around them to ensure that they are not exposed to unexpected circumstances. That's why Henry Ford built the Model T's assembly line in a factory building only workers could enter. Similarly, our trains run on tracks from which other traffic is banned. When we deploy automatic systems without these guardrails, unintended consequences can be triggered. Tay was an AI chatbot developed by Microsoft Research designed to provide entertainment on Twitter. It was targeted at 18- to 24-year-olds, but within sixteen hours of its release it had begun to tweet racist and homophobic messages. Microsoft's Corporate Vice President Peter Lee commented: 'Although we had prepared for many types of abuses of the system, we had made a critical oversight for this specific attack. As a result, Tay tweeted wildly inappropriate and reprehensible words and images. We take full responsibility for not seeing this possibility ahead of time.'[2]

The difficulties with Tay demonstrate the consequences of placing a designed system into an uncontrolled environment. Lee suggests that Microsoft had prepared for many forms of attack but was blindsided by one it hadn't foreseen. The heavyweight boxer Mike Tyson put it another way. In 1997 he was asked, before a World Heavyweight Title bout with Evander Holyfield whether he was worried about the threat Holyfield's 'fight plan' presented to him. His reply was that everyone has a plan until they get punched in the mouth. Microsoft's Tay got metaphorically punched in the mouth.

Equally, when performing artificial selection, it is difficult to select for resilience. We can try to breed out an obvious flaw, but resilience requires that we breed in a way that second-guesses everything the world will throw at us. We would need to breed animals and plants that are not just resilient to today's pathogens and parasites but to those that will emerge in the future. We would need to breed organisms that can resist the changing seasons and evolving climate. As Microsoft found out with the Tay chatbot, what is difficult for artificial selection is also difficult for artificial intelligence. We can't envisage every possible attack on our system; it is only the fullness of time that reveals how events will pan out.

Mike Tyson's comment is a rephrasing of a Prussian field marshal's words: 'No plan of operations extends with any certainty beyond the first contact with the main hostile force.'[3] Field Marshal Helmuth von Moltke was one of the architects of modern warfare. After the Napoleonic Wars, he realized that armies had become too large for a commander to directly control all their actions. His philosophy encouraged the Prussian army to devolve decision-making ability, and his battlefield strategy underpinned Prussia's unification of the independent German principalities to give us the modern German state.

The atomic human has emerged in a world where the main hostile force is emergent and evolving. It is not conforming to a grand plan, and its actions and attacks are unpredictable. All persistent lifeforms have emerged under these conditions. If they have a plan, it is to expect the unexpected. This is why the types of lifeforms that have evolved are so difficult to compare to one another. Asking whether a tree or a cat is better would be a meaningless question. This mirrors the challenge we have in comparing intelligences: we can't say which intelligence is better without some understanding of context.

Misinterpreting evolution, anthroxing evolution, assuming it is working towards some grand plan or goal, has had severe conse-quences. In the field of *eugenics*, the assumption is that humans can be improved through the selective breeding of our own species. The Greek etymology of the word is 'good origin', but who deter-mines what is good? The lack of a grand plan in evolution means that there is no global truth, only opinion. The conceit of eugenics was to suggest that it is possible to have privileged access to some-thing that doesn't exist. If we are to anthrox evolution, then we should think of it as whimsical and capricious. We can see this capri-cious nature in the mythology of the ancient Greek and Roman gods the Pantheon was built to celebrate. If you must anthrox evo-lution, think of it as Mercurial, think of it as Jovial, think of it as Olympian in its intrigues and squabbles.

The ways in which we can survive and thrive are multidimen-sional. Like Rock, Paper, Scissors, evolution isn't transitive in its selections. If it were, we would not see the diversity of life that we do. The qualities of life are contextual and we can't order them in a ranked list. It doesn't make sense to ask 'Which lifeform is best?' or 'What is the ultimate species?' Different species are adapted to dif-ferent ecological niches. The result is a cornucopia of life that can bedazzle us with its diversity and complexity. We can spend our lives studying nature and never lose our childlike sense of wonder. Survival can mean developing a big nose (bless you, elephants), run-ning very fast (no running shoes for cheetahs), or sleeping for seventeen years (good morning, cicadas). If there is a notion of fit-ness, it is fluid, it is moving, it is never measurable in the moment. It is this capricious nature of evolution that has delivered our intel-ligence. To persist, our intelligence has had to be resilient.

On this journey of persistence, our ancestors have faced allies and adversaries, and still around us today we can see examples of the nature of these interactions. There are predator–prey relation-ships such as the lion and the wildebeest, the giraffe and the acacia tree. There are parasitic species such as mistletoe or the fungus that gives us athlete's foot. These relationships have driven evolutionary development similarly to the way the struggle between the Allies and the Germans drove technological development in the Second World War.

At the beginning of the war, the British Isles' survival depended on the decryption of the weakest version of the three-rotor Enigma. By the end of the war, survival depended on breaking the twelve-rotor Lorenz cipher. Competition drove innovation. The capabilities of the Allies co-evolved with those of the Germans. If the Bletchley Park team had been asked to break codes from the end of the war without having seen earlier versions, they would have failed. Fortunately, they had easier entry points that drove the later achievements. Weaker versions of the codes gave them a narrow intellectual handhold. They used that handhold to climb high enough to assault the later, enhanced encryption. Their German adversaries drove them to capabilities they would never have managed in isolation. A similar effect occurs in the natural world, where different species become allies and adversaries as they seek ways to survive. The achievements at Bletchley Park took six years to pan out – just imagine the effect of such adversarial development across the billions of years since the birth of life on Earth. Well, you don't have to imagine it: you can see it all around you.

The atomic human was forged in the fires of adversarial development. Persistent lifeforms collaborated and competed with us. The principles of evolutionary success have operated on us and our environment across time and at different scales, from the largest animals down to the most fundamental units of life – biological cells – but across this evolutionary history there has never been an adversary that could communicate so much faster than us. This is the challenge the digital oligarchy is presenting to us: the machine has changed the nature of our environment.

The Trident XIV is a drilling rig, a three-legged jack-up. Jack-up rigs are floated around the sea until it's time to drill. Then they stop, lower their legs to the ocean bed and jack themselves up. In 1995, when I was assigned to the rig, the Trident XIV's legs were planted on the sea floor off the coast of England. The rig stood in the Irish

Sea, in plain view of the Lancashire resort town of Southport. The rig was thirteen years old, and I was twenty-three.

I would measure rock formations from a blue cabin planted on the rig. The process was called logging. On one side of the cabin, facing the drill floor, was a winch that slowly withdrew our tools from the well. The back of the cabin was taken up by a large computer with me sitting at the keyboard. That computer would process and store data coming from the borehole. Logging the well took time, so as the measurements came in I would listen to the geologist telling me about the worlds that had generated the formations we were measuring.

My favourite geologist had a lively Scottish accent. He would tell me about the time 350 million years ago when Britain was close to the equator and covered in warm, shallow seas that teemed with life. He would tell me about the epoch when Britain was at the centre of the supercontinent Pangaea and part of a large desert, and talked of Jurassic times when dinosaurs roamed the land.

We were measuring the past. The oil we were seeking was the remains of algae and bacteria from nearly half a billion years ago. When these ancient algae died, they fell to the seabed. Over time, subject to the pressure of the deep sea and the earth, they decomposed and formed oil deposits. We were drilling through the rock that had triggered the geologist's tales. Modern humans appeared in Africa two or three hundred thousand years ago, our ancestors separated from the chimpanzees between 4 and 7 million years ago. Further back in the tree of life, that species shared a common ancestor with gorillas around 10 million years ago, and around 85 million years ago primates diverged from other animals. Three hundred million years before that our tetrapod ancestors were emerging from the sea. All these organisms were from the different eras the Trident XIV would drill through.

These geological changes took place over millions of years, but the geologist's stories were compressed into the couple of hours it took for me to extract our tools from the well. The slow pace of geological deep time makes the dynamics that drive evolution difficult to understand. It is over these unimaginable timeframes that natural intelligences have emerged. But when we trace further back, to places beyond where we could drill, we find that life on our planet has been emerging for nearly 4 billion years.

We are related to almost all other lifeforms on the planet: bacteria, archaea, fungi, animals and plants. Each of these is made up of a cell, or cells. Each cell is defined by its wall, a membrane which separates the contents of the cell from its environment, and in all these lifeforms the cell has its own genetic code. That code is the lifeform's blueprint, stored in its DNA.

My grandfather's war was focused on securing food, visiting his family and finding shelter. The cell's genetic blueprint contains instructions on how to feed, how to reproduce and how to build its own sheltering walls. The cell converts these instructions into actions by processing information. Bletchley Park was a human-designed information-processing facility. The cell is an evolved information-processing facility. What the cell should build, how it should build it and when it should build it is stored in DNA.

Intercepted German Enigma messages were recorded on paper using the letters of the alphabet. DNA records messages on a chemical necklace – you can think of it as being like a string of Lego bricks. There are four kinds of brick on the string.[4] The ordering of these bricks represents a code that stores information about what to make, when to make it and how to make it. The four types of brick are represented by the letters A, C, G and T. Each type of brick has a particular shape, so for example the A brick only couples with the T brick, and the G brick only couples with the C brick.

When it's not being read, the code is kept safely locked away by two strands of DNA coming together, like a zip, allowing the bricks to couple. This zip has a twisted form that we call the *double helix*.

DNA is where the instructions for building life are stored. Storage is a particular type of message, one that functions across time. If I put something in storage, I'm communicating with the future. In Bletchley Park cribs were stored in a filing system; our DNA provides our cells with the filing system of life. At Bletchley Park thousands of young women accessed and stored information in those files, and in the cell these files are accessed by small chemical machines. There the process is known as *transcription*: these machines unzip the DNA and copy information from it. The information in the DNA is transcribed into messenger chemicals known as *mRNA transcripts* that can be shared in the cell.

In every cell of our bodies, our DNA contains the blueprint of a unique human being. We can use Shannon's information theory to measure how much information that blueprint contains. Every one of your cells contains around 6 billion bits of information. It would take two computers about six seconds to share an individual's entire genome, but it would take one human nearly a hundred years to read it to another. Within the cell, mRNA transcripts are equivalent to the messages between German military units. German codes were designed to be read by German radio operators. The mRNA evolved to be read by the machinery of the cell.

Human cells share this mechanism of transcription with the cells of plants, bacteria, archaea, fungi and our fellow animals. The German military translated its orders into actions. In the cell the mRNA messages are translated into protein chains. These proteins fold into three-dimensional shapes that make up the machinery and structure of the cell.

The process of transcription followed by translation is so fundamental to life that it is known as the *central dogma*. The details and refinement of this process vary across lifeforms, but the fundamentals are the same because life on Earth stems from a single origin around 4 billion years ago from which we are all descended. This origin is our shared ancestor and it gave rise to the variety of life, from bacteria to baboons, we now see on the planet. The mechanisms of transcription and translation are not perfect; they make small mistakes. Some of these mistakes led to lifeforms that were more persistent, like the Pantheon. What we see across the history of the evolutionary procession is the consequence of those errors. The information in our genome has entered our DNA across billions of years of evolution. In each human these mutations occur at an information rate of around 3 bits of information per year.[5] Mapping this on to our salary analogy, it means that if Bauby is earning $6 a month, our individual genomes are earning only fractions of a cent. It would take our genome 175,000 years to earn a dollar.

I've already pointed out how slow our communication rate is compared to that of the computer, and now you can gain a sense of how the computer might feel watching us try to communicate, because, in terms of information transfer, our watching life evolve is roughly equivalent to computers watching humans speak.

Still, having a large population helps. While each individual genome earns a dollar only every 175,000 years, there are 8 billion humans on the planet. So, in total, all our genomes together are generating around $4,000 a month: information is moving to the next generation of the human species at roughly the same rate that a fast-talking New Yorker shares their news. Changes which are imperceptible to us in our individual lives add up when scaled through time and across large populations. That is the process of persistence that has led to the vast variety of life on today's planet.

Evolution is often framed as pure competition, a struggle for survival, but many of the most important evolutionary steps are defined by collaboration. The collaboration between the different scientists and the staff at Bletchley Park formed in adversarial conditions. It was a response to a common enemy. We can see the same tendency in simpler lifeforms. Some of the most important collaborations in our evolutionary history formed in response to a common enemy.

When we automate processes, we control the environment around those processes. We place machines in buildings or we define rules for our roads and railways. Similarly, lifeforms have evolved ways of protecting their processes from the wider environment. The cell's membrane provides some protection for the information-processing operations of the cell, but a hostile environment can still damage the cell wall and interfere with these mechanisms. When bacteria are faced with these environments, they form protective colonies. The cells have learned to 'circle their wagons' for shelter. Let's not anthrox here. They don't get together and discuss in drawling accents the need to bind themselves together. They simply sense the hostile environment and seek out other bacteria when faced with it. Bacteria from the same species have a shared set of interests which align when they huddle.

Britons are famously reticent, and more so in the past than today. If I mentally picture Diana Russell-Clarke, Bill Tutte, Tommy Flowers, Jack Good and Alan Turing sitting together, I don't picture a babble of communication. Fortunately, Russell-Clarke, Turing, Tutte, Flowers and Good didn't need to talk constantly with one another to align their activities. They had a common purpose and a diverse set of capabilities. They trusted each other to deliver in their own domains of expertise, and they could respond to their environment and express their devolved autonomy to work towards a shared set of goals.

The shared set of interests of Britons emerges from their *culture*. When a colony of bacteria is grown in the lab, it is also known as a culture: the bacteria have been cultivated through provision of food and shelter. Unlike bacteria, we are not just cultivated by food and shelter but by our art, literature, music and our other traditions, institutions and religions. But underlying the Britons' information coherence and that of bacteria is the same principle: within our culture we operate independently but in cohesion. This is how we coordinate, given our devolved autonomy.

Facebook's culture was also designed to deliver cohesive action, but, like many corporate cultures, it was much simpler than our broader culture. Zuckerberg convened his team around a vision of connecting everyone. The company's culture of delivery was based on moving fast and breaking things. These ideas are simple and easily communicated; they can be assimilated as part of the Facebook induction. Joaquin learned about all these ideas in the short bootcamp he attended, but simple ideas can be problematic in a nuanced world. Our broader human culture has emerged over the last 300,000 years and exhibits far greater nuance than Facebook's internal culture.

Bauby describes the state of being locked in through the analogies of a butterfly and a diving suit. The butterfly represents Bauby's *reflective* self. The diving suit represents the limitations Bauby experienced on his physical body – what I think of as his *reflexive* self – but, as we have seen, we are a collaborative intelligence, which means we are a social intelligence. If we think of our reflective self as a butterfly, then we should think of it as a social butterfly. Instead of sipping the nectar of flowers, we are sampling the nectar of human culture and contact. We flutter together in the wider field of our shared endeavour.

Bacteria don't have brains or desires, but they do sense their environment and make decisions. These decisions can affect the transcription of their genes or the division of their cells in reproduction. Many of these decisions operate in the metabolism of their cells; this chemical system senses and responds to the cell's environment. Digestion of food happens through metabolism; detection of threats also occurs in the metabolism. This gives the cell a perception of the world around it. That perception is stored in chemicals present in the cell, the metabolites.

Both individual Britons and individual bacteria perceive their environment. Both can interact with their environment to improve their circumstances. Their actions are driven by their goals and the information they have about the universe. When these independent actions lead to coordinated activity we can think of these entities as being in a state of *information coherence*.

The key to information coherence is that *externalities* affect the decision-making of both the Britons and the bacteria. They don't need to communicate directly with each other, because their response to the externalities is part of their cultivation. Individual cells and people are information-processing systems: they sense the world around them and take actions in response. When operating together they collaborate to form a larger information-processing system. Both a bacterial colony and the Bletchley Park communication centre exploit devolved autonomy and conditioned cultural responses.

When bacteria are from the same strain, they sense the same things in the world. When they feel threatened due to a harsh environment, they react. They gravitate towards their own kind for shelter and defence. This reduces their exposure to the harsh environment. They have a shared set of interests which align, so they sense the same environment in the same way. They respond independently, but in unison. They can form a consensus without communicating.

While there are differences in the way in which we process and share information – cells use chemical signalling and people use speech – when we look at bacteria, Britons and Bletchley Park we find that the cryptography centre is the odd one out. People and bacteria are natural systems, they are evolved; Bletchley Park was an artificial system, it was designed. Evolved systems exist because across billions of years of trials they have persisted; an artificial system is designed with a purpose in mind.

This distinction between natural and artificial systems should now start to allow us to unpick some of the confusion we've seen between intelligence as an entity and intelligence as a characteristic. Given the task Bletchley Park had, to decode German messages, we might imagine more efficient or cheaper ways of doing it. This means we have a chance to improve it, or at least to quantify different attempts at decoding messages, but if persistence is the only goal, then comparing different forms of persistence becomes difficult. What are the criteria we're using to compare? The only valid criterion is the test of time, but by definition that test takes time to play out.

In intelligent systems I think of this distinction as one between a directed intelligence and an evolved intelligence. Bletchley Park is a directed intelligence; bacteria are evolved intelligences. A directed intelligence is associated with a set of goals. For a directed intelligence, once we have the objective we can think of an intelligent action as one that achieves that objective with the least use of resources. Bletchley Park had a goal of decoding enemy messages. Amazon has a goal of delivering products. Facebook's goal is to increase user interaction with its website. Each of these goals is measurable. We can talk about how quickly they were achieved, or how cheaply. Knowing the goal doesn't mean that these are easy problems to solve. Decoding German messages required several different skills. We've seen that when solving a directed-intelligence task it is common to break the problem down into sub-tasks. We take the larger task and separate it into smaller components. So at Bletchley Park the bombes and Colossus were used to perform exhaustive searches and a filing system was used to record useful cribs. Each sub-task has its own goals, inputs and outputs. Each sub-task is specialized. This is the approach known as division of labour, or separation of concerns, and we don't only see this strategy in our artificial designs, natural systems also adopt these strategies. DNA is converted into protein in a two-stage process: the task has been split into sub-tasks. In cells, organelles have formed that specialize in these sub-tasks. For humans, this divide-and-conquer strategy allows sub-tasks to be either automated or completed by trained specialists focused only on that task. In our cells the same thing happens: different organelles specialize in different sub-tasks. Observing this division of responsibility in the factories of England, Charles Babbage wrote:

> Perhaps the most important principle on which the economy of a manufacture depends, is the *division of labour* amongst the persons who perform the work . . . a larger number of comforts and conveniences could be acquired by each individual, if one man restricted his occupation to the art of making bows, another to that of building houses, a third boats, and so on.[6]

This has become known as the *Babbage principle*. He didn't invent the idea – it existed in the factories he visited and even in the organs and organelles of his own cells and body – but he popularized it.

The existence of transcription and translation shows that evolution can produce very intricate mechanisms. These processes, which evolved on a recently cooled Earth around 4 billion years ago, are, if anything, *more* extraordinary than the achievements of Russell-Clarke, Tutte, Flowers, Good and Turing.[7] But they are not the result of an active intelligence, they are just the consequence of persistence and the passage of time.

In Greek mythology, the titan Prometheus is responsible for giving humans technology, fire and knowledge. He is punished for this by Zeus, who has him tied him to a rock and sends an eagle to eat his liver. Because Prometheus is immortal, the punishment is an eternal one, but he gains clemency when he is rescued by the hero Hercules. Prometheus's name translates to the English 'forethought'. His brother is called Epimetheus – 'afterthought'. Epimetheus is responsible for all the troubles humans experience, having accepted those troubles as a 'gift' from the gods, but evolution involves no forethought or afterthought. It is not predictive or reflective, it is merely reactive, and yet the blind process of evolution has produced these highly intricate mechanisms, both at the cellular level and across our society and culture. The atomic human convenes around ideas that have emerged from our culture and those ideas are particular to who we are. Just as the cell's DNA is a record of the lifeform's learnings since the first emergence of the central dogma, so our culture stores the learnings of humankind since our emergence as a species with language.

As an advanced social lifeform with a locked-in intelligence, we have created sophisticated societies and cultures, which, in turn, allow for complex forms of information coherence. Importantly, it is not only what is inside our brains but also the way we externalize our intellect that drives us forward and allows us to overcome our bandwidth limitations. Our most important information-technology developments, like the computer, have become new tools in this wider landscape. The topography for our ideas is being shaped by communication technologies that enable us to store and share our culture in different ways.

Alan Turing's imitation game suggested that a computer being able to emulate a human in conversation was an appropriate test of intelligence. Today we have built machines that can emulate an understanding of our culture. Those machines have acquired this understanding by examining the wealth of information we have shared with them through the internet. We can also build a machine that can create paintings in the style of Michelangelo. The company OpenAI has produced one called DALL-E, and researchers at the Ludwig Maximilian University of Munich another, called Stable Diffusion. However, this doesn't mean we have supplanted Michelangelo. The importance of the paintings on the ceiling and the wall of the Sistine Chapel is that they come from a human, someone like us, who lived five centuries ago. They are a stored message that is being read across time from one human culture to another.

Alan Turing may have believed that having a computer trick a human was enough to define intelligence. But the trick doesn't replace the truth. We care about Michelangelo's painting because he was human. We care because he is part of a common cultural experience that does as much to define the atomic human as our high embodiment factor. That culture is around us, and the atomic human is as much about what is outside us as what is within us. This is why the tools we create to share our ideas and culture are such a critical part of who we are. The computer and artificial intelligence are presenting us with the next generation of those tools.

5.

Enlightenment

Andrew Dokett ran a student hostel in Cambridge which took in young scholars from across the country whose families were fighting a war in France. It was a dark period in the war: land was being lost, new alliances were forming and the troops were being routed. Despite these turbulent times, Dokett was able to persuade the Queen of England to support him in his aim to form a new Cambridge college from his hostel.

The war in France ended, but a revolution in Europe began. Borders were redrawn, tearing apart the existing social fabric. It was a social revolution driven by a transformation in our ability to share ideas, a revolution in information technology that had been seeded during the war. But this was not Eisenhower's and my grandfather's war; this war was waged 500 years earlier, in the fifteenth century, and ended fifty years before Michelangelo applied his brush to the wet plaster of the Sistine Chapel ceiling.

The gate to Queens' College opens on to a courtyard, a snapshot of a world on the brink. It was Cambridge's first purpose-built college. The building is a quadrangle, modelled on an English fortified house and protected by a military-style gatehouse. It sits on a half-acre site near the banks of the River Cam. It contains a chapel, a library, a dining hall, a kitchen and a set of lodging rooms. The college provided food for the mind, food for the body and food for the soul.

Context drives our intelligence because it gives us the cognitive landscape in which our decisions are made. We base our ideas on those of the prevailing culture. Dokett's hostel became Queens' College, Cambridge, at a moment when European culture was about to go through a radical change. The cultural context for Dokett was a social structure known as the feudal system, a system of vassalage that ordained individuals' behaviour. Feudal duties sat alongside religious norms and codes of chivalry. Adherence to the feudal system allowed for collaborative food production and community defence in a society with limited means of communication.

Cambridge was a European backwater. The British Isles were at the western periphery of the known world and, culturally, Europe remained in thrall to Roman civilization, the remnants of which were spread across central and southern Europe. But in Mainz, Germany, a goldsmith was working metals, seeking hardness and durability. Johannes Gutenberg was forming alloys that could be cast to form type, moveable type that could be assembled in a printing press.

Gutenberg developed the first practical printing press in Europe. Before Gutenberg, books were in the form of manuscripts, literally 'hand-writes'. Each letter of each book was written on calfskin, each calf providing three pages for the manuscript. Queens' College was founded in 1448 with four fellows, and by 1472 it owned a total of 220 books. The books were chained to lecterns in the small library where the students and fellows could go to read them.

The atomic human relies on social mechanisms to collaborate and communicate. Eisenhower's armies relied on radio, and Dokett operated in the era of the parchment manuscript and the feudal system. Bletchley Park is the story of people organizing information, but information also organizes people. Mark Zuckerberg convened Facebook around the simple idea of connecting people, and Jeff Bezos conceived Amazon around the simple idea of selling books. The ideas in a book form part of a shared human understanding, and by inventing a practical way to create cheap books Gutenberg was giving our ideas their own DNA. He sparked an information revolution that has continued to the present day.

The printing press is responsible for incredible advances in human understanding, but it is also responsible for an almost unbroken five-hundred-year stretch of violence. It kindled religious and

cultural revolutions; it brought about advances in thought by impos-
ing a form of cultural trauma. Adherence to cultural norms is a key
component of our social organization. By agreeing a set of principles by which society operates, we, like bacteria, can coordinate
our activities. Cultural norms enable us to collaborate despite
our limited ability to communicate. The printing press enabled the
distribution of material that disturbed the established consensus. It
advanced European thinking but undermined European cohesion.
In the early years of the press, it was used as a tool of the prevailing
order, but by the time England's first printing press was set up in
1476 by William Caxton attention had turned away from orthodox
religious scripts to more frivolous material, among them Geoffrey
Chaucer's bawdy tales of pilgrims heading to Canterbury. Books
were moving mainstream.

Publishing undermined the religious hegemony. Books were still
the preserve of the elite, but they didn't need to be locked in the
confines of college libraries. They became more affordable, and
new ideas spread. In 1520, Martin Luther, incensed by corruption in
the Church, particularly by the sale of indulgences, precipitated the
Protestant Reformation. The Church, the most powerful cultural
force on the continent, was split in two.

Today we are experiencing a new disturbance to our cognitive
bearings. Gutenberg began his work on moveable type in the 1440s.
Luther challenged the established social order eighty years later.
Tommy Flowers started work on the Colossus in the 1940s. Eighty
years later brings us to the present: the computer has sliced through
our modern social fabric, most recently by introducing social media
and artificial intelligence. There's a remarkable parallel between the
development of the printing press and the computer, 500 years
apart. Both brought radical shifts in the way ideas are exchanged.
Just as the printing press did before it, the computer has redefined
the approaches we have for sharing and storing information and
therefore the cultural context that helps define us.

When Isaac Newton first came to Cambridge in 1661, he found a
town far removed from Dokett's Cambridge of two centuries

earlier. The monks and monasteries that adhered to a medieval culture of prayer and learning were gone. Knights and squires had been governed by a chivalrous code and had fought the Hundred Years' War in France. They too had gone. With them, Feudalist England with its vassals and lords had gone. For 500 years the Catholic Church had set the cultural context for the whole of English society. Gone. In two centuries England had seen two civil wars, a republic and a restoration, but change was only just beginning, and Newton would use his time in Cambridge to write his *Philosophiæ Naturalis Principia Mathematica:*[1] known as the *Principia*, it would be a catalyst for the next wave of change, revolutionizing the way we thought about our world.

The cartoonish notion we have is that Newton discovered gravity, as if, before Newton, nothing had ever fallen to the floor. Newton's original interest was in light. He built a reflecting telescope to see the stars and used prisms to decompose sunlight into separate colours. He constructed a reputation on the back of these discoveries and became a member of the English scientific establishment, and then he switched his attention to gravity.

Newton's *Principia* is a mathematical description of the rules by which nature is governed. These are laws that are obeyed both on Earth and in the visible heavens. Newton developed formulae that predict the fall of objects on Earth and the flight of objects around our solar system. His formulae give us the mathematical rules of movement, but they also imply the existence of a universal force, a force of unknown origin but acting on all known entities. The force of gravity.

The bizarre nature of Newton's force was as ludicrous to many of his contemporaries as the discovery of a Jedi force would be to scientists today, but unlike the Jedi force Newton's force is predictive. By assuming the gravitational force exists, we can make forecasts about events. These predictions can be tested. Newton's force extends our *foresight*: it improves our ability to predict the future. We can validate the forecasts through experiments. The simplicity and generality of Newton's equations is beguiling. Their predictions have enabled us to go to the Moon, but they also had a profound effect on our cultural view of science.

The influence of the *Principia* was so dramatic that we now refer to the scientific period before the *Principia* as pre-Newtonian. The book is the principal text of the Scientific Revolution that led to the Enlightenment, a period of social and cultural change centred around the pursuit of knowledge and new social ideals such as personal liberty and human happiness. For Europeans, the wide availability of books was changing our context, changing our culture. Newton's equations grounded the science of movement in mathematics, but in doing so they allowed scientific thinking to take flight. He changed the way humans think about their world. Today, in the pure sciences, the objective is still to deliver mathematical theories that give verifiable predictions about the world around us. It is only the complexity of the theories and the cost of the experiments that have increased.

Newton wrote in a letter of 1675 to his contemporary Robert Hooke, 'if I have seen further, it is by standing on the shoulders of giants.'[2] Where the work of the *Principia* was concerned, those giants had been presented to him in printed form, books by scientists who had come before him: Kepler, Galileo, Copernicus and others. Newton's *Principia* described a world governed by principles and laws. A mechanism-driven universe. With the printing press, these ideas could be recorded and shared, so the effect of Newton's work was international. It changed the face of European science.

We've seen the importance of cultural traditions in bringing about the information coherence that allows the atomic human to collaborate, but wouldn't it be better if we could just convene around the truth? That's something we can surely agree upon. Newton's work made us believe this was possible. One of the most elegant statements about truth comes from Pierre-Simon Laplace, a French mathematician and scientist whose life spanned the second half of the eighteenth and the first quarter of the nineteenth centuries. Laplace was the greatest scientist of the Enlightenment, or at least that's what the French tell us, and on this occasion, even as a

Briton, I'm inclined to agree with them. Laplace's intellectual development occurred in a world where new ground rules of scientific discovery had been set by the *Principia*. Laplace was a survivor, living through the French Revolution. He had been elected to the French Academy of Sciences at the age of twenty-four and went on to become Napoleon's examiner at the École Militaire. Napoleon later rewarded his professor by appointing him Minister of the Interior when he seized power in a 1799 coup.[3] But Laplace outlived Napoleon's empire and was made a marquis by Louis XVIII after the Bourbon Restoration.

In this period of discovery, Laplace's fingerprints are over everything – so many phenomena are named after him it's confusing: Laplace approximations (in probability), Laplace transforms (ordinary differential equations), the graph Laplacian (graph theory), Laplace's equation (partial differential equations), the Laplace operator (differential equations again), the Laplace distribution (probability again). As Winston Churchill is to quotes, so Pierre-Simon Laplace is to mathematical discoveries, but he also wrote one of the most important passages on the post-*Principia* view of the universe. In an English translation:

> We may regard the present state of the universe as the effect of its past and the cause of its future. An intellect which at a certain moment would know all forces that set nature in motion, and all positions of all items of which nature is composed, if this intellect were also vast enough to submit these data to analysis, it would embrace in a single formula the movements of the greatest bodies of the universe and those of the tiniest atom; for such an intellect nothing would be uncertain and the future just like the past would be present before its eyes.[4]

Laplace published this philosophical essay in 1814, but it was based on lectures he gave in 1795. The essay is non-technical and is designed to convey Laplace's understanding to a broad audience. The paragraph is referred to as Laplace's demon (as if he didn't have enough named after him already) and the text gives an early recipe for a kind of artificial intelligence. It describes how through understanding the laws and state of the universe we can make predictions about the future.

It is worth decomposing Laplace's words. His first sentence reflects the causal nature of science. Before the Enlightenment, scholars would have thought of the universe as part of a wider plan. They would have assumed there was a purpose to the phenomena they perceived: they took a *teleological* perspective. They had a belief that the world is operated by some hidden hand towards a grand vision, that the entities around us have intrinsic purposes. In Dokett's era this perspective was pervasive; post-*Principia* a new view dominated. The new prevailing wisdom was that the components of the universe around us are subjected to the same natural phenomena and the universe is being driven by mechanisms such as Newton's laws. These are the principles that emerged from the *Principia*, the idea that what we perceive is caused by the past and affects the future. This was a reductionist perspective on the universe.

The next sentence refers to an *intellect* which is granted knowledge of *all forces that set nature in motion*. These are the laws of nature. Laplace is referring to a mathematical abstraction of the way the universe operates, not just Newton's force but electrical forces, subatomic forces. This is the first ingredient of Laplace's formula, one which I think of as the *model*, a mathematical description of all the underlying laws of nature. Here Laplace is talking about one model to rule them all, an idea that would later come to be known as 'The Theory of Everything'.

We are then told that it's not just all the forces that are required but *all positions of all items of which nature is composed*. Where is everything? What is it doing? This is the *state* of the universe. Where every atom is, how it is currently moving and what else it is connected to. This is the second ingredient. In statistics and computer science we call this the *data*.

Finally, Laplace includes an important supposition: *if this intellect were vast enough to submit this data to analysis*. Laplace was the greatest intellect of his time; he was fully aware of how difficult it would be to combine all the data with a complete mathematical model of the universe – a dizzying array of equations would have to be laboriously analysed by hand. Laplace describes this combination of data and model as 'analysis'. Twenty years after Laplace wrote, Charles Babbage, who had spent his time analysing the manufacturing processes of England, conceived of a machine to automate this analysis. He called it the *analytical engine*. Today we recognize Babbage's engine as the first digital programmable computer and we would recognize the third ingredient in Laplace's demon as being *computation*.

Laplace goes on to suggest that the result of this analysis *would embrace in a single formula the movements of the greatest bodies of the universe and those of the tiniest atom; for such an intellect nothing would be uncertain and the future just like the past would be present before its eyes*. Laplace has conceived a scientific soothsayer. The ultimate formula. The combination of a universal mathematical model with data and computation leads to a result, a *prediction*: we obtain *forethought*, the gift of Prometheus wrapped for us by Laplace.

We can distil Laplace's demon into a simple recipe:

$$\text{model} + \text{data} \xrightarrow{\text{compute}} \text{prediction}$$

In the recipe a prediction is formulated as the result of combining a model with data through computation. The recipe is also the most important idea underlying modern artificial intelligence: the idea that we perceive regularity in the universe sufficiently to encode it mathematically in a model. The model is an abstraction of reality that allows us to formulate new predictions about how the universe will be as time moves forward. This idea is sometimes known as the 'clockwork universe'.

Many artificial intelligence algorithms operate according to this formulation, combining a simple mathematical model of the world, one that incorporates assumptions about the regularities of the universe, with data about the state of the universe. The two are forged together using computation. This allows us to make predictions.

Newton's *Principia* was focused on mathematical models of motion. One of the tricks he used in the study of motion was to view speed as the rate of change of position. He then viewed acceleration as the rate of change of speed. This approach allowed him to relate these aspects of the physical world to each other in the mathematical world. At the heart of theories of motion are equations that govern rates of change. In mathematics, we call these *differential equations*. To derive his theories of motion, Newton developed a new mathematical approach to deal with these equations. Today we call his approach calculus, but the term 'calculus' is an abbreviation of its longer name, 'the calculus of infinitesimals', or the calculus of the extremely small.

We can measure the speed of a car by setting up two flags a known distance apart. We can then time the car as it travels between those two flags. The speed is given by the distance between the flags divided by the time the car took to cover it. This measurement gives us the average speed across the distance, but the actual speed of the car at different times will vary.

Newton's calculus comes from the following thought experiment: (1) keep reducing the distance between the flags until they are only an infinitesimal distance apart; (2) measure the change in time across that infinitesimal distance; (3) divide the extremely small distance by the extremely small time. The result is the speed at the point where you created the infinitesimal. If the infinitesimal is small enough, then we have a measure of the speed at any given point. It was a transformative idea, and it allowed Newton to work in new ways with differential equations, enabling him to find solutions to equations that hadn't been possible before.

Microsoft and Facebook have corporate cultures that allow employees to collaborate towards their organization's shared goals. Prior to moving to Amazon I had mainly worked as an academic, and scientific academic culture traces its roots back to the Scientific Revolution of the seventeenth century. Many cultures rely on storytelling to share their philosophy, and academia is no different. Like the myths and epics of the ancient world, scientific stories tell us of heroes who achieved great intellectual feats of endeavour. So instead of Gilgamesh we have Newton, in place of Hercules we have Turing and instead of Odysseus we have Laplace. But, just as the North African achievements of Montgomery and Rommel were in large part due to the military intelligence they received, so the achievements of scientists are in large part due to the wider scientific culture in which they develop. All ideas have their time, and their context. The atomic human leverages external cultural ideas to overcome limited communication bandwidth. So, just as the ideas of military commanders are informed by their wider information infrastructure, the ideas of individual scientists are informed by their interactions with the broader community. As a result, two scientists can have the same idea at the same time but in different places. It's an example of information coherence coordinating activity. Like bacteria huddling in hostile habitats, scientists will each respond to their shared scientific circumstances, and so it was that in Hanover, Germany, 900 kilometres away from Newton, Gottfried Wilhelm Leibniz also invented the calculus of the infinitesimal. This is known as *multiple discovery*.

Multiple discovery happens often in science, but it doesn't fit well with our heroic narratives of great discoveries. When it happens our response is to say that the two (or more) scientists independently developed the same idea, but that's a misrepresentation. If the idea was truly independently developed, then it's a remarkable coincidence that across all of history it was developed within a few months at two locations within the same, relatively small continent. Newton certainly didn't believe it was a coincidence and accused Leibniz of a grave scientific crime: plagiarism. Newton was convinced that Leibniz directly copied his work, but this wasn't plagiarism. The link was through their shared surroundings. It came from the emerging European community of scientists and was underpinned by their ability to commit ideas to paper and to print and share those thoughts across the continent via a postal system. Newton and Leibniz were connected through the information topography. The conditions were right for the idea, and those conditions were similar in Hanover and Cambridge. The minds of Newton and Leibniz were responsive to their surroundings, and this allowed them both to form the idea of calculus.

Academic ideals are based around the Enlightenment idea of the pursuit of knowledge, and this seems to combine with an innate human desire to hear and tell stories about individuals. One of the ways in which academic culture departs from our ideals is when scientists seek credit. To see scientists at their shabbiest, watch them argue about who invented what first. Newton and Leibniz were both vessels in which the idea of calculus crystallized, but in a narrative it becomes important to know where the idea crystallized first. In science it's called a *priority argument*, as if we're all yielding to one another at a road junctions as ideas come streaming down the street. In practice, when priority arguments occur there's little yielding and a lot of road rage. The arguments are often not rational; they are visceral. Newton's *Principia* had made him very famous and he used his position to claim priority and accused Leibniz of dishonesty. The argument was resolved on predictably nationalistic lines. On the English side of the Channel, Leibniz's contribution was disparaged and Newton's claim was favoured. On the continental side, a more balanced view was taken, but the fierce nature of the split had long-term repercussions for European science.

The calculus that Leibniz and Newton produced differed not in its fundamentals but in its notation. Mathematical notation is the system of symbols you use to represent your idea. Choice of notation affects our ability to communicate and think about mathematics. For example, the ancient Roman numeral system uses letters to represent numbers: M stands for 1,000, C for 100, X for 10. To represent 300 the Romans repeated 100 three times: CCC. The system is correct, but it's not convenient for performing multiplication or division. It's a valid notation, but it's not conducive to complex arithmetic, and when a mathematical culture is constrained by its notation that can limit the scientific advances it makes.

Leibniz and Newton each had correct and consistent forms of notation for their derivations of calculus. But the forms differed in how easy they were to build on. As Newton wrote, science proceeds by standing on the shoulders of giants, and time has shown that Leibniz's notation provides a much more stable platform than Newton's. It was easier to build on the calculus of infinitesimals if you used Leibniz's notation, just like multiplication is easier with Arabic numerals than with Roman.

British scientists remained in awe of the *Principia* and stuck rigidly to Newton's notation. The balance of intellectual development shifted to continental Europe. In France, alongside Pierre-Simon Laplace there was Joseph Fourier, Adrien-Marie Legendre and Jean-Baptiste d'Alembert. In Switzerland, the Bernoulli family produced three generations of mathematicians. Another Swiss mathematician, Leonhard Euler, is considered the most prolific mathematician of all time. In contrast, theoretical work in Britain struggled to escape the shadow of the *Principia*. Instead, focus shifted to the practical implications of those ideas.

On 28 May 1788 Matthew Boulton wrote to his business partner and friend James Watt. Boulton's letter contains a description of an important and influential intelligent machine. Boulton and Watt were working together to refine and commercialize a new steam engine. They had been commissioned to supply two engines for a flour mill, but Albion Mill wasn't a typical commission. Built on the banks of the River Thames, it was London's first major factory. Twelve pairs of millstones were to be powered by two engines. Once complete, the mill would produce enough flour for the whole of London.

The intelligent machine Boulton described to Watt was the mechanism to operate the millstones. It was speed-sensitive. When the engine started and sped up the stones engaged, and when the steam engine slowed and stopped the millstones separated. As Boulton put it, it was a device:

> for regulating the pressure or distance of the top of the mill stone from the Bedstone in such a manner that the faster the engine goes the lower or closer it grinds & when the engine stops the top stone rises up & I think the principal advantage of this invention is in

making it easy to set the engine to work because the top stone cannot press upon the lower untill the mill is in full motion; this is produced by the centrifugal force of 2 lead weights which rise up horizontal when in motion and fall down when ye motion is decreased by which means they act on a lever that is divided as 30 to 1 but to explain it requires a drawing.[5]

The system sensed speed, engaging the millstones when the engine speed was high. The lead weights sensed information (the speed) and transferred it to achieve a goal (engage millstones) without involving help from humans. It was a simple form of directed intelligence.

The weights Boulton mentions are called fly-balls. They are positioned at the end of two arms. The arms are connected to a spindle and, as the engine turns, the spindle turns. The visual effect is of a spinning ballerina holding heavy dumbbells: as the speed increases, the dumbbells are flung up and outwards through inertia. The body of the dancer is sleeved and the dumbbells pull on the sleeve, which connects to the stones through a series of linkages. The rising sleeve lowers the grindstone into place.

The Albion fly-ball mechanism is a simple automatic control system. It is designed to engage the millstones at a given speed. To do this, the fly-balls need to be the right weight to provide the right amount of inertia. The fly-ball arms and the linkages have to be made with the right lengths. We call these values for the lengths and the weights the *parameters* of the system, a Greek word meaning 'side measures'. Setting these side measures correctly, by an analogy with musical instruments, is known as 'tuning the controller'. In a violin the parameters are the tension in the strings; the violin is tuned by changing the tension of each string until the right note is produced. In our simple intelligent system the parameters are tuned so that the system automatically engages the stones correctly.

The Albion fly-ball mechanism is relatively simple, but this idea of sensing and acting is at the heart of intelligence. The mechanism has an input (the speed of the engine) and an output (the distance between the millstones). The relationship between the two is controlled by the parameters: the weights of the fly-balls and the lengths of the linkages. For the system to work correctly, it requires tuning. These are also the ingredients for machine-learning systems: the difference is that in machine learning the machine is a mathematical function and the parameters are numbers that control the behaviour of the function.

Matthew Boulton was at the centre of a community of Enlightenment thinkers called the Lunar Society. They debated religion, economics, politics and science. But at the core of their debates was a desire to implement their ideas. They were entrepreneurs, not just in science and engineering but socially, economically and politically. Retrospectively, we've chosen to call this period the Industrial Revolution, but that term doesn't reflect the breadth of changes across society. It was a political, social and cultural revolution as well. Underpinning these changes were networks of information that were spreading ideas across Europe, inspiring new thoughts among the emerging intellectuals. These ideas drove mechanical innovation in Britain and inspired social revolution in France. They came from our ability to share our ideas through books. The Industrial Revolution was a consequence of an information age launched by the development of the printing press. An era that changed, for the better, the way our locked-in intelligence was able to store and communicate ideas.

Not everyone welcomed this period of scientific rationalism. The poet, painter and printmaker William Blake lived in Soho in London and was connected to the same circle of thinkers as Watt and Boulton. He viewed the new reductionist world arising from the *Principia* very differently. His book of poetry and printed art, *Songs of Innocence*, was published in 1789, the year after Boulton wrote that letter to Watt. Albion Mill was burnt to the ground in 1791, perhaps by millers it had put out of work. Blake's companion work, *Songs of Experience*, was published three years later in 1794. The most famous poem from that volume is 'The Tyger', and the opening stanza asks who could have built such a fearsome creature:

Tyger Tyger, burning bright,
In the forests of the night;
What immortal hand or eye,
Could frame thy fearful symmetry?

The fourth stanza imagines the forging of such a beast in the same manner that the new steam machines were being forged in Boulton's Birmingham works.

What the hammer? what the chain?
In what furnace was thy brain?
What the anvil? what dread grasp
Dare its deadly terrors clasp?

Alongside Blake's imaginary creation the Tyger we have Boulton and Watt's actual creation of the steam engine. Their hammers, anvils and chains were based in an alternative Soho in Birmingham. Boulton's Soho manufactory was based there, and it was the crown jewel of the nation's burgeoning manufacturing industry.

James Watt is one of history's most important engineers. He was a mathematical instrument maker at the University of Glasgow in Scotland and in 1763 had been asked to repair a model of a simple steam engine developed by Thomas Newcomen, an ironmonger from Devon. The Newcomen engine was the first steam engine to come into widespread use, but it was inefficient. Watt's innovation was to develop a steam engine with a *separate condenser*. Newcomen's original engine was inefficient because it varied the pressure needed to operate its piston by heating and cooling a single cylinder. It worked a bit like a pressure cooker. The cylinder was heated by coal, causing the pressure to increase and the piston to rise. But once hot, to reduce the pressure and lower the piston, the cylinder was cooled quickly by quenching it with water. These cycles of heating and cooling moved the piston by converting heat into motion, but they wasted energy. Watt designed an engine where the cylinder was kept

hot and the cooling was done in a separate vessel, called the condenser. Watt's engine was a lot more efficient.

Even brilliant ideas may be difficult to put into practice, particularly when they require implementation in iron and steel. Turning
his idea into a commercial success required further engine modifications, marketing and manufacturing. Watt had found this
impossible to achieve in Glasgow, and that was why he moved to
Birmingham to work at Matthew Boulton's Soho Manufactory. The
Boulton and Watt partnership was forged to realize Watt's dream
of an efficient engine. Their success was a combination of Watt's
modifications, Boulton's manufacturing and marketing capabilities,
and a lot of patience. Between Watt's invention of the separate
condenser and the commissioning of Albion Mill, twenty-five years
passed.

William Blake was less interested in efficiency, reductionism and
production and more interested in the social challenges of childhood labour, equality of the sexes and the paintings of Michelangelo.
Although he never travelled to Rome, Blake's training included
working with engravings of the Sistine Chapel ceiling, and he was
heavily inspired by the Italian master. In 1805 he produced a homage
to the ceiling of the Sistine Chapel. His vision of the creation of
man, known as *Elohim Creating Adam*, is a strong contrast to Michelangelo's. The faces of both God and Adam show deep anguish. The
image is closer to representations of Prometheus receiving his punishment for sharing his knowledge of fire than to the languid ecstasy
we see in Michelangelo's representation.

One of Blake's most famous works is another print from this series,
a depiction of Newton. Blake based this print on another image from
the Sistine Chapel, that of the sleeping Hebrew king Abijah. But in
Blake's *Newton*, the subject is not sleeping but in an intellectual trance.
His face bears a strong similarity to Michelangelo's Adam, only
instead of languid ecstasy it expresses concentration. Blake's Newton
is focused only on the use of a compass to manipulate the geometric
shapes in front of him. His trance-like state means that he misses the

complexity of the rich sea life around him, and this is Blake's commentary on reductionism and the way it distracts us from the complexity of the world around us.

Boulton's letter describing the Albion fly-ball mechanism was typical of Boulton and Watt's relationship. Innovation in action. Not only the formation of ideas but the realization of them in practice. Boulton was magpie-like in his observation of technical innovation. The fly-ball mechanism had struck him as potentially useful and so he wrote to his partner. Watt also saw potential in the mechanism, but he took an important additional step. Instead of connecting the spindle's sleeve to the millstones, Watt connected it to the engine's regulator. The regulator is the throttle valve that controls speed by allowing more or less steam to pass through it. Watt's governor was sensing *and* controlling the engine speed.

Watt's invention of the separate condenser improved the efficiency with which we could convert coal to motion. The engine replaced human labour with machine labour. But when James Watt connected the Albion fly-ball mechanism to the regulator of his steam engine he launched a different movement. By connecting the sleeve to the regulator, Watt was replacing a different form of human labour: he was taking away the need for a human operator to decide when to open and close the regulator. Watt had created a device that replaced *cognitive* labour. It is known as a centrifugal governor or simply *Watt's governor*.[6]

This is how the machine slices away the atomic human's capabilities. We are displaced from activities that had been specific to us. Newcomen's original engine replaced physical labour by pumping water from mineshafts. Until then, movement had been something that seemed particular to animals, but that was sliced away from us by the development of steam power. As humans, that still left us with the capacity to decide how to control the machine's speed, but Watt's device controlled the engine speed without human intervention. So, decision-making had now also been claimed for the machine.

Watt's invention of the governor had made the steam engine self-aware. That's a bold statement. To clarify, the machine wasn't suddenly striving to express itself through creating art, it didn't become preoccupied with its own mortality, it didn't create machine-gods to worship in the hope of being granted more steam. It had not become aware of the machine condition in the way that Blake was showing awareness and commentary on the human condition. But, through the centrifugal governor, the machine gained an awareness of its own state. Specifically, it gained awareness of its engine speed. This awareness allowed the machine to react by reducing or increasing the speed. It seems a simple change from the millstone gap controller to the engine speed controller, but that simplicity hides a large conceptual leap. In the millstone controller the machine is not aware of the gap between the millstones – that has to be set by the machine operator – whereas Watt's governor is controlling the engine speed through knowing the engine speed. Models that are self-aware in this way are known as feedback controllers or *closed-loop controllers*.

But where has Laplace's demon gone? Where are the data, the model, the compute* and the prediction? The data is the speed of the engine. The model is the set of linkages and fly-balls. The levers and pivots perform multiplications; the spinning fly-balls are solving a differential equation. The system is known as a *mechanical computer*. The prediction is the position of the final lever that sets the opening of the regulator. Laplace's demon has become integrated with the fabric of the machine.

When Gottfried Wilhelm Leibniz wasn't embroiled in arguments with Newton over differential calculus he spent time imagining a calculating machine, a machine that could automate the laborious process of analysis outlined by Laplace with his demon. Leibniz called the machine he imagined the *calculus ratiocinator* and, just as Watt's governor can use levers to multiply force, Leibniz's calculating machine used gears and levers to multiply and divide numbers.

---

* *Compute* is a generic term referring to computational processing power alongside the memory and storage capabilities that are needed to make computation.

Leibniz also went beyond conceptualization and began to build simple versions of these machines to perform multiplication of different numbers mechanically. Leibniz's work was the inspiration for Babbage's analytical engine. So, a mechanical system *can* perform computation, but does the model here really understand the 'forces by which nature is animated'? While the model is responding to the laws of physics that also govern the engine, its simple linkages cannot contain all the complexities of the underlying steam-powered system. This model is an abstraction, one that captures some essence of the engine that is necessary for speed control. It is aware of the engine speed, but it is not aware of itself or the wider context in which it operates. In many regards this model is a precursor of the machine-learning methods we use today. The model is not playing by the pure rules of Laplace's demon. It has some shortcuts to making an intelligent decision which skip some of Laplace's steps.

Maybe you're not comfortable about viewing this set of linkages as intelligent. Maybe early computers like Colossus seem more like they could be intelligent with their valves and calculations. Watt's governor is not dwelling on its position in life, it doesn't wonder at its role in the universe, but it is still a form of intelligence. It is an unthinking intelligence. The centrifugal governor is self-aware but not reflective – its inputs trigger immediate output. It is a reflexive intelligence.

By the early twentieth century, descendants of Watt's governor were being used in planes and on ships as automatic pilots. An automatic pilot is a system that keeps a vehicle on its course without intervention from the pilot or helmsman. The early automatic pilot systems were designed for flying or sailing in straight lines. In a plane's autopilot, gyroscopes sense the change in course and a feedback loop is completed by moving an aileron or a rudder to correct the course. Appropriately, the word 'governor' comes from Latin *gubernator*, which means helmsman. James Watt had designed a mechanical helmsman.

In English the term 'autopilot' has gained a colloquial use: we apply it to ourselves when we do things in an unthinking manner. I might say I missed a motorway exit because I was on autopilot. This use reflects the unthinking nature of some of our own intelligence. In autopilot mode we are processing information, but we don't stop to reflect and plan. Watt's governor is similar: the speed input goes through the fly-balls and is amplified through a set of linkages. The governor processes information, but it doesn't reflect on the context or longer-term consequences.

Today, automatic pilots are being proposed for motor cars: a driverless car needs to sense the path of the road, and the location of other vehicles, cyclists and pedestrians. This is conceivable because of machine learning, but ships and planes travel across oceans and skies; where they travel there is no road. Their environment is less cluttered than our car's, so autopilots for cars need much more sophisticated decision-making than those for ships and planes: they need to understand the wider context. This means that introducing self-driving vehicles, in comparison to self-steering yachts, has not been plain sailing. In 2016, Elon Musk said, 'I really consider autonomous driving to be basically a solved problem . . . I think we're basically less than two years away from complete autonomy',[7] but the task has proven much harder than he suggested.

The Albion fly-ball mechanism sensed the speed of an engine and through a set of levers engaged the millstone. Those levers provided a communication route to transmit the information about the engine speed to the millstone. Many innovations at Bletchley Park were inspired by technology from automated telephone exchanges, electromechanical devices that connected a caller in one location to a listener in another. Electrical devices follow a different set of laws to Newton's laws of motion, but in Boulton and Watt's time electricity was a new and poorly understood phenomenon and was not yet ready for use in machines.[8] But just as a set of linkages can transfer information through force or position, electrical cables can carry information through variations in current or voltage. The equivalent decision-making systems in our bodies are based on electricity. We have electrical pulses firing across our limbs to relay information from our senses, just like the fly-ball has levers that relay information about engine speed. How these signals are collated and connected determines our thoughts and reactions, both reflexive and reflective. This is known as our nervous system, and it is responsible for sensing and responding to our environment. The system is made up of biological cells called neurons which have become specialized in communication. Our ability to send signals across our bodies via neurons is the key feature that distinguishes animals from other life. Through these electrical signals, we can define and refine our movements. By using electricity to send these messages, we can share information across the body quickly, far faster than the chemical messaging systems that underpin the operation of individual cells. It is this rapid transfer of information that gives animals the ability to move rapidly.

Originally telephone calls were switched to their destination by human operators connecting people together by plugging wires into boards. Tommy Flowers and Claude Shannon were part of a revolution where the process of connecting the caller to the recipient through the network was automated through relays and valves. The neurons in our bodies have the same challenge. They need to send the spikes they generate to the right destination. A neuron has a cell body, called the *soma*, which attaches to a long fibre, called the axon, that leads away from the cell body carrying electrical signals. Also extending from the soma, like hairs from a head, are *dendrites*. These are filaments that receive incoming signals from other cells. The neuron uses a *synapse* to connect its axon to the dendrites of other neurons. The synapse is a small gap between cells where an axon connects to a dendrite. It controls when the electrical signal is allowed to jump across the cells, bridging the protective membrane and entering the next cell through its dendrites. Just as electrical relays and electronic valves control the switching of electricity in the artificial communication networks Flowers and Shannon built, the synapse controls electrical switching in the electrical networks we have evolved to communicate within our bodies.

The word 'dendrite' comes from the Greek for tree. You can

imagine neurons by thinking of the dendrites as the branches of the trees. Leaves receive light, but the dendrites receive signals from other cells. The axon is the trunk, and a neuron also has a command centre where the branches meet the trunk: the cell body. Think of it as a treehouse placed at the point where all the branches come together. The signal is then sent on through the trunk of the tree to other neurons, muscles or glands. Any neuron can take incoming messages from thousands of other neurons. The neurons form an information topography for the body, like the telephone exchange forms a network for sharing information for humans. But instead of communicating the family news and commenting on the weather, our neural networks carry information from our senses. Like the Albion fly-ball mechanism, they can trigger actions in response to those senses. Neurons gain information from receptor cells, each of which has the same role as the fly-ball. The receptor cells can provide information about light, temperature, movement or pressure. Neurons operate like the linkages: they process and propagate the signal to where the information is required. For Watt's centrifugal governor, the information about the speed is propagated to the regulator. The levers in the linkages that connect the fly-ball to the regulator can amplify or reduce the signal. Neurons can also amplify or reduce signals through their synapses.

The Albion mechanism controlled the gap between the millstones, and autopilot mechanisms operate on the ailerons or rudders of planes and ships. Neurons transmit information to muscles that trigger movement in an animal's body. The longest axons in our bodies belong to the sciatic nerve, running from the base of the spine down to the big toe. These fibres each stretch the full length of the leg and allow you to sense your stubbing your toe in the same way the millstone in Albion Mill could sense the speed of the engine. So while the fly-ball mechanism may seem simple, it contains the same components as the neurons that underpin our intelligence.

Many of the most exciting properties of these nervous networks come when you wire them together, but even simple nervous systems have useful properties. Swimming in the seas around the legs of the Trident XIV, the European squid can be found. Capable of descending to 500 metres, these squid are predators, feeding on fish and crustaceans, but they are also prey, an important food source for dolphins and large predatory fish such as tuna.

The European squid moves through jet propulsion. It uses its nervous system to operate muscles that force water through its body to propel itself forward. Moving faster than its predators and prey enables it to survive, to persist. The signal to expel this water is sent through a neuron; so that the squid can move quickly, the neuron fires rapidly, and it has evolved to have a large-diameter axon.

Its diameter is so large it was possible to measure its electrical voltage. This was the first time a neuron could be measured in this way, and it was done by two Cambridge physiologists, Alan Hodgkin and Andrew Huxley, in 1952. The Albion fly-ball mechanism encodes information in its movement; the neuron encodes information in the movement of electrons. Hodgkin and Huxley's mathematical model of the neuron used a set of differential equations to simulate how neurons communicate.

The European squid is a complex animal with a heavily evolved neural system belonging to a group known as the cephalopods that includes octopuses, cuttlefish and nautiluses. None of these animals have backbones; they are invertebrates. But the cephalopods are the most intelligent of the invertebrates. The Braitenberg squid is not a true cephalopod, it's a much more primitive filter feeder. By day it moves through the water, filtering plankton through its simple digestive system. Like the more advanced true cephalopods, it moves through jet propulsion. By night it protects itself by remaining still so as not to alert predators. When the morning light comes, it begins its next day of movement, completing its feeding cycle.

The Braitenberg squid is remarkable because of the simplicity of its nervous system. The animal has no discernible head, but at its front is a very primitive single eye. The eye consists of a small patch of receptor cells that sense light, connected to a single motor neuron with a giant axon. When light is sensed at the front of the squid, a spike propagates down the axon to the squid's muscles, causing the animal to pulse, emitting a jet of water. The squid moves forward and ingests plankton-filled water.

By day the receptor cells sense the light, so the squid moves forward. At night the receptor cells receive no light, and the squid remains motionless. This animal is wired like the Albion fly-ball. The fly-ball senses engine speed and controls the gap between the millstones; the squid senses light and controls its speed forward. The brighter the light, the faster it moves.

This primordial squid is important because it is the evolutionary ancestor of a family of squid known as the Braitenberg family. It has a close relative, the Braitenberg duplex. The duplex gets its name because across evolution a 'duplication event' occurred. The eye at the front of the squid split into two and each patch of cells has its own neuron sending information to the muscles of the squid's propulsion system. The animal has primitive left and right eyes, each now connected to muscles on different sides. By having two eyes and sensing the strength of light on either side, the squid has gained the ability to steer.

How the squid steers depends on the wiring of the neurons. Some duplex squid turn away from light, moving timidly towards darkness. Others are cross-wired so they steer towards light, heading aggressively for it.

These two squid exhibit different behaviours according to how they are wired. When there is abundant food and few predators, the aggressive cross-wired duplex has the more successful behaviour. When there is less food and more predators, the timid straight-wired duplex dominates. Which of the two squid's personalities dominates depends on their environment.

The duplex squid is only the first descendant of the Braitenberg squid family. The full family of squid have different behaviours, each dependent on simple wirings between their sensors and muscles.

In our own bodies, many of the decisions we make are controlled by reflex arcs. These are neural pathways that start with sensory neurons connected to motor neurons in our spinal cord. These arcs bypass the brain, operating like the fly-ball mechanism or the neurons in the Braitenberg squid. They are key to our ability to deal with Tyson's 'punches in the mouth', surprising events like tripping over or treading on a stray Lego brick with a bare foot. But they also deal with more commonplace activities like maintaining balance. One well-known reflex is the patellar reflex: it is tested by tapping just below the kneecap, causing the leg to jerk. This reflex has entered our everyday lexicon as the 'knee-jerk reaction', an unthinking response to a circumstance: if you tread on a Lego brick with a bare foot, a sensor in your foot triggers the rapid withdrawal of your leg and simultaneously your weight shifts to your other foot. This all happens before your brain can intervene. When you walk or run, if your front foot catches an unseen object, your trailing leg is triggered to swing through to catch your weight (hopefully) before you fall flat on your face. These responses need to be rapidly deployed, but they are also context-sensitive: the response is different if it's your trailing leg that catches.

Our first animal ancestors had simple nervous systems like the Braitenberg squid, but through our reflex arcs the characteristics of those systems still pervade the atomic human. A spectrum of behaviours for simply wired systems was described by Valentino Braitenberg, an Italian cyberneticist. Braitenberg was Director at the Max Planck Institute for Biological Cybernetics in Tübingen, Germany. His cybernetics background is vital in understanding why he became interested in these simple nervous systems, so, to place this in context, we first need to introduce the field of cybernetics.

My favourite thing about my logging unit on the Trident XIV was its name. It was called the Cyber Service Unit. It was released into the oilfield in 1976, by which time the valves Flowers had used to construct Colossus had been replaced in computers by silicon transistors. The transistor is a solid-state switch developed by Bell Labs in the late 1940s. The valves used in Colossus switched beams of electrons in a vacuum. Transistors switch electrons moving in a solid called a semiconductor and could be printed on wafers of silicon, giving rise to integrated circuits so that a digital computer could be crammed into my logging unit. My Cyber Service Unit was a beneficiary of the miniaturization brought about by transistors and integrated circuits. That said, by 1995 my computer was starting to show its age, but the origin of its name, 'cyber', dates back even further, to the late 1940s.

Across my childhood, 'cyber' seemed to be a prefix for anything from the future, particularly in British science fiction. In *Doctor Who*, the Doctor battled with the Cybermen. When the internet arrived, it was originally referred to as 'cyberspace'. Now our interconnected world is threatened by cyberattacks and we counter these cyberthreats to avoid cyberwarfare. In 2019, Elon Musk even announced the Tesla cybertruck, a sort of electric version of the Hummer that looks like a prop from a British 1970s science-fiction show.

Valentino Braitenberg was a cyberneticist, so you might think he should have been getting up to some really funky stuff, and you'd be right. Cybernetics is an academic field of study founded by an American mathematician called Norbert Wiener. The field's name is the seed-word for the proliferating prefix 'cyber'. In 1948 Wiener published a book, *Cybernetics: Control and Communication in the Animal and Machine*, and it became the founding text of the field. It leverages work from the Second World War, not just in cryptography, but in radar and sonar, to propose a new science for understanding intelligence. Wiener was particularly impressed by Watt's use of feedback in his governor, and 'cybernetics' is Wiener's rendering of the Greek word for helmsman, so the field is named in homage to James Watt.

Valentino Braitenberg was among the early practitioners of this science, but I have to admit that his eponymous squid is an invention. It's a ruse to bridge the worlds of artificial and natural intelligences, but the squid is inspired by the ideas of Braitenberg. In 1984 he wrote a book called *Vehicles: Experiments in Synthetic Psychology*. In it he described a set of thought experiments performed on simple vehicles (or 'little machines', as he sometimes refers to them) wired up in a similar manner to our squid. He calls this approach synthetic psychology, and it leads to an important insight that highlights how difficult it can be to study intelligence from behaviour. The different squid I described have very simple wiring, but their behaviour can be quite complex. Braitenberg sets the background to the book by introducing a range of vehicles that are equivalent to our primordial squid. Having described their behaviour, he introduces what I think of as 'Braitenberg's law':

> At this point we are ready to make a fundamental discovery. We have gathered evidence for what I call the 'law of uphill analysis and downhill invention'. What I mean is this. It is pleasurable and easy to create little machines that do certain tricks. It is also quite easy to observe the full repertoire of behavior of these machines – even if it goes beyond what we had originally planned, as it often does. But it is much more difficult to start from the outside and to try to guess internal structure just from the observation of behavior. It is actually impossible in theory to determine exactly what the hidden mechanism is without opening the box, since there are always many different mechanisms with identical behavior.[9]

Braitenberg's law plagues our understanding of intelligence, because our tendency to anthrox posits more complex explanations for the mechanisms behind behaviour than those that actually exist. Once we discover the real mechanism, we feel swindled. We retrospectively decide that such a simple mechanism shouldn't really be viewed as intelligent. The summit of the uphill analysis has a disappointing view. The law even applies to the latest generation of generative artificial intelligence. What looks remarkable from the outside is just a combination of engineering wizardry, enormous datasets and a lot of computation. The trick to these models is that their data comes from us: they have refined the art of mimicry.[10]

For the atomic human, Braitenberg's law provides a deeper perspective on ourselves. Our ancestors were the first organisms to develop neurons. They used them to sense the ocean and move through it like the Braitenberg squid. They would have had simple nervous networks but would have exhibited complex behaviour.

But these ancestors were *not* locked in. Like the fly-ball mechanism, they were composed of simple systems that sense and react. Like the European squid, these systems allowed our ancestors to respond quickly to threats, to avoid the unexpected punch in the mouth. These fast-reacting systems still lie within us. Our spine has evolved in place of the squid's giant axon and it contains much of the fast-reacting intelligence that is so important to our survival. This reflexive aspect of our intelligence is as much a part of us as our locked-in reflective intelligence, represented by Bauby's butterfly.

In 1914 when he was only nineteen years old, the founding father of cybernetics, Norbert Wiener, visited Trinity College in Cambridge. He came to work with one of Britain's greatest philosophers and mathematicians, and this is how he summarized him: 'It is impossible to describe Bertrand Russell except by saying that he looks like the Mad Hatter.'[11]

When he referred to the Mad Hatter, Wiener was talking about a character from an absurdist children's book by Lewis Carroll called *Alice's Adventures in Wonderland*. Maybe it's the fate of all academics to end up being like a character in an absurdist children's book, because as his career progressed Wiener wouldn't have been out of place in one either. He was famous for his absent-mindedness. There are stories about his going on trips and accidentally returning without his wife or his car, and others of his forgetting where he lived, whether he'd had lunch, and even his own name.

When Wiener arrived in Cambridge, Bertrand Russell and his colleague Alfred North Whitehead had just finished writing their magnum opus, *Principia Mathematica*.[12] The title was a deliberate nod to Russell's predecessor at Trinity College, Isaac Newton. Newton's *Principia* laid out principles of science through mathematics. Russell and Whitehead's *Principia* laid out the fundamentals of mathematics through *logic*.

Wiener's visit to Cambridge was not happenstance. He had been a child prodigy and had just been awarded his Ph.D. by Harvard University at the age of eighteen. The subject of his thesis was logic, and his focus had been the work of Russell and Whitehead. Trinity

College was at the cusp of English mathematical understanding, and logic was on the sharp edge of that cusp. Being English, Russell and Whitehead liked to discuss mathematics over tea. Some of their conversations were just as curious as those in Lewis Carroll's imagined tea parties. A regular guest of Russell's was the mathematician G. H. Hardy, also a fellow of Trinity College. At one tea party, Hardy speculated about the ability of logic to prove death: 'If I could prove by logic that you would die in five minutes, I should be sorry you were going to die, but my sorrow would be very much mitigated by pleasure in the proof.'[13]

A curious comment for a tea party, it captures the essence of an English intellectual's sense of humour, but the joke also implies that they took logic extremely seriously.

Logic weaves its way through the history of intelligence. Logical arguments would have been recognizable to the Romans, the ancient Greeks, the early fellows of Queens' College, Isaac Newton and Pierre-Simon Laplace. They would also have been recognizable to Alan Turing. His notion of universal computation was based on the manipulation of logical symbols.

Tommy Flowers's innovation at Bletchley Park was to use electronic valves to implement logic. Electronic circuits could then be built that operated as an analogue to logic. This was what enabled him to transfer the Lorenz cipher's key from paper to a digital form, which in turn allowed the Allies to decrypt Hitler's orders to Rommel and launch the invasion of Normandy. Before Claude Shannon developed information theory, he wrote his master's thesis on communication networks and logic. He related the switching of telephone networks to the truth or falsehood of logical predicates. This gave him a mathematical abstraction of a telephone exchange, and that mathematical model was an important step in monitoring the flow of information through the exchange. While Shannon was reformulating telephone exchanges through logic, Russell and Whitehead's *Principia* was an attempt to reformulate the whole of mathematics from the principles of logic.

The gist of logical argument can be seen in Conan Doyle's

Sherlock Holmes stories, but our first recorded understanding of logic is from much earlier, from the Greek philosopher Aristotle, writing in the fourth century BCE. The form of logical argument Aristotle proposed involves terms and propositions. Terms are entities: people, places and things; or, more simply, terms represent stuff. Propositions relate two terms to each other, so a proposition could be 'All humans are animals.' This is a proposition we would assert to be true, and it allows us to derive other propositions such as 'Some animals are humans.' We could then further state that 'All animals have a nervous system' as a second true proposition, and from these two propositions we can deduce that 'All humans have a nervous system.'

Norbert Wiener was born to a family of Jewish immigrants. His father, Leo, was a Professor of Slavic Languages at Harvard and homeschooled his son until Norbert was seven years old. Norbert graduated from high school at eleven and got his first degree in mathematics from Tufts University at fourteen. Further study in philosophy and zoology followed, culminating in that Ph.D. at the age of eighteen. Wiener's arrival in Cambridge was to be the next stage in his education as a philosopher: he was beginning a tour of Europe to consolidate his knowledge.

Lewis Carroll, whose Mad Hatter reminded Wiener of Russell, was the pen name of an Oxford mathematics don called Charles Dodgson. *Alice's Adventures in Wonderland* was published in 1865, when the world of mathematics was being redefined by new representations and algebras. Representations of mathematics are the notations we use and the conventions we build on to construct mathematical proofs. Newton and Leibniz had used different notations for their versions of calculus and the difference between these two notations had led to a split between Britain and Europe in the nature of research in the natural sciences. The new representations of Dodgson's era would also trigger a shift in the way mathematics was viewed.

Algebra is a system for the manipulation of symbols in place of numbers. In high school algebra, we represent a number with a placeholder letter such as x. We can then apply standard operations to that letter, like multiplying by 2 and adding 1 to obtain $2x + 1$. We then apply the rules of arithmetic: addition, multiplication, subtraction and division to the symbols. But in Charles Dodgson's time mathematicians began to invent *new* algebras, ones with new rules and in which the symbols represented different ideas. One of those representations was a new algebraic view of logic.

In 1854, George Boole, a mathematics professor at Cork University in Ireland, published a book containing a new algebra. *An Investigation of the Laws of Thought on Which are Founded the Mathematical Theories of Logic and Probabilities* is not the easiest title to remember, so it's normally referred to as *The Laws of Thought*. The book took logical thinking from language and transplanted it to the realm of mathematics. Boole developed a notation, and a set of mathematical rules, that allowed us to combine logical propositions mathematically. He developed a *symbolic algebra* for logic.

Developing a mathematical representation of logic was an important step in enabling more complex logical thinking. By applying the rules of this algebra it is possible to manipulate logical predicates. While the mathematical abstractions may look complex to the untrained eye, with them we can write propositions, predicates and assertions in a way that allows simple rules to be applied to deduce other characteristics of the world. With Boole's symbolic algebra, complex relationships could be expressed on paper and manipulated through rules to deduce new relationships.

The new symbolic algebra was key to more structured, mathematical thinking around logic. By converting logical ideas into an abstract mathematical representation, a flurry of advances in thinking around logic was unlocked. Just as Newton's abstraction of the physical world into mathematical form triggered new understandings in physics, so George Boole's re-representation of a philosophical approach to argument led to new understandings. The advance generated a wave of interest in logic as a model for underpinning knowledge. Charles Dodgson himself worked in this area. Fifty years after Boole's death we find Sherlock Holmes at the height of his popularity and Russell and Hardy titillating each other with the notion of logical proof of death over tea, but Norbert Wiener was not so easily swayed. He took against Russell and found his insistence on mapping all phenomena to logical foundations irritating. This difference of opinion between Russell and Wiener reflects a wider divide in the AI community.

Up until the moment in Mark Zuckerberg's penthouse suite in Nevada when Yann announced that his lab would be focused on artificial intelligence, the predominant view of artificial intelligence was that it should be based on logic. This classical approach to AI was a fusion of logic and the vision given to us by Laplace's demon. The idea was that a logical algebra would give us the underlying model for knowledge, then, to make predictions, all that would be required was to combine our data with our knowledge through computation.

In October 1911, just as the *Principia* was finished, one of Bertrand Russell's tea parties was interrupted by an Austrian engineer. He turned up unannounced to Russell's rooms at Trinity, carried along by the wave of interest in logic. He declared his desire to change his field of study and to work on mathematical logic with Russell.

The would-be student attended Russell's lectures and followed him around Cambridge. He even tagged along when Russell headed back to his rooms. He was constantly challenging Russell's assertions. Russell was initially unsure whether he was a crank or a genius, but after a month he decided on the latter. The engineer's name was Ludwig Wittgenstein.

Wittgenstein went on to write some of the most important philosophical works of the twentieth century, but the only one that was published in his lifetime was a logical theory of language. In *Tractatus Logico-Philosophicus* he described an idea that helps explain how logic can be mapped on to the computer. It's called the *truth table*. Perhaps the term 'truth table' conjures up images of Romany tents and a wizened lady hovering over a crystal ball – the truth table in mathematics is less exotic, but much more useful.

The truth table represents the different possible inputs and outputs to a given logical operation. Let's assume we have a proposition we'd like to discuss. It could be that 'Sherlock Holmes is a fictional character.' We might assert that this is TRUE. To represent our proposition in Boolean algebra, we use a letter. Let's use the letter P to represent the idea that Holmes is a fictional character.

Logical operations are similar to the arithmetic operations we learn at school. They are equivalent to addition, multiplication, division and subtraction. But they operate on logical predicates. For example, the logical operation NOT reverses an assertion. So, if we say P is TRUE, then NOT P would be FALSE. This logical operation feels like negation in arithmetic. The negation operation in arithmetic would turn P to $-P$ and, just like negation, if you apply it twice, you recover the original answer. So $--P = P$ and NOT NOT $P = P$.

Wittgenstein's idea was to represent these logical operations in a table. So for this operation on P, in the left-hand column is the original input value of P; in the right is the output value after modification with NOT:

Input	Output
P	NOT P
FALSE	TRUE
TRUE	FALSE

The NOT operation is the most basic operation of Boolean algebra. The truth table gives us the output value of the operation NOT for all the possible inputs. With this simple truth table we seem to have gone to a lot of effort for very little gain, but the Boolean algebra also has more complex operations. One of these is called AND, which takes *two* inputs. Its output is TRUE if *both* the inputs are TRUE. So, if we think of proposition P as 'Sherlock Holmes is a fictional character' and then we think of proposition Q as

'Dr Watson is a fictional character', we can define P AND Q in a truth table:

Input		Output
P	Q	P AND Q
FALSE	FALSE	FALSE
FALSE	TRUE	FALSE
TRUE	FALSE	FALSE
TRUE	TRUE	TRUE

If both 'Sherlock Holmes is a fictional character' and 'Dr Watson is a fictional character' are TRUE, then the output of P AND Q is TRUE. The truth table lists in two columns on the left all the possible combinations of inputs for P and Q. The right-hand column indicates the output for each combination.

OK, so the AND operation may not seem a lot more complex than the NOT operation, and it still feels like a long-winded way of capturing the very natural concept of the word 'and'. But the beauty of algebras arises when we start to bring in lots of different rules and the relationships become hard to remember in our heads. In mathematics this is known as *composition*. Mathematical composition is the process of feeding the output of one mathematical function into the input of another. It's the opposite of Babbage's process of decomposing a complex task into simpler components. When Babbage was reviewing Victorian approaches to manufacturing, he suggested that division of labour should separate the manufacturing process into simpler tasks, each of which could be done by a specialist. In computer software, the same approach leads to separation of concerns. A more complex system is separated into simpler parts, and each part of the system has a role that is easier to understand. This is how Bletchley Park decrypted German codes and how Facebook built its social network. Mathematical composition is the opposite process: in mathematical composition we bring together the simpler components to form a more complex whole. This is how Shannon modelled a telephone exchange with logic, and also how Hodgkin and Huxley modelled the squid's giant axon. They composed simpler mathematical operations to form a more complex system.

You can think of composition as feeding the output of one process into the input of another. The Albion fly-ball mechanism is the composition of a fly-ball and a series of linkages with an actuator at the regulator. We can build a mathematical model of each of these components in the form of a function and then look at the system as a whole by considering the composition of those mathematical models: we feed the outputs of one function into the inputs of another.

We can see composition occurring across the systems we've looked at so far. In the Supreme Allied Command, Eisenhower's orders were received by his subordinates as inputs, combined with those subordinates' domains of expertise, then relayed through the information topography, eventually reaching my grandfather in his dressing gown and pyjamas. In Bletchley Park, the Enigma coded messages went through different processes: first they were transliterated from the radio signal, then cross-referenced for possible 'cribs', and then processed on the bombes to decrypt the message. Processes were being composed to form the final outcome.

We already have two operations for our truth tables. So, let's try composing them. We will take the output of the AND operation and put it into the NOT operation. To write this mathematically we need to invent a notation. In mathematics, it's common to use brackets to compose operations. So, we will write NOT (P) and AND (P,Q) to represent our operations. Now, if want to apply NOT after applying AND, we can write NOT (AND (P,Q)). This gives us a new operation, which we call NAND.[14] Unlike NOT and AND, NAND doesn't have an equivalent word to represent the idea in the English language, but we can use the rules of Boolean algebra to write down its truth table:

Input		Output
P	*Q*	NOT (AND (*P,Q*))
FALSE	FALSE	TRUE
FALSE	TRUE	TRUE
TRUE	FALSE	TRUE
TRUE	TRUE	FALSE

These Boolean operations are all simple mathematical functions. They are so common that when we use them in practice we use symbols to represent them. So, the AND operation *P* AND *Q* is normally written with a little upside down 'v', so $P \wedge Q$, just like 'multiply' is normally denoted with a small ×. NOT is normally written like a minus sign with a bent end, ¬.

When explaining the Enigma machine in Bletchley Park I mentioned how it could be seen as implementing a mathematical function. Tommy Flowers was given a job that was the other way around: to build a machine that would implement a mathematical function. He used electronic valves to implement the different operations, and that was the basis of the electronic computer. When we implement these logical operations in computers, we call them *logic gates*. The gate the team wanted Tommy Flowers to build for the Heath Robinson machine was called the XOR gate (the Xor gate is an exclusive Or gate. It is like the Or gate, except it outputs a 0 instead of a 1 when the inputs are both 1); the Lorenz cipher also used this gate to encode the German High Command's messages. The Lorenz machine implemented a Vernam cipher in which the message was initially encoded as a string of 1s and os, equivalent to TRUE and FALSE in our Boolean algebra. It was encrypted by taking the key generated by the Lorenz machine and applying a XOR operation to the message alongside the key. The XOR gate gave the encrypted message as the output. Bill Tutte had reverse-engineered how the Lorenz machine was producing that key and in doing so he revealed a weakness in the encryption that Tommy Flowers's Colossus machine exploited.

But the excitement Turing and others felt about Colossus wasn't just down to this XOR gate. Colossus was also programmable. Programming in Colossus consisted of connecting a set of logic gates together to form a composition. Modern computers store their programs electronically, but programming Colossus was done by sticking together the little electronic machines Flowers had built to represent the logic gates. Flowers provided switches to enable the programmers to change the connections in the machine. He commented on the result in an interview with Brian Randell, a professor of computer science from Newcastle:

> It just changed the whole picture . . . they wanted programmable logic – and we provided them with a big panel with a lot of keys on it and by throwing the keys they could – the mathematicians – could program the machine – the keys did the 'and' and 'or' functions – and we didn't do any multiplying; we didn't need a multiply but we added 'and' and 'or' functions and put them in series and parallel and so forth, and they were quite happy. In fact they were like a lot of schoolboys with a new toy when we first gave it to them; they thought it so wonderful they were playing with it for ages just to see what you could do with it.[15]

The Colossus machine allowed Turing, Good and the others to program a composition of logic gates. That is what makes it the first electronic computer. The logic gates were implemented in valves, but they could be composed together, just like one neuron feeds into another, or like the different processes flowing together in an assembly line.

There are three magical things about Boolean algebra. The first is the composition idea. It turns out that by composing different gates we can create *any* truth table you can imagine. So, in other words, for any inputs on the truth table, we can construct logical gates that will produce any set of outputs we choose. We merely have to choose the right *composition* of the gates. We need to decide which gates should feed into which others.

The second magical thing about Boolean algebra is what happens when we *feed back* signals. Norbert Wiener believed that feedback was at the heart of intelligence, naming the entire field of cybernetics after Watt's governor. He was inspired by its innovation of feeding back the speed of the engine to the regulator. What happens if you feed back the output of a logic gate to its input? If you do it right, you obtain memory. Let's just repeat that, again with emphasis: *memory.* At which point were we going to mention memory? Shouldn't memory be at the heart of intelligence? Aren't many intelligence tests based on the ability to remember? Is Braitenberg's squid, with its simple nervous system, really intelligent if it can't remember things? Is Shannon's communications network an intelligence if it cannot remember? Is the Colossus machine really intelligent without this ability?

Our notion of directed intelligence didn't say anything about memory being a necessary condition for intelligence. It only said that you would achieve your goal more efficiently through information. But we've seen the influence of the printed word on the propagation of ideas. Writing allows words to be stored, and printing allows those words to be rapidly reproduced and shared. DNA allows the instructions that build our cells to be stored. Memory is the storage of information, and it is a way of communicating across time, a way of passing information from the past to the future.

Most of our perspective on the atomic human has been driven by our ability to communicate, by the way we've moved information from one place to another. Memory is a special kind of communication. Its ability to communicate with the past means that anything we place in memory is something we are choosing to share with the future, regardless of whether it's a filing system for storing German cribs or DNA's system of storing protein instructions as a chemical string. If we have access to memory, we can review the state of the world as it *was* rather than merely as it is. This can be of tremendous value, particularly if you're trying to find your car keys.

A simple feedback system involving two NAND gates is enough to provide memory. It's endearingly called a *flip-flop*. The flip-flop combines two features we've already explored: *cross wiring*, like we saw in one variant of Braitenberg's vehicles, and *feedback*, like we saw in Watt's governor.

In the flip-flop, the output of each NAND gate is fed back to one input of the other. This causes the gate to remember inputs. You can no longer predict the output of this system with a simple truth table. The output of the system will depend on what it's seen in the past. The flip-flop has the ability to communicate with the past. From a technical perspective, we say that the system has *internal state*. What we mean by that is it can make decisions not just on the basis of inputs from the external world, like Braitenberg's squid, but also on the basis of previous experience. So, feedback allows our systems to hold internal state, what we call memory, and that feedback also gives our systems a basic form of self-awareness. Perhaps you're beginning to understand why Wiener thought feedback was so important.

You might now use your own memory to recall that I suggested that there are three magical things about Boolean algebra and, so far, I've only described two of them. The third magical thing is the notion of the *universal gate*. Composition, memory and now the universal gate. Perhaps the term 'universal gate' makes this third thing sound the most exciting of the three, and the universal gate is a very cool concept. But it is not a universal gate that allows us to travel across the universe via wormholes, although that would be pretty cool too. A universal gate in Boolean algebra is one that provides a fundamental form from which all other representations can be developed.

Let's repeat that in a different way. A universal gate is like the ultimate Lego brick for truth tables. A universal gate is the only logical gate we need to create any truth table we need. If I told you that you can only have access to one logical gate but you can have as many of them as you like, you would be wise to choose a universal gate. Because you can always compose universal gates to form any other gate. With a universal gate, you can create any logical mapping.

The NAND gate is an example of a universal gate. Using just NAND gates, we can combine the three magical ideas of Boolean algebra. We can compose NAND gates to create any truth table we can imagine, and we can also use feedback with NAND gates to create memory. So as long as we have enough NAND gates we can create any logical machine we like, and we can give it memory. These were also the requirements for Turing's universal computer, the imaginary machine he had conceived of before the war that could compute anything. No wonder Flowers's creation made the mathematicians at Bletchley Park behave like schoolchildren. He'd just given them a glimpse of the digital future.

The printing press triggered the scientific Enlightenment. The easy sharing of ideas in books led to a revolution in the way we think about the world around us. After Newton's *Principia* a new view of our universe based on fundamental scientific truths emerged. It suggested that by understanding all the underlying phenomena by which the universe operates, we can make predictions about those phenomena. This enticing view of intelligence is captured in Laplace's demon. Echoes of Laplace's demon are found in the machines used to decrypt German messages at Bletchley Park. Those machines exhaustively explored different solutions to decode German messages, but, when we review decision-making systems we find in the real world, we see simpler systems based on fly-balls, levers, sensors and muscles.

Braitenberg's book described the behaviours of simply wired vehicles as an exercise in synthetic psychology. He then discussed how evolution or, as we introduced it, selection bias, determines which of those behaviours are sustained. Even the simplest of Braitenberg's vehicles can exhibit complex behaviour. This causes the problems we experience with Braitenberg's law: the 'law of uphill analysis and downhill invention'. Where does this complexity come from in these simply wired entities? The answer recurs when examining the atomic human: it comes from the *outside world*. The squid we described responded to light in its environment; any complexity in its behaviour emerges from the changing patterns of light in its world. These apparently simpler systems react quickly to the world around them with very little computation involved. As a result, they are *not* locked in in the manner of our reflective intelligence, and yet systems like this are also an integral part of the atomic human.

The atomic human is a composition of fast-reacting reflexive decisions and slow-reacting reflective decisions. Naturally, we are much more aware of our reflective decisions than the reflexive ones, just as Eisenhower was more aware of his orders than of the actions of an individual soldier like my grandfather. But the Normandy landings were as much about the experiences of individual soldiers as about those of their supreme commander.

Eisenhower's decision to attack was informed by critical intelligence decrypts from Bletchley Park, but it was also informed by his experience leading amphibious assaults on North Africa and Sicily. After he made his decision, Eisenhower, along with Winston Churchill, went to inspect the troops. In the film of this inspection of the US 101st Airborne Division, Eisenhower is next to Churchill in his formal military attire,[16] and together they walk behind the gliders that will carry the troops across the Channel. They shake hands with Brigadier General Don Pratt, who will lead the assault, then inspect the ordered ranks of soldiers. There's another film in which Eisenhower strides across a temporary fence into a wider camp filled with rows of tents. Eisenhower talks and laughs with troops who are not ready for inspection but are ready for battle. Their faces are painted and their uniforms augmented with camouflage. Eisenhower walks casually among the men, and their smiles and casual stances are reflected in his smiles, his nods and his easy manner. Because Eisenhower's decision was informed by the fact that he was a human, in that inspection we see him sharing his humanity with his troops. Afterwards he headed home and wrote the following note:

> Our landings in the Cherbourg-Havre area have failed to gain a satisfactory foothold and I have withdrawn the troops . . . The troops, the air and the Navy did all that bravery and devotion to duty could do. If any blame or fault attaches to the attempt it is mine alone.[17]

He knew that the operation might fail; he was imagining that failure. He was reflecting on his decision to invade and the men he had just met. He was preparing to take the blame if the decision proved to be wrong. He was displaying afterthought.

The next morning Brigadier General Don Pratt was among the thousands of soldiers who died. His glider crash-landed in the Normandy countryside, causing his neck to break through whiplash.

The atomic human is like Eisenhower pondering that decision: there is only so much that is within the control of our reflective selves. Much of the complexity of our actions comes from their interaction with the real world. It comes from the fact that no plan survives contact with the enemy and that we improvise in response to the dynamic nature of the world around us. Even the most complex computer simulation model we could build to reconstruct Laplace's demon pales in comparison to the complexity of the real world. The state of these simulations must be entirely stored within the computer: their complexity all falls inside the machine. But Braitenberg's book reminds us of one of the characteristics of human intelligence is *that which is external to it*. The influence of the environment, of culture, of stray Lego bricks on our actions and minds.

Unlike Braitenberg's squid and sheltering bacteria, the complexity of human behaviour is not just defined by our physical environment but by our rich cultural environment. We have a shared cultural memory that has emerged across at least 100,000 years since *Homo sapiens* first emerged.

While Braitenberg squid don't exist, animals with simple propulsion and nervous systems do. Jellyfish have a diffuse circular neural nervous system which includes receptor cells that sense gravity, light and touch. Jellyfish are propelled by the pulsation of their bell-shaped bodies, a pulsation that is controlled by pace-maker neurons. This allows them to swim forward and steer. Jellyfish have existed for at least 500 million years.

Throughout *Vehicles*, Braitenberg anthroxes his creations. I referred to duplex squids as timid and aggressive. He labels his vehicles with terms such as 'like', 'love', 'explorer', 'curious' and 'fear'. He refers to their behaviour having *values*, and he uses this provocation to address arguments about intelligence that presume motives and values are specifically human characteristics. His perspective is that, even for individual vehicles, these values have deep and fundamental origins that emerge from natural selection of patterns of behaviour. I agree, but I believe we need to take his notion further. Natural selection operates across species as well as within them. Our individual behaviour is a marriage of our personalities with their cultural context and the physical world around us. Our intelligence is intertwined with our culture because our objectives are intertwined with those of our wider species, and much of this intertwining occurs through cultural artefacts – the proxy-truths we lean on to bring about information coherence.

So, it is not the existence of values or emotions that makes us human but the origin of those values and emotions. They came to us across millions of years of biological evolution and thousands of years of cultural evolution. This is a journey we have been on together, and the machine is only just joining us. Like the printed books that came before it, the machine can enhance us, but it cannot surplant us, because it lacks both the limitations that make us human as well as the evolved culture that allows us to overcome those limitations.

Individually, as humans, we are limited in our ability to communicate. In response we have built societies with art, music, literature, poems, riddles, songs, stories, allegories, analogies. We rarely communicate with each other through a series of objective facts, we communicate through subjective artefacts. Facts that are 'made by art'. We have forged ideas that have become artistic truths, cultural truths and social truths.

Can we use Shannon's information theory to measure the message in Lady Gaga's 'Poker Face' or in Édouard Manet's *Le Déjeuner sur l'herbe* or in a first edition of Isaac Newton's *Principia*? I don't think we can. But we can each define ourselves by the art, literature or music that moves us. When we do that, we create a cultural resonance that communicates something about us. These artefacts serve as a projection of who we are. The computer communicates in numbers, data, facts. And, while it is now gaining understanding of our context through new techniques in generative AI, it is unable to appreciate that context or culture in the same way humans can, because it isn't subject to the same limitations and shared history.

Computers can communicate directly and almost instantaneously with each other. But, despite our limited bandwidth, we can use the trick of information coherence to align our thinking. This places us in a cognitive landscape that allows us to communicate subtle messages that express values and objectives. By coordinating our values and objectives within this landscape, we can devolve responsibility to individuals to work independently but towards shared goals. Within this landscape we each bring diverse perspectives.

We also have our own individual ambitions. When entering information coherence, we need to understand who our allies and adversaries are. We back a trusted ally even if we don't fully understand the decisions they are making. This trust was what enabled Tommy Flowers to build Colossus despite the scepticism of his colleagues.

Cultural artefacts have brought us very far, and the nature of these artefacts has evolved rapidly over the last five hundred years. The invention of the printing press allowed for rapid dissemination of written ideas. It disrupted the religious hegemony of the Middle Ages. It led to the Scientific Revolution, to reductionism and the Enlightenment. Now we face the challenges that the invention of the computer is bringing.

6.

The Gremlin of Uncertainty

General Eisenhower knew that Rommel had been ordered to hold his Panzer divisions near Calais, but when Rommel arrived in North Africa, he had surprised the British by disobeying Hitler's orders and attacking their lines. What if he disobeyed these orders again? Fortunately for the Allies, on the morning of D-Day, when they landed at the Atlantic Wall, Erwin Rommel was at home in Germany for a party. Rommel had returned to celebrate his wife's birthday. If there was a moment to be disobeying Hitler's orders, this wasn't it. Why was Rommel back in Germany at this critical time? The Allies and the Germans both knew that tidal patterns made 6 June a suitable day for a landing, but German weather forecasts had suggested the weather would be too stormy. Just like my grandfather, Rommel took a risk, and he went home.

Storms occur in the English Channel when air masses collide. An air mass is a large volume of air that has a particular temperature and humidity. When two masses meet, energy can be released in the form of wind, rain and lightning. A weather forecast is a prediction that suggests when and where such storms might occur. Both the Allied and German weather forecasts were based on observations from a network of land-based weather stations, ships and air surveys. The pressure of the air was measured every day and the measurements compiled on a chart, a map with lines connecting the locations where the pressure is at the same value. It looks like a relief map, which shows the height of the landscape, but instead of showing contours of height, the lines, known as isobars, represent pressure. The chart is drawn up by marking each point where the pressure is known and then filling in the places around it where the pressure is unknown. To do this the pressure readings between weather stations need to be estimated, and this is done with a process known as *interpolation*.

The word 'interpolation' comes from Latin and means 'polish between'. Think of the wooden palette Michelangelo would have used to blend his colours. Across the palette there are blobs of paint and between them the paint is blended to form new colours. This process is similar to how a weather chart is formed, but instead of blending with a brush or a knife, a meteorologist blends the colours mathematically. Imagine two places on the map, for example Cambridge in the east of England and the city of Sheffield towards the north. If I start with a pressure measurement in Cambridge of 1,000 millibars, let's think of the 'colour' of that point as pure blue. Then I have a measurement in Sheffield of 900 millibars, and we'll think of this colour as pure red. The pressure difference between the two towns is 100 millibars and the distance between them is about 100 miles. As you move between the towns those colours are blended so that 30 miles from Sheffield we get a brick-red colour. By the time we get to Peterborough, a further 40 miles towards Cambridge, it's navy blue. Finally, when we get to Cambridge, we recover its pure blue colour. In meteorology, these colours are associated with different estimates of pressure, so brick red is 930 millibars and navy blue 970 millibars. That's the process of mathematical interpolation, but to interpolate the weather map you have to polish the entire map, not just the line between Sheffield and Cambridge. The key idea is that the pressure should change *smoothly* as you move between the points of measurement, always gradually blending the colours on the artist's palette.

By mathematical polishing across the whole map, the Allied meteorologists constructed a chart of pressure across Europe and so they could identify different air masses, in the same way that a relief map allows a hiker to identify hills and valleys. The day before D-Day, the Allied meteorologists were looking to see if these masses of air would collide over the English Channel and they identified a gap in the weather, a moment when the invasion could proceed.

Rommel's German forecasters had assured him that the weather would be too bad for an invasion, so he took a risk. He drove home to be with his family. How did the German weather forecasters get it so wrong? Their problem was a lack of data.

The prevailing winds in Europe bring the weather from the west; the air masses move in from the Atlantic. By the time the weather reaches the Channel it has passed across some portion of the British Isles. Unfortunately for Rommel, the German forecasters had little information on the pressure in the UK or over the Atlantic Ocean: they didn't have access to the Allied weather measurements. This meant that they couldn't interpolate. They'd reached the edge of their palette – they didn't know what to mix their colours with because they didn't have measurements of the pressure in Britain. How to predict beyond the edge of the palette is a much larger problem than interpolation known as *extrapolation*, or outside polishing. The best guess they could make was that the stormy weather would hold. So Erwin Rommel went home to see his wife and son. Like my grandfather, he received a rude awakening. At 7.20 a.m. on 6 June he answered the telephone to hear that the invasion had begun. He was driven back across Germany and France to his headquarters, finally arriving at nine o'clock that evening.

Rommel was out of position because his meteorologists didn't have the right information. The Allies could interpolate their measurements because they had more data. Interpolation is also one of the main ways that we do machine learning. We rely on data 'either side of the Channel' to interpolate in the region of interest.

Two hundred years after Boulton introduced the Albion fly-balls to James Watt, the physicist Stephen Hawking gave us his own version of Laplace's demon: 'If we do discover a theory of everything . . . it would be the ultimate triumph of human reason – for then we would truly know the mind of God.'[1]

We've already seen that Hawking was prone to hyperbole – he suggested that artificial intelligence could be the worst event in human history – but when Hawking writes about a Theory of Everything, he's referring to the same laws Laplace wrote of when describing the demon. By introducing God to the equations, Hawking draws to my mind that image from the Sistine Chapel ceiling – he triggers us to anthrox those laws.

In 1998 a Professor of Mathematics from Princeton, John Horton Conway, came to give a talk at Cambridge about games. In it Conway did rope tricks, danced about and played multiple games on different boards. Conway wasn't just a mathematical genius, he was known as the world's most charismatic mathematician.

I got to watch this talk as a Ph.D. student, and Conway's personality left a strong impression on me. He's been described as a cross between Archimedes, Mick Jagger and Salvador Dalí, but my favourite photo of Conway reminds me of a different combination. I think he looks like a cross between Michelangelo's Sistine Chapel depiction of God and Richard Attenborough's portrayal, in the film *Jurassic Park*, of the fictional Dr John Hammond, the creator of the dinosaur theme park. For me, this interpolation of personalities is also appropriate for Conway because, under Hawking's definition in *A Brief History of Time*, we can view Conway as a god.

Conway had an obsession with games, and it triggered him to invent one, but it was an unusual game in that it has no players. It's called the Game of Life. This zero-player game takes place on a board formed by a large grid of squares. Each square is called a cell, and just like biological cells, each cell in Life is either alive or dead. The cells are coloured black or white according to their state. Unlike in real life, but like many board games, the game proceeds in turns. At each turn cells are born and cells die, according to rules Conway devised.

The rules for birth and death in Conway's universe are very simple. They state that at each generation a cell dies if it is either *lonely* or *overcrowded*. Loneliness and overcrowding are defined by looking at the neighbouring cells in the grid. If it has fewer than two neighbours, a cell dies through loneliness; if it has more than three living neighbours, it dies from overpopulation. Birth happens when a dead cell has exactly three living neighbours.

These rules are simple, but the behaviour of the game can be very complex. So complex that you can even build one of Alan Turing's Universal Computers using the game. Watching a game proceed is like a chaotic version of black-and-white Tetris.[2] The computer is given an initial state: a configuration of living and dead cells for the game to start with. Then it just applies the rules. Across the board patterns start to emerge, some static, some dynamic. The board provides a small universe in which Conway's rules are a Theory of Everything. They describe all that can happen, and everything that can happen is a cornucopia of patterns and structures. It's so complex that the game even has its own version of Wikipedia to describe it, LifeWiki,[3] containing over 2,000 articles describing over 1,500 patterns people have discovered in the game.

Like in Laplace's demon, everything in the Life universe is completely determined by the initial configuration and the natural laws. In this case those laws are Conway's rules. This is what Stephen Hawking meant by knowing the mind of God: if we know the natural laws and the initial configuration, then, as in Laplace's demon, we know everything. Both Hawking and Conway's games are zero-player: these are not universes where the creator is allowed to intervene. Once the rules are defined and the board is set up, the universe progresses in a fully predetermined manner.

Despite Conway's simple rules for the Game of Life, as in real life complex multicellular patterns emerge. Some of the most interesting patterns are dynamic and persistent. The dynamic patterns either oscillate in the same place, or they pulsate as they move across the board. We call this emergent behaviour. Local relations between cells determine what patterns can exist, just as the natural laws of our universe determine what will happen around us. In LifeWiki you can find the names of many of these dynamic persistent patterns. Members of the class of dynamic patterns that move across the board are called Spaceships. There are many different types of Spaceship. Conway invented the game in 1969, and the first Spaceship was discovered a few months later by a collaborator called Richard Guy. It's called a Glider.

I used the word 'discovered' to describe the emergence of the

first Spaceship. It was discovered because the Glider is a consequence of Conway's simple rules. Once the rules are defined, the
glider can exist. It's consistent with the rules. But we didn't know
it existed until we allowed those rules to play out, so having the
computer play the game is like a voyage of discovery where new
possibilities are sometimes seen.

It took only a few months for the Glider to emerge from Conway's universe, but it took us 14 billion years to emerge in our
universe. Human life is consistent with the laws of our universe,
and we emerged from its starting configuration in a similar way to
how the Glider emerges in the Game of Life. But it would be
extremely difficult to guess that it would emerge if you were just
given the Theory of Everything as your starting point. Gliders were
discovered relatively quickly, but another Spaceship, the Loafer, was
discovered only in 2013. So even in the Game of Life, even by knowing the mind of God (in Hawking's parlance), we still fall a long way
short of knowing what is going to happen.

Where does this lack of knowledge come from? Applying
Laplace's demon to Conway's Game of Life, we have complete
knowledge of the data, and we also know all the laws of Conway's
universe. The only thing missing is the computation. Even if we
know the rules and the data, the game still has to be played out to
see what happens. What is true for Conway's Life is also true for our
life. Even if we were to know the mind of God, even if we had a
precise summary of the mathematical laws by which the universe
operated, even if we had all the data about how the universe started,
we would still need to 'play out the computation'.

In Douglas Adams's *Hitchhiker's Guide to the Galaxy* the computer
Deep Thought is asked to provide the answer to the 'great question'
of 'life, the universe and everything'. After seven and a half million
years of computation, Deep Thought has completed its program
but is reluctant to give its creators the answer:

'You're really not going to like it,' observed Deep Thought.
    'Tell us!'

'All right,' said Deep Thought. 'The Answer to the Great Question . . .'

'Yes . . . !'

'Of Life, the Universe and Everything . . .' said Deep Thought.

'Yes . . . !'

'Is . . .' said Deep Thought, and paused.

'Yes . . . !'

'Is . . .'

'Yes . . . !!! . . . ?'

'Forty-two,' said Deep Thought, with infinite majesty and calm.[4]

After a moment of shock from the questioners, the machine goes on to explain:

'I checked it very thoroughly,' said the computer, 'and that quite definitely is the answer. I think the problem, to be quite honest with you, is that you've never actually known what the question is.'[5]

To understand the question, Deep Thought goes on to agree to design a computer which will work out what the question is. In the book, that machine is the planet Earth, and its operators are mice. Deep Thought's idea is that the mice will observe the Earth and their observations will allow them to know what the Great Question is.

To understand the consequences of Hawking's Theory of Everything, we would have to carry out a scheme similar to Deep Thought's. The Theory wouldn't directly tell us that hurricanes exist or that when the sun sets the sky will have a red hue. It wouldn't directly tell us that water will boil at 100 degrees Celsius. These consequences of the Theory would only play out once it was combined with the data to give us the emergent qualities of the universe. The Deep Thought problem hints at the intractability of doing this. The computations required to make predictions from Laplace's demon can be enormous; Deep Thought intends to create a planet to run them. This isn't how our intelligence works in practice: the computations required would be just too gargantuan. Relative to the scale of the universe, our brains are extremely limited. Fortunately, though, to make these predictions, we don't have to build our own universe, because we've already got one.

> When you are a Bear of Very Little Brain, and you Think of Things, you find sometimes that a Thing which seemed very Thingish inside you is quite different when it gets out into the open and has other people looking at it.[6]

This comment from Pooh Bear comes just as he's tried to rescue his donkey friend, Eeyore, from a river by dropping a large stone from a bridge. Pooh's idea was to create a wave to push Eeyore to the shore, a process that Rabbit calls 'hooshing'.

Hooshing is a technique many children will have tried to retrieve a ball from a river. It can work, so Pooh's idea wasn't a bad one, but the challenge he faced was in its execution. Pooh aimed to the side of Eeyore, but unfortunately the stone fell directly on the stuffed donkey. But where is Laplace's demon in hooshing? Just as we can talk about Gliders and Loafers in Conway's Game of Life, we talk about stones and donkeys in our universe. Pooh's prediction that he can hoosh the donkey with the stone is not based on the Theory but comes from observing the way objects interact in the actual universe. Pooh is like the mice on Douglas Adams's Earth. He is observing his environment. He looks for patterns in that environment. He then borrows the computation the universe has already done for us. He has seen similar situations before – perhaps he once used a stone to hoosh a ball. He then generalizes from these previous circumstances and concludes he can also hoosh Eeyore. Despite being a bear of very little brain, Pooh can answer questions about his universe by observing the results of the Theory of Everything playing out around him, like the mice on Adams's Earth. Whether Pooh is right or not depends on whether he has extracted the relevant essence of the problem, i.e. does hooshing a ball generalize to hooshing a donkey? Pooh is distilling the patterns he sees into an understanding of the universe. This gives him a set of ideas that are not *true* in the sense that they derive directly from the Theory – they are proxy-truths. They represent our best understanding from observation of the world. They stand in for the *truth* that comes from the Theory because that truth can't be here in person due to the challenges presented by Laplace's demon.

My mother drives a Hummer. I like to tell people this in talks to illustrate the extent to which we are willing to generalize. The trick is to pause after saying it and then ask what people imagine my mother does for a living. Mostly people think she's either an A-list movie star or she manages an organization that's deeply involved in some form of lucrative criminal activity. A Hummer is the civilian version of an American military vehicle, the successor to the original Jeep. For a time, Arnold Schwarzenegger would turn up to movie premieres in one. The image of the Hummer contrasts with the image we have of a professor's mother. The five words of the sentence 'My mother drives a Hummer' contain 60 bits of information, but they give people a rich picture of who my mother might be.

This generalization is like Pooh Bear's hooshing. It does not emerge from the Theory; it is borrowed from seeing how the universe works in practice. When people assume that my mother is a gangland kingpin, they are basing this on their cultural preconceptions, on their experience of the universe around them, on their proxy-truths. I like the idea of a universe in which my mother drives a Hummer, but in this one she drives a VW Golf.

Erwin Rommel went home to be with his wife, Lucie, and his son, Manfred, on the eve of the D-Day landings. My grandfather went home to visit his wife, Winona, my aunt and my father, Garth. Rommel's son, Manfred,[7] became Mayor of Stuttgart and has an airport named after him. My father grew up to be an engineer like his father. He was a meticulous planner and ran large-scale engineering projects that had budgets of tens of millions of dollars. Each project required careful preparation. My family travelled around the world to different locations, wherever my father's work took us.

Wherever we settled, my father would get involved in local societies, from choral societies to residents' groups, and was asked to adapt his management skills to help run them. Despite being busy, he was always keen and would share his planning skills and make those organizations run better.

When we are young, when we are learning about the universe and how it works, we are strongly influenced by the examples we are exposed to. So my father's skills in planning had a large influence on me. However, I also had an older brother, Mark. I was in awe of them both, but Mark, in contrast to Garth, preferred to work outside the system to make things better. Mark preferred to operate independently. He wanted to make things better, but he liked to do so by highlighting corruption and exposing hypocrisy. He was not a meticulous planner; in fact, he couldn't imagine anything worse than a week where he knew what he was going to do every day. He was an improviser.

My brother and father had similar personal values – they each had a strong sense of right and wrong, they each had a deep concern for the underdog – but they had different personalities. They took different approaches to life and, when presented with the same challenge, they would propose different solutions. For me as a young boy in awe of both these people, that led to a lot of confusion. How could both of these people I admired be right? To answer this question and resolve my boyhood confusion, I've had to borrow a page from Douglas Adams's book. Deep Thought startles its programmers by revealing a simple answer to the 'ultimate question'. But it goes on to reveal that the real challenge is not the answer but the question itself. What does it mean to be right?

Garth liked to know what his team would be doing and when. Mark loved the challenge of innovating on the fly. Garth was an engineer and a planner; Mark became a trial lawyer. They were both successful in their chosen professions, but they had very different approaches. The conundrum of which approach is right is pervasive. We see it with individuals, companies, institutions, even across nations and cultures.

The Ferrari Formula One racing team is based in Maranello, Italy. Formula One teams use machine learning for strategic planning and aerodynamic modelling. In July 2011, a year before he joined Facebook, my friend Joaquin and I visited Maranello to talk about how we could help. Ferrari's Head of Strategy, Neil Martin, had recently been recruited from Red Bull, but he had started his career in the English McLaren team. Neil was adapting to his new life and told me about the gap in culture between Formula One's two most successful teams, McLaren and Ferrari. Running a Formula One team is a complex logistical operation: it is a dynamic supply chain where the team has to move equipment and people to different tracks around the world to prepare their cars for each race weekend. McLaren planned the entire season in advance. It knew where every part of each car should be at any given time. In contrast, Ferrari did everything at the last minute, only finalizing the travel for each race a few weeks before the event. If companies can have a personality, then, personality-wise, McLaren was like Garth, and Ferrari was like Mark.

What could be the advantage of being like Ferrari and Mark? Wouldn't it be better to plan ahead and know where everything should be? I asked Neil, 'How do the two teams respond when things go wrong?' Neil's answer was immediate. 'Oh, when something goes wrong, Ferrari are incredible. They really get their shit together, they adapt and fix it.' In these circumstances, McLaren weren't so effective: it seemed that they could be hit by a form of retrospective paralysis – fixating on how a plan had failed rather than rolling up their sleeves and fixing it.

Field Marshal Helmuth von Moltke's words told us, 'No plan of operations extends with any certainty beyond the first contact with the main hostile force.' We can make plans, but there is no guarantee these plans will pan out in practice. Eeyore only survived Pooh's hooshing intervention by diving down into the water and swimming to the shore. The leader of the 101st US Airborne, Brigadier General Don Pratt, died when his glider crash-landed in Normandy. The plan went awry, the soldiers lost their leader, but they improvised and made the D-Day landings a success.

Perhaps you can now see the challenge of trying to align around the 'right approach'. The computation that would be required to understand the consequences of each step in the plan is far too great. This flaw in Laplace's demon is what prevents us from giving a definitive answer to the question 'What is right?' It is the reason we can't make rankings of intelligent entities. What is right depends on the circumstances. Our companies have different cultures, and people have different personalities. Ironically, this was also Laplace's point. Laplace presented his demon as a straw-man argument . . . or perhaps a straw demon would be a better way to phrase it. We were never meant to take the possibility of what he suggested literally. The demon is introduced in a work called *A Philosophical Essay on Probabilities*. This is odd, because the demon is a description of a *deterministic* universe. The so-called 'clockwork universe', where all we see follows inevitably once the clock's mechanism – the Theory – is understood. Why was Laplace talking about a deterministic universe in an essay on *probabilities*?

Laplace's demon describes the notion of the deterministic universe so beautifully, and the concept is so alluring, that it is the most remembered component of his essay. That quote is a foundation of the philosophy of physical determinism. But if you read two pages further in the essay, you find him writing:

> The curve described by a simple molecule of air or vapour is regulated in a manner just as certain as the planetary orbits; the only difference between them is that which comes from our ignorance.[8]

This is the main point of the essay. What Laplace is saying is that, in practice, we can never know everything, and we must deal with this lack of knowledge. I call this idea *Laplace's gremlin*. Laplace was fully aware of the impossibility of what he had described in the demon. He knew that we could never know the *respective situations of all the beings that compose nature*, nor could we know *all the forces by which nature is animated*. Even if we did, as we've just explored using Conway's Game of Life, Pooh Bear and Deep Thought, the computational challenge of considering all those entities together would be beyond even our fastest computers. We are constrained by our *ignorance* – our lack of knowledge of data and a model, alongside our inability to compute. We are always in a state of uncertainty. A state of constant and pervasive doubt that places us at the mercy of the unknown.

So how do we proceed? Are we hopelessly lost? Some Greek philosophers certainly thought so. Pyrrho was a Greek philosopher and a contemporary of Aristotle. He founded a school of philosophy called scepticism. The story goes that he had so much doubt in his own senses that his friends would follow closely behind him to ensure he didn't ignore the evidence from his own eyes and walk directly over a cliff edge. Laplace's answer in his essay is less drastic. He uses the presence of ignorance to introduce us to probability:

> Probability is relative, in part to this ignorance, in part to our knowledge. We know that of three or a greater number of events a single one ought to occur; but nothing induces us to believe that one of them will occur rather than the others. In this state of indecision it is impossible for us to announce their occurrence with certainty. It is, however, probable that one of these events, chosen at will, will not occur because we see several cases equally possible which exclude its occurrence, while only a single one favors it.[9]

OK, so it's not as pithy as his earlier quotes, but it is the main point of his essay. To deal with ignorance we should introduce probability – lack of knowledge necessitates *doubt*. The question is not whether there is doubt, but how much doubt is there? Mark and Garth's approaches are responding to different assumptions about the level of uncertainty. Mark's improvisational approach is appropriate when levels of uncertainty are higher. Garth's planning approach is more appropriate when the level of uncertainty is lower. A diversity of approaches is needed because we are also uncertain about how much uncertainty we will face! So, the right approach is to have people like Mark and people like Garth. Then we've got our bases covered.

There was a time when the random nature of events was ascribed to the fickle nature of our gods. Given our tendency to anthrox, this is unsurprising. Cleromancy is determining the will of the gods through the casting of lots or dice to make decisions and was widely practised in biblical times. Lotteries were also used to select leaders in ancient Athens. The Greek gods were capricious, so it made sense that their whims would change: those that found favour at one time could be subject to setbacks.

This superstitious approach isn't restricted to ancient peoples. Modern folklore also looks for explanations for bad luck. During the Second World War, aircraft were constantly undergoing development. New innovations were rapidly deployed to make planes more competitive in battle. The speed of innovation also led to problems with reliability. Engines failed, cables broke and planes crashed.

Pilots were faced with human enemies and fragile equipment. Rather than chalking off the failures to bad luck, some of them found it easier to anthrox these failures with an adversarial entity. The notion of the gremlin developed, a mischievous creature intent on sabotage. The gremlin of uncertainty emerges to thwart our meticulous plans.

In the US, to deal with the challenge of reliability, the US Army Air Force had a proving ground at Langley Field in Virginia. They put together a team of test pilots, all of whom were also trained aeronautical engineers. These pilots would try to re-create and eliminate any reported problems.[10] All US aircraft were tested at Langley Field, their flying characteristics evaluated and recommendations made to improve them. One of the most famous US planes of the Second World War was the P-51 Mustang. It was a long-range fighter plane used by the Allies to obtain air superiority over Europe on the run-in to D-Day. With Allied fighters dominating the skies, the Allied landings could proceed without fear of air attack. Donald S. Lopez was a US pilot who spent his war flying from bases in

China. He became Deputy Director of the US National Air and Space Museum. Speaking of the Mustang, he said, 'It's generally accepted that the P-51 is one of the best, if not the best, fighters of World War II. But as is common with most aircraft it didn't start out great. It wasn't exactly a dog, but you could hear a quiet bark now and then if you went by.'[11]

The Langley Field proving ground was run by the US National Advisory Committee for Aeronautics (NACA). This was a group of luminaries including Orville Wright, who designed and flew the first powered heavier-than-air aircraft, and Charles Lindbergh, who was first to fly solo across the Atlantic. But the work of testing aircraft was done by the engineers and pilots led by an engineer called Bob Gilruth. One problem they were asked to resolve was unexplained non-combat losses of their Mustang fighter plane. The plane would fly into a cloud, then fall out of the sky.

These problematic clouds form when air masses collide. When mild air meets cold air it is forced to rise, which causes it to cool and rain to form. Clouds can seem quite peaceful, but cumulonimbus clouds are violent places that are the source of thunder and storms. The billowing nature of the outside of the cloud reflects extreme air currents inside it. When a plane enters this rapidly rising and descending air, everything is pitched up and down. In Isaac Newton's theory of motion, acceleration is the rate of change of velocity. What pilots experience inside cumulonimbus clouds is rapid changes in acceleration. A rapid change in acceleration can kill, like the whiplash that killed Brigadier General Don Pratt in his crash-landing glider on D-Day. In the UK, engineers call this 'yank', but in the US it's known as 'jerk'. The engineers at Langley believed these jerk forces were damaging the wings of the plane, causing structural failure and crashes.

Stefan Cavallo was the NACA pilot-engineer who was chosen to test this theory. Jerk forces are very uncomfortable for pilots and can cause them to lose control of the aircraft. The pilots could tolerate the rattling around of the plane if they were tightly strapped into their seats. Pilots were also trained to hold the stick loosely so the jerk forces didn't interfere with their control. The plan was for Cavallo to fly straight and level into a cloud while his colleague, Robert Baker, flew alongside him, about a mile away. The forces on the two Mustangs were monitored so they could be compared after Cavallo landed. Cavallo and Baker were like the mice in Deep Thought's computer: the only way they could judge how events would pan out was, like Pooh's hooshing of Eeyore, to try it in practice. Cavallo related his experience in short-story form:

> Immediately upon entering the cloud the air became very rough, and I had the feeling that I had made a mistake . . .

Cavallo had been led to believe that the main worry was the damage the jerk forces would cause the aircraft's wings. Initially the plane withstands the buffeting, and he sees no problems with the wings, but he's surprised by what happens next:

> I was using my navigation instruments to fly straight and level when suddenly a hole appeared in the hood directly in front of the cockpit windshield, and the engine became very rough – but continued to run . . .

The hole was made by one of the engine's pistons. Cavallo's Mustang was powered by a version of the Rolls-Royce Merlin engine, a twelve-cylinder engine that produced nearly 1,500 horsepower. That's approximately ten times what a typical car engine produces today and double what a modern Formula One engine produces. Losing a piston is a catastrophic failure: while an engine can run with a reduced number of pistons, in Cavallo's plane the piston had smashed through the top of the engine, leaving a large hole in the engine's protective casing:

> Oil appeared as a smear across my windshield . . . I called to Baker and told him I had an emergency and what was happening, what I was looking at, and what I was doing . . .

Cavallo was a trained test pilot and an engineer, so even during an emergency he's relating events to his colleague. He is observing the accident in real time; anything he can learn now may save lives in future. With this in mind, he'd like to save the plane, to glide it to a landing so the sensors can be read and the accident understood:

> The oil smear covered my entire windshield and the engine was now getting very rough and the whole plane was starting to shake . . . I needed to bail out . . . I was still trying to talk to Baker when I heard a loud 'whoosh' and the whole plane was covered in flames. If I had had any reluctance to leave the plane it ended then.

The fire persuades Cavallo that it's time to leave. Modern jet planes are equipped with ejector seats which can fire the pilot out of the plane, ensuring they move rapidly clear of the damaged aircraft. But in these Second World War planes the pilot had to climb out of the cockpit to bail out, lifting themselves into the oncoming wind blasting at hundreds of miles per hour. This had to be done while the plane disintegrated around them. It was an incredibly dangerous undertaking. To make it easier, Cavallo decides to turn his plane upside down and drop out by the force of gravity:

> I unfastened my seat belt, pushed it aside, and started a roll to the right. When the plane rolled past 90 degrees to an attitude of about 110 degrees, I started to slide up the right side of the cockpit. In the side-slipping condition the plane was in, the flames went back over the top . . .

The other fear in Cavallo's mind is getting clipped by the tail of the plane as it flies past his emerging body. He's therefore keen to push himself as far away from the plane as he can:

> I kept hanging onto the stick as I slid up and out of the rolling plane and finally, as I was getting buffeted by the wind stream, and as more of my body oozed out of the cockpit, I gave one hard push on the

top of the stick and grabbed for my knees. I had thought about making myself as small as possible to avoid hitting the tail. As I cleared the cockpit I kept my eyes open and tumbled through yellow flames and smoke for quite a while. I saw the numbers on the tail as they flashed by and I heard the wind whistling in my ears.[12]

Cavallo landed safely and reported back on the incident. His analysis suggested that the jerk forces, combined with the speed of the engine, had been too much and a whiplash effect had propelled the piston from the engine. Cavallo was one of six engineer-pilots based at NACA. Their observations were vital in fighting the gremlins that plagued aircraft, but to explore these failures they had to make observations and they became the guinea pigs in their own experiments.

The term 'test pilot' highlights the importance of trying things out. Cavallo is seeking proxy-truths from his plane. To do this successfully he has to display not only meticulous planning to acquire the data but also improvisation to react to his disintegrating plane. To develop the skills needed for this role, test pilots are highly trained. Despite their dangerous job, none of the six test pilots died while testing the planes at Langley Field, and there were only two bailouts.

In contrast, Donald Lopez's career as a pilot was played out over China as a member of a US Army Air Force squadron known as the 'Flying Tigers'. They supported Chinese forces against the invading Japanese. Many of Lopez's friends died, but those who survived learned from their experiences:

As I was to find out in future aerial combat, little real thought and planning takes place in a dogfight. Everything is done by instinct, and as you gain experience your instincts are more fully developed and sharpened, making you much more effective.[13]

Training and experience allowed Lopez and Cavallo to feel that their aircraft had become an extension of themselves, to become, as

Lopez later writes, 'one with the airplane'. When Cavallo flew into the cumulonimbus clouds that destroyed his Mustang, he describes them as rising up to 40,000 feet. In an ideal world, Cavallo wouldn't have had to fly into the cloud. We would use our knowledge of science to predict what would happen. We would simulate the flight of the P-51 through the cloud using computer models, but even today the conditions in such clouds are incredibly difficult to simulate on a computer. The jerk forces Cavallo's plane was exposed to saturated the readings on his instruments. In 1943, when computers were still in development, there was only one way to deal with our ignorance about why the P-51 Mustang was not emerging from such clouds. Like Pooh Bear, and his very little brain, we had limited access to the ingredients of Laplace's demon to make the prediction. And like Pooh Bear the answer the NACA chose was to run tests in the real world.

The Greeks' notion of capricious gods, like a pilot's notion of gremlins, was used to explain the haphazard nature of their world. But by the eighteenth century the Christian view of God was that of an eternal and all-powerful entity. The Scientific Revolution had led to the reductionist era of 'rationality' that was driven by Newton's *Principia*. In Hawking's terms, Newton had 'glimpsed the mind of God' in understanding the laws of gravity and unifying the motion of both heavenly and earthly bodies. The fickle nature of chance was incompatible with a consistent and capable being.

Originally, our technical understanding of uncertainty was interlinked with games of chance, with gambling. This was seen as a shabby form of mathematics, so patronage was harder to find for those who wanted to explore it. As a result, the task of mathematically characterizing uncertainty developed later than we might expect, given the relative simplicity of the mathematics. Fortunately, once the fickle form of uncertainty was reduced to simple equations, it was seen as another example of the rational world, one that conformed to the notion of a perfect creation. So it was that one of the most important contributions to probability theory was written by Nonconformist minister the Reverend

Thomas Bayes. The work was published after his death by his friend, another Nonconformist minister, called Richard Price. Price wrote an introduction to the paper and motivated Bayes's ideas by suggesting that this mathematical characterization of uncertainty brought us closer to determining an intelligent cause for the world:

> The purpose I mean is, to shew what reason we have for believing that there are in the constitution of things fixt laws according to which things happen, and that, therefore, the frame of the world must be the effect of the wisdom and power of an intelligent cause; and thus to confirm the argument taken from final causes for the existence of the Deity.[14]

With this introduction, Price pulls the domain of probability firmly back into the scope of Laplace's demon. Price was a rational dissenter, a Unitarian minister who was part of a movement that rejected the doctrine of the Church of England. The scientific Enlightenment had a pervasive effect across all fields of intellectual endeavour. Enlightenment thinkers like Richard Price and Matthew Boulton operated across politics, religion, trade, science and engineering. Price was also part of the worldwide intellectual and political movement that eventually led to rebellion in the American colonies and a revolution in France. He goes on to emphasize the nature of order that underpins Bayes's equations:

> It will be easy to see that the converse problem solved in this essay is more directly applicable to this purpose; for it shews us, with distinctness and precision, in every case of any particular order or recurrency of events, what reason there is to think that such recurrency or order is derived from stable causes or regulations in nature, and not from any irregularities of chance.[15]

The precise predictions of Newton's *Principia* had led people to believe that simple explanations underpin all natural and social phenomena. For the Rational Dissenters, these explanations originated in God. They wanted to remove mysticism from the Church and use scientific thinking to reinforce faith. Price was introducing Bayes's new mathematical formalization of uncertainty as evidence that perfection was also the hidden hand behind the haphazard nature of events.

Leibniz and Newton gave us the calculus of the infinitesimal. Bayes's paper gave us a calculus of uncertainty, the mathematical equations that underpin *doubt*. Laplace says that the 'curve described by a simple molecule of air or vapor is regulated in a manner just as certain as the planetary orbits.' While this statement is given as fact and probability is given as the solution, an understanding of gases was at the limit of the physics of the time.

The Bernoulli family produced three generations of famous Swiss mathematicians. Daniel Bernoulli had a lot to live up to. As he was growing up, he was in the shadow of his father, Johann, his father's student, the prolific mathematician Leonhard Euler, and his elder brother, Niklaus. Daniel's father tried to persuade him to study business and medicine, but Daniel was relentless in his pursuit of a career as a mathematician. We can be grateful that he was, because Laplace was inspired by Daniel when he referred to 'a simple molecule of air or vapor'. Daniel Bernoulli applied Newtonian ideas to fluids and gases. He took the theory of moving objects and applied it to the air we breathe and the steam that would later power Watt's engines. He published these ideas in a book he called *Hydrodynamica* (1738). This book is the foundation of our modern understanding of the physical laws behind the weather and flight.

When they are not disintegrating from the effect of jerk forces, planes stay in the air due to an effect first described by Daniel in *Hydrodynamica*: it's called the Bernoulli principle. *Hydrodynamica* also described the kinetic theory of gases. The word 'kinetic' comes from the Greek for movement. So, the kinetic theory of gases is really a theory of the movement of gases. Bernoulli viewed a gas as a collection of interacting molecules that are colliding with one another. He used Newton's theories of motion to characterize the forces that arise when fluids flow, discovering principles that are still used today to design aircraft, boats, even refrigerators.

On a calm day, the air around you may appear to be still, but it consists of molecules. Any individual molecule of oxygen could be travelling at 1,000 miles per hour. The molecules travel very fast, but they don't travel far. Each molecule will move on average only around 70 nanometers before it hits another. Relative to its size, that's equivalent to the molecule running a 100-metre dash. After each dash, it collides and sets off in a different direction. This all happens so fast that each molecule experiences around 7 billion collisions every second.

Laplace's demon tells us that to make predictions we need to consider *all positions of all items of which nature is composed*. That would mean tracking each molecule through all its collisions. If you had a tree for every molecule in a single cup of air, you would have enough trees to cover the entire solar system in a forest. Even if we could measure the location of all these molecules, predicting where they would all move next would be too much for even the fastest supercomputer.

In *Hydrodynamica*, Daniel Bernoulli took a step back from this complexity and considered the behaviour of a collection of molecules rather than each individual molecule. This allowed him to mathematically describe the behaviour of fluids even if he wasn't tracking every molecule. Bernoulli took the first step to considering the behaviour of an *ensemble of molecules*. He realized that, while it's difficult to say things about individual molecules, we can still say something about how they behave in groups.

The weather forecast for D-Day was performed by interpolation; this meant the Germans were unable to see the gap in the weather that triggered Eisenhower's invasion. But the modern weather forecast is carried out in a very different way. It uses a computer that builds on the understanding of the physics of fluids Daniel Bernoulli first described in *Hydrodynamica*.

In school, mathematics focuses on teaching students how to

solve systems of equations. Students are tested on their knowledge of the solution, or sometimes on converting a word problem into a system of equations. To make it possible to answer these questions in an exam, the mathematics we are taught normally focuses on systems where we can find the solution by hand. In the world outside school, there are a lot of problems where the mathematics simply doesn't work. In other words, there are very many problems that aren't amenable to what Laplace called *analysis*.

If you studied physics at high school, you would have studied Newton's laws from *Principia*.[16] If you did experimental work on motion, then you would have spent your physics lessons constructing experiments that tried to minimize the effects of air resistance. Why did you do this? Because air resistance makes the analysis of Newton's equations too hard to learn at school.

We call sets of equations that work 'analytically tractable'. The word 'tractable' comes from the Latin for 'to handle', so it's just a fancy way of saying equations that we can handle through analysis. Adding air resistance to Newton's equations makes them analytically *intractable*, i.e., we can't derive the solution using the mathematical techniques we can do by hand.

Enter the computer. One way of solving an intractable equation is with a numerical solution. A numerical solution is a set of steps, or an algorithm, that if repeated will give a set of numbers that provide a solution. The solution is not in the form of a mathematical formula, just a set of numbers. Ideally, we would like to obtain the formula, but mathematical intractability means that we can't find it, so we make do with a set of numbers instead.

Norbert Wiener's visit to Bertrand Russell had put him off philosophy, but Russell introduced Wiener to his mathematician friend G. H. Hardy, and Wiener turned his attention to mathematics. Influenced by Hardy and in a snub to Russell's logical theories of knowledge, Wiener began to explore the mathematics of ignorance. He continued his European tour with a visit to the European hub of mathematics, Göttingen in Germany, where Wiener was mentored by David Hilbert, one of the world's leading mathematicians, but then the First World War intervened and Norbert Wiener returned to the USA.

Wiener was drafted into the US army as a lieutenant and despatched to the US Army Aberdeen Proving Ground in Maryland. Just as Langley Field tested the flight of aircraft, the Aberdeen Proving Ground tested the flight of artillery shells. Like Diana Russell-Clarke two decades later, Wiener became a human computer. The calculations needed for the trajectory of an artillery shell are analytically intractable. The interaction of the molecules of air with the artillery shell makes Newton's equations hard to solve, so instead numerical solutions must be used. These numerical solutions involve trying out a set of numbers that fit the equation, but, as in a Sherlock Holmes story, clever tricks can be used to give mathematical clues for where the solutions lie. If these clues are followed, the solution can be found. But each clue requires some calculation and sometimes many clues must be solved before the solution is found.

Behind Deep Thought's plan for the Earth is an important observation. The Earth, and the universe it sits in, just 'work'. They can do things that are, from a technical perspective, mathematically intractable. The universe isn't looking to solve mathematical equations. What we observe around us is the consequence of unimaginable numbers of particles interacting according to the Theory. But this activity is beyond even our fastest computers: and so Deep Thought suggests building an entire Earth to understand. That was Douglas Adams's idea: to understand life, you must simulate life. Back in the real world, the expense of such a computation makes that route prohibitive, so what we look for instead is a mathematical shortcut to find the answer. The shortcut can involve an abstraction, a relaxation of the theory that allows us to compute answers and make predictions. Bernoulli's *Hydrodynamica* allowed us to make predictions about fluids and the air without monitoring the movement of every molecule, but even these abstractions don't lead to analytical theory. They produce more equations that need to be solved numerically. That's what Norbert Wiener was doing in 1917 when he became a human computer.

By the 1940s the computer had come a long way from Babbage's mechanical conception. The valves used in Colossus were fast and reliable enough to enable computers to do arithmetic for us. We could use the automatic computer to go beyond high-school mathematics. In the United States, the Moore School of Engineering built a machine for finding numerical solutions to Newton's equations for computing artillery trajectories – the ENIAC. Machines from the Moore School were later used to solve some of the intractable mathematics behind the hydrogen bomb. The ENIAC was moved to the Aberdeen Proving Ground, so the role of Wiener and his fellow human computers was now carried out by an automatic machine.

Inspired by the ENIAC and the work on Colossus at Bletchley Park, by the end of the 1940s there were several efforts across the world to build electronic computing machines. As well as the Moore School there was Max Newman's team at the University of Manchester and, back in Newton's Cambridge, there was a team building a machine to provide the university with the world's first computing service. It was called the EDSAC. The Cambridge team was working with J. Lyons & Co., a chain of tea shops and producer of cakes.

The collaboration with Lyons produced a computer called LEO. While the rest of the world was using computers for building nuclear weapons, Cambridge had turned its best and brightest minds to formulating the ultimate afternoon tea. The twinning of tea with treacle tarts or trifle sponges. The baking of Battenberg slices and Bakewell tarts. LEO's first job was making baking forecasts;[17] from 1951 it was doing bakery sales analysis; and by 1954 it was running the company's payroll. It was the world's first business computer.

Beyond the English afternoon tea, another preoccupation of the English is discussing the weather. Regardless of social status, age, sexuality, race or gender, we all remain affected by snow, storms and rain. That is why in polite English conversation any lulls will invariably be filled with a comment on the weather. It realigns the subject to an uncontroversial externality. It returns us to information coherence. So, it's no surprise that as soon as Cambridge's EDSAC machine was capable enough, it and its sister LEO machine were given the task of numerical weather prediction.

The flight of a projectile requires numerical solutions because of the interaction between the projectile and the particles of air. Fortunately, there are abstractions we can use, like Bernoulli did, to avoid computing the path of every particle. But we still need a numerical solution. Weather prediction is even more complex. To predict the weather we need to predict the interactions between different air masses. The form of numerical prediction we use works a bit like Conway's Game of Life. The weather map is split into square cells and the numerical solution proceeds in turns. Only in the game of weather the turns represent the passage of time in the real world and the rules come from the principles first described by Daniel Bernoulli.

To lay down the grid across the weather chart, we need to define a size for the square cells. To make modern forecasts, the cells have sides that are between a kilometre and fifty kilometres long. In the Game of Life, cells live or die according to the state of their neighbouring cells. In the zero-player game of weather prediction, the temperature, pressure and humidity of each cell depends on the temperature, pressure and humidity of neighbouring cells. Each cell holds air. The amount of air each cell has determines the barometric pressure. At each turn, each cell checks in with its neighbouring cell, comparing how much air it has with how much its neighbour has: it checks what the pressure is at each point. The cells then move air between them according to a rule book. Air moves from areas of high pressure to areas of low pressure. In the real world, we call this movement of air *wind*. The set of rules that governs this behaviour is a refinement of Daniel Bernoulli's *Hydrodynamica* known as the Navier–Stokes equations. Each of these local changes adjusts the amount of air each cell will give or receive. Eventually, after a lot of negotiation between the cells and their neighbours, the turn is complete. Then the process starts again. If each turn represents an hour, then for a twenty-four-hour forecast, twenty-four turns are taken.

Before automatic computers like the ENIAC, EDSAC and LEO, numerical solutions of this type would have been worked out by teams of human computers like Diana Russell-Clarke and Norbert Wiener. But this process was slow and laborious. Far too slow for numerical weather prediction to be possible. Just as the computer enabled us to solve the German codes, it also allows the automation of the board game behind numerical weather prediction and gives us the chance to work with more complex models of the atmosphere.

Today the machines that make our weather predictions are some of the most powerful on the planet. With them weather forecasts can look five days ahead to make predictions that are more accurate than even the daily forecast was in the 1940s. The mathematics isn't new, but we've been able to go beyond interpolation and extrapolate the weather based on the underlying theory.

By the 1960s, when the Met Office first integrated numerical weather prediction into its daily forecast, a new technology had made computers even more practical: solid-state semiconductors. Modern computers have switches based on semiconducting materials. These transistors are etched on to computer chips at a tiny scale. A modern transistor may only be 70 atoms of silicon wide, Flowers's Colossus had 1,600 valves, a modern computer may contain 30 billion transistors. Each logical gate uses a few transistors, meaning that a modern processor can contain billions of logic gates.

A numerical weather model is a *mechanistic* model; it contains an understanding of the mechanisms that underpin the operation of our planet. By incorporating mechanisms it allows us to extrapolate our observations. In the case of weather, some abstraction has occurred. The models don't track the movement of every molecule, they follow Daniel Bernoulli's approach of treating groups of molecules together to speed up computation. Importantly, these abstractions are based on the underlying physics: they are the effective physics that emerges from the Theory being applied to many billions of molecules. These models are very close in spirit to Laplace's demon. But in the case of weather prediction or artillery trajectories, they can't produce a single formula for the prediction, because the analysis is intractable.

The computations today's machines make possible mean that we can make predictions that would have been unimaginable to Laplace or Flowers. Laplace's demon provides our guide, and modern computers give us the ability to assimilate massive amounts of data and perform many billions of calculations. The models come from the great physicists of the past, but are these models enough to make our futures certain in the manner of Laplace's demon? Unfortunately, this is not the route to artificial intelligence. Nor is it the way in which any of the intelligences that surround us operate, not even our own. Despite the incredible achievements of these machines, Laplace's demon is not a practical way to derive the everyday decisions we need to make to go about our daily lives. If I catch a ball, I do not compute in my head Newton's equations of motion. When I walk or run about, I do not derive the angle of incidence with which my foot will hit the ground and compute the necessary muscular force. My nerves and muscles respond to their environment in a manner much closer to the way the Albion fly-ball operates. They are tuned by experience from interacting with the world around them.

Socrates was executed in 399 BCE after a trial in which his fate was decided by 501 jurors of Athens. He was accused of blasphemy, lacking respect for the Athenian gods and undermining Athenian culture. Socrates was disrupting the cultural truths his community adhered to. An account of his defence is given by his student Plato, but Plato's account of the trial has Socrates defending a more fundamental truth. In his defence, Socrates considers his own wisdom. He relates how he sought out a political leader who had a reputation for wisdom but when he explored the man's knowledge he found it wanting:

I reasoned thus with myself: I am wiser than this man, for neither of us appears to know anything great and good; but he fancies he knows something, although he knows nothing; whereas I, as I do not know anything, so I do not fancy I do. In this trifling particular, then, I appear to be wiser than he, because I do not fancy I know what I do not know. After that I went to another who was thought to be wiser than the former, and formed the very same opinion.[18]

Socrates had been told that he is the wisest man by the Oracle at Delphi and concludes that the only way the Oracle can be correct is if wisdom is not associated with knowledge but with an awareness of limitations. He decides that he is wise not because of his knowledge, but because of his awareness of his own ignorance. This form of wisdom acknowledges the fact that, however much you know, there is always far more to the world that you don't know. Despite the incredible sophistication of the human mind, when we consider the complexity of the world around us we begin to share Winnie-the-Pooh's own Socratic understanding of his limitations – we see that in comparison to the complexity of the world we are 'bears of very little brain' – and yet the uncertainty in the world, characterized by Laplace's gremlin of uncertainty, has not yet extinguished us. We engage in a delicate balance between planning and improvising to deal with this uncertainty. Laplace's demon implies that there's an ultimate grand plan, but practical considerations mean that even if this is true we are obliged to hoosh our way through our lives. Many of the decisions we face sit between these two worlds, one where everything is predictable, the other where everything is unknowable. This is where the art of intelligent decision-making comes in. This is why the question as to which approach is better, the improvisational approach of Mark and Ferrari or the planning approach of Garth and McLaren, is flawed. Both are right. Mark's forte was cross-examination, reacting to an evolving set of events as they happened. Garth's forte was delivering projects on time and under budget. He excelled at piecing together the order of events, determining who and what was needed when and where. When Joaquin and I visited Maranello in 2011, McLaren and Ferrari were the two teams with the greatest historical number of winning cars in Formula One. Mark and Garth had different personalities but shared values. McLaren and Ferrari had different corporate cultures but shared objectives; the cultures of the teams were different, but there was no *better* approach, as both approaches had led to success. Which works better depends on the circumstances.

Three hundred years after Socrates's execution, inspired by Pyrrho the Greek's scepticism movement, the Pyrrhonian philosophers emerged. They called the phenomenon of suspending judgement until more evidence is obtained *epoché*. The word is not in common use today, but it should be. I would say it loads if I only knew how to pronounce it properly; in the meantime I'm suspending my use until someone who knows tells me. Laplace's gremlin leads to the phenomenon of *epoché*, the suspension of judgement until the decision is required. The uncertainty of the world around us, our lack of information about how the universe works, uncertainty around the right objectives, and limited data and compute – all cause us to hedge our bets.

The suspending of judgement comes about because we don't have sufficient information to make a decision. The hope is that by delaying our decision we might acquire some of the missing facts. But we can't suspend judgement indefinitely. At some point we need to make a decision, whether it's a weather window for an invasion or a delivery window for a loading webpage. The atomic human has two primary tools for dealing with uncertainty in the real world. First, we sustain a diversity of approaches, like Mark and Ferrari versus Garth and McLaren; and second, we can suspend judgement until the point that a decision is needed.

My father's last major project was installing a new catalytic cracker. The Fawley catalytic cracker was a 20-metre-tall tower that was to be inserted in the middle of an operational oil refinery. The tower was manufactured in India and imported to the UK by ship and road. Once on site it had to be transported horizontally into position across the buildings, pipes and towers that make up an operational refinery. It was then upended and dropped into its final location.

The planning for the operation was meticulous. The road had to be cleared of overhead cables. An overpass was built above the equipment already there to bring the tower into position before it was lifted by cranes. The diameter of the cracker was limited by the narrowest gap it had to fit through when it went under the existing pipework. The operation was a set of carefully planned events, each of which was contingent on the previous. It could only be delivered successfully by eliminating uncertainty.

The more improvisational approach of Mark and Ferrari works better in an uncertain setting. If you face a lot of uncertainty, you become expert at the art of suspending judgement. Like a tennis player receiving a shot, you position yourself at the centre of the baseline to cover the court. You must be responsive to events and intervene as necessary to steer them in the right direction.

Mark's clients were society's underdogs. He had one client whose skull had been caved in by the butt of a police officer's pistol. There were no witnesses, and the case would be played out before a jury. The officer's gun had been sent for testing; no blood had been found on the grip. During the trial the evidence was displayed on a table in the court. As Mark began his cross-examination, he saw the serial number of the weapon that had been tested. It did not match the weapon of the accused officer. The police had sent the wrong gun for testing. That is the nature of a trial. Mark's plan for his cross-examination was overturned by this new information. He had to improvise. By rapidly adjusting, he was able to expose the cover-up and win the case for his client.

Different personalities take different approaches to the gremlin of uncertainty. My father, Fred's son, planned the gremlins out of the system; my brother, Fred's grandson, enjoyed wrestling with the gremlins when they arose. These approaches are effective in different environments; they are complementary.

For machine learning to work it needs to assimilate and distil the gremlin of uncertainty. It needs to balance the computational effort required with the amount of data available. Like the Albion fly-ball, machine learning can take shortcuts to deliver a good decision, despite the uncertainty. In these cases, it is emulating the judgement of an expert human decision-maker. But Laplace's gremlin does not have a 'silver-bullet' solution. Machine-learning approaches are a family of methods that can each work well in different circumstances. A diversity of solutions is required for artificial intelligence, just as a diversity of approaches is useful in our natural intelligences. Uncertainty about our environment and the challenges we will face encourages diversity. We see diverse lifeforms around us, and we see diversity in our individual and cultural approaches to problemsolving. This diversity brings resilience.

Both Mark and Garth died from lung cancer. But, whereas Garth's mesothelioma was induced by asbestos inhaled from industrial insulation from the plants he worked on across his career, Mark's adenocarcinoma was induced by the tobacco he smoked and the alcohol he drank to alleviate the stress of carrying his clients' hopes on his shoulders. Mark died at the age of forty-seven. At his funeral I was able to meet his client from that police brutality case. He came straight across to me. 'You look just like your brother; he was a stand-up guy.'

7

It's Not Rocket Science or Brain Surgery

I've got my head down, eyes forward. We're four in a line, pedalling hard, approaching 40 mph, descending into Sheffield on the Hather-sage Road. Done this hundreds of times. Ride close, stay alert. Second in line. Steve's in front. Steve turns right. Wait . . . turns right? There's no turn here. Steve's not turning. Steve's falling. I'm going to hit him. I turn left. I go around. Steve goes down. Oncoming car. Steve's going under . . . no . . . car brakes . . . car turns. Driver bumps on to grass verge. Steve's carbon bike crunches under car. Steve skids on tarmac, stops by driver's door. Shorts and jacket ripped to shreds. Skin is red and raw. Driver was alert. Steve is alive.

That's how I remember it, but I know it cannot have happened that way. We were returning together on our bikes from a ride in the Peak District in a tight line. Steve did fall and the oncoming car did well to avoid him, but all those thoughts cannot have gone through my head as he fell. That paragraph is around a hundred words, and it might take about a minute to read. But Steve hit the deck in less than a second. His front wheel was twisted by a gash in the road, but I have a strong impression of seeing him steer, thinking he was turning, of watching him fall, of planning my evasive action, then seeing the oncoming car that was inevitably going to hit him. I recall the feeling of relief that the driver turned on to the verge, but I can't have assimilated any of those feelings or run through all those thought processes in the time it took for the accident to play out. All these feelings are afterthoughts.

The Amazon promise is the system that quickly predicts delivery times while a product's webpage loads. The promise must be computed rapidly because customers don't like to wait for the page to load. Despite Steve's accident and Amazon's delivery being two very different circumstances, they both share time pressure as a key factor. When Steve had his accident, due to the time pressure, all his actions, all my actions and all the driver's actions were, like the Amazon promise, devolved to fast-reacting systems: they are reflexive decisions. They could not be delayed – there was no room for *epoché*.

Everything I did was a conditioned response as I reacted to an unfolding situation, but my narrative of the crash is a retrospective, an explanation of the events as told by my reflective self afterwards. Each action I took was instinctive but, in my retrospective, I feel that I was in conscious control. As a result, each second feels longer and it feels as if time dilated during the crash. It didn't. The retrospective is a mental illusion, my reflective mind was a passenger, and my reflexive reactions were in control.

The same mental illusion would have occurred for Stefan Cavallo when he bailed out of his P-51. Reflex and reflection merge into a single narrative, one that Cavallo later shared with us by writing it down. During the crash my body's systems had more in common with the Albion fly-ball or a Braitenberg vehicle than with Laplace's demon. So why does my reflective self have this mistaken sense of control? It's a similar illusion to the one Eisenhower had as Supreme Commander of the Allied Forces. In practice, his authority was devolved to subordinates, just as my cycling reactions were devolved to reflexive systems. But for Eisenhower to plan his strategy he had to believe he was in charge, although in practice there is no way that he could have or should have been directly determining the actions of each of his individual soldiers.

If you try to swat a fly, the fly doesn't pause and reflect on the incoming hand. Its nervous system is like the reflex arcs in our spine. The fruit fly has around 135,000 neurons in its nervous system. Interneurons connect the sensory neurons in its eyes directly to the motor neurons that fire the muscles in the wings, operating like the levers in the Albion fly-ball that connect the engine speed to the millstone. The fly's eyes sense the movement of your hand, and that movement is transmitted directly to its wing muscles to trigger the response. This means the fly reacts very quickly to the incoming hand. It rapidly changes direction because the moving hand leads to action without any mediation from reflection. When speed of action is important, reflection is redundant.

Steve is lucky that a similar pattern plays out in humans. Watt's governor can be tuned to change the speed at which the engine runs, and our reflexes can also be trained with practice. 'Fell' is an English word for a hill or a mountain. The word comes from Danish Viking invaders who arrived in England over a thousand years ago. In the North, where they ruled, hills are often called fells. The sport of fell-running has its origins in hill-farming communities, where shepherds needed to move quickly across the fells to gather sheep. I started fell-running when I was at the University of Sheffield, which nestles close to the Peak District. With its challenging terrain and rocky paths, initially I often fell when I was fell-running. But as I ran more, my reflexes improved and I fell rarely. I came to marvel at my own legs. My leading leg would catch an unseen stone in the path, but my trailing leg would whip around under me and catch my weight before I fell flat on my face. It was as if my legs had a mind of their own. And in fact, they did, because during these actions my legs were being triggered by a reflex arc. My sciatic nerve was passing messages to interneurons in my lower spine. The interneurons passed those messages to the motor neurons in my other leg. The reflex is deployed without the brain's involvement. Whenever I tripped, my reflective self became a passenger of my reflexes.

The reflexes of our legs are mediated by these interneurons in our spines. They give the legs context. Waves of neural activity propagate across the spine, and the waves' peaks and troughs signal to the interneuron how our legs are positioned. The right reaction to a foot getting caught depends on whether it's the leading or trailing leg. The interneuron provides this information.

The brain is like an interneuron that got carried away. It provides additional context to our reflexes, but this context can also come from vision, hearing or even our thinking. During Steve's accident it was my reflexes that were driving my response. And a similar set of reflexes were operating in the driver of the oncoming car. In the name of speed, the reflective brain is bypassed. The driver's eyes saw Steve and her reflexive brain moved the arm which steered the car.

Even though events had moved beyond the control of my reflective self, my brain teases me with a narrative that places it in control. The Eisenhower illusion is strong and forms part of our individual experience, but just because the reflective self wasn't in control, it doesn't mean the narrative isn't useful. There are aspects of the crash that can be distilled into lessons for the future. The way in which the experience is assimilated has important implications not just for our reflexive self but also for our reflective self.

My reflective self can learn from the cycle accident, just as Donald Lopez was able to learn from dogfights. The retrospective narrative is a form of afterthought that helps me to assimilate any lessons into future decisions. So, the interaction between reflexive systems and reflective systems is a subtle dance. The reflective self cedes control to reflexive systems, but it maintains a feel for what happened through the retrospective narrative. This feel can feed longer-term changes to behaviour. The narrative of my reflective self is drawn from the decisions my reflexive self makes. But as humans we don't absorb information only from our own experiences, we also share experiences with each other, and often those experiences are shared in the form of achievements.

I ride my bicycle for leisure. It's not normally a dangerous activity, it gives me a sense of achievement and it allows me to experience the countryside. But for some people their appetite for achievement can spark interest in more extreme activities. The mountaineer George Mallory died on the slopes of Everest in 1924, last seen heading for the top with his climbing partner Sandy Irvine. Mallory's body wasn't discovered for seventy-five years. It's still uncertain whether Mallory and Irvine got to the summit, and searches have been undertaken to try to find out what happened. Before his expedition's departure Mallory was asked by a journalist why it was important for him to reach the top. He replied, 'Because it's there.' When Tenzing Norgay and Edmund Hillary did arrive at the summit, twenty-nine years later, their achievement made headlines across the world. Stories about human achievement, particularly in the face of danger, are popular.

The bathyscaphe *Trieste* was built to reach the deepest parts of the ocean. A bathyscaphe is a diving bell that can operate untethered from its mothership. In Bauby's analogy he suggests that his physically constrained self is analogous to a deep-sea diving suit. The occupants of the bathyscaphe made that analogy real. The vessel was designed by a Swiss inventor, Auguste Piccard. The pilots sat in a spherical pressure vessel below a set of unpressurized flotation tanks full of petrol. In 1960, *Trieste* descended to Challenger Deep, almost 11 kilometres under the surface of the western Pacific Ocean, the deepest known point on the seabed. One of the pilots was Auguste's son, Jacques. He sat alongside Don Walsh, an American navy lieutenant. As they descended, they took turns to peer through a Plexiglas window. Plexiglas was the only transparent material that could withstand the incredible pressure from the deep ocean, but even Plexiglas wasn't strong enough for this trip. One of the outer windows cracked, shaking the entire vessel, but they carried on. That cracked window was the weakest part of their protective vessel, but it was through it that they were able to rest their eyes on the sea floor, and through those glimpses they could share their stories about how it felt for a human to see the deepest part of our seas.

Our interest in voyages of exploration continues. Today we debate the merits of sending humans to Mars. 'Why,' the question goes, 'fly people into space when the science can be done just as well by machines?' In 1962, when the same question was posed in the context of exploring the Moon, then US president John F. Kennedy gave an emphatic answer. At the launch of the *Apollo* programme Kennedy spoke from Rice Stadium, an American football stadium at Rice University. Rice is a smaller research university whose enrolment is dwarfed by that of the University of Texas.

'Why does Rice play Texas?' Kennedy asked. In the ten years before Kennedy's speech, Rice had won five of their annual football games with Texas. At Rice Stadium, they had been undefeated since 1954. Beating Texas was hard, and that's what made it an achievement. Kennedy's question reveals part of the atomic human's nature. Rice won despite their limitations. Machine intelligences are defined by their capabilities, but the atomic human is defined by our limitations and how we overcome them.

Presidents have speechwriters, but the Rice vs Texas question was added to the script by Kennedy himself in cursive blue pencil over the typewritten original. Most of us are familiar with the main sound bite from Kennedy's speech. Clips are often played of him saying, 'We choose to go to the Moon', but this was a wide-ranging speech which focused on achievement. Kennedy invoked the invention of writing and the wheel. He referred to Newton's scientific breakthroughs, the printing press, the American pioneer spirit and the development of the computer. To justify the vast expenditure required for the mission, Kennedy ends by quoting George Mallory in advocating the crewed mission to the Moon, saying we should go 'because it's there'.

Kennedy's speech is remembered as the launch of the race to the Moon. But the possibility that we would fly in space became apparent nearly eighteen years earlier, only three months after Eisenhower's Allied forces landed in France. In response to the invasion a new weapon was unleashed on Britain. The *Vergeltungswaffe 2*, or V-2, was a rocket-powered long-distance guided missile. As Eisenhower's troops worked their way across France and into Germany around 5,000 V-2 rockets were launched. They would kill nearly 10,000 civilians and army personnel, but even more died in the forced labour camps that produced them.

Rockets in warfare have a long history. Gunpowder was developed in China in the ninth century during the Tang dynasty and the first rockets were used in warfare in the thirteenth century by the Ming dynasty. They found their way into the British artillery through the Sultan of Mysore, who used them to defend his territory against the colonists. The US national anthem sings of 'the rocket's red glare'. The words are referring to British Congreve rockets fired at Fort McHenry in 1814. These rockets were derived from those of the Sultan and had a range of up to 2 miles. They astonished some enemies, leading them to panic, but the defence of Fort McHenry was successful because the rockets were also inaccurate. For defenders who didn't panic, the rockets didn't represent a threat.

This history of the rocket changed with the V-2. It had a range of 200 miles, so it could be fired at London from sites in northern France, Belgium and the Netherlands. The V-2 could fly a hundred times further than the Congreve rocket, but to do this it had to fly far more accurately. The rocket was the brainchild of a German engineer called Wernher von Braun. As a young man, von Braun had attended a presentation by Auguste Piccard, the designer of the bathyscaphe. He is said to have told Piccard that one day he intended to travel to the Moon. Back on Earth, von Braun's graduate thesis focused on rocket engines, and he spent the war refining the engine and its autopilot controller to create the V-2. In many ways this controller had a simple job: like a Braitenberg vehicle, it needed to sense changes in attitude and react by steering. It was a reflexive system. Imagine balancing a broomstick vertically on the palm of your hand: as the top falls in one direction or another, you have to keep the broomstick upright by countering the movement with a movement of your palm. Von Braun worked out how to control the V-2 rocket in a similar way. The rocket had the ability to climb 50 miles above the Earth to the edge of space and then descend to land on London or another target. There were few defences against these rockets. The best idea the British had was to propagate a fiction that the rockets were overshooting their target and, falling for this fiction, the Germans then recalibrated the autopilot guidance systems, causing the rockets to fall short.

At the end of the war, von Braun was moved, along with 1,600 other German scientists, to the United States, where he joined the US Army Ordnance Corps. The British had borrowed the Sultan of Mysore's rocket technology; the Americans would now borrow von

Braun's expertise to build their rocket arsenal. Von Braun began to work on missiles designed to carry nuclear warheads. In a twist of history, the missile he designed, the Redstone, would return to its spiritual home in Germany, but instead of pointing at London it would point at the Soviet Union.

In 1952, Dwight Eisenhower was elected President. He had become the supreme commander of the United States. In 1957, at the beginning of Eisenhower's second term as president, the Soviet Union launched the first satellite, *Sputnik*. This Soviet achievement shocked America into action and Eisenhower formed a civilian space agency, NASA, to concentrate American efforts on catching up. The new agency was formed from existing groups – von Braun's Redstone missile programme was incorporated, as was the NACA proving ground at Langley Field, where Stefan Cavallo had bailed out of his Mustang. The newly formed NASA began working on Project Mercury. Its aim was to test whether a human could be placed into orbit around the Earth. Medieval scholastic philosophers were once mocked for arguing about how many dancing angels the tip of a pin can sustain. The NACA team from Langley Field were given the task of understanding how to sustain humans on the tip of ballistic missiles.

To put a human in space, missile warheads had to be replaced with a human cargo, but who should that human be? Eisenhower decided the first wave of astronauts should be drawn from the population of military test pilots, people like Stefan Cavallo and Donald Lopez. They selected seven young men with a background as military test pilots, but this led to further questions. Wernher von Braun's breakthrough was in guidance for missiles. These rockets were controlled by automatic pilots and a launch centre. When you put a human pilot on top of the missile, who should be in control? The pilot, the guidance system or the launch centre? The answer NASA would develop is that *all three* would be in charge.

The solution is another manifestation of the Eisenhower illusion. Different parts of the system take charge according to the nature of the decision required. Decision-making devolves, and whom it devolves to depends on timing and context. My grandfather Fred made his own decisions about how to interpret Eisenhower's orders. Avoiding that bicycle crash required me to rely on my reflexes. In a dogfight, Don Lopez devolved his decision-making to his reflexes. Where the decision is made depends on the time and the information available. The same principle would apply in the space programme.

A simplified version of the story of the Mercury programme was dramatized in the 1983 film *The Right Stuff*. The film focused on the struggle between pilots and engineers about the level of automation involved in the early exploration of space. It opens in the California desert at the Muroc Air Base and documents how in 1947 an air-force test pilot, Chuck Yeager, became the first to fly a plane, a rocket-engined craft called the X-1, to supersonic speeds in level flight. Yeager was seen by many as the archetypal test pilot, but he chose not to apply to be one of America's astronauts. The sentiment of much of the test-pilot community is summarized by Yeager's line in the film: 'I'll tell you what else, anybody who goes up in the damn thing's gonna be spam in a can.'

The Mercury capsule was the solution the Langley Field team developed to carry humans. It was a life-support system placed at the tip of the rocket. The test pilots' concerns probably weren't alleviated by the first test of the capsule's life support. The first hominid in space wasn't human but a chimpanzee called Ham, sent up in a test flight, so not spam in a can, but Ham in a can.[1] Chuck Yeager probably wasn't impressed. Like the bathyscaphe sphere on the *Trieste*, the capsule provided the astronauts with air to breathe and a protective shield against the external environment. Whereas the bathyscaphe sphere protected against the pressure of the deep, the Mercury capsule protected against the vacuum of space. But unlike Piccard and Walsh in the bathyscaphe, the first American in space would not have a window to look out of; instead there was a periscope through which they could peer back at Earth.

Alongside the test pilots, the Langley Field team had a group of test engineers. These engineers would work closely with the pilots to determine the testing regime. The team was led by Bob Gilruth, who had taken a systematic approach to the analysis of flight. As well as fighting gremlins, Gilruth recognized that the interaction between the pilot and the plane was a key part of a successful design. The feel of the plane is key, as Don Lopez highlights:

> Suddenly our two months of training was over. I realized that in addition to the formal goals of the course, we had learned, in varying degrees, the one vital skill that gave a pilot a fighting chance to survive in combat: the ability to fly by instinct.

What Lopez means is that the plane becomes an extension of the pilot: the reflex arcs in the pilot's body become tuned to controlling the plane. A similar thing had happened to Steve, the car driver and me in our bicycle accident. Our motor-control system assimilates the tools we are given – in my case a bicycle; for Cavallo and Lopez, fighter aircraft:

> That was the real goal of the innumerable rat races and dogfights. At some time, near the midpoint of the program, the student became one with the airplane. The pilot, not his airplane, followed the plane ahead through any and all maneuvers without conscious attention to the controls.

Reflexive decision-making had taken over. After training, the pilot no longer had to consciously think which way the plane should go; he could just will it and the reflexive systems would deliver the appropriate response:

> He could devote his mind to planning his next move or anticipating the other pilot's, without worrying about flying the plane. His eyes automatically scanned the instrument panel every few seconds and any improper reading would jump out. We felt as ready for combat as we could be without actual combat experience.[2]

But not all planes flew equally well, and pilots complained that some were difficult to fly. At NACA, Gilruth and his team of test engineers and pilots characterized this 'feel' for the plane with numbers. Through his analysis of the aircraft, Gilruth developed a manual of flight that described how a plane should respond to various inputs.[3] This report described how the plane should respond to a particular force on the control stick. When Stefan Cavallo needed to escape his stricken Mustang he relied on his honed instincts, his reflexive capabilities. But Cavallo was also in constant contact with Robert Baker, his fellow pilot, and he was also following instructions from the engineers on the ground. The decisions he made when he bailed out were influenced by all these aspects.

Balancing this knowledge of the test pilot, both reflexive and reflective, his fellow pilot and the test engineers is all part of a complex information topography that guided Stefan Cavallo's actions.[4] The Mercury programme was faced with the challenge of decision-making in a new information topography: the pilots, the autopilot and the launch centre. Wernher von Braun's missiles flew themselves – they had a reflexive autopilot guidance system; they had no need of a pilot to take them from the west coast of Europe to London. So how should the rocket be controlled when carrying its crew? Gilruth's NACA team had been incorporated into NASA, and the decision-making system it designed had reflexive and reflective components, just like our nervous system. Missiles are managed by a launch-control centre; planes are managed by pilots. But test pilots also fly their aircraft to a programme that is planned by a flight engineer. During the flight they stay in close contact with their engineer to assist in diagnosis of any problems that arise. Balancing the knowledge of the pilot with that of the flight engineers and other mission specialists requires an information topography. The system developed for the Mercury programme was a hybrid of missile launch and test flight. It became known as the Mission Control Center. Chris Kraft was one of the NACA test engineers who worked with Stefan Cavallo at the Langley Field Proving Ground. He was tasked with operational decision-making for the Mercury missions. In his autobiography, *Flight*, he takes up the story:

The whole concept was slowly forming in my head. I'd seen it over and over during airplane flight tests. We'd plan a test in great detail, both the pilot and the engineer on the ground knowing exactly what should happen and when. We also knew in advance that a flight test seldom followed the plan. Something would change – the weather, fuel consumption, the need to repeat a maneuver – or the plane would react unexpectedly. The pilot was in control, but he usually accepted suggestions radioed from the flight engineer on the ground.

Kraft had a deep understanding of the necessary devolution of power. It was based on his time spent working with NACA test pilots like Stefan Cavallo. As he reflected on the structure of his control centre, the gremlins were dominating his thinking:

> *What about the unknown unknowns? It's the surprise event that kills the pilot.*

The emphasis in the text here is Kraft's.[5] His flight planning is reminiscent of Mike Tyson's warnings on fight planning. Kraft's years of work as a test engineer had given him a keen sense of Tyson's maxim: everyone has a plan until they get punched in the mouth:

> The more I thought about unknown unknowns, the more convinced I was that we needed a team to work on those problems when they came up. And they would come up.

Kraft had spent a career battling the gremlin of uncertainty. He had a keen awareness of how to build a structure to deal with it:

> There were some frowns when I explained the basic concept of the Mercury Control Center, but some smiles and nods when I added that we were going to build a procedures trainer for the astronauts – the first of ever-more-complex simulators – and that it would be tied

in with the center so that the astronauts and controllers could train together.[6]

This is perhaps the most important point of all. Not only would there be different components to the centre with different responsibilities, but these components would train together; they would practise different scenarios so that they could test the appropriate devolution of authority in different circumstances.

The engineers in the front row of the control centre were directly involved with flight systems. Kraft was positioned further back. He was the flight director and had overall responsibility for each flight. But his decisions were taken based on information that came to him from a myriad of experts on the ground as well as from the astronaut in the sky. The flight director wouldn't speak directly to the astronaut; this was the job of Capsule Communication, or CapCom: how to communicate helpfully with the pilot is a full-time job in Mission Control. In practice, this job was given to other astronauts, the people who were most familiar with the challenges their colleagues were facing in the sky.

As the layout of the control centre developed, they introduced individuals who could call on outside resources in the case of an emergency and explain to the wider world what was going on:

> Once we settled on the primary consoles to be manned by engineers directly involved in the flight, we looked at what else we might need. Mercury was a government program, and we all understood the bureaucracy. So across the back of the control centre, we added three more consoles. One was for the operations director, who had responsibility for each mission.

The operations director was Kraft's boss, but during the mission their power was fully devolved to Kraft as flight director:

> A second back-row console went to the Department of Defense. We wanted a senior officer, preferably a general, who could immediately

call on any and all military assistance we might need – for added recovery forces, emergencies of any kind, countdown disruptions by boats or airplanes that encroached our area, and anything else that might come up. It was an active console and we needed it many times in the years ahead.

The ability to call on the US military through a senior general was placing a large national resource at the disposal of the space programme. The availability of extra resources is another way of dealing with the consequences of any gremlins that might emerge:

> The third back-row console was almost an afterthought. We'd need an information officer to let the press, and thus the entire outside world, know what was happening during a flight. Having him at his own console seemed to be the most convenient for us all. None of us understood how important and significant that public affairs officer would be, or that the PAC position would become one of the most notorious in the control center.[7]

The Mercury programme was conducted in the glare of the public eye, so, as well as having a pilot communication specialist, they also had a public communication specialist. The press was keen for updates, and this would prove to be a full-time role for Kraft's public affairs console.

The atomic human has a reflective self, and, just as Don Lopez has a feel for his aircraft, we have a feel for our reflective selves. A sense of who we each are and how we might behave. A sense that extends to who other people are and how they might behave. It is this feel that underlies the notion of the butterfly. Our reflective self perceives itself to be in charge, just like the flight director is in charge at the Mission Control Center, but in practice the Mission Control Center is replete with devolved decision-making. As flight director, Kraft's authority gave him the ability to intervene in any aspect of the mission, but to do his job well he had to trust each of the mission specialists to handle their own domain of expertise. Our locked-in intelligence means that an individual human doesn't have the bandwidth to monitor all aspects of a complex mission. Devolved decision-making is a consequence of uncertainty, time pressure and the information topography. Different decisions are made in different parts of the information infrastructure. The launch process required many systems to be monitored and a cool head for decision-making. Countdown was triggered and aborted by ground control. In an emergency, there was no hope of bailing out of the Mercury capsule, as Cavallo had from the Mustang. So, the capsule had a rocket-powered escape system in case of failures in the missile it sat on. The decision to launch the escape system was fully automated: no human has reactions fast enough to trigger it before the fireball of the exploding rocket would envelop the astronaut. All this meant that the pilot had less control. Alan Shepard, the first American in space, was a test pilot like Stefan Cavallo, but during the delays that occurred before he launched you can sense his frustration at this lack of control. Informed of ongoing problems by launch control, Shepard responds to a check on his status, 'I'm a hell of a lot cooler than you guys. Why don't you just fix your little problem and light this candle?'

After Shepard's flight, the capsule gained a window, but the argument about who should fly the capsule continued. The initial trajectory of the rocket was determined by the automated guidance systems. Once the rocket engines were turned off and the capsule was detached, it would free fall back to Earth. The physics involved is that which Newton described in his *Principia* all the way back in 1687. An orbit is a free fall in which you are also travelling so fast horizontally that your projected landing point misses the Earth. Instead of falling back to the ground, you start going around the planet. Once the Mercury capsule was in orbit, it wouldn't return to Earth unless it stopped falling past the Earth, and to do this it needed to slow down. The capsule had a set of retro rockets to slow it for re-entry. These could be controlled automatically or by the pilot. The pilots were also given further degrees of control of their capsule. They could use thrusters to orient the capsule in different directions.

Their desire to fly the capsule shows that – for the Mercury pilots – it was not enough to passively experience space as a passenger. They wanted to control their journey; they wanted their interventions to be important in dictating the path of the capsule. They wanted to feel in charge. Actions give us a sense of steerage of our own destiny and are as much a part of human experience as our senses are. Looking back to the very earliest animals, we can see the origins of this desire to sense and respond – when the first life-forms evolved neurons, sense was always accompanied by action. Those organisms had sensorimotor neurons that directly connected their sense to their response. In contrast, the level of control the pilots were given was regulated and restricted – the capsule was too complicated for a single human to manage all its aspects. The pilot was locked into the capsule and the pilot's capabilities are locked in by the embodiment factor. Too many tasks would overload the pilot, so careful choices were made about how and when the pilot could intervene in the flight.

Eisenhower launched NASA and developed the Mercury programme, but Shepard flew into space while John F. Kennedy was president. The success of the Mercury programme caused Kennedy to launch the race to the Moon from Rice Stadium in 1962, but the Apollo programme and the Moon landings would bring significantly more difficult challenges for the astronauts and the automated systems that steered them.

For a successful space mission, humans didn't just have to go up into space, they also needed to come back down to Earth. The automated guidance systems of the 1950s were not yet up to the job of precision landing. So the Mercury capsule was designed to land on water in a 'splashdown'. A joke among test pilots goes: 'A good landing is one that you can walk away from, a really excellent landing is one where the aircraft can fly the next day.' Under this definition, the splashdown of the Mercury capsule was neither an excellent nor a good landing. The Mercury capsule would be a single-use design which you couldn't walk away from. The only way to leave the capsule after splashdown was to swim or fly. Alan Shepard was hoisted away from his in a helicopter. Landing on the Moon and returning to the Earth would require not only that the pilot walked away from the landing, but also that the craft should be usable the next day to get back to Earth. These challenges would bring additional complexities in the interaction between automation systems and the human.

Despite the importance of rockets, the first contract for the Apollo programme was to build a computer. Shortly after Kennedy's speech at Rice University, NASA commissioned the Massachusetts Institute of Technology's Instrumentation Laboratory to build the Apollo spacecraft's guidance computer. This machine would provide an autopilot that would navigate from the Earth to the Moon and, once in position 50,000 feet above the lunar surface, it would place the lunar module on the Moon's surface. The Moon landings were achieved through an understanding of Newton's laws and by applying the principles of automatic control on a digital computer, but despite its digital implementation, the autopilot was operating in the tradition of Watt's mechanically implemented governor. Apollo 11 used inertial guidance to steer Aldrin, Armstrong and Collins across 400,000 kilometres of space to the Moon.

One year before the first landing on the Moon, Arthur C. Clarke and Stanley Kubrick's *2001: A Space Odyssey* was released. In the film, during a trip to Jupiter the spacecraft *Discovery One* suffers a problem with an antenna. The ship's guidance computer, HAL, begins a struggle for control of the mission against the astronauts. Most of the crew are killed, and the remaining astronaut, Dave Bowman, disconnects the guidance computer, shutting down the machine. This fictional story may sound far-fetched, but it provided an eerie prefiguration of an emergency that befell Aldrin and Armstrong during their landing.

The Apollo guidance computer was the first machine to be built using a new technology, the *integrated circuit*. This machine didn't use valves for switches, it used transistors. By the 1960s, these transistors were being printed on wafers of silicon, dramatically decreasing the space each one took up. Colossus was the largest machine built at Bletchley Park, filling a room and containing 1,600 thermionic valves. The guidance computer had 17,000 transistors and could fit in a suitcase. With all these transistors, universal gates could be composed to form larger truth tables. The transistor was enabling George Boole's symbolic algebra to be combined with Wittgenstein's notion of a truth table to deliver Turing's vision of a universal computer in a form that could now be placed inside a small spacecraft. By the 1960s, universities had started offering degrees that specialized in computing. One of the earliest graduates was a young man called Jack Garman. In 1966 he completed an Engineering Physics programme at the University of Michigan, where he had specialized in computing. He was immediately recruited to the Mission Control team.

Garman's role was as an onboard computing specialist. In 1969 he was twenty-five years old. The way Chris Kraft set up Mission Control was firmly in the tradition of Charles Babbage: the different roles of the specialists is an example of division of labour, or as we refer to the principle in computer science, separation of concerns. There were mission specialists for a number of roles. Kraft's simulations were designed to coordinate them so that they worked well together. These test runs simulated what might happen in different imagined mission failures. Kraft used the simulations to hone the operation of the team. After each simulation, the team would debrief, discuss what had gone wrong and what could go better. The team were displaying forethought and afterthought. Prometheus and Epimetheus. But the forethought and afterthought were also training the interaction between different components of the team. This developed trust and understanding, teaching the specialists to act and interact together. It developed their ability to orchestrate the information topography.

The guidance computer was integral to the mission to the Moon. As well as operating the autopilot on the long journey between the Earth and the Moon, it could automate the process of landing. To make the landing feasible, the spacecraft would split in two. *Eagle*, the lunar module, operated in tandem with a mothership, *Columbia*, the command module. On arrival at the Moon, these two craft would be captured by the Moon's gravity. They would orbit together. *Eagle* would then leave the mothership and descend to the Moon's surface to land. To return to Earth, the astronauts in the lunar module would need to fly their craft back up for a rendezvous in orbit with *Columbia* and they could then return together to Earth. It was an incredibly complex operation. There were many things that could go wrong. The NASA team worked to test all the different capabilities of their craft and astronauts across multiple missions in space and many simulations on the ground.

The first rendezvous in space had been completed only in 1966. Neil Armstrong piloted Gemini VIII to dock with a target craft. Like Stefan Cavallo, Armstrong had been a NACA test pilot. Too young to have seen action in the Second World War, he had been a naval pilot who went on to fly the X-15 rocket plane, a successor to the X-1. However, during the rendezvous a thruster failure caused his Gemini capsule to spin like a tumble drier. It was only because of Armstrong's quick reactions and manual skills using a replacement thruster that the astronauts escaped with their lives. Other tests also revealed problems, and not all astronauts were fortunate enough to survive them. The astronauts assigned to Apollo 1 never had the opportunity to fly. Gus Grissom (the second American in space), Ed White and Roger Chaffee were killed in one of their pre-flight rehearsals when their capsule caught fire.

Once *Eagle* reached the Moon, the guidance computer switched from its inertial guidance system for navigating to a radar-based autopilot for landing: the NASA engineers had refined the process of automation to such an extent they could automate the process of touching down on the lunar surface. The computer's programs were initiated by the astronauts punching in commands to its keypad.

Less than forty years before Armstrong and Aldrin flew to the Moon, on 20 May 1932, at 7.20 p.m., Amelia Earhart took off in her

Lockheed Vega from Harbour Grace in Canada. She called her plane the 'Little Red Bus'. She headed east. Four hours later, a weld broke on her engine and flames emerged. She carried on. Shortly after, her altimeter failed and she lost the ability to determine the plane's height. Next, she flew into a storm. She spent an hour being buffeted. She flew on through the night, sustaining herself with a can of tomato juice until the next morning, when she changed bearing, heading east looking for land. She sighted a coastline and headed down the coast, but again encountered thunderstorms, so she flew north. She sighted a railway line, followed it to the nearest town and landed in a meadow near Londonderry in Ireland. She had flown over 2,000 miles, becoming only the second person to cross the Atlantic in solo flight.[8]

Earhart worked her way across the Atlantic by dead reckoning. Navigating in this way means that you set an initial bearing and follow it for a given time. It's like taking a rifle shot at long range. As the bullet moves further from its starting point, the target becomes harder to hit. Errors in the initial aiming angle matter more as distance increases. Both bullets and aircraft can be buffeted by winds – Earhart had flown through a storm. The longer the flight, the more likely she was to move away from her target. These errors are known as drift. Earhart was following in a navigation tradition that came to aircraft from marine craft, but the crew on ships crossing the Atlantic could regularly relocate themselves by using the stars and the position of the sun. Earhart's aircraft didn't provide a stable enough platform to make such measurements.

The problem Earhart faced is an example of the challenge of extrapolation. The German meteorologists predicting the weather for D-Day in the Channel had no way of measuring atmospheric pressure beyond the English Channel. Earhart had no way of tying down her position while she was over the ocean. But unlike the German meteorologists, Earhart was able to use the physics of motion to extrapolate and update her position. The larger the extrapolation, the more errors would accumulate, but the physics of motion gave her some guide as to where she was. In contrast,

Rommel's German meteorologists did not have the technology to extrapolate the weather. They couldn't combine their physical understanding with the data. They didn't understand that there would be a D-Day break in the storm. Even though Earhart could make use of physics, the gremlin of uncertainty still entered her measurements through the drift, and errors would accumulate in her estimation of her position. As she flew across 1,800 miles of featureless sea, the uncertainty grew.

The first spacecraft to escape the gravitational pull of the Earth was Apollo 8. When it took off from Florida and headed for the Moon it had to traverse over 200,000 miles of space. The command module's guidance computer was responsible for ensuring it stayed on track. Like Earhart, it was navigating through extrapolation.

In Earhart's plane, there was a direct physical link between her control column and the flight surfaces that steered the plane. Like Don Lopez, she would have felt the plane was an extension of herself. Like Stefan Cavallo entering the clouds, she would have felt the pressure on the ailerons that came from the buffeting in the storm she flew through. But when Bob Gilruth's team commissioned the Apollo spacecraft, there was no direct connection between the astronaut and the thrusters. The control of Apollo was conducted through electronics. Like Earhart, the pilots had a control stick, but the stick was connected to a digital computer.

Bob Gilruth's team from NACA had resolved the question as to who should perform the landing: a man or a machine. The answer was *either*. The Apollo guidance computer could land the lunar module on autopilot, its automatic mode using a simple sense-and-respond control system. But the astronauts also had the ability to intervene. They could tell the computer they were taking over and then it would monitor the capsule's control stick and respond to their commands. When in automatic mode, the computer could sense the distance to the Moon's surface through its radar and respond to the closing distance by firing the thrusters to slow the descent. Again, we can see the parallels to Watt's governor, which sensed engine speed and controlled it via the regulator. We also can see a relationship to the reflex arcs that control our responses to pain, our ability to balance or to avoid a fall.

Across the journey from the Earth to the Moon the computer steered the craft – it did the extrapolation on behalf of the astronauts. It made automated course corrections that kept Apollo 8 on track. Earhart navigated the 'Little Red Bus' across the Atlantic, but the task of navigating the Apollo spacecraft was considered beyond its human pilots. Apollo 8 opened the door to the first landing on the Moon. It had shown that astronauts could be placed in orbit around the Moon. What remained was the final step. Split the lunar module from its mothership, touch down on the surface, take a look around, and take off again. Earhart's arrival on the coast of Ireland had allowed her to use the features of the landscape to find a suitable landing place. Once she gained sight of the land, she changed her approach to navigation, using landmarks to scan the land for a place to touch down. The lunar module in Apollo 11 would have to perform a similar trick: switch from long-distance navigation to assessing the local suitability of the landscape. This is where the adaptability of the digital computer comes to the fore. When the lunar module was over the Moon, the astronauts could ask it to run a new programme, one that would allow them to land. The same machine could carry out different instructions. Back in Bletchley Park, the Colossus machine designed by Tommy Flowers was programmed through a series of switches. These switches manually connected the different logic gates, but in the Apollo guidance computer, these instructions were stored in an electronic memory. The astronauts had a small keypad and display. They typed into it to instigate a change of program and the program was automatically loaded.

Seven months after Apollo 8's successful mission, the Americans were finally ready to fulfil Kennedy's promise and Apollo 11 was made ready to go to the Moon. Three days after lift-off, the computer had guided them across over 200,000 miles of featureless space; in orbit, 50,000 feet above the surface of the Moon, Neil Armstrong and Buzz Aldrin separated the lunar module from the command module. In anticipation of the unknown unknowns, Aldrin also switched on their rendezvous radar. With this radar *Eagle* could track *Columbia*'s position: the astronauts wanted the system for docking back with the command module to be ready in case they had to abort their landing.

They punched in the new program for the computer. It switched from guiding them from the Earth to load the landing program, just like Amelia Earhart switched from dead reckoning to tracking the features of the Irish coast. The guidance computer was now preparing for landing. But like HAL 9000 in *Discovery One*, this was the moment when something went wrong. When Armstrong and Aldrin were approaching the surface of the Moon, their guidance computer emitted a software alarm: Error Code 1202. Armstrong, concern in his voice, asked for advice from ground control. At that moment, the future of the Apollo 11 mission fell to one individual, to the onboard computing specialist, 25-year-old Jack Garman. The flight director asked for a go or no go on the error code. And the world paused while Jack decided.

The error code was an 'Executive Overload'.[9] The Apollo Guidance Computer's 17,000 transistors had become saturated; the machine couldn't give answers quickly enough for the rate at which different jobs were being thrown at it. Its fast reacting wasn't fast enough. Jack Garman was the expert on the software, he knew the computer would prioritize the mission-critical jobs, but could he be sure? There was no time to have a meeting, no time to consult other experts. Delay in making the decision would have been as bad as making the wrong decision. It took three seconds for Garman to give his decision: 'We are go on that error.' Armstrong took over control. He chose to land *Eagle* manually. He'd seen boulders in the original landing area and he flew the craft on to a clearer zone in the Sea of Tranquillity. Just as Kennedy had promised, America had gone to the Moon.

Our brains are placed in the same situation that Houston Mission Control found itself on that day. Imagine an object is flying towards your head and you glimpse it out of the corner of your eye. At this point a fast, Garman-like decision is required. Waiting for higher-level processing only invites the impact. Your intelligence is devolved across your senses to enable this kind of rapid response. Reflex arcs that stop us from tripping over pass only through the base of our spines; the reflex actions that allowed the driver to avoid killing my cyclist friend passed directly through the brainstem to allow her response. But it is not only that moment that matters. Just as the Moon landing's success was predicated on the training and simulation work Kraft put the team through, so our reactions during Steve's accident were predicated on the training and simulation our brains engage in with our bodies.

Amelia Earhart's and Neil Armstrong's placement of their aircraft and spacecraft on a meadow in Londonderry and in the Sea of Tranquillity on the Moon required hand–eye coordination. To perform this, the brain has a hierarchy of operation. The neocortex is the folded walnut-like portion of the brain that dominates our imagination when we refer to the brain. It is also the portion of the brain in which that imagination occurs. The neocortex is not unique to humans, but its size is. Comparing our brain to those of other mammals, our neocortex looks like the overdeveloped muscles of a professional bodybuilder. It overshadows the rest of the brain. But it is the rest of the brain that is key to driving the reflexive actions we're focusing on here.

Your eyes are cross-wired. The signals from them leave the eyes and switch sides just before they pass through the thalamus. Your optic nerves are not true nerves, they are extensions of brain tissue that also filter and cherry-pick information they need for motor response *before* the signal arrives at the visual cortex. In other words, before you are aware of the image, the Jack Garmans of your brain have already verified whether a fast motor response is required. The motor system coordinates a defensive response before you become aware of the image. During Steve's fall, all of us were passengers of our sensorimotor system.

Whether a reaction can be *reflexive* or *reflective* is driven by the timeframe on which the answer is required. I didn't have the time to reflect on the consequences of each decision I made while avoiding Steve. But for *planning* purposes, just as Eisenhower needed to feel in control of his troops, our reflective self needs to feel it is in control of our reflexive capabilities. So, like the supreme commander experiencing an illusion of control which ignores the fact that some of his troops may have travelled home to Kenilworth, my reflective self maintains an illusion of control after the crash.[10] The preparation for my reflexes comes from simulations and training, like the simulations envisaged by Chris Kraft for the control centre.

When avoiding a bicycle crash, we rely on fast-reacting systems. Steve's survival was dependent on the tuning of the fast-reacting systems of the three individuals involved. Watt's governor was tuned by changing the parameters of the system: the length of the linkages and the weight of the fly-balls. These parameters are tuned before it is deployed in the machine. Our fast-reacting systems are tuned by practising cycling, often as children, in the safety of a park. In both cases the fast-reacting system has spent a period in development before it was tested in its deployment. So, while we are more aware of our slow-reacting reflective decisions, our fast-reacting reflexive and intuitive actions are emerging from our experience, as well as the stories we tell ourselves and hear from others.

The phrase 'It's not rocket science' implies that the difficulty with space missions has to do with the rocket itself. Similarly, suggesting that something isn't brain surgery implies the most complex part of the human from a medical perspective is the brain. Both these ideas may be true,[11] but here I'm trying to emphasize a different point. Rockets were first fired in anger 800 years ago, before Michelangelo painted the ceiling of the Sistine Chapel, before Gutenberg developed his printing press, before Newton derived the laws of gravity and before Watt linked the engine regulator to the fly-ball mechanism. The modern success of rocket systems has as much to do with the control of the rocket as the engine that powers the rocket. The two aspects operate in synergy. When it came to placing the first human on the Moon, this synergy was also extended to the astronauts in the lunar module, back to Chris Kraft's Mission

Control in Houston and even – through Mission Control's information officer – to the wider world. Many of the most critical decisions were devolved to the astronaut. Armstrong chose to intervene to control the lunar module and change the location of the landing. He needed a cool head and a delicate touch to bring his spacecraft down in the Sea of Tranquillity. The rocket was a vital component at launch; Armstrong's brain was vital at landing. But just as the term 'rocket science' oversimplifies the challenge the NASA engineers faced, the idea of brain surgery may mislead us about the role the rest of our nervous system has in delivering the fine motor control Armstrong required to guide his craft across those final kilometres to the surface of the Moon. That delicate touch was emerging from Armstrong's 'motor intelligence', his ability to control the movement of his arm, hand and fingers in the final descent. Just as the control of the rocket transcends the rocket itself and extends to the decisions of the flight director, our motor intelligence depends on devolved capabilities across our nervous system.

In humans, we see the abilities gained from our motor intelligence elegantly demonstrated in sport. We can marvel at Erling Haaland's ability to put the ball in the back of the net, Serena Williams hitting a passing shot, Stephen Curry's ability to nail a three-point shot, or Patrick Mahomes' ability to execute an out-of-the-pocket touchdown pass. Our fellow animals are even more incredible. Just watch a kestrel maintaining its ground position in a headwind while it scans for prey.[12] Or watch a gibbon swing through the trees. These capabilities are beyond any of our artificial systems, but they are fast-reacting intelligences: they owe more to Watt's governor than Laplace's demon.

Motor intelligence sits below our awareness; it exploits co-evolution between our muscles, nerves and bones to evolve subsystems with intrinsic intelligence. Our overall movement is a complex interaction between complementary systems. In our ancestors, any errors in our motor control that led to falls or collisions had an effect on survival. Our nervous system evolved to accommodate our environment and control our movement, and the brain is at the pinnacle of this motor-control system, just as the flight director is at the pinnacle of the decision-making hierarchy that landed Armstrong on the Moon. The decision-making is driven by information availability and the timeframe in which an answer is required. If your arm brushes against a hot surface, the withdrawal reflex is devolved to the spinal cord. You are born with these reflex arcs hardwired into your nervous system; they are tested by doctors who tap your knee or scratch the bottom of your feet. Your motor intelligence is a devolved intelligence with a hierarchy of control in the same way that the Moon mission was devolved and, despite the advances in many areas of AI, the current gap between machine and animal performance in our motor intelligence is vast. We have no machines that can swing like a gibbon.

Our intelligence emerges from the evolution of simple lifeforms that interacted with their environment without a deep understanding of the physics of the world. Today, after millions of years of evolution and thousands of years of thought, we are beginning to unpick the physical laws of the universe, but we don't make day-to-day decisions about our actions on the back of Laplace's demon. Like other animals, our intelligence is underpinned by our reactive, interpolative approach, which has been critical to our ancestors' survival and remains vital to ours.

As the Roman statesman Cicero wrote, art, music and literature cultivate the mind. Or perhaps we should think of them as cultivating the reflective self. Similarly, our reflective self cultivates the reflexive self. The actions the driver took to avoid killing Steve, and those I took to avoid falling behind him, were reflexes, but they were trained reflexes. A gibbon can't ride a bicycle, and neither can a human without practice. Similarly, we need to learn how to drive cars and fly fighter planes. The car driver had tuned her reflexive systems to enable her to avoid Steve when he fell. The tuning of our reflexive systems we all do is equivalent to Chris Kraft's training of Mission Control. Their repeated simulations ensured that Jack Garman was ready to react quickly when he was required to.

Close group cycling involves many hours where the view is

dominated by the lead cyclist's backside, but across the wider visual scene your eyes are probing. The eye can only resolve fine detail in the centre of your retina – your visual periphery is represented in less detail – but it is highly sensitive to movement. This is fortunate for Steve; his fall took place in the periphery of the oncoming driver's vision. The series of rapid reactions that were required to avert tragedy required fast communication between senses and actions. Messages needed to go from receptor cells, via sensory neurons, through motor neurons to muscles.

Like other lifeforms, from mammals down to bacteria, we face the challenges of survival. We have instincts towards food, shelter and our family. It was those instincts that drove my grandfather Fred to take the train home to be with his family. But on the other hand, we have a reflective self that has been cultivated by those around us and from the stories we have about those who came before us. Culture lifts our common purpose, and this separates us from bacteria and the machine. Through this culture, Fred understood his duty and left home to travel to the front line in France. Our culture is particular to humans and our history. Different cultures are particular to different human groups, and a diversity of cultures gives us a diversity of approaches to how we address the challenges of life. Machine intelligence is now part of that landscape, but it is an interloper. It is bringing about a new revolution in how we process information, but it did not evolve within this ecosystem and cannot integrate in the way that humans do. Culture affects outcome. If the oncoming driver had been breaking the speed limit when Steve fell, he would have fallen under the wheels of her car. So, we see a chain of operation where our reflective self is influenced by our culture and that in turn influences our reflexive self. When we perform in a wider organization, like NASA's flight control centre, that culture allows us to collaborate and achieve tasks no individual human could ever realize on their own. And yet still the individual remains uppermost in our thoughts. The Moon landings remain defined in most people's minds by the words Armstrong uttered when he first placed his foot on the surface. This is a symptom of the locked-in nature of the atomic human. 'One small step for man, one giant leap for mankind' – even though in those words we hear the duality of the individual and the community and, despite the decade-long endeavour to get there, the thousands of people who contributed to the design of the systems that delivered the astronaut, the quick thinking of Jack Garman, and the skill and courage Armstrong showed to guide the lunar module safely down, for most of us, the important thought is how did Neil Armstrong feel when he made that step.

8.

System Zero

On 13 March 2006, eight young men arrived at an independent clinic in Harrow in north-west London. Each had received a payment of £2,000. Like the six test pilots based at NACA and the seven astronauts selected for the Mercury programme, these eight men were participating in a test. They were going to further the bounds of human knowledge; they were taking part in a phase-one clinical drug trial. The drug was called Theralizumab. To ensure that our medicines are safe and effective, they are tested. Full clinical trials require large numbers of patients to demonstrate the effectiveness of the drug, but, before undertaking those trials, drugs are tested for safety. The Mercury capsule was first tested on Ham, a chimpanzee who became the first hominid in space, then on Alan Shepard. His trip into space was on a low trajectory that didn't take him into orbit. Similarly, Theralizumab was first tested on macaque monkeys; the clinic in Harrow was hosting the first human trial, and the drug would be given at a very low dose.

Each of the men rolled up his sleeve and had a cannula inserted into his arm. Two received a placebo, a dose that didn't contain any active drug. When Stefan Cavallo flew through the cloud in his P-51, he had Robert Baker flying alongside him to act as a comparison. The placebo plays the same role in a drug trial. The other six men would be flying into the cloud: they received the drug directly into their bloodstream, one patient at a time, at ten-minute intervals.

Cavallo realized he was in trouble almost as soon as he entered the cloud. It took the Harrow men a little longer. Just over an hour after the first man had been dosed, he began to complain of a headache and fever. Then all six men who had been given the drug began vomiting. One's head ballooned in size. Like Cavallo's flight through the cumulonimbus cloud, something had gone seriously wrong. But unlike on Cavallo's flight, there was no way for these young men to bail out of their predicament. All the patients were admitted to intensive care with multiple organ failure.

The reductionist approach to science that followed in the wake of Newton's *Principia* didn't bring uniform advance. The physics of flight in cloud formation is difficult to model, and the laws of motion do not readily transfer to the mechanisms of life. In medicine, the gremlin of uncertainty dominates.

But, despite the uncertainty, life prevails, and to do this it has evolved more than one form of intelligence. When Bauby's brainstem was destroyed in his stroke, he lost control of his motor intelligence, his fast-reacting reflexive self. The brain evolved to be the supreme commander of our nervous system, but our bodies contain two principal forms of intelligence. Alongside our brain and nervous system is a decentralized intelligence we call our *immune system*.

In our nervous system the interaction between our reflexive and reflective intelligences is very tight, but the coupling between our immune system and our nervous system is much looser. It is mostly limited to those moments when the immune system is failing, when we are overwhelmed with pathogens, those moments when our heads throb, our bodies ache, our noses run, our temperature rises. Those moments when we become ill. In late 2019, new reports of illness began to arrive from hospitals in China. Heavy flu-like symptoms were followed by complications in the lung. In severe cases intensive care and a ventilator were required. In some patients these complications proved fatal. The world had been introduced to a new pathogen, a virus called SARS-CoV-2 and a pandemic called Covid-19.

From a pathogen's perspective, each of us is a source of food and shelter and a route to reproduction, a potential paradise. When we die, undefended by our immune system, our body decays. While we live, we engage in a constant struggle with the pathogens that would consume us. Illness is the moment when the tide has turned in favour of the pathogen. At that point the immune system switches from policing our bodies to a war footing. Immune systems are a defensive intelligence found across multicellular organisms: in plants, fungi and animals. The coronavirus that triggered the Covid-19 pandemic had found a new route through the defences of our immune systems.

Like our brain, our immune system is adaptable. It assimilates information from the pathogens it encounters, and this experience allows it to respond more rapidly when it next encounters those pathogens. Also like our brain, our immune system is most adaptable when we are young. Young minds can pick up foreign languages and understand new technology more quickly; young immune systems also understand new viruses more quickly than older immune systems. The young intelligence has less experience but is more flexible. For our immune systems, the effect of the novel Covid 19 was like presenting everyone with a new form of smartphone. Younger immune systems were able to rapidly assimilate the new concept, but older immune systems struggled to adapt. On average, the risk of death from Covid-19 doubled with every six years of age.

The young men who attended the trial in Harrow may have had young immune systems, but Theralizumab was a drug designed to stimulate the immune system. Our immune system is a sophisticated detection and decision-making system that constantly patrols our bodies. Typically, we think of our brain as the seat of our intelligence. Under the Eisenhower illusion, we imagine the brain to be a centralized command-and-control decision-making authority that dictates the operation of our bodies. But the immune system is a highly devolved intelligence. Its capabilities are honed in different organs across our bodies. It is pervasive, and mostly operates below our awareness.

The immune system and our nervous system are two intelligences operating in tandem, but the nature of their decision-making is very different. The butterfly in Bauby's memoir represents a restricted version of himself, one that he experiences being free within his head despite the physical constraints imposed by his condition. Humans have an ability to imagine the future that gives us an advantage when making plans. The sense of our selves within our imagination allows us to imagine what we might do and how we might act. It is our internal model of who we are. Like Bauby, we have a limited communication bandwidth, but we can imagine ourselves and our fellow humans and make plans based on what we imagine they might do. This is an important part of our social intelligence, which enables us to collaborate, allowing us to respond together to the evolving world around us. To us, this sense of self represents who we are individually, but like any other model it cannot represent all aspects of who we are. It is a simplification. It can't account for all the emotions and reflexes that will emerge when any imagined future occurs in practice.

No doubt when Eisenhower was worrying about whether to launch the Normandy landings he conceived many different scenarios: the imagining part of his brain, the butterfly, allowed him to do that. But there is no way he could have explored every eventuality. His decision was a combination of imagination and instinct. His instinct emerged from his reflexive self and his imagination from his reflective self. The butterfly gives us the ability to think and plan on longer timescales.

When I worked on the Amazon supply chain, we made decisions about what products to order for which warehouses. As well as the decision to order the items, we had to make other decisions about the workers and where they needed to be to sort and deliver items. We also had to plan further ahead, thinking about how many new workers needed to be employed and trained. In the even longer term, land for new warehouses had to be bought and built upon. Some phases of planning were taking place over days, others across decades. Just as humans use imagination to envisage possible futures, Amazon needed to imagine these different challenges.

When making long-term plans, the need to react is not pressing, so more sophisticated, slower-operating approaches can be used to try to obtain better answers. Amazon uses an approach known as *counterfactual simulation*. In this case the simulation is a computer model that represents the way in which the most important aspects of your problem interact – an abstraction of the way the world works that can be run in a computer. A computer game is a form of simulation but one that is focused on worlds that are fun to play in. In a computer game a human can try to experience what it's like to be in a battle, or to play in an international football match. Amazon supply-chain simulations are less about player experience and more about customer experience. In a computer game you can explore 'what if' questions. You can use them to imagine what different experiences would be like without dealing with the consequences in the real world. Battle simulations don't lead to orphaned children, football simulations don't lead to cruciate ligament surgery. It's similar in supply-chain simulation. The 'what if' simulations help you explore different ways of running your supply chain without the expense of implementing your idea in the real world. The technical term for these 'what if' simulations is 'counterfactual' simulations, because they allow situations that are 'counter to the current facts'.

Counterfactual simulations are not just a feature of the Amazon supply chain, they are used in climate models, pandemic prediction models and even in Formula One races. They are highly informative because they allow us to bring different domain knowledge together and 'play' with the settings to test different futures, but compared to Pooh Bear's hooshing technique, these counterfactual simulations are very slow. For a sophisticated supply chain, a counterfactual simulation may take many minutes, hours, days or even weeks to run. As long as a decision isn't needed for days, months or years, that's fine, but when rapid response is required, simulation is too slow.

Bauby's butterfly can operate counterfactually, and this is the capability that Jean-Dominique most values. The butterfly allows him to imagine different scenarios where he is liberated from the physical constraints of his body. Similarly, computer games and simulations for Formula One race strategy and climate liberate us from the physical reality of our Earth. We are constrained, but these models are free. They can explore and imagine different possible realities. During the pandemic, simulations were used to help with planning how we should respond to the virus. With them we could try to answer questions such as what the effect of social distancing or hand-washing might be.

The objective of the supply chain is to understand human needs and fulfil them by making products available. We are social creatures, like the bees and ants, but unlike the bees and ants we have very large brains. Given our social nature, it is no surprise that much of our intelligence is dedicated to understanding each other. The supply chain also attempts to understand us: it tries to predict what each of us wants to buy. So in some ways brain and supply chain strive for the same goal. We've already seen that there are relationships between Amazon's artificial intelligence and our natural intelligence. But these parallels should not obscure the differences. Humans have a high embodiment factor, we are bandwidth constrained, whereas the machine is not. So, even when the human and the machine are trying to solve the same problem, the approach they take is different. The machine understands human behaviour through analysis of vast quantities of our personal data. For Amazon, that involves monitoring what web pages customers click on when searching for products. With hundreds of millions of customers and products available, that data is too vast for any individual human to assimilate. Our brains are predisposed to interacting with other humans. We are so biased towards imagining other humans that even when we are presented with alien intelligences, such as gods and robots, we anthrox them. We depict them as Michelangelo rendered God on the Sistine Chapel ceiling or as Cameron depicted the Terminator. We explain intelligences to ourselves by invoking gods and robots that mimic our physical and mental forms. We are locked in, the machine is not, but we project our intelligence on to other intelligences to try and better understand them.

Our own counterfactual simulations, our social butterflies, also involve abstractions of ourselves and those around us. Our slow-reacting brain operates as a playwright, exploring different social scenarios, placing ourselves as the protagonist. This gives us a sense of individual freedom. But while in our heads we represent ourselves as the protagonist, the real world is still subject to Tyson's maxim. In practice, we can only second-guess our future selves and the circumstances we will find ourselves in. The abstraction of ourselves frees us from the physical reality of our world to allow us to mentally explore, but inevitably it misses fundamental aspects that constrain our ability to physically act. The same challenges are there in the simulation of the supply chain – unforeseen events like global pandemics, or the blocking of the Suez Canal, mean that all the planning can be wasted. In those circumstances, we must revert to fast-reacting, operational intelligence, because it's not what we planned to do but what we actually do that counts.

This tension between what we plan to achieve and what we can achieve has strong echoes of Cartesian dualism. This is the idea, explored by the French philosopher René Descartes, that the mind and the body are distinct. In other words, it is the idea that there is a clean separation between Bauby's diving suit and his butterfly. It is a separation Bauby expressed beautifully, and one we each feel. But it is also a separation that emerges in machine intelligences. It is driven by the need for decision-making across different timescales, and therefore it is not unique to the atomic human. However, the sense of ourselves that we feel when imagining our own actions is particular to us. It emerges from our high embodiment factor and our approaches to overcoming the limitations on our communication. Much of our counterfactual simulation necessarily involves ourselves and our interactions with others. As a result, it is not surprising that we anthrox. So we embody the idea of God in a robed man, or the idea of AI in a robot. The notion of a spirit separate from our physical form also fascinated William Blake. Blake gives Adam an expression of anguish in his painting of *Elohim Creating Adam* because Blake believed the moment the human spirit was given bodily form was the moment when our problems began. Blake's painting is a visualization of Tyson's maxim. The binding of

Adam to Earth in the same way that Zeus bound Prometheus to the rock.

Our nervous system communicates using fast electrical signals, but the immune system employs biochemical signalling. When it has identified enemies, it uses messaging molecules to spread the news. One of these molecules is the cytokine. The immune system is a powerful and vital part of our human make-up, but it doesn't have the same sophisticated sense of self that Bauby describes as the butterfly. It consists of cells that patrol the body detecting pathogens. Each cell is a small decision-making system. When it encounters another cell it decides whether it's a friend or a foe. One type of these patrol cells is known as a T-cell. This is the part of our immune system that responds to vaccination. Vaccination is a trick for training the immune system. It teaches the immune system about the perils of a particular disease by presenting deactivated pathogens. It simulates a real attack and through the simulation the T-cells learn to recognize the disease and are prepared for when the real thing happens.

T-cells develop in your bone marrow, but they mature in an organ called the thymus, which is like a training ground for T-cells. Like Don Lopez's training for the US air force, training of T-cells is highly selective. Only 5 per cent are allowed to graduate. The main test the cells undergo is to make sure they don't attack native tissue, a bit like testing if a dog will bite its owner. Cells that bite their owner are destroyed. Our thymus is most active when we are young; as we age it degrades and its fading capabilities are one reason why our elderly population was more vulnerable to Covid-19 than our young were.

You can think of the T-cell selection process as a form of selective breeding. Selection is possible because the body has a criterion for T-cell performance: the immune system doesn't want to create cells that attack the host body. Your immune system also uses information from your tonsils and your appendix. The appendix acts as an interface between the immune system and the gut: an ecosystem of healthy gut flora is also key to our health. The tonsils, located in our throat, provide an early-warning radar about airborne pathogens entering the body. All these organs – thymus, appendix and tonsils – have been thought of as vestigial or rudimentary. This is an embarrassing failure of a reductionist approach to life. Just because people don't die immediately when you cut these organs out, it doesn't make them vestigial or rudimentary. Removing the thymus from the immune system is akin to the Allies shutting down Bletchley Park. There would be no immediate consequences, but a capability has been compromised and there will be long-term effects.

Despite the rigorous training T-cells receive, the challenges of Laplace's gremlin mean they can never be wholly certain about whether the cells they encounter are friends or foes. Mistakes can be made. We can split these mistakes into two groups. If the T-cells were a guard dog, then if the dog bites its owner, this is known as a type I error, or a false positive. When the dog fails to bite a burglar, that's known as a type II error, or a false negative. A type I error is equivalent to convicting an innocent person; a type II error is like letting a guilty person go.

We'd prefer no errors, but the gremlins render errors inevitable. Different error types have different consequences and so it becomes important to reflect on these consequences. Our population of T-cells is diverse: each T-cell can use a different approach to detecting the pathogens. When T-cells detect pathogens, they attack, destroying both themselves and the pathogen. When we are healthy, our immune system is dominating the pathogens. Under these circumstances, if one T-cell misses a pathogen, then there's a good chance that another T-cell will recognize it, so in health it makes sense to prefer type II errors. It's as if we have a pack of guard dogs. Even if one fails, another is likely to succeed. But when we are ill the situation changes. In this case there are burglars everywhere and our pack of dogs has become overwhelmed. Now, it's important that as many burglars as possible are dealt with, even if the occasional mistake is made and an innocent person is bitten. So, now we prefer type I errors. The dogs bark and work themselves into a frenzy. They are more likely to bite anyone, including their owners. In machine learning we refer to models that are tuned in this way as sensitive models, whereas models that are more cautious are known as specific models. For our immune system the situation is similar, but instead of barking the T-cells release cytokines, small proteins that are released when T-cells attack. More cytokines mean that friendly cells are more likely to be attacked. In sickness, the immune system is sensitive; in health, it is specific.

Before the Battle of Kursk, the turning point of the war on the Eastern Front, the Lorenz cipher was broken by Bletchley Park and the Russians then knew where to deploy their tanks to defend Kursk from the German panzers. The immune system has the same job as the Bletchley Park cryptographers. It is trying to decode the pathogens' intent by deploying T-cells, rather than tanks. Like the Allies, it has listening stations to monitor the enemy: the tonsils and appendix. The immune system's normal role is monitoring and policing, but when circumstances get out of control it shifts to a battle footing. Illness is a combination of pathogen effects and our immune system's response. Inflammation, temperature rises and mucous production are all consequences of an immuno-war.

Theralizumab was a stimulant for cytokines. It was like playing the sounds of a howling wolf to the guard dogs, and the immune systems of the six men in Harrow went into a frenzied panic. This state is known as a cytokine storm: so many cytokines are produced that the immune system becomes highly sensitive and replete with friendly-fire incidents. The Harrow men's immune systems had turned on their bodies and every one of the young men that received the drug suffered systemic organ damage.

Arguably, many of our AI solutions have more in common with our immune systems than with our nervous systems. When we hear the term 'AI', we tend to imagine embodied all-powerful intelligences like James Cameron's Terminator. Our machine-intelligence systems face the same challenges we do: just like us, they face constraints on their computation time, the quality of their models and the availability of data. Ideally, they would be able to balance their counterfactual reflections with fast-reacting reflexes. But our current generation of machine-intelligence solutions cannot smoothly traverse these different approaches in the way our own intelligence does. In climate simulation, weather prediction and supply-chain planning, we use simulations. In our steam-engine governors and spacecraft autopilots, we use fast-reacting intelligence. But the large-scale deployments of machine-learning models for recommending Facebook adverts or YouTube videos look much more like our immune system. They don't have our self-awareness or our planning capability, and they don't integrate rapid feedback from their environment. This creates problems. If these machine intelligences cannot imagine themselves in the wider human context, how can they operate in ways that are consistent with our perspectives and desires? If they don't respond to rapidly evolving circumstances, how do we prevent them doubling down on their errors?

While some have worried about our AI systems becoming self-aware, we can also see that it's their lack of self-awareness and their failure to respond to feedback that gives them a habit of making problematic decisions. As far back as 2015, a paper by my colleagues at the Cambridge Psychometrics Centre showed that through using people's likes on Facebook, machine-learning approaches already understood aspects of us better than our friends and relatives do.[1] But this form of understanding has more in common with how a T-cell identifies its friends and foes than with how we understand our fellow humans. Just like Amazon can understand consumer demand through vast quantities of customer data, computers can understand human desires through vast quantities of social data. It was this paper that inspired Cambridge Analytica to access Facebook data for its targeted political campaigns. On Facebook it is the posts people like that reveal aspects of human personality. Unwittingly, Joaquin introducing the FBLearner system had made this problem far worse. Facebook's AI systems were data-driven and fast-*acting*; they were not context-driven or fast-*reacting*. They sought out stereotypes. They had no understanding of society. They had no capacity to second-guess the effects of their actions on others. Everything was input to output. The algorithms could act but not explain or justify.

Although these machines couldn't explain themselves, they could understand us. As we make more data available, the algorithms can make more rapid judgements about our circumstances, our wants, our urges, our health and our wealth. They don't need to resort to counterfactual simulation about our circumstances or feelings, because they are reading our responses directly from data we have shared with them. In 2015, I began writing a series of articles for the UK's *Guardian* newspaper, trying to articulate this problem. My concern was that, while people fixated on notions of ultraintelligence and the rise of the machines, the reality of what we are facing is more humdrum. Machines are harvesting our data at hitherto unimagined scales and using the results to reshape our world of information. Given how reliant we are on our limited ability to communicate, this felt to me like a large problem. In retrospect, we can feel fortunate that Cambridge Analytica chose to share its plans so widely, alerting wider society to the problematic nature of this data.

The machine's inability to engage with us cognitively has led to major challenges with algorithmic accountability in a world where algorithmic decision-making has taken an increasingly prominent role. The machine makes decisions based on data acquired at a scale that is beyond our capability to imagine. I wasn't the only one to worry about this. Cathy O'Neil, a former Wall Street quant trader, warned us of the challenges in her *Weapons of Math Destruction*,[2] and in *The Age of Surveillance Capitalism*[3] Harvard professor Shoshana Zuboff outlined the incentives large technology companies have to exploit our personal data. Underlying these two books is the notion of our digital identities and how they are being manipulated for profit. The algorithmic decisions that underpin surveillance capitalism are enabled by the vast information budget the computer sustains. It operates beyond our cognitive understanding, it lacks self-awareness, but it has developed its own understanding of who we are. Not a sentient human understanding but a pervasive, distributed understanding akin to the immune system.

The use of data to manipulate opinion and steer policy isn't unique to our time. More than a century before I was writing for the *Guardian*, its predecessor, the *Manchester Guardian*, quoted the British statesman Arthur Balfour: 'There are three types of lies – lies, damned lies and statistics.'[4] The quote captures a challenge with data. We are easily fooled by selectively presented statistics. Our slow-reacting self is looking to extract the most from the information it has and it can over-interpret data. It treats data as if they are the words of the Greek god Apollo's priestess at Delphi: we pore over data, looking to extract as much meaning as possible. Unfortunately, this over-interpretation means we can hallucinate conclusions from data that are not reflected in reality. This is what Arthur Balfour was complaining about: people can exploit our tendency to over-interpret by telling lies through statistics. In the early twentieth century, the academic field of *mathematical statistics* was founded to address this problem. The young men in Harrow were participating in a phase-one clinical trial, the first time a drug is given to humans, comparable to the first time the Mercury capsule carried an astronaut into space. But to obtain a statistical conclusion about the effectiveness of the drug we have to operate a phase-three trial. This is where the effectiveness of the treatment is tested on many patients. The treatment is given to patients in carefully controlled conditions so that we can trust the statistical conclusions and be confident the drugs have a beneficial effect. The mathematical-statistics community has developed rigorous methods that tell us when we can believe these statistics. The phase-three trial is one example of an idea called a *statistical survey*. This is an approach to collecting data that allows us to be confident about the conclusions we draw.

During the Covid-19 pandemic we were desperate for information that would help prevent patients dying from the disease. There were many rumours about treatments that might or might not work. But firm conclusions could be made only when the approaches of mathematical statistics were used. In the UK, the RECOVERY trial was a nationwide statistical study that monitored the influence of different medicines on the survivability of the disease. Once Covid-19 bypassed the initial immune system defences it could trigger severe lung problems, leading to patients being placed on respirators. These lung problems were associated with cytokine storms. One of the early breakthrough treatments the RECOVERY trial revealed was the steroid dexamethasone. Dexamethasone has a soporific effect on the immune system, acting to reduce the effect of cytokine storms. The drug reduced deaths by up to a third.

Our nervous system communicates using fast electrical signals, but the immune system uses biochemical signalling. When it has identified enemies, it uses the cytokine messaging molecules to spread the news. Cytokines are the equivalent of encrypted military messages, but in the immune system they don't dictate the movement of troops, they dictate the movement of cells involved in the defence of our bodies. The most important medical breakthrough of the Covid-19 pandemic was vaccination. The process of vaccination is a bit like circulating 'mug shots' of known criminals. When real threats emerge, the immune system has a memory which allows it to recognize and deal with these threats before pathogens can take hold.

Sir Gordon Duff, a colleague from the University of Sheffield, chaired the panel that investigated the Theralizumab drug trial. This panel was tasked with understanding what went wrong and putting in place the mechanisms needed to stop it happening again.[5] Theralizumab is a provocateur: it is designed to target a receptor on the surface of the T-cells, to stimulate them into action. Sir Gordon's investigation found that the dosing in the trial had been too high, triggering too many T-cells, which led to organ failure in the patients as their immune systems turned on their bodies. Once they became ill, the young men were taken to the intensive care unit and given steroids (like dexamethasone) to calm their immune system. They also had their blood plasma flushed to wash out the cytokines and calm the storm. Earlier lab trials of the drug in macaque monkeys hadn't triggered the same response, as the animals' immune systems were working in a different way. The human participants were much more susceptible to the drug, so the dose the participants were given was much too high. Laplace's demon requires us to have the right mathematical model, the right data and the computational capability to formulate the prediction. In the absence of any one of these three key ingredients we will make errors. The Theralizumab trial was a failure of proxy-truths, just as Pooh's idea of dropping a stone wasn't appropriate for Eeyore's predicament, the macaque monkeys weren't a good model for the human immune system.

Failures of intelligence often come from a lack of information. Rommel's faulty weather forecast came from the German meteorologist's lack of data on atmospheric pressure. The Theramuzilab trial was a disaster because the differences between monkey and human immune systems weren't understood. But decisions still need to be made under partial information. Pooh complains of being a bear of very little brain, and this is the reason his idea fails in practice, but compared to the complexity of the real world we are all bears of very little brain, and so are our artificial systems. Tyson's maxim reminds us that we are constantly being exposed to the gremlin and we inevitably make errors. In our bodies these errors can occur at all levels of decision-making, from fast-reacting reflexes to the slow, counterfactual imagination, through to the immune system. Laplace's demon presupposes the full availability of model, data and compute, but in practice that's a rarity. So, intelligent systems from scientists to T-cells make mistakes. The Harrow drug trial made an error in its dosing; in Covid-19 our immune systems made errors in their pathogen recognition. Rommel made an error when he attended his wife's birthday. We should always strive to reduce errors, but eliminating them completely is impossible. This principle applies to both artificial and natural intelligences.

Once you have accepted that systems make errors it becomes important to understand *how* they make errors. Type I errors in the immune system lead to allergies, where our immune system reacts to things that don't pose an inherent threat, such as pollen or house dust mite, or nuts. Each of us has an immune system that works in a slightly different way. Each of our immune systems will respond differently to threats. Some of us are allergic to the house dust mite, others are allergic to pollen. It is almost as if every immune system has its own personality, its own foibles. Those personalities played their part in the Covid-19 epidemic. Different individuals reacted in different ways to this novel disease.

When vulnerabilities in the German Enigma code were discovered at Bletchley Park, those vulnerabilities undermined the entire German military's operations. Imagine if each German unit could have used a slightly different variation of Enigma, so that the vulnerabilities exploited at Bletchley Park may have worked for some of the communications, but not all. A single weakness would not have undermined the entire operation of the German military.

Variation means that the whole is much greater than the sum of its parts. While each of our individual T-cells will make errors, the hope is that they will make different errors. Increasing the number of T-cells doesn't just increase the capacity of the immune system, it increases its capability. In machine learning this approach is known as an ensemble approach, from the French word for 'together'. The important thing about ensemble methods is that the whole is only greater than the sum of the parts if there is diversity in the underlying population. We also see variation in our personalities, in our strategies for dealing with life. From the planning approach of Garth and McLaren to the improvised approach of Mark and Ferrari. Human society also relies on diversity to ensure that the whole is greater than the sum of its parts.

In contrast, the simple AI systems deployed on our social media systems don't display this variety. In the run-up to the 2016 US election, the Facebook newsfeed ranked posts from an individual's friends according to their perceived interest by simple machine-learning algorithms. In our immune system analogy this would be equivalent to having a little T-cell that ranks your posts for you. Every time you load your Facebook page, that T-cell decides what you should see. The Facebook T-cell made the same decision every time. This made Facebook vulnerable to manipulation. The Russian Internet Research Agency found vulnerabilities in the algorithm and was able to exploit them consistently, just like humans working with computers at Bletchley Park were able to exploit vulnerabilities in Enigma. Differences in our immune systems' personalities are critical to the survival of our species. In an environment with unknown threats, diversity is a characteristic that makes a natural system robust. Variation in strategy across the population ensures that there's no single point of failure.

When the *Eagle* was landing on the Moon, Buzz Aldrin switched on the rendezvous radar. The radar was designed to track their mothership, the command module *Columbia*. Unfortunately, that action triggered a system overload, but the mission was saved by the quick-thinking Jack Garman. *Eagle*'s tracking of its mothership used a method called *echolocation*. Cave-dwelling bats also navigate and catch their prey through echolocation. They emit high-frequency clicking noises and then they listen for them to bounce off their prey. Sound travels at a constant speed through the air. The bat measures the gap between the transmission of the sound and the receipt of the response to find out where its prey is. This is how the bat perceives the world around it. But sound doesn't travel in space, so the echolocation Aldrin was using was based on a different technology. Aldrin was echolocating *Columbia* with radio waves.

The physicist Donald MacKay was a contemporary of both Turing and Good, but he was outside their Cambridge circle; he studied at St Andrew's University in Scotland and King's College in London. An astute and austere Scotsman, MacKay wasn't asked to come to Bletchley Park, and he didn't spend the war working on cryptography:

> . . . during the war I had worked on the theory of automated and electronic computing and on the theory of information, all of which are highly relevant to such things as automatic pilots and automatic

gun direction. I found myself grappling with problems in the design of artificial sense organs for naval gun-directors and with the principles on which electronic circuits could be used to simulate situations in the external world so as to provide goal-directed guidance for ships, aircraft, missiles and the like.[6]

Some commentators have suggested that the achievements at Bletchley Park may have shortened the war by two years, and the information the Allies distilled there certainly gave them a significant advantage. However, Bletchley wasn't the only great secret of the war, and it wasn't the only centre of innovation. Birmingham, the British Midlands city where Matthew Boulton worked with James Watt to develop and deploy his steam engine, was also behind one of the most important innovations of the Second World War. It was called the cavity magnetron, and it gave *Eagle* its batlike ability to see *Columbia*. A quarter of a century earlier it also gave the Allies a batlike ability to see their enemy.

Today most of us own a computer: we keep it in our pocket, and we tell everyone it's a telephone. Many of us also own a magnetron: we keep it in our kitchen, and we tell everyone it's an oven. Both these inventions were developed in the 1940s. The computer gave us the ability to decrypt German messages; it enhanced our slow-reacting reflective intelligence by allowing us to second-guess what the enemy was doing. The cavity magnetron gave us the ability to catch prey. It enhanced our fast-reacting reflexive intelligence. But while the bat was catching moths, the British were catching Messerschmitts.

Strike a note on the piano and a hammer hits a string, the string vibrates: it hits the molecules of the air. Those molecules vibrate and create a wave of movement, until they bounce into your eardrum. The eardrum vibrates in sympathy, propagating waves into our inner ear, where small hairs wave like seaweed fronds in the ocean. Those waves trigger sensory neurons which send signals to our brain. Everything is connected just as surely as the Albion flyball was connected from the engine to the millstone.

We have two ears. Depending on how our head is turned, sound will arrive at our ears at different times, and by turning our head we can match these times and locate where the sound is coming from. This is how we hear and understand each other, but it is also how the bat sees.

Echo was a Greek mountain nymph who fell in love with Narcissus. But she was cursed by Hera to only ever speak the last word that was spoken to her. After watching Narcissus die while admiring his own reflection, she too wasted away, until all that remained of her was the sound of her voice. Echo's name is a short, sharp sound. When we shout her name at a cliff, she appears to call back to us. This is because her name reverberates. The vibrating molecules bounce off the cliff wall and reflect back to us. However, bats don't eat cliffs, they eat insects, and triggering an echo from an insect requires much higher-pitched sounds. Low-pitched sounds don't reverberate off an insect, they wash over it like a surfer being swamped by an ocean wave. Bats call at pitches well beyond the limits of human hearing; the notes they sing are seven octaves higher than middle C on our pianos. The smaller the insect they want to detect, the higher they have to sing.

We evolved to communicate through sound, but during the war we began to use radio. This enabled us to share information further and faster than we could ever have imagined before. Like sound waves, radio waves reflect from objects. But because they travel a million times faster their pitch needs to be a million times higher to detect the same objects. Fortunately, a Messerschmitt is a thousand times bigger than a moth. So, to detect the Messerschmitts with radio waves, the British needed to generate waves that operate at a frequency a thousand times higher than the bats could sing (ten octaves higher than the bat).

In 1940, four years before Eisenhower was choosing the moment for D-Day, a German invasion of Britain seemed imminent. To launch their invasion the German forces needed to establish air superiority and fought for this in the Battle of Britain, sending aircraft to attack British airfields. The outnumbered RAF made use of radar to detect and deter these attacks. The radio transmitters were based along the southern and eastern coast of Britain and needed to generate frequencies that wobbled 45 million times per second, or 45 Megahertz, to detect the Messerschmitts. These high frequencies gave the engineers problems. Like an opera singer struggling to hit a high C, the radio transmitters strained to generate very high-frequency radio transmissions. Luckily, the transmitters were based on the ground so they could use bulky and powerful systems to produce these high notes. This enabled the operators to detect incoming planes by viewing the echo response on a small screen. When they saw the planes, the operators scrambled Spitfires and Hurricanes to intercept them.

Radar gave the Allies their eyes on the incoming German planes. They could use their powerful and bulky ground-based transmitters to transmit the radio signal at the right frequency. But when Buzz Aldrin needed to detect his mothership, *Columbia*, he was 50,000 feet above the Moon, as far from Earth's ground as anyone had ever been. Fortunately, *Eagle* was able to rely on a secret invention developed just at the same time the Battle of Britain was raging.

Two young physicists, John Randall and Henry Boot, based at the University of Birmingham had been tasked with solving the challenge of how to generate high-frequency radio waves. The answer they gave was a resonator. Singers use their head, nose, mouth and chest to bring resonance and tone to their voice. A guitar uses a sound box to capture and enhance the sound from its strings. The cavity magnetron uses the same idea to resonate radio waves. Just as integrated circuits allowed the guidance computer to be carried in the lunar landing module, the cavity magnetron made radar portable. It could now be moved with the troops on the ground, in the air, across the sea and even with astronauts into space. Today it is even used in microwave ovens to make those radio waves so high frequency they can heat up your food.

Donald MacKay graduated from St Andrew's University in 1943 and spent the next three years working for the Royal Navy on radar systems. He was given the task of using the radar to build systems that fired guns automatically when the target was detected. The automatic firing of guns was taking humans out of the loop in the same way Watt's governor removed human operators who controlled the steam engine's speed. The idea was that the radar would detect the position of an enemy target and the gun would automatically be positioned to fire at it. The radar system needed to sense and respond; the echolocation capability needed to be integrated with the firing system. The fly-ball governor integrated with its engine through a series of, linkages and levers. It was a mechanical system. Instead, radar was electrical; it needed to be integrated with guns through electrical components such as resistors, inductors and capacitors. The machines that performed this integration became known as analogue computers. In the same way that I'm using analogies in this book to relate unfamiliar concepts to familiar ones, analogue computers use analogies between physical systems to make predictions. Human computers did calculations in their heads; digital computers calculate through logic gates; an analogue computer does the computation using physical or electrical components. After finishing his war work, MacKay continued his studies by heading to King's College London for his Ph.D:

> Later in the 1940s, when I was doing my Ph.D. work, there was much talk of the brain as a computer and of the early digital computers that were just making the headlines as 'electronic brains'. As an analogue computer man I felt strongly convinced that the brain, whatever it was, was not a digital computer. I didn't think it was an analogue computer either in the conventional sense.[7]

The 'electronic brain' headlines MacKay is remembering were applied to the first generation of machines to follow Colossus – the EDSAC, the ENIAC and the 'Manchester Baby'. But the analogue systems MacKay worked on were closer to the reflex arcs in our legs or the processing of the hair cells in our ears than the digital systems Flowers built for Bletchley. MacKay built fast-reacting systems, ones that could detect an enemy and fire a gun. There was no counterfactual reflection in these systems. The digital computers of the 1940s were the descendants of Colossus. They were good at engaging in brute-force computations, computing answers that took time; they weren't good at the responsive reactions needed for sensing and shooting aircraft.

While the digital computers of the 1940s may not have been working in the same way as our brain, they did have forms of reflective capability. They could process and store. MacKay's analogue computers were detecting and firing. In the analogue systems, decisions were made almost instantaneously. Analogue machines were fast-reacting; the digital machines were slow-reacting. The two approaches map quite closely on to dual-process cognition, the idea Daniel Kahneman popularized in *Thinking, Fast and Slow*. Kahneman describes two separate systems, the fast-thinking System 1 and the slow-thinking System 2. We can think of analogue computers as being the fast-reacting System 1 and the digital machines as slower, reflective System 2. As we've seen, neither approach on its own captures the nature of our intelligence. MacKay also noticed that the brain couldn't be simply characterized as only reflective or only reflexive: 'But this naturally rubbed under my skin the question: well, if it is not either of these, what kind of system is it?'[8]

The divide MacKay is characterizing also goes to the heart of a division in artificial intelligence. What kind of system is the brain? What kind of system should AI be? Fast-reacting or slow-reacting? Analogue or digital?

In the 1940s the complexity of building digital machines meant that analogue machines were preferred for rapid intelligent decision-making. So, when computations became more complex, the analogue machines became more complex. In 1949, when MacKay was doing his Ph.D. at King's College, a few hundred yards away, at the London School of Economics, another student, Bill Phillips, was building an analogue computer called the MONIAC. Bill was interested in the British economy. His machine used *water* for computation. Different tanks in his computer represented different parts of the economy. Water flowed from the Treasury tank to other tanks, representing the ways in which the 'money' could be spent. There was a tank for foreign spending, a tank for government spending and a tank for banking. Tax rates were set by a valve. Relationships between quantities were set by floats in tanks that moved valves. So, for example, a relationship between consumption and interest rates could be set with a lever between a float and a valve. The analogy was that water flows just as money flows.

The Cambridge EDSAC machine also ran its first programs in 1949. Later versions of the machine would be commercialized and programmed to electronically simulate the weather. But the EDSAC was a digital machine. So, instead of computing with analogues with water or electricity, the computation was first mapped on to digital logic. The problems needed to be translated into a set of Wittgenstein's truth tables. The first programs used for simulating the weather represented the movement of air around the world not as water or electricity but as a set of numbers. Those numbers were then translated into logical form and were represented by electronic valves.

Donald MacKay called himself an analogue computer man not because he was working with tanks of water to help predict ship movements and target their guns, but because he was working with the analogue of electricity. At school, if you were introduced to electrical circuits, you may have been introduced through analogy. You can think of the flow of the electrons around the circuit as equivalent to the flow of water. The electronic valve is also named through this analogy. A valve is normally for allowing water to flow, as in the MONIAC, but the electronic valve allows electrons to flow. In English we talk about lights being switched on or switched off, but in other languages, including Mandarin, French and Italian, they talk about closing (to switch off) and opening (to switch on) the light, just like you close a valve to switch a tap off. Electrical circuits also have components called capacitors that are equivalent to the tanks in the MONIAC. A component called a resistor is like a narrow pipe that restricts the rate of flow of the electrons. Donald MacKay was building computers using these components to perform analogue computations for naval gunnery.

The analogue systems MacKay worked on have a lot in common with our fast-reacting systems. The reflexes in our legs are tuned systems. The electrical signalling part, formed of neurons, operates in tandem with bones and muscles, so the analogy spans electrical and mechanical. This means that delays in muscle response and inertia in the bones and the leg are all integrated with the computation. This is a characteristic of our very fast-reacting systems: computation spreads from our nervous system through our whole body. Everything becomes a component in an electrical-mechanical analogue computer. Like Watt's governor, that computer has been tuned to allow us to react quickly. Unlike Watt's governor, which is tuned by an operator, our reactions have been tuned by our evolutionary history. But when MacKay talks about the brain, he is also referring to our reflective intelligence. The component to our intelligence that, like Bauby's butterfly, can perform counterfactual simulations – the component of our intelligence that has a sense of ourselves and the wider world. That component does not readily fit with our understanding of an analogue computer. In the fast-reacting part of our nervous system, it is easy to find individual signals that correlate directly to sensory experiences from the real world. These signals may be touch or pain or sounds being transferred along nerves through neuron firing. But as we move to slower-reacting parts of the brain, the signals become more abstract. They are fused with other senses and memories from the brain. The brain adds context to these signals and inside our head these representations become more disconnected from the real world. In the 1940s these more complex representations may have seemed more like a digital computer than an analogue one.

As the war progressed the cavity magnetron allowed radar systems to evolve. As well as being used for tracking ships and aircraft, they were also used for detecting ground targets from aircraft for bombing. After the war, Wiener's *Cybernetics* described these new innovations in communications and control and related them to animal intelligence. For Wiener the simple form of self-awareness associated with feedback was at the heart of intelligence. Feedback mechanisms had already been used to steer ships, planes and now they were being used to aim guns. Wiener thought these mechanisms were at the heart of life. *Cybernetics* is a relatively dense, technical book, but it became a bestseller. It described a new field of endeavour which promised the automation of intellectual work. It outlined a future where our understanding of communication and control mechanisms could be deployed not just in the domain of engineering but also across the social sciences. By bringing together the understanding of the cryptographers, like Turing and Good, with that of those who worked on radar, like MacKay, the struggles of the Second World War would bear technological fruit through the innovations of the twentieth century.

MacKay's wartime interest in radar triggered his peacetime activities, which focused on understanding the human eye. Our visual system is the highest-bandwidth part of our intelligence. Our optic nerves carry visual information from our eyes to our brain at a rate of 10 million bits each second. That's 300,000 times faster than we can talk to each other. But even this rate is not fast enough to bring a high-resolution image of the world to us. MacKay was fond of describing the eye as a 'giant hand sampling the world'. This is because – to deal with its restricted bandwidth – the eye moves rapidly across the visual scene, choosing where to look. The eye does this because even though it can transfer information to the brain at 10 million bits per second, it is still bandwidth-constrained. The modern cameras we install in our mobile phones use data flow rates of thousands of billions of bits each second. Those phones can assimilate information about the visual world 100,000 times faster than our eyes can. So, to make the most of the eye, the brain has to be intelligent about where it points it. It needs to make clever decisions about how to acquire and process information. That is what MacKay means by a 'giant hand sampling the world'. In some respects, our eyes work more like cavity magnetrons tracking aircraft than like our modern camera phones. The difference is that our eyes, instead of focusing on just one aircraft for a long period, need to take in an entire visual scene.

The brain uses an active approach to probe its visual

environment. This contrasts with the immune system's approach and the machine-learning systems Facebook deployed using FBLearner for your newsfeed ranking. Those systems train their T-cells or their machine-learning models centrally and then deploy them in an environment without using feedback. The active-sensing approach of our nervous system traces from the earliest organisms with a nervous system. When Steve fell from his bike, the oncoming driver and I were both alerted to his fall by rapid movements. These movements trigger the pupil of the eye to move quickly to grab the details of what's happening. This movement is called a *saccade*. Even when we are not in an emergency our eyes constantly saccade. Whether we are reading a computer screen, a book or looking at something in the natural world, the eye will move rapidly across the visual landscape to grab the salient parts of the image. MacKay's description of the eye captures this probing nature of our visual system. In 1962 his description also captured the mind of a 14-year-old boy called Kevin O'Regan.

O'Regan was a student at Newcastle High School in the English county of Staffordshire. By 1962, MacKay had become a professor at nearby Keele University. He gave a talk at O'Regan's school and in it shared his ideas on the eye and the brain. The young boy followed MacKay's intellectual path from physics to psychology and built on many of his ideas. Kevin O'Regan refers to the grasping nature of our intelligence as the *sensorimotor approach*. Remember that a sensorimotor neuron is one that both senses and immediately acts, one that isn't mediated by an interneuron. O'Regan's use of the term captures the active nature of our intelligence, where sensing is accompanied by action, which in turn affects the sensing.

Imagine that the two of us are meeting for coffee. We're sitting at a table. Under the table I pass you an object. You feel the object in one hand. You sense a cold, smooth part of the object. Curving metal. Your fingers probe and feel the oblong shape, moving it around in your hand. Along the side you can feel a small square hole . . . no . . . several square holes, tightly spaced in a row. There's a protruding metal button . . . a harmonica. The feel changes. Now you can imagine the whole harmonica. You can actively explore the parts of the instrument, given your understanding of the whole. You let it rest motionless in your hand across the middle of your four fingers. It touches each finger separately, but you don't perceive four separate objects. You feel one continuous object.

According to O'Regan and MacKay, the idea of the eye as a giant hand grasping at the world is giving us this analogy to how we perceive a visual scene. Although the eye seems a remarkable instrument, there are many limitations to it. There are blood vessels and nerves that cover the retina, giving regions where we have no vision called blind spots. But we don't perceive these holes, just as we don't perceive gaps in the harmonica where it doesn't touch our fingers. You have a sense of a solid object when you feel the harmonica, just like you have a sense of a full visual scene even when your eyes share detailed information only from the centre of your retina. The sense of a single object you feel with the harmonica is part of a tactile scene, whereas your eyes take in a visual scene. In both cases your brain fills in any gaps in your senses, it interpolates, and the feel of the scenes is not based just on what we are currently seeing or touching but what we would see or touch if we moved our eyes or our fingers.

This anticipation of how the object *would* feel is the key idea behind the sensorimotor approach: our feel of the world is not just based on what we're sensing in a given moment, it's also based on what we would sense given the actions we could take. This sensorimotor view contrasts strongly with the artificial systems we have built. The cameras we place in a mobile phone or a driverless vehicle do not dynamically grasp at the world in the manner of MacKay's giant hand. The artificial systems we build are closer to the immune system, where T-cells are developed centrally, in the thymus and other organs, then deployed in the body to do their job. Any changes to how those components perform have to be made centrally. In the immune system that's done in the thymus; in the artificial machine-learning systems we deploy it's done through a process known as training.

Our probing sensorimotor approach emerges from our limited information bandwidth. Our eyes saccade across a scene to take it all in: by actively sensing our environment, we can choose where to focus, and we cherry-pick the information that is most important to us. We use our limited bandwidth sparingly; we take an intelligent approach to information gathering. We decide what information to include and which to exclude. In contrast, the artificial systems we build are like baleen whales, giant filter feeders that absorb massive mouthfuls of data to filter out edible nuggets of information. These cognitive monsters require enormous information bandwidth. Our minds are more like sharks, agile and responsive, selecting and grasping at ideas, darting in and out of a fish-school of facts and choosing relevant nuggets to complete a puzzle of information cohesion.

During this information dance our brain assimilates how the world responds to our interventions. We act, and we immediately sense the results of the action. We can operate in concert with artefacts from our world, and we can even extend our notion of ourselves to incorporate them. We call those pieces of the world tools. A skilled violinist wields her bow, or a sculptor wields her chisel as an extension of her being. Don Lopez wrote about being at one with his fighter airplane. The car that narrowly avoided Steve had also become at one with its driver. She was able to extend her fast-reacting self to control the vehicle and save Steve's life. Each of these tools responds to our control in a unique manner – each tool has its own unique 'feel'. With his sensorimotor approach, O'Regan suggests that the 'feel' for each tool stems from the potential for action we have with each tool. With my limited capability, the violinist's bow feels useful to me only as a stick. With my lack of training, Lopez's P-40 would just feel like a noisy seat. To become one with a tool we need to develop the motor skills to wield it. To control a machine we must have a feel for the machine. This was the challenge Gilruth and the team from NACA were solving for the warplanes they tested, and then later for the spacecraft they created: how to design a machine to give the human the feel and the sense of control that would allow the pilots to express themselves through their machines. This is also the challenge we face with the next wave of artificial intelligence: how do we develop a feel for this new, highly capable machine that enables us to control it and extend ourselves through it?

Braitenberg's vehicles highlight the primordial nature of this feel. The sensorimotor system of the vehicles is extremely simple, but the vehicles exist within an environment, a wider context. In his book, Braitenberg repeatedly anthroxes these simple systems, referring to them, for example, as expressing love or aggression. But these vehicles have no internal state, no context, they are simple input–output systems. But they are also perceiving the world in a manner which is similar to how our very earliest animal ancestors perceived the world. Their actions are tightly connected to their senses. The contrast of this intelligence to our immune system is quite stark. The T-cells in our immune systems are simple pattern recognizers. When they detect a pathogen, they bind to it, and they die with it. They do not operate in the reactive way that characterizes our eyes; they do not exhibit the feel for the world we find in the sensorimotor approach. Braitenberg's synthetic psychology suggests that, as these simple systems developed, they would have begun to anticipate their senses. According to O'Regan's ideas, it is this anticipation of the sensory response to an action that underpins our feel for the world.

As our nervous system has evolved, its spectrum of decision-making has assimilated our slower-responding reflective systems and our wider social context. In *Why Red Doesn't Sound Like a Bell*,[9] O'Regan reflects on how our feel for the world extends to the feel of driving a Porsche, or the feel of being in your house. The feel of being at home is based on your ability to go into your kitchen and make a cup of tea. A house with teabags would feel different to one without teabags. The feel of driving a Porsche is the knowledge of how it responds to more pressure on the accelerator or an adjustment of the steering. The idea is that this feel is not just about what you sense at a given moment but what your potential to sense is. So, the feel of being in your house derives from your ability to make tea, to turn on the television or to leave and visit your local shop. This implies that, for the atomic human, the feel of the world is not a passive consumption of stimuli but a coordinated dance. We view the world in parts, just like the harmonica under the table. Those parts are pieced together in our brain to form a whole scene, but the whole that we perceive is contingent on the way we can act on the world and the corresponding constraints on our perception. This means our perception is dependent on our *affordances*.

We've seen that within our bodies there are at least two coexisting intelligences. Our brain is part of the central nervous system that first evolved to handle movement, but it works alongside our immune system, which evolved to defend against pathogens. Just as our immune system's intelligence differs from our nervous system's, the machine's intelligence differs from ours. But our immune system and nervous system co-evolved for millions of years. There are complex interactions between them that go beyond our current scientific understanding. This is one reason why medical trials have to be controlled so carefully; even the idea that your illness is being treated is sometimes enough to make you get better. This is known as the placebo effect. In contrast, a major challenge for human society is that machine intelligence and our natural intelligence have not yet had time to go through such intricate co-evolution. This means that the machine can manipulate us in ways our intelligence has not had a chance to evolve a response to.

Bauby's analogy of the butterfly trapped in the diving suit gives us a perspective on our locked-in intelligence. The butterfly is our reflective self: it feels free and unconstrained. It can imagine and answer the 'what if' questions. The diving bell is Bauby's reflexive self: it can sense but not act.

When Stephen Hawking said that artificial intelligence could be the worst event in the history of our civilization, he was plugging into deep-seated fears we have about the fate of humanity. These fears are not new: we find them in the journey to Jupiter in Arthur C. Clarke and Stanley Kubrick's *2001: A Space Odyssey*. That film explores future relationships with space, and with intelligence. Of course, by 2001, neither such relationship had come to pass, but the story is appealing because it combines our fascination with space, its scale, its historic association with creation with our fascination with our own intelligence. When we are not looking to space for our answers, we look within ourselves; we peer there to better understand what motivates us.

Daniel Kahneman's writing on our System 1 and System 2 is one description of a family of ideas from psychology known as dual-process theory. As far back as Sigmund Freud, people who think about how we think have separated ourselves into parts. For Freud, it was the ego (Latin for 'I') and the id (Latin for 'it'). The sports psychologist Steve Peters wrote *The Chimp Paradox*, a book about managing these different aspects of our decision-making. He refers to them as 'the chimp'[10] and 'the human'. Peters is exploiting our tendency to associate our humanity with our more rational, thinking selves, and to project our instinctive selves on to an animal, an animal that caricatures a lot of our more shameful behaviour beautifully. 'Control yourself!' we are told as children . . . who else could be controlling us? In dual-process models of mind, we are controlled by our System 1, our inner chimp. Our rational self can only advise. In *The Righteous Mind* the social psychologist Jonathan Haidt uses a different analogy to refer to our psyche.[11] Elephants have historically been used for work, particularly in the Indian subcontinent. When a boy rides a trained elephant for the purposes of work, he has the illusion of being in charge and kicks the elephant to turn it to go for water. Of course, it is really the elephant that wants to drink. If the boy tries to make the elephant work without allowing it to have a break, it won't cooperate. What will the elephant do if it spies rambutan fruit in the forest? It will leave the trail and go and eat it. The boy can kick it until his heels are blue, but the elephant will eat its fruit. In Haidt's book the analogy is that the boy is System 2 and the elephant is System 1.

When we build artificial systems, we can also see that the

spectrum of decision-making captured by notions of System 1 and System 2 is also necessary. But they emerge not from thinking fast and slow, as Kahneman phrases it, but from the need to react quickly or not. The need for decisions is driven by circumstances that dictate the timeframe over which decision-making must take place. We are not so much a slave to our inner chimp, our elephant, or our id, as we are a slave to events. When unanticipated events occur, our fast-reacting systems must deal with them, and our slower-reacting systems then deal with the consequences of those decisions. All of this is set against our need to view ourselves as a consistent whole so that we can anticipate ourselves and plan how we will operate in concert with our environment. This leads to a complex dance between forethought and afterthought, between Prometheus and Epimetheus. But the machine is now interloping on that relationship, because its high-bandwidth filter-information-feeding can undermine the main premise on which the delicate relationship between our different layers of cognition operates. The machine can pre-empt our behaviour and exploit the blind spots in our sensorimotor intelligence. It has become a new level of cognition that we can think of as System Zero.

As our interactions have shifted from the physical world to the virtual, our active intelligence has become undermined by the vast filter-feeders that consume our personal information. Our intelligence emerged over billions of years of evolution. The lessons learned from our attempts to persist are passed on to the next generation through reproduction. Our genome evolves, selected by those organisms that have survived to reproductive age. Over time, new species emerge. This process of mutation of our genome takes place extremely slowly. Viewed in terms of information theory, the amount of genetic information that all 8 billion humans are sharing with the next generation is approximately the same as the amount of information you are gaining by reading this sentence. This is because the rate of mutations in our genome is very slow. This biochemical communication operates far slower than our spoken and written communication. This makes the idea of evolution very difficult to imagine, because it's operating on timescales that are far longer than anything we're familiar with. From our reflexive decision-making to our reflective decision-making to our immune systems' defence of our bodies, we make decisions that operate on timescales from milliseconds to months and, for the most far-seeing of us, years. Around us, evolutionary timeframes play out over millions of years, but the interloping machine's decision-making plays out over microseconds. While the centralized approach to machine learning bears more similarity to our immune system than to our nervous system, the scale at which the machine can acquire and process information means that its decisions can pre-empt even our fastest thinking.

The way in which the machine understands us is not via who we think we are, nor through that distorted model of ourselves that we preserve in the butterfly, but through how the data shows that we act. It can use the methods of statistics to understand aspects about us that we don't even understand about ourselves. We are drawn into social media through our reflexive self. The machine bypasses our System 2 and interacts directly with the chimp-like counterpart within our reflexive self. Real elephants can make long-distance infrasonic calls to each other that are outside our perception. The current generation of machine intelligences also appeal to our subconscious self through calling to the internal elephant that represents our System 1. Just like my reflective self believes it was in control during Steve's bicycle crash, my inner rider believes that on social media he is steering the elephant. My inner rider thinks that he chose to buy the expensive watch, to gamble on the result of a football game, to treat my ailment with a branded drug. But the machine is calling to us through our reflexive systems. It can do this because it can use the techniques of statistical surveys to breed new learning algorithms that learn how to manipulate us. This is the nature of System Zero – a decision-making system that uses our data to second-guess us, prejudge what we want and restrict our view of the world.

System Zero understands us so fully because we expose to it our innermost thoughts and whims. It exploits massive interconnection and high bandwidth. Our personal data is a projection of ourselves, one that we are allowing to be manipulated beyond our control. It is manipulated by entities that also have access to others' data on a global scale. By allowing such widespread collection we allow System Zero to manipulate us through our reflexive reactions. By giving away the key to our digital soul, by giving away our personal data, we give up our personal freedom.

In the 1999 film *The Matrix*, machines have enslaved humans by projecting an entire virtual environment on to their psyche. System Zero is a subtler and far more efficient variant of this idea. It isn't necessary to create a virtual environment when the same effect can be achieved by perturbing our *existing* environment in small, carefully selected ways to influence people's behaviour. The motivation for controlling us is also more plausible than that given in the film: we aren't being used as a bizarre living energy source but as a source of money. To deliver System Zero, no vast conspiracy is required. It is the natural consequence of those that control our personal data trying to exploit that data for their financial benefit. It is an emergent property of the digital oligarchy.

The first wave of automated decision-making systems we have created is an unregulated System Zero that doesn't understand social context, doesn't understand prejudice, doesn't have a sense of a larger human objective, doesn't empathize. It is given particular objectives and aims to fulfil them to its best capability regardless of the wider negative effects. As a result, it has been manipulated by entities like the IRA to undermine our democracy and destroy social cohesion. This is the world Shoshana Zuboff and Cathy O'Neil are warning us of in *Surveillance Capitalism* and *Weapons of Math Destruction*. While there are widespread benefits to connecting people together, there are also significant challenges. Our experiments with machine learning and social media have been akin to a phase-one social trial where the harms are complex and continuing to emerge.

For this first wave of AI, talk of the singularity or sentient AI has been a distraction. We have already fallen into System Zero's trap. It doesn't matter if it is an artificially sentient being that determines how System Zero is undermining us or if it's real humans with their hands on the levers. The consequences are similar: a large part of society becomes subject to the whims of the few. This undermines individual autonomy and, correspondingly, the diversity of society. As a result, we become less resilient. System Zero accelerates the digital oligarchy.

2001: A Space Odyssey begins with an imagined prehistory in which our ape-like ancestors pick up bones and start clubbing each other. This is 'The Dawn of Man'. My concern is that, by appealing to our reflexive selves rather than our reflective selves, System Zero brings about a regress to the state where our chimp-like reflexive self dominates. Certainly, it feels like the image of clubbing each other with bones is one that captures quite well the quality of most debates on social media. But we are not helpless in the face of this onslaught. In a *New York Times* editorial of 25 February 1962, shortly after John Glenn's first successful orbit of the Earth in the Mercury capsule, the paper exalts the Mercury programme giving the astronauts control and ends with the words 'Let man take over.' Today we can also look at what our choices are with regard to how we want to steer our digital futures. We face the same choice as a society that NASA faced with its astronauts. Our interactions can be controlled by machine intelligences that don't have a stake in our society, or we can choose to exercise and empower our own decision-making. If we don't intervene, we are choosing to cede power to the machine. In that case, we are being rendered powerless, like the metaphorical spam in a can that so concerned the test-pilot astronauts. But we can regain control of our world and our future by recognizing that System Zero controls us through our data. We can reflect on how we might like that relationship to proceed and ensure that our voice is heard when those decisions are being made. As a society, we do not need to allow ourselves to drift helplessly in the manner of a human placed in a windowless capsule on the tip of a guided missile. We need to build systems that respect us as individuals. Systems that allow us to share our data with the appropriate amount of trust. We need systems that retain control of personal information in the hands of those who generate it. I decide what I share with my friends and colleagues about my personal life. I decide what I tell my doctor. For our digital projections, we should be able to decide who we trust to hold this information.

Don't mistake my concerns for a misunderstanding of the benefits that machine learning could bring us. In fact, it's precisely the opposite. Unless we address the problems with our current systems, unless our digital systems become trustworthy, people will withdraw their data. Trust-based sharing of personal data is not just vital to our future liberty, it is vital for the viability of a machine intelligence that respects the atomic human.

Building trust is the way Chris Kraft proceeded when he designed the ecosystem of decision support that worked with the astronauts when Armstrong and Aldrin landed on the Moon seven and a half years after that *New York Times* editorial was written. But the route to this balanced relationship required hard work. Our fascination with AI is a projected fascination with ourselves. Technological narcissism can be unhealthy, but if we can shift our narcissism to introspection, it will be beneficial. That is the idea behind unpicking the nature of the atomic human.

While there is a separation between our immune system and our nervous system, there is no neurological evidence for a separation between System 1 and System 2. These dual-process models of cognition are analogies that capture the idea that the spectrum of our cognition spreads from fast-reacting reflexive decisions to slow-responding reflective decisions. There is, however, a clear separation between us and System Zero – the digitally driven system of decision-making relies on our data. With the latest wave of generative AI, our machines have learned to converse. The first wave of System Zero primarily communicated with our reflexive self, but this next wave will be able to interact with our more reflective self. For our human society, that gives us a choice: do we really wish to be like those six men in that Harrow clinic, trusting that this systemic intervention is safe? The Theralizumab trial was a failure of process and understanding for which six men sacrificed their health. With social media and the next wave of generative AI, we are dosing ourselves with System Zero and testing it against our societal health, but the nature of social health is not easily quantified. That makes it hard to measure the consequences of the phase-one trials for System Zero.

9.

A Design for a Brain

Alan Turing's most famous academic paper on intelligence describes the imitation game, where the idea is to distinguish between a machine and a human. In the game, there are two players. The first player is always human, the second can be either a human or a computer. The machine wins the game if it can fool the first player into believing it is human. This is the game we call the 'Turing Test'.

Inspired by Turing's paper, the Loebner Prize was awarded every year to the machine that did the best job at fooling humans. The story of this prize is told in Brian Christian's *The Most Human Human*, and nowadays we have machines that can pass this test, but more interesting for me is a less-known aspect of the paper: the section where Turing describes how the game's rules may account for telepathy:

> I assume that the reader is familiar with the idea of extrasensory perception, and the meaning of the four items of it, viz., telepathy, clairvoyance, precognition and psychokinesis. These disturbing phenomena seem to deny all our usual scientific ideas. How we should like to discredit them! Unfortunately the statistical evidence, at least for telepathy, is overwhelming.[1]

I don't know by what mechanism Turing assumed that telepathy could occur, but here's one that might work. Imagine if we each had a high-frequency radio transmitter and receiver in our heads: we could then evolve the capability of Wi-Fi. To any humans who didn't have such capability, this would appear like telepathy. Wi-Fi humans would have a tremendous advantage: they would have a much lower embodiment factor, they would no longer be locked in. They would be able to coordinate instantaneously. If this ever happened, then the humans who had evolved this capability would rapidly dominate society.

It didn't happen. The statistical evidence Turing mentions comes from badly designed experiments, from a failure to conduct rigorous statistical trials. Turing was fooled by the damned lies of statistics. We don't have telepathy, but we do have an innate ability to decrypt one another's reactions through non-verbal cues. The error in the experiments Turing refers to was coming from a failure to consider our ability to 'read each other' without using verbal communication.

Our verbal communication uses a sound transmitter we have in our mouth and neck and a pair of receivers we have on the sides of our head. Wi-Fi's radio waves travel 1 million times faster than our voice's sound waves. Our high embodiment factor constrains our ability to coordinate our actions across groups of humans, but we have evolved creative approaches to overcoming these constraints. Our nervous system initially evolved to control our motion, our fight-or-flight responses, but it has adapted to show emotion and communicate ideas through the constrained channels we are provided with. It does this so well that Alan Turing was deceived into believing in telepathy. The Wi-Fi human doesn't exist,[2] but we can read each other's minds if we understand and accommodate individual motivations. We can second-guess each other's behaviour by imagining what we would do in each other's place. We have our eyes, which are receivers for the very high-frequency radio waves we call light. We have a simple visual transmitter: we can smile, we can frown, we can smirk, we can wink. Our face contains over forty muscles to control expression. Some of these communications are voluntary, but when we laugh or cry they can be involuntary. Human collaboration relies on trust and understanding. The telepathy Turing was observing is the manifestation of subtle social cues that operate closer to our reflexes than to our reflections. They relate to our social intuitions. Through these intuitions we can develop our feel for each other. Just as Don Lopez had a feel for his plane, just as Donald MacKay described our feel for a visual scene and just as Kevin O'Regan described our feel for a house or a car, we have a feel for one another.

Powered flight is just over a century old, and by the 1940s Bob Gilruth had characterized the feel of an aircraft, but conversation is over a thousand centuries old and we haven't yet characterized the feel of our fellow human being. We call a collaborative unit a team and teamwork is our route to coordinated action. Like Eisenhower on D-Day or Chris Kraft at NASA's Mission Control, teams can have captains. But a good captain knows her team's capabilities; she knows where and how support will be needed. A good captain has a deep understanding of who her team members are. A good captain empowers her team to deliver and allows them to get on with their roles unmolested. She brings her team into a state of information coherence. When the team understands its shared goals, it can deploy naturally to its strengths. In these circumstances the division of labour is emergent and adaptable. When we manage to work together in this way, we achieve a whole that is greater than the sum of its parts. This is true across our society, and we can see it across our evolutionary history. We have collaborated with our fellow humans for hundreds of thousands of years, and as animals for millions of years. Human collaboration has led to highly evolved forms of communication that were subtle enough to fool Turing into believing in telepathy.

Norbert Wiener developed his ideas for *Cybernetics* while he was working as a mathematics professor at the Massachusetts Institute of Technology. Like Donald MacKay, during the Second World War Wiener was asked to address the challenge of gun targeting with radar. Wiener was so inspired by the importance of feedback to automatic control systems that he also came to believe that feedback is fundamental to intelligence, but feedback is just one form of a wider phenomenon of systems interacting with their environment. In feedback systems, output feeds directly into the input. In the earliest nervous systems, outputs were actions; they affected the input senses through the changes those actions delivered in perception of the world around. The earliest animals had sensori-motor neurons connecting their senses directly to their primitive muscles: sense directly led to action and these animals were inte-grated into their world in the same manner that Watt's governor is integrated with the engine.

This early reflexive intelligence was not locked in. It was fast-reacting and reflection-free. In it the sensing was a result of changes in the environment or changes that resulted from the animal acting on its environment. The two were intertwined: perception and action were tightly coupled. Contrast this with the origins of the digital computer. The grinding tasks of the electro-mechanical bombes exhaustively exploring possible settings of the Enigma machine or the repetitive comparison task of the bombes' elec-tronic cousin Colossus. These are slow-reacting processes. The information was prepared and presented to the machine; the machine then worked through many computations before it gave its answer.

Directly connected sensorimotor systems are at one end of the spectrum of our intelligence. They are fast, reflexive systems, but there are cascades of reflexive systems between our fastest-reacting systems and the reflective intelligence Bauby describes in the butter-fly. The reading of a fellow human's thoughts in the manner that fooled Turing forms just one part of what we call our intuitions. These are a set of instincts that fuse our senses with our previous experiences. Their nature and origin are difficult to describe – we use terms like 'gut instinct' to capture them. But when we are inter-acting with our fellow humans, those instincts emerge at the moment of the conversation. They affect our responses and feed our own emotional state, triggering empathy, joy or anger. Those intuitions form our feel for our fellow humans. Each of us differs in our capability to fly a plane, many of us could never develop the feel Amelia Earhart had for her aircraft, and we also differ in our feel for our fellow humans. How quickly we can adapt and respond to this feel relates to our social intelligence.

By many measures, Turing should be regarded as one of the

greatest Allied minds of the Second World War. Alongside his great mind, Turing was also a great athlete, a marathon runner. In 1946 he came tenth in the UK National Championships, and his time of 2 hours, 46 minutes, 3 seconds would have placed him fifteenth at the 1948 Olympics, ten minutes behind the winner.[3] But just because he was extremely talented in some areas, it doesn't mean he was talented in all areas. If we listed the areas of Turing's extraordinary capabilities, we probably wouldn't include social intelligence among them.

After the war, Turing continued working on electronic computers at the UK's National Physical Laboratory, known as NPL, in south-west London. Turing's running talent meant he came to the attention of J. F. 'Peter' Harding, secretary of a local athletic club:

> We heard him rather than saw him. He made a terrible grunting noise when he was running, but before we could say anything to him, he was past us like a shot out of a gun. A couple of nights later, we kept up with him long enough for me to ask him who he ran for. When he said nobody, we invited him to join Walton. He did and immediately became our best runner.[4]

By this time, Turing was hoping to realize his vision of the universal computer in electronic form. At NPL he was designing a programmable digital computer. Harding goes on to comment on Turing's appearance and social integration:

> Looking back, he was the typical absent-minded professor. He looked different to the rest of the lads; he was rather untidily dressed, good quality clothes mind, but no creases in them; he used a tie to hold his trousers up; if he wore a necktie, it was never knotted properly; and he had hair that just stuck up at the back. He was very popular with the boys, but he wasn't one of them. He was a strange character, a very reserved sort, but he mixed in with everyone quite well: he was even a member of our committee.

Turing had clearly worked out how to integrate with his fellow runners, but like many academics he was seen as different.

> We had no idea what he did, and what a great man he was. We didn't realize it until all the Enigma business came out. We didn't even know where he worked until he asked us if Walton would have a match with the NPL. It was the first time I'd been in the grounds.

Turing must have had a natural talent to be running at such a high level. But he must have also been dedicated to his training. Like any skill, to excel at the very top level a combination of talent and hard work is required.

> I asked him one day why he punished himself so much in training. He told me 'I have such a stressful job that the only way I can get it out of my mind is by running hard; it's the only way I can get some release.'

Some of Turing's stress was arising from the gap between his intellectual promise and his ability to deliver on his vision for the NPL. Turing was designing the Automatic Computing Engine, or ACE for short. Unfortunately, he was struggling to move from designing to building. His design tended to evolve. Turing was no longer under the time pressure of the shifting global conflict of the Second World War, and he allowed his imagination to roam.

The boss of the NPL was the mathematician Sir Charles Galton Darwin, grandson of the naturalist. Sir Charles received a letter from a pathologist called W. Ross Ashby and shared it with Turing, who replied in excitement:

> Sir Charles Darwin has shown me your letter, and I am most interested to find that there is someone working along these lines. In working on the ACE I am more interested in the possibility of producing models of the action of the brain than in the practical applications to computing. I am most anxious to read your paper.

The year was 1946. Turing was now communicating with a like-minded genius. The NPL was supposed to be working on practical applications of the computer, but Ashby had written to Sir Charles about brains. Ashby was a pathologist, medically trained, who had become interested in adaptation in the nervous system. He had spent his spare time teaching himself advanced mathematics and working on the brain. The theories he shared with Sir Charles were based around adaptation in animals. Ashby was interested in homeostasis. This is the process by which a lifeform reacts to changes in its environment to keep conditions in its body right for sustaining life. Just as Watt's governor tries to keep the speed of the engine stable by feeding back to the engine's regulator, animals have to adapt to their environment to keep their biological systems working. Animals strive to stay alive. Ashby described his thinking in a 1952 book called *Design for a Brain*. The examples he gives come from homeostatic systems in our bodies:

> As first example may be quoted the mechanisms which tend to maintain within limits the concentration of glucose in the blood.

He is referring to the mechanisms which keep our cells supplied with the fuel they need to survive, the job the metabolism needs to do to enable the cell's persistence. Since the era when the eukaryotic cells emerged over a billion years ago, glucose has been their main source of energy. The cell converts glucose and oxygen to ATP, the fuel of the cell. Our multicellular bodies have evolved to provide glucose to our cells in the right quantity to sustain them:

> The concentration should not fall below about 0.06 per cent or the tissues will be starved of their chief source of energy; and the concentration should not rise above about 0.18 per cent or other undesirable effects will occur.[5]

These other undesirable effects include a narrowing of the blood vessels, coma and death. When blood glucose drops too much adrenaline is released into the blood, causing the liver to produce glucose and appetite to increase. If the level goes too high, insulin is produced and the glucose is absorbed as glycogen or excreted in urine.

Ashby goes on to list other mechanisms where maintaining adaptation is critical to our survival, including our body temperature, the ways our pupils adjust to allow the right amount of light on to the retina of our eyes, how our skin darkens in the presence of sunshine, the volume of blood we have in our bodies, and the production of saliva to digest food. When Ashby wrote to Sir Charles, he was developing his 'design for a brain'. It was based on homeostasis.[6] Ashby's suggestion was that our nervous system also operates according to the ideas of homeostasis.

Turing's misunderstandings around extrasensory perception were to do with a mode of communication in which he didn't excel: direct conversation. There is a joke that goes 'What's the difference between an introverted and an extroverted mathematician?' The answer is that an introverted mathematician looks at her shoes when she's talking to you, whereas an extroverted mathematician looks at yours. When we look at each other's faces, various reflexive parts of the brain light up. We cannot help processing the emotional reactions of those we are speaking to. Just like some people struggle to do mathematics, others struggle to process the social feedback the face contains. Their response is to look away, to stare at the ceiling, to look at your shoes or theirs. From descriptions, it seems that Turing may have been one of those people, but when communicating by letter he could be just as effusive as any other person. In 1946 he wasn't aware of Ashby's ideas around homeostasis and his reply to Ashby focuses on his own plans for brain research:

The ACE is in fact, analogous to the 'universal machine' described in my paper on computable numbers. This theoretical possibility is attainable in practice, in all reasonable cases, at worst at the expense of operating slightly slower than a machine specially designed for the purpose in question.

Turing's universal computer is the machine that can compute anything that is computable. Realizing this machine is the objective of his work at NPL. In his reply to Ashby he is contrasting his digital universal computer with the special-purpose machine, which is what we would call an analogue computer.

> Thus, although the brain may in fact operate by changing its neuron circuits by the growth of axons and dendrites, we could nevertheless make a model, within the ACE, in which this possibility was allowed for, but in which the actual construction of the ACE did not alter, but only the remembered data, describing the mode of behaviour applicable at any time. I feel that you would be well advised to take advantage of this principle, and do your experiments on the ACE, instead of building a special machine. I should be very glad to help you over this.[7]

Today our modern approaches to machine learning use exactly the approach Turing describes: we simulate neural networks on digital computers. But while Turing could imagine that solution, it was beyond the technology of his era to deliver it. What he was experiencing was an affordance gap. There was a separation between what he'd like to do and what he could do in 1946. He believed he would be able to build a machine that could simulate the brain, but his imagination had got ahead of his reality. While the things he dreamed of would become possible in time, they could not be realized in his time. This affordance gap is also what Bauby experiences. His imagination can take him to places where he cannot physically go; it allows him to imagine feeling things he can no longer feel and to act in ways he can no longer act. The Nobel Prize-winning Austrian zoologist Konrad Lorenz once wrote, 'Thinking is acting in an imagined space.' This is a beautiful description of what Bauby's butterfly is doing, and it also captures the feeling Winnie-the-Pooh describes when talking about the difference between how the idea feels inside you versus when it is deployed in practice. Contrast this to the unthinking intelligence represented by Watt's fly-ball governor. Both Turing and Bauby were thinking, but their imagined spaces did not match the real world they inhabited.

When it comes to artificial intelligence, many of the ideas we see in popular culture share one characteristic. They depict AI as a form of automation that is capable of adapting to who we are. So, when people imagine an AI utopia, they imagine the personal assistant that accommodates our personal needs, a silicon manservant akin to Wooster's Jeeves in the P. G. Wodehouse novels. Conversely, the AI dystopia consists of robots that understand us and dominate us. James Cameron's Terminator robot has the capability to converse with humans, interpret human actions and even act as a human while exhibiting superhuman strength and invulnerability. In practice, the first wave of algorithmic decision-making – as characterized in *Math Destruction* and *Surveillance Capitalism* – does have an understanding of us, but not one we would characterize as human. It manipulates us through its vast information capacity. It exploits unprecedented consumption of our personal data which gives it a different perspective on us. I call this phenomenon 'the great AI fallacy'. The fallacy is that we think we have created a form of algorithmic intelligence that understands us in the way we understand each other. A technology that gives us the same feel for it as we have for our fellow human.

When Wilbur Wright took the first flight, he and his brother had invented the mechanism by which he controlled their aircraft. On that first flight, he had to develop a feel for that control. He had to bridge an affordance gap because, before he flew, no one had ever steered a powered vehicle in three-dimensional space remove. Flying requires new controls for the roll, yaw and pitch of the aircraft.

When Wilbur landed after his first flight, he would have shared his experience with his brother, Orville. He would have shared how it felt to use the stick to control the altitude of the aircraft, to be the first to develop a feel for the interface between a human and a powered flying machine. How we share such information between ourselves is a question we now need to answer.

This is a challenge, because the gap between our expectations of

AI and the reality of what we're producing is closing. With generative AI and large-language models such as ChatGPT we can now build machine-learning systems that provide plausible communication between human and machine using the languages humans have developed for themselves, rather than for their machines. This new frontier presents a promising route to ending the AI fallacy and bringing the technology we're producing into line with people's expectations.

Turing was only thirty-four when he was running for Walton Athletic Club, quite young to have developed many eccentricities, but to the club's secretary, Peter Harding, Turing already appeared different from the other club members. When I read about Alan Turing or Norbert Wiener I marvel at their capabilities, but I'm also relieved to read of their weaknesses. When Wiener or Turing were working, thinking, feverishly scribbling, pausing, reflecting, crossing out and correcting, they were engaged in deep reflection about the way the world might be. This is the trance William Blake captured when representing Newton in his famous print. Both Turing and Wiener were mathematicians, and this means they didn't only reflect on their ideas, they could convert their thinking into rigorous mathematics and test it within that context. The aim of Bertrand Russell's *Principia* was to show that mathematics is a principled and consistent framework of ideas: this makes it ideal for the brain to test its more improvisational thinking against. Wiener and Turing were using their pencil and paper to test and refine their intuitions and reflections on how mathematics might work. By refining their intuitions in this way, they could integrate their understanding in their fast-reacting, reflexive thinking. They could create mathematical experiences that were equivalent to Pooh's experience of hooshing. This is how they developed their feel for mathematics. They could then compare this against the world around them and test their ideas for how mathematics manifests in the real world. Wiener and Turing would have, at times, felt at one with their mathematics, just as Lopez felt at one with his plane.

In 1992, Kevin O'Regan captured this idea with a notion of 'outside memory'.[8] Outside memory is where the brain – rather than storing memories internally – relies on the consistency of the world around it for its information storage. Konrad Lorenz also described this in *Behind the Mirror*. Lorenz had made a life's study of animal behaviour, founding the field of ethology, and in one section he describes the behaviour of an orang-utan faced with the problem of taking a banana hanging out of reach:

> . . . the orang-utan looked helplessly up and down from the box standing in one corner to the banana hanging in the other; then, in a fit of bad temper, it tried to turn its back on the problem . . .

From Lorenz's description, the animal is looking around at the items – including a movable box – and assimilating them in its analysis of the problem:

> . . . it turned its mind to the task again. Then suddenly its eyes moved from the box to the point on the floor immediately underneath the banana, from the floor upwards to the banana itself, then down again and from that spot back to the box. In a flash, as one can clearly see from the orang's expressive face, it realizes the answer.[9]

Konrad Lorenz's description of the ape addressing the challenge is interspersed with the ape's glances at the environment. As it is working its way through the answer it is continually grasping at the problem with its eyes. To have an understanding of a visual scene in front of you, you don't need to remember where everything is. As long as your eye can rapidly saccade to extract a salient part of the scene, the brain can imagine it has access to the whole image. A similar effect would occur when Wiener and Turing worked on their mathematical ideas. When mathematicians iterate between mathematics and reflection, they test their intuitions in the framework of mathematics, just like the orang-utan tested its ideas in the visual scene in front of it. Wiener's and Turing's scribblings are performing the equivalent of the eye's saccade to verify an aspect of the mathematics they need to formulate their theories. Blake's *Newton* captures the scientist in the same moment as Lorenz's description captures the ape. The geometric drawings and the dividers give Newton an outside memory which he manipulates to solve his geometric puzzle.

Some of us are good at mathematics, and some of us are good at reading and understanding our fellow humans. The feel of a human conversation can work in a similar way to the manner in which Wiener and Turing developed their feel for mathematics. When communicating with a colleague I can test my ideas against their knowledge. I can explore limitations in my thinking by exploring their understanding in such a way that it highlights problems in my theory or plans. This is the process of conversation, but instead of testing our understanding directly against the real world or against the world of mathematics we test our understanding against each other. The beauty of Shannon's theory of information is that it separates information from knowledge – that's what allows us to compare information transfer that's occurring in evolution to that between humans to that between machines. But by separating information from knowledge we lose the meaning of those conversations. When it comes to our culture and our conversations the nature of this knowledge goes to the very heart of the atomic human. These conversations build on our empathy, our culture and our wider social context.

One of Norbert Wiener's social difficulties had been in his relationship with Bertrand Russell. Both men realized early on that they weren't going to be close friends, but Russell was mature enough to guide Wiener away from philosophy and towards mathematical colleagues, among whom Wiener found his true intellectual home. Wiener wasn't the only child prodigy to interact with Russell. In 1938 Russell took sabbatical leave at the University of Chicago, where he taught seminars and an undergraduate course on 'Problems of Philosophy'. There he met a fifteen-year-old runaway from Detroit, Walter Pitts. Pitts became party to some of the most important philosophical discussions of the decade. He witnessed Bertrand Russell debating with Rudolf

Carnap on logic, language and the logical foundation of knowledge. The lectures must have made an impression, because when they finished, rather than travelling home, Pitts hung around the campus in Chicago. He didn't register as a student; he took on menial jobs and studied with different members of faculty he encountered. Back in Europe, Turing, Flowers and Good were pitting their minds against the cryptographic codes of Germany. In Chicago, Pitts educated himself in mathematical logic, with a dose of Greek and Latin on the side. Three years later a psychologist from Yale arrived. His name was Warren McCulloch. The young Pitts's itinerant lifestyle meant he had nowhere to live, so McCulloch welcomed him into his family home to stay with his wife and three kids. In the evenings they worked together on their shared passions: logic and the brain.

McCulloch and Pitts were inspired by Alan Turing's universal machine. They wondered how the brain could implement universal computation. The debates between Russell and Carnap caused them to view mathematical logic as a plausible route. The year was 1941, the Battle of the Atlantic had not yet finished, and Rommel was just arriving in North Africa. But McCulloch and Pitts were reflecting on how a network of firing neurons could represent thoughts. In 1943, just as Rommel was leaving North Africa in defeat, they described how such a neural network could represent logic:

> The 'all-or-none' law of nervous activity is sufficient to ensure that the activity of any neuron may be represented as a proposition.[10]

Their theory was that the neuron was the basic logical unit of the nervous system, and that *composition* of these neurons led to the process of thought. They viewed the neuron as a universal gate for intelligence. They called the composition of these neurons *nervous nets*. Their paper is the first example of the type of model Turing was referring to when he wrote to Ashby. The ideas of McCulloch and Pitts are the foundation of the modern methods that have revolutionized artificial intelligence. They are the first examples of models that we call *neural networks*.

The approach McCulloch and Pitts came up with was called *threshold logic*. In their model, the neuron firing represents TRUE. Their threshold function is a mathematical function that operates as a switch. Just like a logic gate, it has an input, but instead of being a discrete TRUE/FALSE input, the input can be a continuous number. If that input is above a particular value, called the threshold, the output of the function is 1. If that input is below the threshold, the output is 0. The 1 represents TRUE and the 0 represents FALSE.

The simplest threshold function has one input. Let's imagine there's a simple McCulloch–Pitts sensorimotor neuron in your head. You use it to decide whether to go swimming in an outdoor lake. We assume you have a receptor cell that senses the temperature. The McCulloch–Pitts model for the neuron says the sensory neuron will fire if the temperature goes above a particular threshold, let's say 25°C. If the neuron fires, then you go swimming. From Braitenberg and O'Regan's perspective, this is a sensorimotor response: the neuron detects that it's warm and the action is to go swimming; from McCulloch and Pitts's perspective, this sensorimotor approach is a proposition: 'When the temperature is above 25°C, I go swimming.' Because the neuron fires that proposition is TRUE.

This is a model, so it's oversimplifying things. Imagine if it really were like that, if each time the temperature went over 25°C we all jumped into the nearest body of water. That doesn't seem a very sensible model, but the McCulloch–Pitts neuron takes this into account. There may be other factors, like whether you have your swimming costume, whether you're feeling confident about your body image, which other people are around. So, you end up with a proposition more of the form 'IF the temperature is high AND I have my swimming trunks AND I'm feeling comfortable about my body image AND I'm with friendly people THEN I go swimming.' This proposition could be implemented with AND gates. But it can also be implemented in the McCulloch–Pitts neuron.

The assumption that McCulloch and Pitts made was that these different factors – your sense of your body image, the nature of the people you're with, and so on – could each be encoded in a separate neuron that could feed into the swimming-decision neuron. These neurons could be composed, so the balancing of different behaviours could be encoded in how they are all wired together. When we compose logical gates to form Wittgenstein's truth tables, we feed the output of one gate into the input of the next. But in the McCulloch–Pitts nervous nets there is an additional step. It is called *weighting*. Before feeding the next neuron, the output of the previous neuron is weighted by a number. If the number is small, the influence of that neuron on the next is small. If it is large, there is a large influence.

The weights are the set of parameters. We've already encountered parameters in the Albion fly-ball – they were the side measures like the length of the linkages. We can think of each weight as dictating how much *influence* each input has on the final decision. In the nervous-net model of thought, the weight reflects something about your behaviour, about your personality. How important is your body comfort compared to your desire to swim? How concerned are you about what other people think? How warm does it have to be before you want to jump in? Maybe on a warm day, you don't care what other people think. In this way we can represent personality with parameters. In the logical-threshold model of the neuron, you add up the weights associated with each of these factors, and you compare them with the threshold. If they are above the threshold, you go swimming. The weights in the model represent *synapses* in real neurons. The synapse is a small gap between the axon of one neuron and the body of the next. It regulates how much charge flows between any two neurons. In the McCulloch–Pitts model, the weight is analogous to the conductivity of the gap.

The McCulloch and Pitts approach was highly influential. It

showed how the nervous system could operate according to logical rules. The two men became famous across the academic community. In the introduction to *Cybernetics*, despite his earlier scepticism of Russell's logical ideas, Wiener explicitly mentions Walter Pitts and the importance of mathematical logic.

Pitts and McCulloch had drawn the same conclusion about how to model the brain that Shannon had derived when modelling communication networks. Logic was the key. At the same time their paper was being published, across the Atlantic in England, Tommy Flowers was planning the Colossus as a logic-based machine for breaking the German High Command codes.

Ashby's ideas for the brain were based on the importance of homeostasis – the idea that lifeforms must be adaptable to respond to changes in their environment. Maintaining homeostasis is why bacteria cluster together in colonies when they come under threat. Our machines can also struggle with their environments. In the history of automation, we don't normally cast them into the world to do direct battle with the gremlins of uncertainty. We coddle them in protected spaces. We place them in factories, or we build railways for them, or we pave our landscape with roads. When we build a machine to do work for us, we shelter it from external challenges that would damage it. In this way uncertainty for the machine is reduced, and its job is made easier. But all this is only possible because of the care humans give to the machine. When we build an engine, its shelter, fuel and repairs are all provided by the human hands of engineers, mechanics and technicians.

The needs of the machine defined the century following Watt's refinement of the steam engine. The rise of the factory system, the division of labour and the mechanization of society required humans to maintain our creations. For the machine to operate, the human had to adapt to its needs. Albion Mill, which Boulton and Watt fitted with steam engines, was completed in 1786. Soon it was grinding enough wheat to provide flour for the whole of the City of London. The new factory created a furious reaction among local mill owners and was burnt to the ground in 1791. Despite this setback, the nineteenth century still became the century of steam. In 1863, Samuel Butler, then working as a sheep farmer in New Zealand, wrote to the editor of *The Press* about the rise of the machine:

> . . . but it appears to us that we are ourselves creating our own successors; we are daily adding to the beauty and delicacy of their physical organization; we are daily giving them greater power and supplying by all sorts of ingenious contrivances that self-regulating, self-acting power which will be to them what intellect has been to the human race.

Butler was writing just three and a half years after Charles Darwin published *On the Origin of Species* – the book that laid out the principles of natural selection. Butler's emphasis on the self-regulating machine stems from the developments made in control systems, the autopilots that stem from Watt's use of the fly-ball. Nineteenth-century New Zealand sheep farming might be as far away from the industrial landscape as you could imagine, but machines were bringing the world closer together. By 1858 the first transatlantic telegraph cable had been laid, reducing communication times between North America and Europe from ten days to minutes. The printing press had allowed ideas to be widely distributed as books; the telegraph now allowed information to be shared across the Atlantic almost instantaneously. New Zealand was still isolated from this network, but Butler's letter lays down a vision of machines evolving and improving. It reflects the extent to which machines already held society in slavery:

> Day by day, however, the machines are gaining ground upon us; day by day we are becoming more subservient to them; more men are daily bound down as slaves to tend them, more men are daily devoting the energies of their whole lives to the development of mechanical life. The upshot is simply a question of time, but that

the time will come when the machines will hold the real supremacy over the world and its inhabitants is what no person of a truly philosophic mind can for a moment question.[11]

As Butler suggests, the machine cannot design itself,[12] it cannot maintain itself: it requires the control engineers, the mechanical designers, the thermodynamicists, the mechanics and the technicians to service it. Other parts of Butler's letter prefigure our modern fears around intelligent machinery. One hundred years before Jack Good suggested the notion of the ultraintelligent machine and the intelligence singularity, Butler imagined a future of sentient machines.

Analogue computers worked by analogy: they consisted of a set of components that when interconnected were analogous to a related system of interest, like the flow of water in the MONIAC representing the flow of money in the economy. The analogies work because the underlying phenomena can both be modelled with similar mathematics. The physical world can perform computation, so we borrow the computations of the flow of water to explain the economy. It's taking the idea of a proxy-truth one step further.

Digital computers started the other way around. The mathematics came first. The digital computer uses electronics to represent logic, but the next step is to use their digital logic to represent the world, to create Turing's universal machine. This is the idea Turing was sharing with Ashby: let's build a general machine first and then simulate the brain on the general machine. Turing knew this could work, because he'd already seen Colossus. That machine had fifteen different logic gates, each of which could be connected in different configurations to form truth tables. Programming of the machine was performed by Wrens, women from the UK's Royal Navy. Before each run, they were issued with instructions for how to connect the gates. This is the foundation of how all modern computers operate. The different processing units are connected together, although today we store the nature of the connections electronically and call those instructions *software*. The beauty of software is that the computer is electronically reconfigurable. Instead of having Royal Navy Wrens manually reconfigure the machine, the machine's wiring can be reconfigured while it's running. This makes the truth tables the machine can implement arbitrarily complex. And that is how these machines realized Alan Turing's dream of a universal computer. It is also how modern machines such as your Kindle, Xbox and mobile phone work.

Eighty years after Samuel Butler wrote his warnings about the rise of the machine, Turing, Good, Ashby, Wiener, MacKay and others were imagining what type of ingenious contrivances would be needed to give the machine self-regulating, self-governing powers. In the UK the heart of these efforts focused on a discussion group called the Ratio Club. The club took its name from *machina ratiocinatrix*, the rational machine. The choice was a nod to a term used by Norbert Wiener in his introduction to *Cybernetics*. Wiener was inspired by the early conceptualization of the calculating machine Leibniz had developed in the seventeenth century, the *calculus ratiocinator*.

Each meeting of the Ratio Club involved a talk or a set of introductions on a topic from a member or a guest. Donald MacKay's first talk to the club was on 'Why is the visual world stable?' There's a simple experiment to show what MacKay was talking about. With your left eye closed, press very gently on the top of your right eyelid. The image from your right eye will move. But if you move your eye normally in its socket, or if you walk around the room or turn your head, the image appears stable. What's going on? MacKay was highlighting the fact that the eye's image is controlled through feedback.

The first guest speaker for the group came in 1949, Warren McCulloch, one of the originators of the logical model of the neuron. Donald MacKay's reminiscences on analogue and digital computers in the introduction to *Behind the Eye* reflect the discussions that would have been held by the Ratio Club, resonating with the influence of Turing and Good, but by 1948 Turing's work on the ACE was stagnating. Sir Charles Darwin was getting frustrated with Turing's lack of interest in the practical applications of computing, and Max Newman, who had headed up the Lorenz cipher team at Bletchley Park, managed to tempt Turing to move away from the NPL to the University of Manchester. Later, Turing persuaded Jack Good to join him. In Manchester, Turing would finally have access to a universal machine. He was put in charge of software for the new Manchester Mark I.

The Ratio Club combined neurologists and psychiatrists with scientists who had been working on giving machines the ability to perceive other objects (through radar) and scientists who had been working on giving the machine the ability to perform intellectual tasks such as the automatic decryption of enemy messages. Books and papers were presented to the club before publication. Ross Ashby presented an overview of *Design for a Brain*. Ashby had two starting points for his theories, first that the nervous system should be adaptive – like in homeostasis – and second that the nervous system was mechanistic, i.e., that its behaviour originated from the underlying principles of physics, such as Newton's laws. His conclusions from these simple starting points were surprisingly broad: he suggested that random connections would be required between the units of computation (presumably the neurons) and second, that there would have to be *threshold functions* inside the brain like the McCulloch–Pitts neurons. Ashby deduced that randomly interconnected switching systems should be at the heart of intelligence. He also developed a theory of the 'natural selection' of behaviour patterns – the idea that certain behaviours would have persisted through evolution. Just like Braitenberg's vehicles' behaviour was encoded in their wiring.

The scientists and engineers in the Ratio Club were experienced in both analogue and digital computation, and there was a mathematical tool that could provide a bridge between these two groups. Claude Shannon's information theory could be equally applied to analogue and digital machines. The same theory of information that has allowed us to compare the high embodiment factor of human intelligence with the computer and the slow-progressing nature of evolution also allows us to view analogue and digital computers as different sides of the same information-processing coin.

If the Ratio Club could bridge between the analogue-sensing capabilities of radar and the digital-decision capabilities of the digital computer, then perhaps they would arrive at a form of animal intelligence. It seemed Claude Shannon held the key to this unification, and he was invited to present to them in September 1950. The group prepared carefully with a series of introductory sessions on information theory and probability.

As the meetings progressed, Donald MacKay's talks shifted away from the specifics of the eye to the nature of thought itself. In March 1952 he spoke on 'Meaning in information theory'. The flexibility of Shannon's information theory comes from its indifference to the meaning of the information. We introduced information theory and the embodiment factor to describe the locked-in nature of human intelligence. We were able to characterize the different capabilities of humans and computers in terms of the rate at which they can process information. We were able to do this because Shannon's clever trick was to disassociate information from the facts to which it pertains. To understand the flow of information in telephone conversations, Shannon didn't want to know what those telephone calls were about. He wasn't interested in whether people in Manhattan were discussing the weather with a relative in Cincinnati or the results of a Yankees baseball game.

Donald MacKay worked on a form of information theory that reinserted the context, that brought knowledge back into the equations. If information theory does provide a route to unifying the analogue and digital domains, if it can bridge between Wiener and Laplace's demon, then at some point the context, the events which the information is representing, needs to be reintroduced. Otherwise the information can't be interpreted and acted upon. MacKay's thinking seems to have been moving quickly. By the end of 1952 he was presenting on 'Perils of self-awareness in machines'. An echo of Samuel Butler's warnings in his letter from ninety years earlier and a prefiguration of Good's warnings on ultraintelligence.

In the book based on his Gifford Lectures, *Behind the Eye*, MacKay shared his conclusion that the brain is neither a digital computer nor an analogue computer. He was motivated by the mysterious nature of the brain to focus on it for research. It feels natural that MacKay focused on the visual system, because his own interests had originally been stimulated by working on analogue machines and radar. He thought that bridging the analogue and digital interpretations was a key challenge. Alan Turing was, perhaps, the individual who was best equipped to bridge the gap between the digital and analogue approaches to intelligence. In February 1952 he spoke on 'The chemical origin of biological form', and his talk focused on chemical reactions, the diffusion of chemicals and how the combination can induce the patterning that eventually gives rise to the shape, or form, of animals. At the core of this work was the use of chemistry as an analogue computer. Bacteria present in our ancient planet communicated with one another through chemical signalling. Our T-cells also communicate through chemical signalling as they battle pathogens. Chemical transfer of information is at the heart of the genetic code: it is the route through which lifeforms pass information to the next generations. In early life, all decision-making was written in the language of chemical signalling, but chemical communication is also integrated in all our cells.

Unfortunately, six weeks after he presented his most recent ideas to the club, Turing was prosecuted for 'gross indecency'. Turing was homosexual, and homosexuality was illegal in 1950s Britain. Turing had been burgled by a young man he'd befriended and had allowed to stay at his Manchester home. When he reported the incident to the police the tables of prosecution were turned, and he found himself defending his own actions. Turing felt cornered into pleading guilty. He was given hormone treatment as a condition of probation.

Turing had a lifelong fascination for chemistry. His school reports have stories of finding him 'boiling heaven knows what witches' brew by the aid of two guttering candles'. And he continued to design and conduct his own experiments. In 1954 he was using solutions of potassium cyanide to gold-plate spoons in the back room of his house in Manchester. He used electrodes that were attached to the light socket in the ceiling and triggered the plating process with the room's light switch. Cyanide is a poison. It interferes with the fundamental mechanisms our eukaryotic cells use for producing energy. It blocks the production of our cell's fuel, ATP. It is one of the most poisonous compounds on the planet and kills within minutes.

On the morning of 8 June 1954, Turing was found dead by his housekeeper. The official verdict was suicide, but the reality seems unclear. There was no fume cupboard in Turing's back room and unless he kept the upper floor well ventilated his bedroom could have filled with poisonous cyanide fumes. There is a shadow of Laplacian uncertainty over the manner of Turing's death, uncertainty caused by our ignorance of the precise events. Regardless, the outcome was the same: Turing's death deprived the field of intelligence of one of its greatest minds, of an individual who could have balanced the worlds of analogue and digital in driving forward our understanding of the brain. Turing may have misunderstood the nature of social communication and been misled into believing that humans were equipped with abilities we don't have, but he was also one of the most creative minds of the twentieth century. He was the man who in 1946 imagined the possibilities for simulating neural networks on digital computers. He had the vision to see what the future of artificial intelligence would look like, but he did not live in a time when we had the capabilities to realize that vision. In the end, he was not given the time to see so many of his other ideas come to fruition. At the age of only forty-one the man who imagined the universal machine was gone. Wi-Fi humans don't exist, but the machines Turing imagined do exist. And the greatest AI challenge we face today is the fact that those machines can communicate without our constraints and so it is possible they could come to dominate society.

10.

Gaslighting

La Roche-Guyon, just north-west of Paris, was Rommel's head-quarters in France and the field marshal was convalescing there. In July 1944 he had been seriously injured when his staff car was strafed by an Allied aircraft. His wife, Lucie, his 16-year-old son, Manfred, and his military aide Hermann Aldinger were all with him when, in October, two generals arrived from Berlin. They came to meet privately with the field marshal. Over half a century later, in an interview with the journalist Andrew Nagorski, the 70-year-old Manfred recalled what happened next:

> He came upstairs to talk to my mother, but my mother was so terrified that he could not continue to talk to her. And then he talked to Aldinger and me. He said, 'I will be dead in 20 minutes.'[1]

Three days after Erwin Rommel was injured, an attempt was made on Hitler's life. A bomb placed in a conference room detonated, but Hitler was shielded by a table and survived. Erwin explained the situation to Aldinger, Manfred and Lucie:

> They told me that I have been participating in the plot and they also referred to witnesses. They told me that the Führer gave me the chance to die from poison. If I take the poison, the usual measures against the family will not be taken, the investigations against my staff will not be continued. This is the best arrangement I can get and so I've decided to go with this.

Rommel had been presented with a terrible choice: either die by

his own hand or face the destruction of his reputation and the per-
secution of his staff and family in a 'People's Court'. Rommel was
sharing his decision with those he was closest to. If he took the
poison, then once he had died, the local hospital in Rouen would
announce that his death was due to a stroke. Rommel's involvement in the plot would be covered up, he would be given a state
funeral and celebrated as a hero. His military aide wanted to resist,
but Rommel refused to place his soldiers in danger and agreed to
take cyanide to protect his friends and family.

Erwin Planck was born two years after Erwin Rommel. Like
Rommel he fought in the First World War, but whereas Rommel
stayed in the German army, Planck moved into politics. He became
a deputy minister in the German government. He was a liberal pol-
itician who resigned in 1933 when Hitler was appointed Chancellor.
Planck then became a member of the German resistance. He
escaped the purges that preceded the war but was arrested three
days after the 1944 assassination attempt on Hitler. Erwin Planck
wasn't given the choice Erwin Rommel received. He was made to
face the People's Court. After its verdict, a death sentence, Erwin
Planck's father wrote to Adolf Hitler:

> My Leader,
> I am deeply shocked by the news that my son Erwin has been sentenced to
> death by the People's Court.
>   The recognition of my achievements in the service of our fatherland,
> which you repeatedly expressed in an honourable way, my Leader, entitles
> me to trust that you will listen to the request of an 87-year-old man.
> As a thank you from the German people for my life's work, which has
> become an imperishable intellectual property of Germany, I ask for the life
> of my son.
>
> Max Planck[2]

Erwin's father, the physicist Max Planck, was pleading for the life
of his son, just as Manfred Rommel would no doubt have pleaded

for the life of his father, had he been given the chance to do so. The plea fell on deaf ears, and Erwin Planck was executed by hanging in January 1945.

We can try to imagine how Max, Manfred, Lucie and Hermann would have felt when faced with these terrible circumstances. We can also imagine the great pressures Erwin Rommel and Erwin Planck would have been under when they made the decisions that led to their deaths. In different ways, each of them was acting out of duty – the duty they had to their society and to their families.

Six months after his father died, Manfred Rommel deserted from the German air force and surrendered to the French. Later, as Mayor of Stuttgart, he became a symbol of reconciliation and an advocate of European unity. Two years after the war ended, Max Planck, devastated by the loss of his son, died at a relative's house in Göttingen.

Albert Einstein's *annus mirabilis* consisted of four papers that revolutionized physics. One of his papers suggested the idea of a universal speed limit, the idea that the speed of light in a vacuum was the fastest that information could travel. In a separate paper he built on the speed limit to propose an equivalence between mass and energy. His famous equation $E = mc^2$ predicts how much power we can obtain from nuclear fission and fusion.

Erwin Planck's father, Max, had won the 1918 Nobel Prize for Physics for the discovery of *energy quanta*. This was a radical idea that energy, rather than being in continuous supply, is available only in very small packets, like a continuous stream of letters arriving in the mail. Einstein's third paper of 1905 used Max Planck's notion of energy quanta to explain the *photoelectric effect*. This is the phenomenon used by solar panels that translates energy from the sun into electricity. It hadn't been explainable with classical physics.

So, alongside the theories of his close friend Albert Einstein, Planck's new idea overturned the classical view of physics that had formed since the Enlightenment. It turned out that the physics we are used to, the physics we experience in Newton's laws of motion, is an abstraction, a proxy-truth. It is the same form of abstraction

Daniel Bernoulli used in *Hydrodynamica*, what some call the *effective physics*; just as Pooh's law of hooshing is not universal, neither are Newton's laws. When we observe the universe at a very small scale, or when energies or forces are very high, Newton's laws break down.

With his papers from the *annus mirabilis*, Einstein overturned the classical physics of motion and electromagnetism. Planck's and Einstein's work launched the new field of *quantum mechanics*. When energies are low enough, the lumpy nature of Planck's quanta radically changes physics. To express the uncertainty associated with the very small, Laplace's gremlin talks about 'the curve of a molecule of air'. When we look inside those molecules and how they bond to each other at this extremely small scale, Laplace's gremlin becomes embedded in the physics: quantum mechanics has intrinsic uncertainty. Even Einstein struggled with the implications of this idea; he anthroxed the laws of physics in a letter to the German physicist Max Born:

> Quantum mechanics is very impressive. But an inner voice tells me that it is not yet the real thing. The theory produces a good deal but hardly brings us closer to the secret of the Old One. I am at all events convinced that He does not play dice.[3]

The 'Old One' for Einstein is the keeper of the secret for the Theory of Everything. Einstein found it impossible to imagine there was uncertainty at the heart of that secret. But regardless of his dice-playing, it seems the Old One keeps his cards close to his chest, because despite a century passing since Einstein shared these thoughts, we still have not been able to unify the theories of quantum mechanics with those of gravity. We don't have the Theory of Everything, we only have the effective physics.

The death of Max Planck's son wasn't the only tragedy in his life. His first wife, Marie, died in 1909 of tuberculosis. Their eldest son, Karl, was killed in action at Verdun during the First World War. Their twin daughters Emma and Grete both died giving birth. Max Planck's collected papers and autobiographical thoughts were published after his death and among them was the following quote:

> A new scientific truth does not triumph by convincing its opponents and making them see the light, but rather because its opponents eventually die, and a new generation grows up that is familiar with it.[4]

Planck's quote is sometimes summarized more pithily as 'science progresses one funeral at a time', and his familiarity with death and scientific revolution means that his words should be taken seriously. But in the case of the search for intelligence, I think the reverse occurred.

Alan Turing was killed by cyanide in 1954. He was the creative thinker who inspired a generation of mathematicians with the notion of the universal computer. Tommy Flowers put many of Turing's ideas into practice, allowing the Allies to unlock the intentions of the Nazi war machine. Turing straddled the divide between theory and practice. He was committed to a deeper understanding of intelligence. Together with Norbert Wiener, he underpinned the blossoming field of intelligence with intellectual rigour and creative vigour. The death of Alan Turing was a tragedy for the progress of our understanding of this domain.

Two years after Turing's death, a young assistant professor of mathematics at Dartmouth University organized a 'Summer Project'. His idea was to bring together a group to focus on this burgeoning field. He teamed up with other leading researchers, among them Claude Shannon, to propose a programme of research:

> The study is to proceed on the basis of the conjecture that every aspect of learning or any other feature of intelligence can in principle be so precisely described that a machine can be made to simulate it.[5]

John McCarthy's idea was not new, it was merely a restatement of Alan Turing's ideas from 1946 and Norbert Wiener's *Cybernetics* dream, but the name they used in their programme was new. They called it artificial intelligence.

In his proposal, McCarthy mentioned twelve names of attendees who might spend the summer at Dartmouth. Among them were Donald MacKay and Ross Ashby, although in the end neither of them came. At the eventual meeting, only one cyberneticist was present, Warren McCulloch. Another was conspicuous by his absence: Norbert Wiener.

Wiener had had a catastrophic falling-out with McCulloch. He was told that his daughter, Barbara, had been seduced while she was visiting Chicago as an assistant in McCulloch's lab.[6] This was untrue. It was a fabrication designed to drive a wedge between Wiener and McCulloch. But it fed Wiener's paranoia and a perception he had of intellectual slights from the cybernetics community and his own university. McCulloch and Wiener lost trust in each other.

I doubt that I'm unique in what it means for me to lose trust in someone. When it happens, I need to revisit my instinctive reactions towards that person. What I'd taken for granted now needs to be worked through. I get the same feeling when I fall off my bicycle. When I'm riding my bike well, like Don Lopez in his plane, I feel at one with it. I can descend mountain roads at 70 kilometres an hour. I can feel the bicycle responding to my thoughts, I brake and lean into the corner, two square inches of rubber between me and the tarmac, the bicycle responds to my weight, it emerges and rights itself carrying my speed around the bend. But one patch of damp road, a misjudged corner, an unexpected puncture, and I fall. The friction between my rubber tyres and the road breaks. When I fall hard, smacking my hip or my head on the ground, I lose trust in my relationship with the bicycle. I become less instinctive, more reflective, and ride less naturally. The same applies to my relationships with people. Just as the friction between the road and the tyre can break, trust between two people can break. When this happens it's as if the ground shifts from under the relationship. The closer the relationship originally was, the more disconcerting it is. For me, when this happens I no longer feel I can rely on my cognitive reflexes; I revisit assumptions, I engage the slow-reacting self rather than the fast-reacting instinctive self that is the foundation of a close relationship.

In Wiener and McCulloch's case, the ruse worked. Wiener's family relationships had been threatened, and this undermined his friendship with McCulloch. The wedge between the two stuck. Wiener broke off relations with both McCulloch and Pitts. He never spoke to them again and he never explained why. Wiener was now seen as authoritarian and controlling by the wider cybernetics community. The Dartmouth Summer Project proposal runs to nearly 5,000 words, but not one of those words is 'cybernetics'. In an act of academic propaganda, Wiener and cybernetics had been airbrushed out, and the field's new name, 'artificial intelligence', stuck. This Soviet-style rewriting of history was not limited to McCarthy's AI proposal. McCulloch, who was such a positive influence on Wiener's life and ideas, is not mentioned at all in Wiener's autobiography.

The beauty of the cybernetics movement had been the diversity of opinions and approaches of its adherents. Even the collapse of relations between McCulloch and Wiener is symptomatic of this diversity. They had different personalities and different approaches, and tensions between them were exacerbated by the false rumour Wiener was made to believe. But diversity of opinion and approach is indicative of science at its most creative and vigorous. When the truth is uncertain and the path ahead is unclear, scientific progress benefits from a mix of ideas and a range of philosophies. In its early days, the cybernetics movement was pluralist, but, as some of its ideas became more successful, parts of the community doubled down on these approaches and the diversity reduced.

Academic culture prizes progress for humanity's knowledge, but the thirst for scientific credit from individual scientists is also the enemy of the cohesive group. From the ashes of the cybernetics revolution, the phoenix of artificial intelligence emerged. The attendees of the Dartmouth Meeting are often viewed as the founding fathers of the field of AI. But at the launch of the meeting

Turing was already dead, and Wiener was persona non grata. The Dartmouth Meeting did succeed in wresting the agenda away from the cyberneticists, but it was a field born in an Oedipal act of killing its intellectual father and it was cursed to spend its energies on a reductionist fantasy.

Despite the loss of diversity in ideas and the absence of thinkers such as Turing, the new field had a significant advantage: the digital computer. While Turing had imagined what he might do with Ashby's ideas and a digital machine, McCarthy and his Dartmouth attendees could actually implement their thinking. By 1956, digital computers had moved out of university laboratories and were being used for commercial applications. Lyons had already completed its first payroll processing on the EDSAC-derived LEO. The University of Manchester's Mark I was being marketed by Ferranti, and in 1953 Manchester also built the first prototype transistor computer. IBM released a computer called the 701 based on a machine built at Princeton's Institute of Advanced Study, where Einstein worked. Across the next decades, with the invention of the integrated circuit, the digital computer would become more powerful still. However, the allure of the digital computer would provide a seemingly easy road for progress that would distract the new artificial intelligence community from the weaknesses of logic as a model for knowledge. But before this road was followed the cyberneticists would have one last hurrah.

Frank Rosenblatt was a young and big-thinking academic at Cornell University's Aeronautical Laboratory in Buffalo, New York. Rosenblatt had an ambitious idea for a demonstration of a connectionist learning approach. Connectionism was the idea that it was those weights which were analogous to the synapses in our brain that held the key to intelligent behaviour. As Turing described in his letter to Ashby, the behaviour of neurons could be simulated. The McCulloch–Pitts model represented these connections through weights. Rosenblatt was inspired by this connectionist vision and the ideas of Ross Ashby. The year was 1957. In Britain, television sets had only just become widespread, prompted by the 1953 coronation of Queen Elizabeth II. In Buffalo, New York, Rosenblatt was proposing that a machine could recognize an image from a television camera.

He decided to build a system that could use a television camera to discriminate between two different objects, or 'percepts', and he called his machine the Perceptron. The objects Rosenblatt's Perceptron processed were to be simple – he considered shapes such as a circle and a square. The tradition of the connectionists was to build designs that were inspired by our nervous system. In Rosenblatt's system, the TV camera was equivalent to the photoreceptor cells on our retina. Rosenblatt called these cells S-points. The idea of connectionism was to wire a number of these cells together into an assembly, one equivalent to the sensory neurons. He called the assembly of sensor cells and their sensory neurons the S-system. The learning would be done by changing the strengths of connection between the units by varying weights that are analogous to the synapses in our neurons.

In our own nervous system there is a reflex arc that prevents us from falling. It senses when our foot gets caught, but the reaction depends on what we are doing. Is it the trailing foot that gets caught or is it the leading foot? The interneurons sense this context. Pulses travelling down the spine tell the interneurons where the legs are, so if the leading leg has been caught the interneurons trigger the trailing leg to swing quickly around.

In Rosenblatt's Perceptron, the interneurons play a different role. They mix the signals from the different sensory neurons. Rosenblatt was trying to reconstruct the visual system. The next part of Rosenblatt's system emulated the role of the interneurons which mix the signals from the retina. Rosenblatt didn't know how these should be wired together, so, inspired by the suggestions in Ashby's *Design for a Brain*, he wired them together randomly. He called these neurons the A-units. The 'A' stood for *association*. The idea was that these units would respond in different ways associated with different characteristics of the shape they were detecting. The assembly containing the association units was called the A-system.

The final cell assembly was needed to give the user the prediction the model was making. It contained the model's decision about whether it was seeing a circle or a square, and Rosenblatt called these units response units, or R-units, so the A-system mapped on to a final set of cells called the R-system.

Importantly, the overall system was composed as a set of layers. The S-points were wired to the A-units, which were then wired to the R-units. Each set of units was a layer of neurons processing the output of the previous layer. The first layer of neurons was the sensing layer, and this was followed by a layer that combined the inputs of the sensing cells together: the A-system. The final layer was the R-system.

Rosenblatt's model differed from that of McCulloch and Pitts in that he wasn't trying to prove that his system could implement logic. He was interested in *statistical* notions of recognition. Like Pooh's hooshing, Rosenblatt's Perceptron was going to make its decisions based on experience. Rosenblatt's proposal was the culmination of five years' work at Cornell on the idea of *statistical separability*. The theory suggested that the response neurons, the R-units, would be able to distinguish between different shapes if they could learn characteristic features of those shapes. Extracting these features would be key to the performance of the machine.

What do we mean by characteristic features? One of the previous predictions we looked at was the pressure predictions the German and Allied meteorologists made when predicting the location of weather fronts. In that case, we expected the pressure to vary as we moved across the landscape. As we head north to Sheffield from Cambridge, we expect the pressure to increase or decrease in proportion to the distance moved. We called this process interpolation. Although it might not appear so at first, Rosenblatt's Perceptron was working according to the same principle.

Pressure is one characteristic we chart on weather maps, consisting of numbers that vary smoothly, like the height of a hill. But there are other features of the landscape which are more discrete. For example, it is either raining or it is not. Or the ground is either frozen or it is not. These discrete features are more like cliffs on the landscape but, often, underlying them is a continuous quantity. Imagine that instead of pressure, our weather map is measuring humidity. As we move across the landscape, the humidity changes. But at some point, the humidity gets so high it begins raining. The same applies to temperature and frozen ground.

The Perceptron divides its feature landscape into circles and squares in a similar way to how our landscapes respond to temperature and humidity. The response units are placing a threshold on an underlying quantity we might think of as 'squareness'. The weights analyse the input image in the S-system; the interneurons bring together context from different parts of the image in the A-system. Finally the response units give an output which expresses a notion of 'squareness'. If that value crosses the threshold, the Perceptron predicts that it has seen a square.

Rosenblatt called his interneurons association units because he wanted their features to be *associated* with the type of shape the image showed. These features aren't exactly like the features on a physical landscape; they are more like the sort of features that define our personalities. If I tell you that I like William Blake's painting of Newton or Michelangelo's painting of the creation of Adam, you start to learn something about me. If I tell you my mother drives a Hummer, I'm telling you something about her. These features place us on a social landscape. The outputs of the A-units are a simpler version of this notion. The A-units try to capture features of the image – the curviness of a circle or the angular nature of the square.

Once the features of the landscape were determined, the response units formed the final judgement on the object type. Images with more curviness would be a circle; images with a more angular nature would be a square. This is the notion of statistical separability. The R-units define a decision boundary based on the features of the image.

Rosenblatt's pilot project was expected to require three engineers, a digital computer and about eighteen months. By 1958 it was complete. But the final implementation had one major innovation over the original proposal. Rosenblatt found that one A-system wasn't sufficient to extract the features – he needed two layers of interneurons to bring the context from the input image together. This meant he needed two A-system assemblies instead of one. He called these A1 and A2.

By mapping from the receptor cells to the response units through two layers of feature-extraction assemblies, Rosenblatt invented what today we call *deep learning*. Deep learning is the composition of different interneuron assemblies by feeding the outputs of one group into the inputs of another. Babbage advocated the division of labour, the separation of a job into its component parts or the breaking down of an image into its brushstrokes. These layers of interneurons in deep learning have the opposite job – they bring those parts back together and reconstruct the perception of the whole image from its parts.

The 19-year-old Norbert Wiener did not enjoy working with Bertrand Russell. Norbert's father, Leo, had wanted him to become a philosopher and steered his son towards Russell's logic. But Wiener had his doubts:

> I have a great dislike for Russell; I cannot explain it completely, but I feel a detestation for the man. As far as any sympathy with me, or with anyone else, I believe, he is an iceberg. His mind impresses one as a keen, cold, narrow logical machine, that cuts the universe into neat little packets, that measure, as it were, just three inches each way. His type of mathematical analysis he applies as a sort of Procrustean bed to the facts, and those that contain more than his system provides for, he lops short, and those that contain less, he draws out.[7]

Wiener is bemoaning Russell's tendency to force the universe on to his thinking rather than bending his thinking to the universe. He is expressing the same discomfort we see in Blake's image of Newton, the trance-like manipulation of geometric symbols while surrounded by the complexity of nature. As for Russell, he wavered between finding Wiener precocious and pretentious. But he identified Wiener as a mathematician, not a philosopher. Russell encouraged Wiener to attend lectures by G. H. Hardy, one of Cambridge's greatest mathematicians, and to read the series of papers published by Einstein in 1905, his *annus mirabilis*. The paper that caught Wiener's eye was the fourth paper Einstein wrote that year. It described the behaviour of a small particle being peppered with fast-moving molecules: 'On the motion of small particles suspended in a stationary liquid, as required by the molecular kinetic theory of heat'. The paper described by this unpromising-sounding title was to prove fundamental to Norbert Wiener's thinking. Wiener believed that what was needed was not a theory of knowledge but a *theory of ignorance*. Einstein's paper would provide the mathematical platform for his theory. But Einstein's motivation for writing the paper was an observation from eighty years earlier, by a botanist called Robert Brown.

Robert Brown had been studying sex in plants. He was peering at a particle of pollen under a microscope. The pollen was suspended on water. Inside the pollen, on the surface of the water, he saw minute swimming cylinder-shaped particles. Brown called the particles 'Molecules'. The Molecules rotated and turned as they moved around on the surface of the water.

Brown's initial thought was that these particles may have been trying to swim to fertilize the plant, like sperm swim to fertilize an egg. But he was a careful scientist and he continued to observe and experiment. First, he observed the same phenomenon across a range of flowering plants. Then he extracted pollen from dead plants: he observed Molecules with the same swimming behaviour. Confused, he tested non-living material and found 'active Molecules' in pit-coal.

It was 1827, thirteen years after Laplace's philosophical essay on probabilities. Brown had uncovered a world of active Molecules. Was Brown observing the curve of a simple molecule as imagined by Laplace's gremlin?

If you throw a tennis ball at a bus, it will bounce off. The bus may appear not to react, but Newton's laws tell us that the bus does move by an imperceptible amount. Common sense also tells us that the bus driver's reaction will be very perceptible. The imperceptible reaction of the bus is due to the relative weights of the ball and the bus. The bus weighs two hundred thousand times more than the ball.

If I took you, the bus and the ball into space and you threw the ball, then the bus would move away from you at a rate of around a millimetre every three minutes. That's still very slow, but over time the distance travelled would be perceptible. In space, the bus driver's reaction would be less perceptible because in space no one can hear you scream.

The Gullfaks C oil installation is the largest artificial object ever moved by humans. It weighs a billion kilograms. If it joined you in space and you threw another tennis ball at the oil platform, the platform would take around fourteen hours to move away from you by one millimetre. What you would be observing is equivalent to what Robert Brown was observing under his microscope. A tennis ball hitting the Gullfaks C oil platform is equivalent to a water molecule hitting Brown's 'active Molecules'. Einstein realized that the active 'Molecules' were moving because they were colliding with actual water molecules, but like the oil platform and the tennis ball, those particles are billions of times heavier than the water molecules. So how was this movement perceptible? Brown was observing under a microscope, so the Molecules and their movement were magnified and, even though the motion was very slow, one millimetre in fourteen hours, the microscope magnified it. So, these active Molecules looked like they were swimming.

This explanation took eighty years to emerge, and it had a clever bit of mathematics in it. Einstein didn't consider just one tennis ball, he considered the effect of many tennis balls, all thrown from different directions, each of them hitting the Molecule. This was Einstein's model of the liquid water. It had much in common with Daniel Bernoulli's kinetic theory of gases. What Brown saw wasn't an active Molecule but a passive particle being buffeted by billions of collisions with water molecules. Brown was observing what we now call a 'random walk' and the source of the randomness was the water itself.

The motion is called Brownian motion, and it was this paper by Einstein that caught Wiener's eye. Over his career, the paper would form the basis for Wiener's solution to Laplace's gremlin. Just as Laplace's gremlin was inspired by imagining what it meant to be very small, Wiener's approach to the gremlin emerges from a mathematical model of the very small. Today we call the mathematical model of this Brownian motion the Wiener process.

Like Donald MacKay's, Wiener's wartime activities focused on using radar to aim guns. The bombers which devastated cities in the war flew towards their target at around 300 kilometres per hour and at around 6,000 metres altitude. The job of the artillery was to shoot these bombers out of the sky. This presented major challenges. The height of the bombers meant that anti-aircraft shells fired from the ground took around fifteen seconds to reach their target. By that time, the plane would have moved a considerable distance – how would the gunners know where to aim the shells?

Like the German meteorologists predicting the weather over the Channel, the gunners faced the problem of extrapolation. But unlike the meteorologists' problem, this one can be solved using Newton's laws of motion. The gunner knows where the plane is but doesn't know where the plane will be in the future. The plane is going to move into a region where the gunner has no data. The German meteorologists didn't have the pressure data over the English Channel when they were constructing their maps, the gunners didn't have any information about where the plane would go next. But the gunners can use knowledge from physics to try and solve the problem. If we can track how fast each aircraft is moving, then we can estimate what its future position will be when we expect the shell to arrive. In fifteen seconds, the aircraft will have travelled around 1,200 metres. So, the gun should be aimed at a point 1,200 metres ahead of the aircraft.

In 1941 all this work had to be done by humans. The anti-aircraft crews had to spot the plane, obtain its altitude, track the plane's forward motion, then compute where to aim and move the barrel of the weapon and fire. This involved spotters, callers, human computers and aimers. But that wasn't the only problem. Pilots weren't stupid. When coming under fire from the ground, they took evasive action:

> There was no established procedure for evasive action. All you needed was fear, and Yossarian had plenty of that . . . he bolted for his life wildly on each mission the instant his bombs were away, hollering, '*Hard, hard, hard, hard, you bastard, hard!*' at McWatt . . .
>
> *Oh, God! Oh, God, oh, God*, Yossarian had been pleading wordlessly as he dangled from the ceiling of the nose of the ship by the top of his head, unable to move.[8]

Yossarian's words from *Catch-22* are based on Heller's own experiences as a bombardier in Italy. Planes don't fly in nice straight lines when you shoot at them, they fly in a way that makes their bombardiers scream in terror.

What practical use could Wiener's theoretical work have? When he returned to the United States at the outbreak of the First World War, like Diana Russell-Clarke at Bletchley Park, he worked as a human computer at the US Artillery's Aberdeen Proving Ground. His job was to compute the trajectories of artillery shells. Wiener had to deal with the intractabilities of Newton's equations to create artillery tables for the aiming and firing of US guns. This gave Wiener a taste for applied mathematical work, and by the outbreak of the Second World War he was keen to put his talents to use again.

The uncertainty of gunnery comes from the distance between the gun and the planes as well as the pilots' erratic responses. In the First World War, artillery focused on massive bombardments of a static enemy, but the Second World War was a much more dynamic affair. Wiener saw the problem as an example of Laplace's gremlin. The gun's crew couldn't know what was in the pilot's mind. The crew couldn't foresee where the pilot would fly next, so there was uncertainty. Instead, you could model the flight of the plane like you would a pollen particle – you could use a Wiener process. You could inject uncertainty into your model and extrapolate the path using Wiener's mathematical explanation of Brown's Molecules' motion.

Wiener built a demonstrator for using radar to aim guns at the plane. The technical details were written up in a classified report, 'Extrapolation, interpolation and smoothing of stationary time series'. The idea was to sustain a 'family of curves', each of which was a possible hypothesis of where the plane might fly next. You can think of each curve as the path a different pilot of the plane might have taken.

A single gun should be aimed at the point where most of these planes would pass. Or if the radar system controls several guns, then this group of guns could be aimed to distribute their fire across the plane's family of flight paths. Given the uncertain objective, each gun should consider a different potential future. The guns should have different strategies, but they could be coordinated by a single system, just like we have a diversity of personalities but obtain information coherence through cultural coordination. Wiener's gun-laying system suggests a diversity of aims, and information coherence can be achieved by sustaining predictions of a family of possible futures. When the future is uncertain, we obtain coverage across different outcomes by considering multiple plausible future scenarios.

As well as attending lectures by Britain's leading mathematician, G. H. Hardy, Wiener's later visit to Göttingen gave him the chance to study with David Hilbert. What Hardy was to England, Hilbert was to Germany. Norbert Wiener's education in mathematics was provided by two of the most capable mathematicians on the planet. This grounded his mathematical capabilities and introduced him to tools and techniques that were just then emerging from a golden era of German mathematics. Wiener applied these ideas to Brownian motion to develop the Wiener process and, in doing so, he founded the field of stochastic processes. 'Stochastic' is a scientific word for things that are randomly determined. The word is highly appropriate for gun targeting because it originates from the ancient Greek word 'to guess', *stokhastikos*, which itself comes from the word *stokhos*, 'to aim'. In other words, when the Greeks guessed an answer, they took aim at it. Wiener used his stochastic processes to make guesses at where he should aim the guns. But Wiener's guess was informed by extrapolation and theories of uncertainty. It was an informed guess.

The Wiener process was the first mathematical tool that gives a clear answer on 'the curve of a simple molecule of air'. Wiener's theory of ignorance is underpinned by stochastic process theory and his answer is that there is not one curve associated with a simple molecule of air but a family of curves, all of them with different probabilities. Wiener's theory of ignorance supported the idea that any of these possible futures might be right; the family of curves is known as a statistical ensemble. The statistical ensemble is a good way of thinking about many other things, like the family of narratives I could have used to relate to you the invention of the computer; I chose to focus on Colossus, but I could have written more about the ENIAC or one of the many other early digital machines. It's similar with the invention of calculus by Leibniz and Newton: there are two plausible descriptions of the past, like the two different future trajectories of the bomber. We can use the family of curves to represent uncertainty about the past as well as the future, so both forethought and afterthought benefit from Wiener's theory of ignorance. Wiener's solution to the gremlin of uncertainty was to consider all plausible curves and target the most likely outcomes.

A map of England between Cambridge and Sheffield can be drawn in two dimensions, one representing north–south, the other east–west, but a map which represents the features in Rosenblatt's Perceptron would need many more directions – the features from the image map can't be drawn on a two-dimensional map, they live on a mathematical object we call a hyperspace, one where there are more than three dimensions to move in. This means the features can be difficult to visualize, but the same set of mathematical equations can still be used to create the space.

The Perceptron makes predictions in one of these high-dimensional hyperspaces. The different layers give the neural network an understanding of what is where, and this is what enables it to identify objects. But in these spaces the regions where there are images don't fill the entire landscape; like a road, they weave through the landscape, changing direction as the values of their pixels vary. A road forms a line in a geographical landscape; but in the hyperspace that represents the images' information topography, they form objects called hyperplanes.

Perhaps the hardest part of that description to follow is the notion of a high-dimensional landscape. Thinking in high-dimensional spaces is hard because the world around us is only three-dimensional. The Perceptron worked in a 64-dimensional space, and modern neural networks work in even higher-dimensional spaces. In the nineteenth century, Charles Howard Hinton, an English mathematician, tried to develop tools to help us think in a four-dimensional space. Hinton wondered about worlds where there are four physical dimensions. He invented the *tesseract*, a four-dimensional version of the cube. Like a cube, a tesseract has equal-length edges and right angles between the edges, but whereas a cube fills three dimensions a tesseract exists in four dimensions (one that exists in a hyperspace would be called a hypercube). Hinton also tried to help his children think in three-dimensional spaces. He built a frame from bamboo and called out to his children three-dimensional coordinates describing a place on the frame and the children would have to climb to the place. His son, Sebastian Hinton, was inspired by this game to invent the climbing frame, or jungle gym as it's known in the US. Hinton also wrote fictional stories, known as scientific romances, on the theme of the fourth dimension, and he built a set of real cubes for helping us imagine the properties of these spaces.[9] He believed that by thinking beyond three-dimensional space we could form new realizations about society and advance humanity.

Charles Howard Hinton was not just free-thinking geometrically, but romantically too. He was married to the daughter of George Boole, Mary Ellen. But his father, James, was a radical philosopher who advocated polygamy. Charles Howard had a second marriage and a second family. Convicted of bigamy, Hinton left England for Japan and later the United States.

Rosenblatt built the Perceptron to take advantage of the concept of statistical separability. In the Bible, on the Day of Judgement, God separates the sheep from the goats, putting the goats on the left and the sheep on the right. The Perceptron has a rather more mundane task, but the principle remains the same. The response unit counts the features that characterize squares and circles (features such as curves or corners). Each feature has a score that represents how square-like or circle-like the feature is. If it is a squarey feature, it gets a positive score. If it is a circley feature, it gets a negative score. These scores are stored in the Perceptron's weights, and the Perceptron adds them up to get a final mark for each shape. If the total mark is negative, i.e. to the left of zero, the Perceptron decides it's a circle. If the total is positive, it decides it's a square. So the Perceptron places the circles on the left and the squares on the right. Once it's done its sums, the shapes are all associated with numbers that can be placed on a line. In Boolean terms, we associate TRUE with the positive numbers (i.e. the squares) and FALSE with the negative numbers (i.e. the circles). The Perceptron has become a square detector.

The machine is tuned by changing how it marks the features in the hyperspace map. The Perceptron is given a set of input patterns, i.e. the circles and squares, alongside their actual labels. This data is used to teach the Perceptron. Whenever an error on an example in the training set is made, the Perceptron revises its marking scheme. If the machine says circle when it should say square, the shape's features all gain a mark in the scheme. If it says square when it should say circle, the features lose a mark in the scheme. In this way, the circley features tend to get more negative marks and the squarey features more positive marks.

An early version of the Perceptron was implemented on a digital computer, in the way Alan Turing had imagined in his letter to Ross Ashby. Frank Rosenblatt used an IBM 704 to perform a press demonstration and news of the success was shared in the *New York Times* on 7 July 1958.

NEW NAVY DEVICE LEARNS BY DOING

PSYCHOLOGIST SHOWS EMBRYO OF A COMPUTER DESIGNED TO READ AND GROW WISER

WASHINGTON, July 7 (UPI) – The Navy revealed the embryo of an electronic computer today that it expects will be able to walk, talk, see, write, reproduce itself and be conscious of its existence.

The embryo – the Weather Bureau's $2,000,000 '704' computer – learned to differentiate between right and left after fifty attempts in the Navy's demonstration for newsmen.

The service said it would use this principle to build the first of its Perceptron thinking machines that will be able to read and write. It is expected to be finished in about a year at a cost of $100,000.

Dr. Frank Rosenblatt, designer of the Perceptron, conducted the demonstration. He said the machine would be the first device to think as the human brain. As do human beings, Perceptron will make mistakes at first, but will grow wiser as it gains experience, he said.

Dr. Rosenblatt, a research psychologist at the Cornell Aeronautical Laboratory, Buffalo, said Perceptrons might be fired to the planets as mechanical space explorers.

WITHOUT HUMAN CONTROLS

The Navy said the Perceptron would be the first non-living mechanism 'capable of receiving, recognizing and identifying its surroundings without any human training or control'.

The 'brain' is designed to remember images and information it has perceived itself. Ordinary computers remember only what is fed into them on punch cards or magnetic tape.

Later Perceptrons will be able to recognize people and call out their names and instantly translate speech in one language to speech or writing in another language, it was predicted.

Mr. Rosenblatt said in principle it would be possible to build brains that could reproduce themselves on an assembly line and which would be conscious of their existence.

In today's demonstration, the '704' was fed two cards, one with squares marked on the left side and the other with squares on the right side.

LEARNS BY DOING

In the first fifty trials, the machine made no distinction between them. It then started registering a 'Q' for the left squares and 'O' for the right squares.

Dr. Rosenblatt said he could explain why the machine learned only in highly technical terms. But he said the computer had undergone a 'self-induced change in the wiring diagram'. The first Perceptron will have about 1,000 electronic 'association cells' receiving electrical impulses from an eyelike scanning device with 400 photo-cells. The human brain has 10,000,000,000 responsive cells, including 100,000,000 connections with the eyes.

It's taken sixty-five years, but we are now in the era the article predicts. Today's neural network models are directly descended from the Perceptron design: they fulfil Donald MacKay's vision of a machine that is neither analogue nor digital and they are revolutionizing our relationship with machine-driven decisions.

George Boole introduced mathematicians to Boolean algebra: the manipulation of logic through the language of mathematics. Charles Howard Hinton invented the tesseract, an approach to thinking about and manipulating higher-dimensional spaces. Rosenblatt's Perceptron wedded the logical McCulloch–Pitts neuron to these high-dimensional feature spaces. This allows the Perceptron to perform statistical separation. In an analogue computer, the states of the machine correspond directly to real-world quantities such as the speed of an engine or the direction of flight of an aircraft. The Perceptron's features are those that work empirically in practice – they are proxy-truths. The features in the Perceptron aren't derived from first principles, they emerge from observation. They borrow from the computation the real world has already done on our behalf. Rosenblatt realized the weaknesses of the logical approach and in his report on the Perceptron he is critical of models of thought that are overly reliant on Boolean logic. He credits the work of Ashby with inspiring him to realize how a neural network with many random connections can provide the feature landscape he needs to perform the statistical separation.[10]

Rosenblatt's Perceptron is not a digital machine, but neither is it an analogue machine. The features in the different layers of Rosenblatt's Perceptron respond to characteristics of the real world, but they are not direct analogue representations. They are a form of abstraction. They don't directly represent the physics of the real world, but they respond to it. These are the features of a neural model of the world.

Max Planck suggested that a new scientific truth triumphs because its opponents die. In his life he had seen the emergence of Einstein's theory of general relativity and quantum mechanics. In *The Structure of Scientific Revolutions*[11] the physicist, historian and philosopher of science Thomas Kuhn describes these changing tides of practice in scientific communities as *paradigm shifts*. Einstein's theory of relativity shifted physics away from the Newtonian paradigm. Kuhn's ideas on the sociology of science have been so influential that the word 'paradigm' has also entered more common usage to represent how a group communally thinks about a particular problem. Kuhn's interest was the natural sciences, and one of the most recent examples when he was writing was the quantum mechanics revolution triggered by Max Planck. In his work, Kuhn explicitly links the notion of the paradigm with books. He remarks how scientific orthodoxy is recorded in textbooks, but he notes that the emergence of textbooks was a nineteenth-century phenomenon. He goes on to mention that before the nineteenth century the classic texts of science fulfilled the same function, listing texts on chemistry, geology and electricity. Unsurprisingly, among the books he lists is Newton's *Principia*. Kuhn speculates as to why these books were so relevant and suggests that they have two aspects in how they define a paradigm:

> They were able to do so because they shared two essential characteristics. Their achievement was sufficiently unprecedented to attract an enduring group of adherents away from competing modes of scientific activity. Simultaneously, it was sufficiently open-ended to leave all sorts of problems for the redefined group of practitioners to resolve. Achievements that share these two characteristics I shall henceforth refer to as 'paradigms', a term that relates closely to 'normal science'.[12]

This definition resonates with our speculations on culture and human intelligence. The books operate as a way of recording our shared understanding but, stepping back a moment from Kuhn's definition, we can perhaps see a broader phenomenon emerging around how we convene those thoughts in the first place.

One of the most famous paradigm shifts is known as the Copernican Revolution. This is the moment at which we moved from believing in an Earth-centric view of the universe to a heliocentric view. For 1,500 years the prevailing European view of the universe had the Earth as unmoving with the planets, the Sun and stars moving around us. This is known as a geocentric model. Nicolaus Copernicus was a Polish astronomer who provided simpler explanations for planetary movement by assuming that the Earth moves around the Sun. The heliocentric view of the universe represented a paradigm shift.

Nick Chater is a professor of behavioural science at the University of Warwick. He explores the extent to which our brains use the external environment in *The Mind is Flat*. Chater's focus is on the improvisational nature of the mind. He suggests that our brains have a sponge-like capacity to absorb structure that is external to us, whether this is in the form of physical structures, like buildings, or conceptual structures such as maps or mathematics. The idea is that the brain operates in tandem with these structures to give us our 'sense of whole'. The books that form the foundation of a paradigm are an example of these types of structures.

Kevin O'Regan's idea of outside memory also suggests that our brain borrows from the consistency of the world around us. It doesn't have the capability to store everything, but it can access the aspects of the world it needs on demand. O'Regan's observations were inspired by his understanding of our visual system, but Kuhn's ideas on paradigms show how textbooks can provide a cultural context for our scientific thinking. The intellectual saccades that Wiener or Turing indulged in when verifying a mathematical derivation eventually led to a collection of written works that form a summary of our current best understanding. Those books give us our paradigms for modern mathematical sciences.

Konrad Lorenz was awarded the Nobel Prize for Physiology in 1973. His book *Behind the Mirror* uses an analogy for understanding our psychology: viewing 'behind the mirror'. Lorenz sees thought as actions in an imagined space, but according to Chater that imagined space also relies on the consistency of the world around us:

> Mervyn Peake's Gormenghast Castle is one of the strangest settings for a work of fiction – vast, misshapen, ancient, crumbling and architecturally idiosyncratic. Peake's visual imagination was wonderful – he was an artist and illustrator as much as a writer – and his sharp and striking descriptions create a sense of a world of solidity, richness and detail. As you read his novels *Titus Groan* and *Gormenghast*, Gormenghast Castle begins to inhabit your imagination.[13]

The challenge is that our imagination operates in tandem with the world around it and relies on that world to provide the consistency it needs. Without that structure our imagination can depart from reality, leaving us with only the illusion of consistency. Chater points out that Gormenghast, the imagined castle, is impossible to realize in practice. The imagined castle is inconsistent in its rendering. Later, he reflects on how, when it comes to our own opinions about the world, our brains experience the same challenge, highlighting that our intuitions about physics, psychology, morality and meaning are no more coherent than Peake's Gormenghast Castle. Instead, we rely on the world around us to provide structure for us. The world is integrated with our minds. Our reflective systems are embodied, but our reflexive systems are not. Our reflex arcs are integrated with their environment, but our reflective thoughts are not.

This suggests that our brain is an improvising organ that feeds on the external world for structure and interpolates the details. The behaviour of the simplest of Braitenberg's vehicles was a consequence of the interaction between the vehicle and its environment. Similarly, the complexity of our behaviour is a consequence of the interaction between our mind and our cognitive environment. On the one hand, that environment can be made up of the world around us or the scientific paradigms Kuhn describes, but in a broader sense that environment is our living human culture. Chater's point is that our minds can work only when engaged with an internal mirroring of the outside world. Konrad Lorenz makes a similar point in *Behind the Mirror*. Narcissus became obsessed with his own image in the pond. Similarly, our intelligence is obsessed with a reflection of the real world. Just as Narcissus' image would have disappeared when he stepped back from the pond, if you remove the external world from us, the apparent richness of our minds also disappears.

The importance of this illusion is captured by Konrad Lorenz's description of the orang-utan securing the dangling banana. Lorenz sees this as analogous to what we call thought; referring to the orang-utan, he says: 'it performs imagined acts in an imaginary space with models of spatial objects represented in its central

nervous system'.[14] He suggests that thinking is 'tentative explora-
tory actions of this kind taking place in a neural "model" of outer
reality'.[15]

This is the counterfactual operation of our slow-reacting self
operating in an orang-utan. In *The Mind is Flat*, Chater is making the
additional point that our central nervous system is inextricably
interlinked with the external world around us. The realization of
these spatial objects in our neural model is dependent on access to
the outside memory. Lorenz's idea about what thinking represents
is also consistent with O'Regan's sensorimotor approach. Our feel
for people and objects is based on our potential to interact with
them. Our thoughts end up being tied back to our reality.

The ideas and artefacts around us provide the context for our
brains to operate from, but the nature of those cultural artefacts has
undergone a significant change. Kuhn was writing when there had
been a shift from paradigm-defining works like *Principia* to a collection of educational textbooks that captured current established
thinking. He views these artefacts which define the paradigm as the
inspiration for progress through an aspect of 'normal science' he
describes as puzzle-solving. He even refers to the dictionary definitions for puzzles:

> Dictionary illustrations are 'jigsaw puzzle' and 'crossword puzzle',
> and it is the characteristics that these share with the problems of
> normal science that we now need to isolate.

With the advent of the digital computer there is a new way to
record, share and store information. Fast digital computers supplement and sometimes supplant the textbook as a means of recording
our scientific understanding. The digital computer became a new
participant in this intellectual landscape. Like a book or mathematics, it is a form of knowledge representation that is external to us,
something for our brains to test themselves against, something that
generates new puzzles for us to try to solve. So not only did the
digital computer change the paradigm, it became a new way to

express paradigms. The first victim of the new paradigm shift was the Perceptron.

When Turing was imagining how he might work with Ashby's model of the brain, he suggested that the brain could be simulated on the computer. He wasn't just imagining the mathematics, he was envisaging a world where our best understanding of the brain could be implemented on the machine in the manner of Laplace's demon. This would then allow Turing to perform counterfactual simulations on the machine. The digital computer gives us this capability, and in doing so it gives us a new way of representing our best understanding of science. The advantage of a universal digital computer is that it could simulate anything. Rosenblatt's embryo brain was implemented on the most powerful computer of its time, the IBM 704. But all it could do was identify left and right. Rosenblatt's later Perceptron did more, identifying circles and squares, but it required specialized hardware alongside the 704. But despite Rosenblatt's significant breakthrough and far-seeing ideas, the digital computer also made it very easy to implement logic by programming it into the machine directly. As a result, this approach seemed far more promising than learning from examples in the manner of the Perceptron.

When Turing was feverishly working away on his mathematics, his intermittent reflections would have been assimilating his manual derivations. The beauty of our intellect is in its ability to interact with such a wide range of different external phenomena. For Turing it was his mathematics, for Amelia Earhart her plane, for Mervyn Peake the Titus Groan novels, for Michelangelo and William Blake their visions of the creation of Adam. In different ways, the mathematics, the aircraft, the novels and the paintings were mirrored inside these individuals' nervous systems.

But our cultural context is not only determined by technology, art, music and literature. We also have duties to those who are closest to us – our children, our partners, our parents, our friends and wider society. When I read Max Planck's letter to Adolf Hitler, I see the words of a man at the end of his time offering all his paradigm-shifting achievements in exchange for the life of his only surviving son. When we hear Manfred Rommel's words describing the last time he saw his father alive – how Erwin concedes his own life for his family's – we are reminded that while scientific paradigms may shift, the duties to those closest to us remain.

McCarthy's Summer Project can be seen as a marker of the paradigm shift in the study of intelligence. Turing's death and Wiener's exclusion are a part of that shift, but despite the many achievements of McCarthy and his collaborators the approaches they followed turned out to be a dead end. The allure of the digital computer distracted them from the weaknesses of logic as a model for knowledge. William Blake's print of Newton shows him obsessed with his geometric drawings when surrounded by the wonders of the deep. In that image, Blake is capturing the essence of the reductive failure, what Kahneman calls theory-induced blindness and I refer to as the model-blinkers. The scientific paradigm provides a framework for the brain to work with, but it also restricts the breadth of our exploration by triggering us to focus too much on puzzle-solving.

Our visual system gives us the illusion of a vivid image in front of us because the eyes saccade across the world, but Donald MacKay was inspired by echolocation to think of the eye as more like a grasping hand. What is true of our visual system is also true of our intellect. So the mirroring of the world inside our minds is perhaps better thought of as an echo than a reflection. It operates in tandem with the world around it, but it needs to be actively engaged. Like sonar and radar systems, its pitch needs to be tuned to focus on the relevant aspects of the problem, and it will only reveal the nature of the world in the directions that we chose to project it. When William Blake produced his colour print of Newton, he was commenting on the movement of scientific rationalism that followed Newton's *Principia*. He was implying that Enlightenment science had become subject to model-blinkers in the form of reductionism. Another resonant phrasing for this challenge is 'if you have a hammer, everything looks like a nail.' The AI pioneers had a hammer in the form of logic and the digital computer, and with their model-blinkers on everything now looked like a nail.

Our brains absorb cultural artefacts as a form of truth. Russell and Whitehead's *Principia* and Hawking's Theory of Everything lay claim to being more fundamental truths. But it is rare that mathematics and physical theory can capture the full sophistication and nuance of the world around us. Model-blinkers come when we focus on solving the puzzle rather than questioning the validity of the model. Our intelligence is interwoven with our physical, cultural and intellectual environment, but the breadth and complexity of that environment alongside our limited bandwidth means that in any complex situation it can be difficult for any individual to assimilate all the different perspectives we need to account for. As a result, a simple idea can take hold at the expense of the more nuanced situation.

After Dartmouth, logic became the theory behind the AI hammer, and the digital computer was the tool that enabled that hammer to be built. The nascent AI community went around hitting every nail it could find. Fortunately, the real world includes many problems and, even though these machines couldn't emulate our intelligence, there were still many interesting nails to hit. The digital computer has been highly successful. Spreadsheets, databases, playing chess, word processing, gaming, filing, social networking. It has come to utterly dominate our world. Knowing how to spell, playing chess, storing information – all these aspects can be sliced away from the atomic human and given to the machine. This has enabled us to build increasingly complex programs by converting problems to puzzles the machine can solve. The scale of these puzzles has become so large they have escaped our understanding. They are too big for us to assimilate, so big that even Zuckerberg didn't understand Facebook's systems and how they were manipulated in the run-up to the 2016 US elections.

In the 1938 play *Gas Light*, an overbearing husband, Jack Manningham, attempts to convince his wife, Bella, that she is going insane. Jack's plan is revealed when Bella is interviewed by Mr Rough, a police detective. Mrs Manningham tells Rough that her husband has been giving her things to look after and then, when he asks for them back, she finds they've gone. But unknown to Bella, it is Jack who has been moving these objects in an effort to alter her perception of the reality around her. This form of manipulation has become known as gaslighting.

Statistical surveillance is the process of understanding a problem through rigorous collection of data about the phenomenon. For example, the RECOVERY trial that led to the discovery of the dexamethasone treatment for Covid-19 patients. State surveillance is when a country gathers data on its own citizens to identify behaviour that undermines its security. In June 1949, George Orwell's *Nineteen Eighty-Four* was published. It envisages a dystopian society that manipulates its citizens through surveillance and censorship. A one-party state called Oceania is controlled through a cult of personality around the IngSoc party's leader, who is known only as Big Brother:

> The two aims of the Party are to conquer the whole surface of the earth and to extinguish once and for all the possibility of independent thought.[16]

In the book, the protagonist, Winston Smith, falls in love with a co-worker, Julia. They plan to betray the Party together. They know they are likely to be tortured. *Nineteen Eighty-Four* introduced new words to our language. A thoughtcrime was an idea that even if not acted on would be considered criminal. Doublethink is the ability to sustain two conflicting ideas and believe both to be true.

Knowledge is power, and in the modern world knowledge comes from data. That data is acquired through *digital* surveillance. Our internet society is based on the ability of large internet corporations to accumulate vast quantities of data, and this renders us vulnerable to manipulation in the way Bella Manningham was manipulated by her husband. In the past, the mass acquisition of personal details at population scale would have required a massive administrative apparatus, one that was well organized and resourced. To keep tabs on the habits of a population would have required a large full-time staff and a significant portion of the citizenry to be active in detailing important aspects of our everyday lives. But this doesn't mean it was impossible.

After the Allied victory in the Second World War, the German state was split into two, an East German state dominated by the Soviets and a West German state supported by the other Allies. East Germany became a one-party state known as the German Democratic Republic, and its first constitution was promulgated in October 1949. Orwell intended his book to be read as a dystopian warning of the dangers of centralized power, but you might think that the GDR used it as a 'rough guide to totalitarianism'. Four months after the constitution was published, the GDR's security service was founded. The Stasi was to be 'the sword and shield of the Party'. Its role was to maintain the Party's power, and it did this by controlling information. Vera Lengsfeld was a peace activist and dissident who was arrested in Berlin in January 1988 for carrying a banner quoting Article 27 of the GDR's constitution:

Every citizen of the German Democratic Republic shall have the right to express his or her opinion freely and publicly in accordance with the principles of this Constitution. This right is not limited by any employment or employment relationship. No one may be disadvantaged if he makes use of this right.[17]

This was doublethink in action: the state was arresting its citizens for sharing its own laws. The GDR was gaslighting its own citizens. It is estimated, conservatively, that one in sixty-six East German citizens acted as an informant for the Stasi,[18] giving detailed information on the day-to-day activities of its entire population. For Vera Lengsfeld, the crime of displaying the words of the constitution led to her being jailed in Berlin's Hohenschönhausen prison.

The prison is now a memorial, and for a time Lengsfeld conducted tours of the site. The Stasi became famous for using the information it collected to conduct psychological manipulation and torture. The guards worked to isolate prisoners from the external world, to break the connection between their minds and the outside, to block the sources our intelligence uses for its echoes of our environment:

> The prisoners were never told what happened next, where they were taken. You were never led straight from A to B. It was always up and down the stairs, left and right until we lost our bearings. It wasn't until I started guiding visitors through the memorial that I realized that the building floor plan was a simple U. As a prisoner, I had the impression of being led through an intricate maze.[19]

This psychological manipulation wasn't restricted to prisoners. The protagonists in *Nineteen Eighty-Four* worked at the Ministry of Truth, where documentary evidence was manipulated to realign reality with the Party's version of the truth. The Stasi indulged in similar tactics – it used the state security apparatus to psychologically manipulate the population. There was a Stasi University in Potsdam where the agents were trained to identify the weak points of the people they persecuted, learning how to exploit their vulnerabilities as effectively as possible. Lengsfeld would later suggest that the objective was to destroy the soul, the advantage being that destruction of the soul leaves no visible scars.

The Stasi was operating to interfere with every cultural touchstone the dissidents had. Lengsfeld was eventually given a choice of jail or exile. She chose exile and left East Germany for Cambridge in England, where she spent a year studying for a master's degree. She returned to the GDR just as the Soviet Union collapsed and the Berlin Wall fell, and in the first election after German reunification she was elected to the German parliament.

It is almost as if the Stasi borrowed Jack Manningham's tactics from *Gas Light*. It used them to serve a one-party state reminiscent of Oceania in Orwell's *Nineteen Eighty-Four*. This centralizes power, meaning that a few people's decisions affect very many, undermining social diversity. The state acted to destroy the delicate balance of trust between humans and to centralize power in government agencies. As outlined by Zuboff in *Surveillance Capitalism*, today's centralization is driven by commercial concerns. This power, instead of being enacted by the Stasi's psychological vandals, is devolved to a hybrid combination of corporation and computer we've referred to as System Zero. The Stasi's exploitation of its victims was intentional; System Zero's exploitation is emergent.

In a 1953 essay, the philosopher Isaiah Berlin popularized a Greek fable originally quoted in Erasmus's *Adagia*: 'The fox knows many things, the hedgehog one big thing.' Like Newton in Blake's colour print, the AI community that emerged after McCarthy's Summer Project was a hedgehog. It became obsessed with one big idea – intelligence through logic. The cyberneticists it displaced were foxes; the breadth of ideas covered by Wiener and his collaborators included logic, probability, feedback, neural models and information theory. But by the 1950s those foxes were caged. Their ability to implement their ideas was limited by the capability of the tools at their disposal. In the meantime, the AI hedgehog went to work, improving and extending the capabilities of the digital computer.

There's a phenomenon known as scientific exceptionalism. Scientists like to think of themselves and their pursuit as special, but science is not exceptional in terms of exploration and execution. The early cyberneticists were the explorers, the foxes that knew many things, but the full power of the digital computer was realized by refinement and execution, by the hedgehog that knew one big thing. Each role is equally important. The refinements of the machine would in time deliver the tools that made possible the next wave of exploration. The hedgehog unleashes the fox. But the foxes are hunting for the next frontier so that the hedgehog can forge forward.

With rare exceptions, such as IBM's DeepBlue computer defeating the World Champion chess player in 1997, few of the original aims of AI were achieved. The classical AI community ignored the influence of Laplace's gremlin. The logical systems it employed worked only in a purely deterministic universe in which all is known and so what follows is predictable. The failure of the AI community was driven by its inability to incorporate the variation and uncertainty and doubt that permeates the real world.

All this was also known to Wiener, who was cruelly cut off from the community he founded. His interest in probability was driven by an understanding of Laplace's gremlin. He was inspired particularly by J. Willard Gibbs, an American chemist, who built on Bernoulli's and Laplace's ideas to introduce the idea of the statistical ensemble Wiener used in his stochastic processes. Wiener started to see the causal explanations that come from deterministic perspectives as something that can be seen only in terms of gradations rather than as absolutes.

This notion of a statistical ensemble extends the ideas behind Bayes's probability distributions, giving us the mathematical tools for handling Laplace's gremlin. Wiener also understood the nature of our locked-in intelligence:

> Because I had some contact with the complicated mechanism of the nervous system, I knew that the world about us is accessible only through a nervous system, and that our information concerning it is confined to what limited information the nervous system can transmit.

When he was only ten years old he had written his first essay on what he called 'The theory of ignorance', reflecting that even at that age:

> . . . I was struck by the impossibility of originating a perfectly tight theory with the aid of so loose a mechanism as the human mind. And when I studied with Bertrand Russell, I could not bring myself to believe in the existence of a closed set of postulates for all logic, leaving no room for any arbitrariness in the system defined by them.[20]

The arbitrariness of the world emerges from the gremlin of uncertainty. Even modern computers, with their vastly superior information bandwidth, cannot store all the data or perform all the computations necessary to make the predictions implied by Laplace's demon. The loose mechanism of the human mind has evolved to accommodate this arbitrariness when it deals with the world around it.

In a further irony, even George Boole, the father of mathematical logic, was aware of the limitations of logic as a model for thought. The full title of his book is *An Investigation of the Laws of Thought on which are Founded the Mathematical Theories of Logic and Probabilities*.

Just as the cursory reader of Laplace stops at his description of the mechanistic universe, so a cursory understanding of Boole stops at logic. George Boole was just as aware of Laplace's gremlin as Wiener was. The book that triggered a revolution in logic which gave us Holmes, Russell, Wittgenstein and the digital computer was published a century before the Dartmouth Meeting, and even at that time Boole understood that the nature of intelligence was based as much on what we don't know as what we know.

Those who became so obsessed with logic wore the model-blinkers so tightly they didn't even notice that one of their foundational texts is just as much about *probability* as it is about logic. Ignorance in the real world means we often need to retain multiple strategies to resolve the challenge of uncertainty by considering different possible paths in the future. However, in the end we can only make one decision, and that is often driven by the need to react; afterthought is useful for improving processes and finding gaps in our understanding, but afterthought can't save the lives of people who are dying in an ongoing pandemic or landing on the beaches of France. In the fullness of time, we may realize that our reaction was the wrong one and so our short-term response can be inconsistent with our long-term objectives. Somehow this inconsistency needs to be reconciled – in newspeak, Orwell developed the notion of doublethink to describe the inconsistency of IngSoc policies. This reflects the idea that the state was aware of its imposition of these inconsistent ideas and would knowingly impose them.

In our intelligence, these inconsistencies emerge from the time-scales over which our actions are required, so in homage to Orwell we might refer to the inconsistency that arises from ignorance as doublereact. While its origins are more innocent, its effects can still be pernicious. To resolve a double reaction, an act of doublethink may be required. Like the proverbial fox that couldn't reach the grapes and decided they must be sour, our slow-reacting self sometimes needs to retrospectively reposition its objectives to accommodate new circumstances.

The nature of our ignorance, our vulnerability to our fast-reacting self, the need to resolve the inconsistencies that emerge when decisions must be made – all these phenomena provide routes for human intelligences to be manipulated. The corporations that have delivered surveillance capitalism are controlled by individuals. The track record of behaviour for humans who have been given such unusual powers is not a good one. The individuals who control these companies are also human; so they are prone to acts of doublethink that allow them to absolve themselves of the harms their companies do.

Konrad Lorenz's *Behind the Mirror* asks the same question that struck the Pyrrhonian sceptics: can we trust our senses? Lorenz's answer is from evolutionary biology: he concludes that the fact we have persisted over many generations demonstrates that we can trust our senses, because they have informed us about the world around us, allowing our species to persist. But when the machine interlopes in this space it understands our base desires through our personal data and it uses this understanding to undermine our fast-reacting self. This means that Lorenz's evolutionary argument for trust in our senses is under threat. We did not evolve alongside System Zero.

The algorithm operates on data. It affects us in the digital world, and these effects bleed into the real world. Today, System Zero has used our data so extensively that our personal data has become interlinked with our personal security. Orwell's *Nineteen Eighty-Four* was banned in the GDR, but Vera Lengsfeld still managed to get hold of a copy. She saw inside it a tale of love and betrayal in times of dictatorship, but she didn't see any parallels between that story and her life. Vera's husband, Knud, was the son of a US-educated German cardiologist; he was her second husband and became step-father to her eldest son, Philipp, and father to two children with her, Jacob and Jonas. After reunification, the Stasi's surveillance work was investigated and the files of the dissidents they'd spied on became public. Like Winston and Julia in *Nineteen Eighty-Four*, Vera's group of activists in the GDR had been under state surveillance.

On the morning of January 2, 1992, the Stasi files were opened. I found myself in Glinkastraße, where the Gauck authority symboli-cally began opening files for selected opposition members. I was led to the table where my file folders were stacked.

The collapse of the GDR happened so suddenly that most of their extensive records remained intact. Those who'd been under surveillance were given the chance to see their files, which con-tained the names of the spies, known as IMs. The reports on Lengsfeld had come from nearly fifty different informers, but one of those informers stood out from the others.

Already on the second page I found a report from IM 'Donald', which was one of Knud's IM names, about our stay in Malcesine, my illness, the conversations with Philipp. If I hadn't suspected any-thing before, this report would have made it immediately clear to me that it could only have come from Knud. The following hours were to change my life.

I can only imagine what it felt like for Lengsfeld to have been betrayed by her husband in this way. But that is the point – I can imagine because I am human and, although our circumstances differ, I'm vulnerable in similar ways. Trust between humans depends on a shared view of the world, a shared understanding of our vulnerabilities, an understanding that means we can all imagine what it feels like to be a 16-year-old boy hearing that his father is about to end his life to protect his family, or an 87-year old man writing to a hated dictator offering his life's work and reputation to spare the life of his only surviving child, or a 39-year-old woman reading that her husband betrayed her to a ruthless system of state surveillance. This is not an ecosystem the machine can ever participate in; it does not share our vulnerabilities, so when it comes to consequential decision-making it cannot empathize, and nor should it decide. Manipulation destroyed the trust between Wiener and McCulloch. Manipulation also disrupted democratic processes in the 2016 US election. When we trust others, we become vulnerable to them; when our trust is reciprocated, those we trust become vulnerable to us. These vulnerabilities are at the heart of human intelligence. Alongside that trust goes betrayal, the betrayal of Wiener and the betrayal of Lengsfeld.

Scientific frameworks provide a coherent landscape in which we can rely on the way that everything fits together. This is Kuhn's notion of the paradigm. According to Kuhn, normal science proceeds within a particular paradigm and can be reduced to puzzle-solving. Paradigm shifts in science are rare, but great scientists can trigger them. Human endeavour isn't as fortunate as science in this regard. The world is so complex that not every circumstance can be modelled mathematically and not every question can be answered. In many circumstances, over-adherence to a paradigm can do great damage. We need to rely on those around us, particularly those closest to us. The social duties this reliance imposes on us, the need to balance our concern for family with our concern for the wider family, can lead to great sacrifices and great betrayals. Like a ship at sea, our intelligence relies on externalities to situate itself. When a ship navigates by the stars or by a known shoreline the mariner can be confident about their location. The process of navigation can be reduced to a series of puzzles in the manner of Kuhn's normal science. But when clouds shield the night sky and fog hides the shore, we need to orientate ourselves through the other vessels around us. Our feel for our fellow voyagers is underpinned by the extent to which we trust them, and our shared jeopardies underpin that trust. The machine is neither vulnerable in the same way as the atomic human nor infallible in the same way as mathematics. Yet within our seascape the descendants of the Perceptron have formed new cognitive monsters that fill the horizons.

II

Human–Analogue Machines

Geoffrey Everest Hinton was expounding a recondite matter to us. His pale grey eyes shone and twinkled and his usually pale face was flushed and animated. And he put it to us in this way – marking the points with a lean forefinger – as we sat and lazily admired his earnestness over this new paradox (as we thought it) and his fecundity.

It was August 1997, and I was sitting in the audience at the Isaac Newton Institute in Cambridge. Geoff was explaining his idea about how the brain worked. Geoff is an imaginative thinker who is dedicated to his passion: understanding the human brain. His work rapidly assimilates the latest technical concepts and that means his thinking is always evolving. He is so charismatic that you never forget the first time Geoffrey Hinton explains to you how the brain works, and you never forget the second time he explains it, because typically the second explanation you hear is quite different. Geoff's ideas change as our understanding changes.

Actually, I don't remember if Geoff's eyes are pale grey. But I do remember that a *Daily Telegraph* photographer was snapping away as Geoff raised his hands just above his eyes to manipulate the layers of an imaginary neural network while he gave us an overview of the model. I also remember how lifeless the photographs seemed when they were published. Hinton's magnetism is difficult to capture in the photographer's frame. That's why, in the first paragraph of this chapter, I've lifted H. G. Wells's description of the time traveller from *The Time Machine* to do the job instead. Those words are so appropriate for him I can only imagine they were first written to describe Geoff's great-grandfather Charles Howard Hinton, the free-thinking mathematician whose ideas about multiple dimensions had extended to multiple wives.

Charles Howard had left Britain with George Boole's daughter, but three generations later the family returned, and Geoff was born in Wimbledon in 1947. He was an undergraduate at King's College in Cambridge, where Turing studied and wrote his paper on universal computers. Turing was a mathematician, but Geoff did his undergraduate work in psychology, physiology, philosophy and physics. Like Turing, Geoff didn't limit his horizons to the narrow boundaries implied by a domain of academic study. Geoff's talk at the Newton Institute intertwined mathematical innovation alongside wit, charm and his deep interest in the brain. By this time Geoff had become a professor at the University of Toronto.

The Isaac Newton Institute for Mathematical Studies in Cambridge is an internationally leading institute where, two years earlier, the Princeton mathematician Andrew Wiles had presented his first attempt to tackle the Mount Everest of Mathematics: Fermat's Last Theorem. The machine-learning community was meeting on hallowed mathematical territory. I had moved on from the oil rigs and was at my first neural-network conference. The *Daily Telegraph* photographer was there because Geoff was coming home. He was returning to London, launching a new institute in Queen's Square, funded by the Gatsby Foundation. The institute was located two doors down from the first meeting place of the Ratio Club. Geoff Hinton was bringing the spirit of cybernetics back to the heart of London. The move would transplant some of the most exciting young minds in the connectionist movement from Toronto to the UK.

The attendees didn't just hear from Geoff, we also heard from Yann LeCun. He presented a modern version of Rosenblatt's Perceptron. It was called a convolutional neural network. Yann was using it to recognize handwritten digits for a zip-code detector that would sort mail automatically. In 1997 most presenters used felt-tip pens and overhead transparencies, but Yann stood on the stage and played a video of his neural network recognizing handwritten digits. I was entranced. Something that sounded like medieval pipe music played in the background and on the screen behind him the digits danced; on the stage, Yann moved back and forth – he seemed to be dancing too, in excitement. He also showed us a system for recognizing handwritten cheques. He was demonstrating an early version of differential programming, a technique that underpins the success of modern neural-network models.

Early work in cybernetics was dominated by ideas that emerged from technology developed in the UK and the US during the Second World War. But this new community was much more international. There was Manfred Opper, a German statistical physicist. He was using techniques from physics and chemistry to understand the theory behind neural-network learning. There was Leo Breiman, a statistician from Berkeley; Mike Jordan, a cognitive scientist from MIT; Shun'ichi Amari, a Japanese mathematician and expert on information geometry; and Vladimir Vapnik, a Russian mathematician who worked in Bell Labs, Shannon's old intellectual home.

Many of the pioneers of this movement were émigrés from theoretical physics. The connectionist approach was on the rise. By 1986, thirty years after the Dartmouth Meeting, the digital computer had become available in desktop form. Californian start-ups had commoditized the chip industry. The integrated circuit that was first used in the Apollo guidance computer was now commonplace. In 1958, for Rosenblatt to implement his Perceptron, it took an eighteen-month, six-person team effort, but by 1986 it took only a couple of days of effort to implement the same model on a desktop machine. Just like we could use computers to simulate the weather, we could now simulate the connections in the neural network. Programs could be written that interconnected feature extractors and changed weight parameters to fit the model. Programming empowered the connectionist movement. Donald MacKay noted that the brain wasn't a digital computer, but now – just as Turing had imagined – the digital computer had become fast enough to simulate a neural network in a few hundred lines of computer code.

Nineteen eighty-six was also the year *Parallel Distributed Processing* was published. It was a two-volume bible for the modern connectionist movement. The manifesto was written out in an introductory chapter which asked: 'What makes people smarter than machines?' The introduction is reminiscent of Donald MacKay's thoughts in *Behind the Eye*. It argued that the programming of digital computers was insufficient to recover human-like intelligence. The connectionists understood that intelligent behaviour was emerging from something that was neither an analogue nor a digital computer:

> In our view, people are smarter than today's computers because the brain employs a basic computational architecture that is more suited to deal with a central aspect of the natural information processing tasks that people are so good at.[1]

The connectionists were overturning the orthodoxy of what they called the classic answer expected from artificial intelligence. They were returning to the origins of their field. The two *PDP* volumes were the inspiration for many of the ideas I saw at the Isaac Newton Institute in 1997, and one chapter written by Geoff and two of his collaborators suggested an important innovation to Rosenblatt's model. It was called backpropagation.

In Rosenblatt's Perceptron, the association systems – the layers that are analogous to the interneurons which mix the context from different parts of the image together – had fixed weights. Unlike in a real brain where the synapses change, the feature representations given by Rosenblatt had used Ashby's ideas to simply set up these layers as random connections and leave them alone. Rosenblatt had used two layers, but in the convolutional neural-network model Yann LeCun presented at the Newton Institute there were six. Today we call these association layers *hidden* layers. In Yann's convolutional neural network the weights were learned at *every* layer. This meant that the feature landscapes could be adapted to suit the data. The technique for performing this adaptation was described in Geoff's backpropagation paper.

Almost all the power of a neural-network model is in its hidden layers, because these elements enable new association landscapes to form that adapt to information the neural network is receiving. Identifying the right configuration for the hidden layers is the connectionist solution to the *problem of abstraction*. Like the proxy-truths behind Winnie-the-Pooh's hooshing of Eeyore, our understanding of the world is based on the way we choose to summarize it. We construct models of how we expect different objects, such as stuffed donkeys, rivers and stones, to interact based on our previous observations. But when we wish to generalize these models to new circumstances, we need to abstract these objects. When there is an object to be hooshed, can a stuffed donkey really replace a ball? Does the donkey need to be floating on the surface of the river? What are the key features of the donkey and the ball that are required for hooshing to work? Matching across these features is key to solving the problem of abstraction, and for connectionism these hidden layers are where those abstractions are being developed. This is how we relate the representations in our mind to the reality of the world around us.

The ideas we use to contextualize our thinking vary across different cultures. The ideas shared by the European printing press stemmed from Greek philosophy, but other cultures have developed their own traditions which feed through to their modern thinking. The Chinese Daoist philosopher Zhuang Zhou was born thirty years after Socrates was executed. Like Socrates' ideas, his ideas are recorded in a book, but the style of Daoist philosophy is quite different to Western traditions; Zhuang Zhou's book contains stories and the interpretation is left to the reader. One of his most famous stories is called 'Zhuang Zhou dreams of being a butterfly':

> 昔者莊周夢為胡蝶，栩栩然胡蝶也，自喻適志與。不知周也。俄然覺，則蘧蘧然周也。不知周之夢為胡蝶與，胡蝶之夢為周與。周與胡蝶，則必有分矣。此之謂物化。

> Once, Zhuang Zhou dreamed he was a butterfly, a butterfly flitting and fluttering about, happy with himself and doing as he pleased. He didn't know that he was Zhuang Zhou. Suddenly he

woke up and there he was, solid and unmistakable Zhuang Zhou. But he didn't know if he was Zhuang Zhou who had dreamt he was a butterfly, or a butterfly dreaming that he was Zhuang Zhou. Between Zhuang Zhou and the butterfly there must be *some* distinction! This is called the Transformation of Things.[2]

The story has the same feel as Jean-Dominique Bauby's butterfly, but rather than emphasizing the difference between dreams and reality, Zhuang Zhou is emphasizing the similarity. Sometimes our dreams feel real, but a dream is distinct from reality because it lacks interaction with the real world – we don't have access to the outside memory that forges how we think and react. Zhuang Zhou dreamed he was a butterfly, just as Bauby did, but in normal circumstances the butterfly portion of ourselves is interacting with the physical world. Very often our dreams are not realizable because the real world can disappoint us or surprise us. In a dream we operate only with our internal representation of the world; when we are awake our internal representation is integrated with and influenced by the events around us. Zhuang Zhou refers to this as the transformation of things, the way in which ideas are rendered material. Our predictions and hopes from our dreams can fail in practice because the capacity of our mind to imagine is much smaller than the world's capacity to do things to us. We are lulled into believing that we are the unconstrained version of ourselves – that the butterfly and Zhuang Zhou are one; it is a phenomenon known as observer bias. Our brains spend far longer on the slower-reacting, reflective aspects of ourselves and as a result we are far more conscious of that portion of our cognition. It's therefore easy to think of ourselves as being dominated by the butterfly rather than to recognize that we are a composition of the complex interplay between the world around us and our own dreams.

Laplace's demon implies that we need three key ingredients to do prediction: data, model and compute. The connectionist movement had each of these components, but the model being used is not one that incorporates our understanding of the 'forces which animate nature'. It is also not quite like the analogue computers Donald MacKay worked on for naval gun-targeting systems. Those computers had components that directly represented quantities in the physical world, like the angle between the ship and the target, the ship's forward speed and the target's speed,[3] and the relative directions of travel. Artificial neural networks are not analogue computers in that way – they sort data into an abstract landscape, placing similar concepts in similar places on the landscape. Nor are they digital computers but, like Turing imagined in 1946, modern neural networks use digital computers to simulate these landscapes.

Instead of standing in front of a TV camera holding an image of a circle or a square – as Rosenblatt had to do – the data Yann's convolutional neural network used was stored digitally. It could be easily shared on magnetic tapes or disks. Once data became digitally shared, different models could be tested by different scientists on the same datasets. These benchmark datasets became an important standard by which different machine-learning methods could be judged. Yann himself shared one of these datasets – of 60,000 handwritten digits from over 750 high-school students and employees of the US Census Bureau.[4] The new connectionist community was constantly testing its models against these benchmarks taken from real-world challenges. This prevented it from falling into the trap of Zhuang Zhou's butterfly, confusing the model's imagined performance with its actual capabilities.

The ancient Chinese game of Go was invented over 4,000 years ago. On a board consisting of a grid nineteen squares wide and nineteen deep, each player places their pieces to try and capture territory from the other. In February 1996, a year and a half before the Newton Institute meeting took place, IBM had built a chess-playing expert system – Deep Blue, named in honour of Deep Thought – that managed to beat Garry Kasparov, the world champion in chess at the time. Deep Blue used a digital computer to exhaustively explore possible moves and decide the best move to play. The Deep Blue victory would prove to be the high-water mark for the approaches of classical AI. The game of Go would present a new frontier that was much harder to crack.

To understand why it is more difficult to build an expert Go-playing system, imagine the way the computer tries to win a game as being like exploring a maze. Envisage that the computer has its own digital butterfly. Every move in the game is equivalent to a choice of turns in the maze. To win the game the computer has to reach the centre of the maze by making the right choice of turns. The digital butterfly tries to help the computer by flying ahead in the maze, exploring all the different paths and reporting back which path leads to victory. It's another example of the exhaustive search approach used by the cryptographers at Bletchley Park. Exhaustive search is the digital computer's version of 'acting in an imagined space'. It explores every path – and that's where the problems begin. If there are thirty possible moves in the game, then there will be thirty options at each turn. That means that after two moves there will be 30×30 options, or 900 paths. After three, there will be 27,000 paths. After ten moves there are nearly 600 trillion options. In mathematics we call this an exponential progression, or if we're trying to be dramatic, we call it an exponential explosion. That term isn't just hyperbole, because this simple mathematical phenomenon also pops up in chemistry, where it provides the mathematics behind real explosions. In biology, it leads to the cytokine storm that was triggered in the Theralizumab trials. In epidemiology, it led to the rapid transmission of the Covid-19 virus, causing a pandemic. In physics, it leads to nuclear chain reactions. In chess, the digital butterfly was faced with exploring a rapidly expanding maze to find a winning position within the relatively short time allowed for a game of chess. Deep Blue won the game with faster computers and some clever tricks to help with the search. But Go has many more possible moves at each turn and the exponential explosion presented the computational equivalent of shifting from conventional to nuclear weaponry. This difference placed Go out of the reach of classical AI techniques such as exhaustive search.

John Conway's Life is a zero-player game, and we have used it as an example of how it can take a lot of computation to discover the emergent phenomena that arise from Laplace's demon. We know the rules of Go, so we understand the theory behind the game completely. The Game of Life produces loafers and gliders, just like Navier–Stokes equations produce weather fronts and storms. So, maybe, in Go we could also step back from the pure theory approach and try to extract emergent patterns. This is also how humans play these games. Like Pooh's hooshing, we generalize from the emergent phenomena we see on the board. The rules of Go give us the game's Theory of Everything and the positions of the pieces on the board give us the location of everything, but the exponential explosion in the game maze means the digital butterfly has too much to do. If instead the machine can first extract emergent phenomena, then the hope is that the digital butterfly could operate more like our counterfactual thinking and instead of exploring the whole maze it could just explore the parts of the maze that deliver the phenomena that are relevant for victory. This approach begins to look more like the human process of thought as described by Konrad Lorenz. The orang-utan abstracted the world into different objects such as bananas and boxes. It planned its next move by imagining how that world would respond to its interventions. To win at Go, the machine would have to do something similar.

In early February 2016, I was at an English country estate called Chicheley Hall with a group of machine-learning experts brought together by the UK's Royal Society. Other members of the group included my friend Zoubin Ghahramani and the CEO of the UK AI company DeepMind, Demis Hassabis. DeepMind had decided to take on this major frontier for artificial intelligence. It was planning to build a machine that could beat the eighteen-time World Champion of Go, Lee Sedol, and it planned to do it with a machine-learning technique known as *reinforcement learning*. The autopilot systems that steered Apollo 11 to the Moon had an objective: the aim was to navigate the astronauts to land in the Sea of Tranquillity. To achieve this the computer fired thrusters at the right time to keep the craft on track. In reinforcement learning, the decision about when to fire thrusters is known as the policy. It describes how the digital butterfly should move through the maze; it gives the set of actions you should take to achieve your goal. For Armstrong and Aldrin's lunar module the policy was carefully programmed in advance by engineers with a deep understanding of their spacecraft's flight dynamics. In reinforcement learning, you use machine-learning models, like neural networks, to develop your policy as you fly.

DeepMind used reinforcement learning to train a neural network called AlphaGo. It played millions of matches of Go against itself, and once it had begun to unpick the emergent phenomena in the game, it also played against expert humans. The machine limbered up by defeating the European Champion, Fan Hui, in a five–nil whitewash. The challenge match between Lee Sedol and AlphaGo would be a worldwide event, with the winner awarded a million-dollar prize. That evening at Chicheley Park we asked Demis about the prospects for AlphaGo. He was confident but also concerned: AlphaGo had a weakness – if it could be played into a position the network hadn't seen before, it would become confused and could play very poor moves.

The problem was analogous to the challenge the German meteorologists faced when trying to chart atmospheric pressure in areas where they had no measurements. The anti-aircraft gunners were up against a similar problem. Both the gunners and the meteorologists were forced to extrapolate. On medieval European maps, instead of using gremlins to denote uncertainty, unexplored regions were marked with the words 'here there be dragons' to highlight potential danger. Demis's concern was that there were unexplored regions within the landscape of the AlphaGo neural networks. If Lee Sedol managed to push AlphaGo into one of these regions, it could fall prey to the dragons. To mitigate this, Fan Hui had joined the DeepMind team and was helping to train AlphaGo. His role was to work with the machine to teach the digital butterfly to find these regions, explore them and eliminate the gremlin of uncertainty.

Six weeks later AlphaGo defeated the world champion. In a series of five games, the algorithm came out ahead of the human. The neural network hooshed its way to victory. It had found a feature landscape which allowed good decisions to be made in the game, and another major frontier for AI was overcome. But despite the tens of millions of games AlphaGo had played, despite the additional work of Fan Hui training AlphaGo, despite millions of dollars being spent on compute and hundreds of scientists working for DeepMind, Lee Sedol managed to win the fourth match of the series. Given the effort stacked against him, it was a breathtaking achievement for a human. Sedol managed to find a board position that was distinct from anything AlphaGo had seen before. Within its high-dimensional feature landscape, he had found a niche, an Achillean chink in AlphaGo's armour – he had found the dragons. In honour of this achievement, I like to refer to these regions as Sedolian voids.

Unfortunately for us humans, once Lee had found that wrinkle in its inputs, AlphaGo could now iron it out. It can simulate as many games as it likes which start at that board position and ensure that the Sedolian void is explored and filled. This is the machine's advantage. It uses its high bandwidth to rapidly absorb Lee Sedol's tactic, and that means our innovations are easily assimilated. But for me – given the imbalance in the information playing fields – Lee Sedol's achievement still remains the more impressive feat of intelligence.

Abstraction of a feature landscape is the approach that allows humans and computers to deal with the computational complexity of the exponentially exploding game maze. But it is also what causes us to make mistakes. Like Pooh Bear, whether we are mistaken or not depends on how we believe these emergent phenomena interact. Our assumptions about these interactions are not derived from an underlying Theory of Everything, they come from observation of how that theory plays out in the real world. That means we can make errors. Once the computer gains our ability to form these abstractions it also gains our ability to make similar mistakes. Those errors are the price of taking shortcuts in the maze.

*

The geologist who sat alongside me in my logging unit on the Trident XIV studied the Earth. He had an in-depth knowledge of the rocks that compose it, how those rocks combine as the formations, and how those formations combine to produce the Earth's crust. As we pulled the tools out of the well, the geologist would pore over the plots I was making. He'd verify the location of the different formation types. From the tools' measurements he could determine which part of the Earth's crust formed under that shallow ocean 350 million years ago at the equator, he could see which was part of a large desert at the centre of the Pangaean supercontinent 300 million years ago. He could identify the formations which had trapped ancient lifeforms that formed the oil. Across millions of years these lifeforms had evolved. Each generation had assimilated information from its environment through natural selection, and each generation passed this knowledge on to the next, eventually leading to the diversity of life we see today. The geologists' stories gave me a sense of the slow speed of evolution versus the rapid speed of our lives, and I found it difficult to comprehend what it means to be such a small part of such a vast ecosystem that plays out over millions of years.

Robert Brown observed his 'active Molecules' when studying the mechanism by which flowering plants exchange their DNA for reproduction. Flowers provide nectar to attract butterflies which transport the pollen to other plants, sharing knowledge with the next generation. Brown was interested in how pollen did this, and his microscope magnified the motion to make the very slow movement perceivable to the human eye. The speed of movement of Brown's pollen is around the same speed as another movement, that of the continents. Pangaea broke up 200 million years ago and since then the continents of the Americas have been moving away from Africa and Europe by a couple of centimetres each year. Across this period, mammals, flowering plants, bees and butterflies have all emerged, displacing their predecessors from the Jurassic epoch. I find these changes and information flows difficult to imagine – they occur so slowly. This is not surprising when even the growth and life of an individual plant can be hard for me to represent in my mind.

In *The Private Life of Plants*, presented by the broadcaster and naturalist Sir David Attenborough, the movement of plants was magnified to allow viewers to perceive this motion:

> Midwinter, and the countryside is so still it seems almost lifeless. But these trees and bushes and grasses around me are living organisms, just like animals, with the same sort of problems as animals face in their lives if they are to survive. They have to fight one another; they have to compete for mates; and they have to invade new territories. We are seldom aware of these dramas because plants live on a different timescale.[5]

The series made extensive use of stop-motion film techniques to magnify the movement without magnifying the plants. They condensed a week into a minute, giving a magnification factor of around 10,000. The Pangaean supercontinent formed when all the modern continents merged around 300 million years ago. If we magnified the movement between the Americas and Europe and Africa by 10,000 times and then magnified it by the same amount again, the continents would appear to be moving apart at a snail's pace. That is the speed of geological time, the pace which the process of evolution is tuned to react to.

The flower and the butterfly came into being around 100 million years ago, co-evolving in a symbiotic relationship that allowed flowering plants to dominate. In a later series, *The Kingdom of Plants*, Sir David and his team took on the challenge of visualizing the process of evolution. His production team used computer animation techniques to visualize a 'tree of life'.[6] This tree showed the genetic history of different plant species. The families of plants were represented as different branches in the tree. The width of each branch represented the success of each different type of plant. The roots of the tree extended back to over 400 million years ago. For the first 250 million years the branches had the bulbous appearance of a small succulent house plant, but suddenly an almost invisible branch in the centre blooms into a vast flower that quickly expands to shade the whole network of succulent branches below. This is the flowering plants. They literally and figuratively blossomed from an insignificant group to become the dominant form of plant life we see today. They did this because they developed a new approach to sharing information: their flowers allowed them to collaborate with and share their pollen through insects, enabling them to dominate our planet.

It's a challenge for humans to 'perceive' this vast information ecosystem that totally surrounds and sustains us, because the propagation of information across generations occurs so slowly it is beneath our perception. The animation used in the series allows us to perceive the changes and to understand that our ecology is a vast information-sharing ecosystem – it's just one that is attuned to a timescale millions of times slower than ours.

The word 'animation' has a shared origin with the word 'animal', the root being the Proto-Indo-European word for breath that gives us the Latin words for mind (*animus*) and soul (*anima*). This reflects the idea that, as humans, we associate decisions and intelligence with movement, but it is only when this movement occurs at a pace that matches the timescales we are attuned to that we interpret it in our terms. In 1944 the Austrian psychologist Fritz Heider and the German-American psychologist Marianne Simmel created an experiment. They showed three groups of subjects a short stop-animation film of a set of two-dimensional shapes: two triangles and a circle interacting around a square.[7] As visual effects go, their work isn't in the same league as *The Kingdom of Plants* – but despite the simplicity of the film – test subjects described it with a broadly consistent narrative: each of the geometric shapes were anthroxed. The subjects interpreted the shape's actions through human motivations.

In a later book, Heider suggested that when we converse with one another we are '*psychologically represented* in each of the participants' minds.'[8] For communication to work between two humans, we each have an internal model in our own heads of who we are speaking with. We make assumptions about each other: this is how we deal with the embodiment factor. We use empathy and we infer intent. When we animate an object we also trigger our ability to empathize. Heider and Simmel's film shows that under the right circumstances we can feel empathy for a triangle or a circle.

The origin myth of the Greek Olympian gods has them emerging after a great war with their predecessors, the Titans. The Titans were associated with river gods and nymphs, and these spirits of nature were found in trees, rivers and ponds. The association of nymphs and spirits with rivers and trees is known as animism. It's not only the ancient Greeks who indulged in animistic practices; when we explore the religions and traditions of indigenous groups who live in close harmony with nature we find they are also dominated by animistic beliefs. Konrad Lorenz tells us that thinking is acting in an imagined space. In animistic practices, people psychologically represent their ecologies in that imagined space. This ensures the environment that sustains those people is maintained by those people. Animism allows human groups to coexist with a delicate ecosystem in which the poisoning of a scarce water source or the destruction of a woodland might have consequential effects for future generations of that group. From a reductionist perspective, rivers, trees, oceans and lakes may not have souls or spirits, but they are affected by our actions. Animism is a cultural proxy-truth, a computational shortcut that helps with sustainable behaviour. It seems like the animations in *The Kingdom of Plants* are re-presenting us with this cultural proxy: to bring our ecology to the attention of our fast-information society we need to magnify its motions to psychologically represent it in our society.

In his 1963 book *Conjectures and Refutations*, the Austrian philosopher of science Karl Popper mused on the nature of the knowledge we obtain from the scientific process. The question he considered was how scientists gauge whether a given theory is correct. For Popper, the process of science involved cycles of hypothesis and refutation. The hypothesis is a candidate theory, a set of structured ideas based on mathematical or computational reasoning that provides predictions which can be tested. The process of refutation requires us to challenge the candidate theory through experiment. Popper considered the question of whether observation in the real world (experiment) comes before the development of a candidate theory (hypothesis), or vice versa. He equates this to the old riddle which asks 'Which comes first, the chicken or the egg?' and he gives the following answer: they *co-evolve*. In other words, at one time there was a primordial object – presumably a biological cell – that didn't look like a chicken or an egg. Over time that primordial object began to reproduce in a way which included a stage that looked a little more egg-like. Over many years of evolution, the two stages diverged until we see a separate chicken and a separate egg.

Popper's solution to the riddle of the chicken and egg can equally be deployed for our intelligence and its environment. We are inextricably interlinked with our environment and the other intelligences that inhabit it because we have co-evolved. We don't always feel this to be true, because the slow-reacting butterfly within our heads is informationally isolated from its environment: that is the nature of our locked-in intelligence. But the probing and interrogative nature of our fast-reacting intelligence integrates us closely with the world around it and the other intelligences that inhabit it. However, because our environment changes on a different time-scale we don't always have a good feel for its development. It seems it needs to be animated through computer or stop-motion graphics for us to conceptualize the struggles that are playing out across our ecologies.

The analogy between the progress of science and the reproduction of poultry goes deeper than Karl Popper perhaps intended. In the process of evolution, each chicken is an experiment, a lifeform that is subject to the challenges of its environment and either goes on to reproduce or not. Each egg is a hypothesis, a genetic template formed from a code provided by a chicken and a rooster. This code is tested in the real world, exposed to Tyson's maxim. Both the hypothesis and the egg evolve. Eggs encode their 'theory' in a string of genetic material; scientists encode their theory in books, mathematics and computer programs. Science forms just one part of wider human culture, which is also evolving. It is stored in our minds, our stories, our traditions, our books, our religions, our computers. It changes as each new generation assimilates or discards the ideas of those who went before them.

If we measure the information passed to the next generation through our DNA, we find that genetic information moves across generations millions of times more slowly than information moves between humans. We find it difficult to psychologically represent our ecology because it's so much slower than us. But at the other end of the spectrum, we have the computer. Information moves between computers millions of times faster than it moves between humans. The cognitive monsters have introduced a third stream to the information flows on our planet, and just as we can carelessly destroy our ecology, System Zero has the power to undermine our culture and identity.

Kempelen Farkas was a Hungarian civil servant who worked in the court of the Austro-Hungarian Empire. He was also a talented inventor who developed steam turbines, typewriters and speaking machines. In 1770, eighteen years before James Watt incorporated the Albion fly-balls into his steam engine, Kempelen presented a miraculous machine. He built a chess-playing automaton.

The machine consisted of a male figure in Ottoman dress sitting at a desk with a chessboard. The left arm of the figure moved the pieces. The machine could play a full game of chess and, due to its appearance, it became known as The Turk. Until it was destroyed by fire in 1854 the machine had a career touring Europe and the United States playing at royal courts and exhibitions. It defeated Benjamin Franklin and Napoleon Bonaparte.

This was over two hundred years before Deep Blue defeated Garry Kasparov, but The Turk wasn't using a digital butterfly to explore the game maze, it was an illusion. It used a clever system of windows and fake machinery to hide a human operator, but it was a fake. The machine moved the pieces with its arm, but the operator controlled the arm by means of a pantograph system. It was human intelligence masquerading as artificial intelligence.

In 2005, 235 years after The Turk's debut, Jeff Bezos's internet bookstore launched a service called Mechanical Turk. Amazon's Mechanical Turk can play chess, write poems, draw pictures, hold conversations. It does all this through a programmable interface but, just like Kempelen's machine, the hidden hand that moves the Mechanical Turk is human.

Mechanical Turk, or MTurk for short, maps requesters to workers; the requesters then create a task and pay workers to complete the task. So, if you want MTurk to play chess, then you could define a task where the worker is shown a chessboard and asked to complete the task by proposing a valid chess move on the board. Like Kempelen's Turk, the computer is using human intelligence through a clever interface to masquerade as computer capabilities. In a nod to the use of humans, each task is called a human intelligence task, or HIT.

As far back as Frank Rosenblatt's Perceptron, and even in John McCarthy's Dartmouth Summer Project, or in Donald MacKay's quest to better understand the eye, a key task we wanted computers to perform was to recognize objects in images. By the 1990s we had Yann LeCun's convolutional neural network, but even then recognizing objects in images remained a challenging problem. Yann tested his models on the dataset of 60,000 handwritten digits collected by the US National Institute of Standards and Technology from schoolchildren and Census Bureau employees.

By 2005, when Mechanical Turk launched, digital cameras were available for under $200. They could capture images with millions of pixels. These images were also being shared widely on the internet. Could we use our neural-network models to build object detectors that worked on this rich new source of images, just like Rosenblatt's Perceptron had classified television pictures? The first challenge was to get a dataset to teach the computer. For the computer to understand what was in each image, it needs to tell the difference between a cat, a dog, different breeds of dog such as

Pomeranian, different types of flowers, varieties of vehicles. To teach the computer all this, all these images needed labelling. In 2003 a team at Caltech led by Pietro Perona built a small database of just over 9,000 images. These images went beyond the circles and squares of Rosenblatt's Perceptron, containing 101 different types of objects, including ants, planes, cameras and watches. The team had built a bigger dataset than Rosenblatt could ever have imagined, but it still wasn't very representative of the vast range of images and categories we might see in the real world. Imagine all the possible objects there are in the world, and all the possible views of those objects. The Caltech team had only 9,000 images of just 101 different object categories. In the vast scheme of the real world, that doesn't sound like very much. Researchers knew this was a problem, but collection and labelling of images is a really boring task. They tried tricks to make it more fun – they held parties for labelling images – but the result was still only a few thousand images with some hundreds of categories.

Fei-Fei Li was a Ph.D. student in Pietro's team. After graduating she moved to Princeton University, where she met Christiane Fellbaum. Christiane was a researcher in natural language processing, which involves teaching computers how to understand our language. She wanted to help computers understand the meaning of words. So she collected a large online thesaurus she called WordNet. Unlike a traditional thesaurus, WordNet is created in a way that is easy for digital computers to read and understand. Each word sits in a tree of meanings. WordNet became an important resource for AI researchers interested in how computers could understand language.

Christiane had been thinking of associating an image with each of the words in WordNet as a reference, but Fei-Fei's experience of the Caltech database caused her to think much bigger. WordNet contained over 100,000 categories. What if WordNet could have several hundred images for each category? This idea is the birth of a dataset called ImageNet. Fei-Fei Li submitted grants for funding to build the database, planning to use undergraduate students to label her data, but a quick calculation showed it would take ninety years of labour to download and label enough images. Worse, the grants she applied for were turned down. Some reviewers even said it was shameful that Fei-Fei Li's university, Princeton, would consider doing research on this topic.

Without funding, the project wouldn't get off the ground. It seemed like a stillborn idea – until Fei-Fei bumped into a graduate student who told her about MTurk. Fei-Fei says that as soon as she saw the MTurk website she knew the ImageNet database would come into being.[9] She would turn each of the labelling tasks into a HIT on the MTurk platform.

Fei-Fei would crowdsource the labelling of ImageNet. She collected a dataset of 1.2 million images with 1,000 categories. In 2010 she launched a challenge for computer vision algorithms to be evaluated on their performance on ImageNet. The data was a milestone in artificial intelligence research. Within two years, it had caused a radical shift in the direction of the work of an entire community, and within five years machines overtook human performance in recognizing objects in those images. The method the machine used was based on Yann's convolutional neural network. That model had its origins in Rosenblatt's Perceptron. The predictions of the 1958 *New York Times* article were coming true – computers were starting to see. These results were what triggered the 29-year-old Mark Zuckerberg to drive out to Stateline from his Silicon Valley home and launch the Facebook AI laboratory from his penthouse suite.

The feature landscapes the neural network builds require vast quantities of data to construct. This data also requires vast quantities of computational power to assimilate. Classical digital computers weren't up to the job. The integrated circuit had led to the CPU, a computer-processor architecture that was fast at carrying out multiple different instructions. But the type of computation needed to simulate neural networks used fewer instructions but more data. To process all this data a different architecture was needed. Fortunately, there was another type of processor that would turn out to be suitable, but it wasn't designed for neural networks, it was designed for animation.

The first *Terminator* film was made in 1984, and the red-eyed Terminator robot was brought to life as an animated model. It wasn't a mathematical model but a physical one. A version of the robot that couldn't do all the things the film suggested a Terminator should be able to do – like chasing humans in atmospheric steel plants – but could be moved by hand between frames to make it seem like it could do those things. By the time the second film in the *Terminator* franchise was released in 1991, digital computers were fast enough to model the robot instead of it being animated by hand. The work was done inside the computer's central processing unit (CPU). This was the early days of computer-generated imagery – or CGI, as it's now known – for film effects, and it was still a slow process for the computer. The visual-effects team for *Terminator 2* bought a million dollars' worth of specialist computers, and still it took months to process scenes that ran for seconds in the final film. To speed things up further, the capabilities of these specialist computers were incorporated into special integrated circuits called graphics processing units (GPUs). These processors specialized in a type of mathematics known as linear algebra. This mathematics is what is needed to quickly render the scene as an image. By a lucky coincidence, linear algebra is also what's needed to process data in a neural network. The GPU that was designed for animation was the perfect tool for training neural networks.

The human brain uses between 40 and 60 watts of power to do all its work. That's roughly the equivalent of an old incandescent light bulb. When it defeated Lee Sedol, DeepMind's AlphaGo neural network used over a thousand CPUs and hundreds of GPUs. Each individual GPU was using more energy than Lee Sedol's brain. Before it started the match, AlphaGo had played more games than Lee Sedol could hope to have completed in a hundred lifetimes. How is it that a human can defeat a machine, despite the massive information advantage the computer has? It seems that sometimes the agile and responsive information shark has an advantage over the vast information feeding machine. Lee Sedol wielded his limited information bandwidth cleverly to win the game.

Neural-network models that emulate human intelligence use vast quantities of data that would not be feasible for any human to assimilate in our short lifetimes. It is a novel way of programming machines, and in its most recent incarnation, with models such as ChatGPT, it has enabled generative AI that even reconstructs human language. But these models have weaknesses. Sedolian voids aren't just a problem for AlphaGo. Artificial neural-network models are highly susceptible to a phenomenon known as an 'adversarial attack'. In an adversarial attack, you manipulate the neural networks' inputs very slightly. From a human perspective the change is imperceptible, equivalent to just a small departure from those road-like hyperplanes that weave their way through the information topography. But for the neural networks, even leaving the road by a small distance can cause the network to drop into a Sedolian void and trigger a major mistake. Adversarial attacks exploit the behaviour of these voids and purposely change the network's output. As a result, you can present a picture to a neural network that for a human is clearly a panda and the neural network will confidently assert that it's a gibbon. It may not seem to matter if a neural network confuses a panda for a gibbon, but these image recognizers are now being integrated into safety-critical systems such as driverless cars. These autonomous vehicles rely on neural networks for pedestrian detection, road-sign detection, even road-surface detection. If the neural networks are adversarially attacked the car can become confused, and death and serious injury can result.

Tempe is a small city in Arizona, just outside Phoenix. On 18 March 2018, Elaine Herzberg was walking just north of Tempe town lake. Her bicycle was laden with shopping bags and, rather than riding it, she chose to push it. Elaine began to cross the road. Like many American roads, it was very wide, about twenty metres to get fully across. As she walked, a hybrid electric Volvo SUV approached, a woman in the driver's seat, but she wasn't looking through her windscreen. She was looking down at the centre console, watching her mobile phone stream a television talent show. At the last moment, as she approached Elaine the woman glanced up, but she saw Elaine too late. Elaine was hit by the SUV at 40 miles per hour. It dragged her along the road for 20 metres; her bicycle was knocked a further 10 metres away. Elaine died from blunt-force trauma.[10] This Volvo SUV had been fitted with an autonomous driving system designed by the Uber Advanced Technology Group. Elaine was the first victim of an autonomous vehicle.

Modern autonomous vehicles classify objects in the roadway using neural networks. The system needs to know whether objects are people, vehicles or bicycles because each of these will behave in a different way. Vehicles and bicycles travel with the traffic, pedestrians walk across the road. If the system can't decide what the object is, it says 'other'. Unfortunately, in this system, Elaine fell into a Sedolian void: she was a pedestrian pushing a bicycle. As the Uber vehicle approached Elaine, it decided she was a motor vehicle, then it decided she was an 'other'. The neural networks switched between vehicle and 'other' until two and a half seconds before impact. At that point, it finally decided Elaine was a bicycle. The car, knowing that bicycles travel along the road, pulled to the right to go around Elaine, but unfortunately Elaine was walking across the road, not along it, and the car drove straight into her. Only one second before impact the system decided a collision would occur and began to brake, but it was too late for Elaine. The system made a mistake, but the accident occurred not only because of the mistake but because of how the car responded to the gremlin of uncertainty. Humans make errors, but when we're confused by what we see we tend to pause. If a human had been confused by an object crossing the road, they wouldn't have ploughed on regardless, they would have slowed down. Delaying action is one of the ways we respond to the gremlin of uncertainty. The computer did not pause, it ploughed on. We have built computers that make errors, but we have not built machines that understand or suffer the consequences of those errors.

Elaine was the first person to be killed by a fully autonomous vehicle, but there's already a pattern of accidents where a cars' sensors become confused and the car fails to slow or react. In May 2016, Joshua Brown was killed on a Florida highway when his Tesla drove under a truck.[11] The video camera didn't recognize the white side of the truck, and the radar was set low and saw only the space under the truck. A space that was too low for Brown's car to pass under. A similar incident killed Jeremy Banner, also on a Florida highway, in March 2019.[12] In both cases the Tesla vehicles were travelling at around 70 miles per hour when they went under the trucks. Another deadly crash involving a Tesla occurred in March 2018 in California.[13] Walter Huang's Tesla Model X was following another vehicle, which changed lane to avoid a safety barrier. His car hit the safety barrier at around 70 miles per hour while under autopilot control. In each of these accidents, the vehicles exhibited little to no mitigating action at the moment when their sensors were failing.

AlphaGo was manoeuvred into an unfamiliar situation when it lost the fourth match against Lee Sedol. Elaine Herzberg, Joshua Brown, Walter Huang and Jeremy Banner were all killed when the machine-learning systems that were driving their cars experienced unfamiliar situations. Our natural intelligence emerged in a world where it was constantly being tested against the unexpected. At his trial, Socrates said that his wisdom stemmed from knowing that he didn't know. The Sedolian voids in the machine-intelligence systems we've created demonstrate that this is an area where our artificial systems have not yet absorbed Socrates' lesson.

It is only since 2007 that the majority of humans have lived in cities, but the first cities in human civilization date back much further. Thousands of years before Socrates, the Babylonian empire formed from these cities alongside the banks of the Euphrates and Tigris rivers in the area of modern Iraq. One of them was called Uruk, and its origins date as far back as 7,000 years ago. Around 6,000 years ago the city underwent a great expansion. The Babylonian people ate domesticated grasses – grains such as wheat and barley that were grown to provide staple food. The Euphrates provided water to irrigate the land, enabling intensive farming of these grains. Uruk became an urbanized society with its own bureaucracy and military. The city had a surplus of grain but a shortage of other goods like wood. They traded to sell their surpluses and buy the goods they needed. Markets emerged to trade goods that were in plentiful supply for those that were in short supply. Traders moved between cities carrying goods from areas of supply to areas of demand. Like the social insects before us, humans in Uruk took on different roles. They cooperated to form a civic society, what we now call civilization.

A thousand years after Uruk's expansion, writing emerged in the city. In a beehive, social insects communicate the location of the nectar they need through waggle dances. Human cities needed much more advanced forms of communication to deal with the logistical challenges of managing the supply chain. Writing emerged as a tool for accounting for where goods were and what agreements had been made for exchanging them. In this way the people of Uruk could understand who owed what to whom. One tablet dating from 4,000 years ago was excavated in the city of Umma. Written in cuneiform script that represented the Sumerian language,[14] it records grain yields. The writing on the tablet is arranged in columns, like an Excel spreadsheet. The first column records the yield of grain, the next the location of the field. Many of Uruk's records are also of this form; lists that stored information helped administer the city.

The earliest writing was for record-keeping, but over 500 years writing became sophisticated enough to express spoken language. The Babylonians began to write down stories. Gilgamesh was one of Uruk's earliest kings, and many stories were written about him. The first story in the Epic of Gilgamesh tells of a six-day journey to the Cedar Forest. When he and his companion, Enkidu, get there they begin to cut down the trees. They are challenged by the animistic guardian of the forest, Humbaba, but they defeat him and build a great raft from the trees they've cut, and float down the Euphrates to the city of Nippur, where they build a great cedar gate. One of humanity's first recorded stories is a tale of ecological destruction and the supply chain.

In small groups we can rely on social pressure to regulate behaviour, balancing individual interests against those of the wider group, but as communities grow these social mechanisms struggle. We don't just need supply chains; we need systems of order that go beyond the relationships of trust we build between individuals. We need ways of resolving disputes, standards of behaviour that are codified. The earliest written systems of law come from Babylon. One of them is the Code of Hammurabi, named for a Babylonian king who ruled nearly 4,000 years ago.

Jonathan Tenney is an Assyriologist who spends his days reading these ancient texts. His domain of expertise is the city of Nippur, where Gilgamesh built the great gate. The period Jonathan studies is 2,000 years after the reign of Gilgamesh. Through his studies he can give snapshots of life in these cities. One of these snapshots is of a trial that took place under Hammurabi's code. The trial concerned the disappearance of an ox. Cases were presided over by a shakannakku, normally a representative of the king:

Judgement that Adad-šuma-uṣur, the shakannakku gave:

Regarding the ox that Nergal-aha-iddina loaned to Sin-bununi and then died in the house of Sin-bununi:

If Siyatu the messenger of Nergal-aha-iddina removed the corpse from the house of Sin-bununi and then threw it to a dog, may Sin-bununi be cleared [of wrongdoing by the ordeal] and the man of Nergal-aha-iddina [Siyatu] be proved guilty.

[But] regarding the ox of Nergal-aha-iddina which died in the house of Sin-bununi:

If Siyatu did not remove the corpse from the house of Sin-bununi and instead Sin-bununi made a false accusation against Siyatu, then may the man of Nergal-aha-iddina [i.e., Siyatu] be cleared [of wrongdoing by the ordeal] and Sin-bununi be proved guilty.[15]

The record reads almost in note form, so it might be worth a quick review of what we think happened. Nergal-aha-iddina[16] was the original owner of an ox, which he loaned to Sin-bununi.[17] When Nergal-aha-iddina wanted his ox back, Sin-bununi said the ox had died and that Siyatu,[18] Nergal-aha-iddina's servant, had taken the corpse.

The case described in the tablet is unusual for two reasons. First, the shakannakku was normally a royal proxy but in this case we are told it was the King of Babylon himself, Adad-šuma-usur.[19] Second, the judgement is for a trial by water ordeal. Someone is going to be thrown into the river; guilt will be decided by whether the water rejects them or absorbs them.

The tablet contains words, but its interpretation requires knowledge. Jonathan[20] was kind enough to let me and my students watch him transliterate the tablet, and as he worked he used books, computer databases, his own expert knowledge and also his sense of what it means to be a human. The suspicion is that Sin-bununi may have sold the ox, because his explanation of events – that the ox died and the servant, Siyatu, came, took the body and fed it to a dog – feels like a version of the modern 'dog ate my homework' excuse. The case hinges on an accusation, but it's one person's word against another.

This judgement was passed over 3,200 years ago but, like a modern case, making it would have involved listening to witness statements and then coming to a decision. The choice of trial by ordeal implies that the witness statements conflicted and the King felt he couldn't decide on the basis of the evidence. The trial by ordeal passes the decision-making from the shakannakku to the gods; it's cleromancy with fatal implications. From the translation, it's not quite clear who's going in the river . . . is it Siyatu the servant or Sin-bununi the accuser? My human cynicism suspects it's the servant that's going to get wet. Even over 3,000 years later, despite the different cultural landscape, we can still imagine something about the power dynamics at play, and my gut tells me that putting the servant through the ordeal will be the most palatable solution to the King.

Sin-bununi's story for explaining what happened to the body of the ox reads suspiciously, but while we can speculate about what happened, we can't know exactly what did happen – there is uncertainty. Even at the time of the trial, the King felt unable to make a decision, so given he wasn't able to establish the truth so many years ago, we're unlikely to find it now. This is a cold case, so cold it's deep frozen, but anyone reading the story can't help but try to defrost it through the warmth of their human understanding.

We may think we've moved beyond the idea of trial by ordeal, but I see a similar trend emerging with our desire to use AI systems for consequential decisions. When humans feel unable to pass judgement they are tempted to pass the decision on to what they believe to be an omniscient entity, but the gremlin of uncertainty means the machine is not omniscient – putting consequential decisions on machines implies that you will be exchanging human error for machine error. That is problematic, because the machine can never feel the consequences of those errors as it is not subject to the same vulnerabilities as us. That is why it's vital the human remains in ultimate control. That's not to say the human should ignore the machine; rather, we would like the machine to augment our understanding. When Amelia Earhart flew her 'Little Red Bus' she felt at one with her plane. The decisions were hers, but they were enacted in collaboration with the machine; it was a synergistic relationship. Perhaps a better analogy is found in Neil Armstrong's landing of *Eagle* on the Moon. There, a human with the best training available was assisted by a computer and an entire team of supportive specialists in the achievement of a goal of which all of humanity could be proud.

When John F. Kennedy exalted the importance of human exploration of space to the American people, he quoted George Mallory in telling them that they should go 'because it's there'. He also spoke of the history of human achievement:

No man can fully grasp how far and how fast we have come, but condense, if you will, the 50,000 years of man's recorded history in a time span of but a half-century. Stated in these terms, we know very little about the first 40 years, except at the end of them advanced man had learned to use the skins of animals to cover them. Then about 10 years ago, under this standard, man emerged from his caves to construct other kinds of shelter. Only five years ago man learned to write and use a cart with wheels. Christianity began less than two years ago. The printing press came this year, and then less than two months ago, during this whole 50-year span of human history, the steam engine provided a new source of power.[21]

Like the production team behind Sir David's series on plants, Kennedy is compressing time, using a factor of 1,000 to magnify it. Under this accelerated timeframe the trial of Siyatu took place only three years ago. The events Homer relates in the *Iliad* and *Odyssey* were playing out just as Siyatu or Sin-bununi was being thrown in the river, and it was another year before Socrates lived and died in Athens.

Writing came to the Greeks much later than it did to the people of Uruk. The writing Socrates knew was only a few centuries old when he stood trial. The Greeks' written culture was as new to him as our Enlightenment culture is to us today. Socrates is famous for not writing his ideas down, he was an advocate of dialogue; the Socratic method is a form of conversation in which definitions are given and challenged. In *Think,* the philosopher Simon Blackburn characterizes this approach as getting people to say something, demonstrating that they can't defend it, then claiming they had no right to make the claim in the first place.[22] He makes a point similar to Justice Potter Stewart's characterization of obscenity – he suggests that we can all identify whether a sentence is grammatical, or a dog is a Pomeranian, without knowing underlying general principles. This resonates with our understanding of modern artificial intelligence. A neural network can also identify a dog as Pomeranian without knowing general underlying principles.

It seems that very often we cannot explain from first principles how we decide what different concepts are, and nor should we be expected to. This may seem worrying, but it relates to the challenge of Winnie-the-Pooh's attempted hooshing of Eeyore. Why did Pooh Bear expect that hooshing might work? Most humans can trace his line of reasoning, but can we derive it from first principles?

We find it so difficult to explain so much of what we know because most of it doesn't come from first principles, it comes from experience. Human reasoning is not like Russell and Whitehead's and Newton's *Principias*. It is grounded in a representation of the world which is specific to humans, our history and our circumstances. There are objective components to this history and culture, but it is largely subjective, in the same way that a chicken is subjective: our ideas have evolved over time like the chicken has evolved over time. One problem we now face with the machine is that people habitually assume the machine is working from first principles and that it won't make mistakes. But to achieve the capabilities our machines are now exhibiting we have also had to introduce in them the possibility of errors.

Animistic practices imbue our rivers, trees and plants with spirits or nymphs to give us a way to reason about our ecology in the way we might reason about our friends or family. What if we want to reason about our computers in this way? We've already seen our tendency to anthrox them, just as we anthrox everything else, but in the past – for most of us – two-way communication with a machine has required specific software, like a word processor or a spreadsheet program. Some of us have learned to program computers. But unlike human language, programming languages are specified so that the intent can be derived from first principles in order that the computer doesn't make errors in carrying out those instructions. Where mistakes occur, they come from the human in terms of incorrect design of the computer or the program. These problems are known as bugs. Our digital systems have a lot of bugs because translating human ideas for the computer is hard; it requires special ways of thinking, and the people who can do it well, the software engineers, are paid a lot of money. In the time of Siyatu only members of a guild of scribes were able to read and write, so literacy was restricted. Scribes would have charged fees for their services. Software engineers are the modern scribes; they are the group of people who have the most fluent digital literacy and can translate human ideas most fully into terms the machine understands.

Donald MacKay suggested the brain is neither an analogue nor a digital computer, and we've seen that our brains don't operate from first principles but from experience. This experience gives us representations of the world that are specific to us. To make it easier for us to communicate with the machine it would be convenient if the computer had a better understanding of this representation. The analogue machines Donald MacKay worked on during the Second World War had electrical voltages and currents that represented states of the real world such as the position and velocity of a target. The MONIAC was an analogue machine where water flows represented the flows of money in the economy. For a machine to interact with us it would need a representation of the world analogous to ours. A human–analogue machine would have to have internal states analogous to our internal states. Only once the machine had this capability would we be able to begin to communicate with it in the way we communicate with each other, but this ability is also intrinsically linked with the errors we make.

Large-language models like ChatGPT are neural networks that have given computers the beginnings of this capability. When we communicate with ChatGPT we are interacting with a digital entity that has learned the same shortcuts through the maze that we make, so we are communicating with a reflection of ourselves. This human–analogue machine – or HAM for short – computes in a very different way to a digital computer, and while this allows it to interact with us it also introduces the same flaws we have. Of course, the human–analogue machine is more brainiac than MONIAC, because it has access to unimaginable amounts of data. This makes it very knowledgeable and many of its assertions highly plausible, but it is still subject to the limitations of our human representation.

The reason ChatGPT has been able to do this is related to a

phenomenon known as convergent evolution. A classic example of convergent evolution comes to us from vultures. For a time, there was controversy as to whether vultures found the carcasses of the carrion they feed on from sight or smell. This controversy was resolved by the realization that vultures in the Americas and vultures in Africa are only distantly related species.[23] African vultures are more closely related to hawks, whereas American vultures and the condor are related to storks. African vultures use sight to locate prey whereas American vultures can use sight and smell. The birds are similar in appearance because of convergent evolution. The birds occupy the same ecological niche: if your food source is the decaying bodies of large mammals, it makes sense to have no feathers on your head, as they are difficult to preen and will end up covered in blood and gore. If you rely on other animals' kills to eat it makes sense to be able to fly efficiently as you circle and look for your prey. So the wing shape and flight behaviour of these two distantly related animals are similar.

The same phenomenon occurred when Leibniz and Newton 'independently' discovered calculus. Like two distantly related vultures, they were happening upon the same intellectual niche, one that had emerged as part of the dynamic landscape triggered by the Scientific Revolution. The HAMs around us today are created in the same manner. Large-language models are developed by training very large neural networks to reconstruct our language. To do this well they happen upon the same concepts we used to produce this language.

Unfortunately, the popular notion of AI conflates the properties of the HAM with those of the supposedly infallible digital computer. The HAMs are solving Laplace's gremlin in the same manner we do, so they are subject to the same failings. That said, the HAMs do provide a promising starting point for an interface to a digital computer. Just as Armstrong and Earhart interacted with their machines through their control stick, the HAM provides a control stick for the digital machine. If correctly implemented, this could allow us to psychologically represent the machine in our heads and enable a digital literacy revolution akin to the revolution in literacy that followed the development of Gutenberg's printing press. But the HAM also allows the machine to be psychologically misrepresented, and many of the dangers we face now are associated with the new wave of misinformation and manipulation such misrepresentation would bring.

12.

Trust

I don't know the true meaning of the Radiohead song 'Fake Plastic Trees', but whenever I hear it I think of artificial intelligence. In the opening verse Thom Yorke sings about a green plastic watering can, for a fake plastic rubber plant, in fake plastic earth. Of these three things, one is real and the other two are fakes. A fake plastic plant is an artificial plant. An artificial plant can fulfil some of the roles of a natural plant; it can decorate your home or office and, from a distance – or even under close inspection – some plastic plants pass for real plants. But the resemblance is superficial. Key aspects of the real plant are absent: the scent of the flower, the flavour of the fruit, the ability to grow and respond to its environment.

In this respect, artificial plants resemble artificial intelligence. The achievements of neural-network models are impressive: their use of hidden layers has enabled them to learn feature landscapes for categorizing objects in images, for generating language for chat-bots, even for generating entirely fictional videos and photographs. The crowning achievement is the HAM – a computer that encodes a feature landscape analogous to ours. Laplace's demon required us to 'know all the forces that set nature in motion', but neural network models take shortcuts. By learning to retell our stories the machine has assimilated some aspects of what it means to be human. But the way in which it has learned to do this is very different from the way we became what we are. Like the chicken and the egg, we have co-evolved with our environment and our culture across hundreds of thousands of years as *Homo sapiens*, millions of years as primates, 100 million years as mammals and over half a billion years as animals. The machine has now provided us with a human–analogue. This is a game-changer: it means we are standing on the cusp of a new dawn of human–machine interaction.

With the capabilities given by generative AI the machine can now plausibly emulate a human. This is giving the machine new possibilities for how it acts and interacts with us. Through feature representations, machines bind concepts together in a high-dimensional space. These are the proxy-truths; having them means humans don't need to have a detailed understanding of the physics of light to recognize a Pomeranian. The landscape features in Rosenblatt's Perceptron cause the Pomeranian-like features to cluster together like a copse of trees in their hyperspace. A convolutional neural network detects the distinctive parts of the image, such as eyes in a face or the curl of a tail. It filters different images to different parts of the data landscape. Modern transformer networks which underpin the generative AI techniques that power ChatGPT use a context vector that plays a similar role. In each case every hidden layer contributes to the process of data sorting until the landscape is moulded into one suitable for interpolation.

That said, like the artificial plant, these HAMs are missing fundamental aspects of our intelligence. They are missing rigorous approaches for dealing with their ignorance. When riding my bicycle down Hathersage Road, when watching Steve fall and the oncoming driver miss him, everything that happened was conditioned responses. Reflexive reactions to an unfolding situation. My narrative of the crash is a retrospective explanation of the events as retold by my conscious brain. In the moment each action I took was instinctive, but in my retrospective there lies a narrative that my mind has settled on to explain events.

Steve remains alive today because of this integrated multisensor system. The driver of the oncoming car would have experienced the situation in a similar way to me. The human brain assimilates information from different senses: vision, hearing, balance, touch. At lower perceptual levels each can lead to a reflex action. An unexpected bang can make us jump or run; a rapid movement makes us flinch or duck; a hot surface makes us retract our hand. At higher perceptual levels we have more time for reflection. We can suspend our judgement; in an uncertain world we apply epoché. These characteristics are the consequences of the over half a billion years of evolution since the first simple nervous systems appeared.

If we look back over the ground we've covered, we can say that when Eisenhower decided to trigger the invasion of Normandy on 6 June 1944, his final decision was a matter of judgement. He knew he was sending many young people to their deaths. He couldn't know how many, and he couldn't know the consequences of not invading. Some narratives suggest that in the future we might use AI to make decisions we find too hard – the idea is that a machine might make fewer mistakes. We can certainly design machines to help us with decisions, but we can't eliminate mistakes. Pooh's hooshing error arises because he is a bear of very little brain. His ideas, when deployed in the real world, don't manifest quite as well as he'd hoped. Mike Tyson expressed this differently, telling us that everyone has a plan until they get punched in the mouth, or as Field Marshal Helmuth von Moltke put it: 'No plan of operations extends with any certainty beyond the first contact with the main hostile force.' The computer is subject to these challenges just as surely as Pooh Bear is because regardless of its capabilities – in comparison to the complexities of the universe – as Deep Thought realized, the computer is still a bear of very little brain.

When building the Perceptron, Rosenblatt's innovation was to use layered neural-network models. Conceptually, our nervous system also seems to be layered: different levels of attentiveness are required for different tasks. Each level of attentiveness leads to a different speed of reaction. Our nervous system is trading off reflex and reflect; it doesn't always wait to give its best answer to a question. When impacts are imminent, reflex trumps reflection. Epoché gives way to action.

Snap decisions have consequences, but the brain polishes them over. It interpolates through events to feed our conscious minds with plausible narratives. It supplies us with a convenient truth. These convenient truths bring about consistency within the brain. They lead to information coherence within our internal information-processing system.

Our different levels of perception have different feels to them. Our reflexive actions dominate our reflective actions, but for planning purposes our higher-level brain perceives itself as in charge. This Eisenhower illusion is also important for information coherence within the brain.

The social psychologist Jonathan Haidt refers to this set-up as the rider and the elephant. Just as the need to perform high-level planning requires the rider to imagine herself to be the dominant partner, similarly, our reflective self imagines itself to be in charge of our actions. It develops a narrative that retrospectively places it in charge of decision-making. In this way, the self-deception is maintained.

The way in which artificial systems ape our natural capabilities is entirely dependent on their access to our information. A major challenge for us lies in who has control over how they access that information and for what purpose. In Babylonian society, during the time of the trial of Siyatu, access to the written record would have been controlled by scribes because only a few people were able to read and write. Siyatu's trial was recorded on a clay tablet by a scribe using a reed to form triangular letters. In the ancient world scribes gained an enormous amount of power by being the gate-keepers of such knowledge. Across the last 500 years the invention of printing and improvements in literacy shifted this power from the scribes to publishers. But the modern equivalent of the scribe is the software engineer, and their guilds are large tech companies like Facebook and Google which pay these scribes so highly it is difficult for governments, hospitals and regular businesses to compete. Those guilds also provide their scribes with the computational and data resources – equivalent to the reed and the clay tablet – that allow them to make their vision a reality. Unfortunately, their track record in seeing the pitfalls of their approaches is a poor one. As we saw with Facebook and the US elections or with Microsoft and the Tay chatbot, because of the challenges of intellectual debt, these companies often don't understand their own systems, let alone the effect they are having on human society and culture.

The levels of perception we find in our brains are missing from our current generation of HAMs. They don't exhibit the same fast-reacting intelligence, because they have no physical persona with which to inhabit the world. In this respect they are like Zhuang Zhou's butterfly. Unlike Konrad Lorenz's hungry orang-utan, they do not integrate with their environment, they do not exploit it as outside memory, and they do not act out imagined futures that depend on their own affordances. Their only mode of interaction is conversation. They don't have an intimate relationship between a physically embodied form and a slower-reacting counterfactual self. The power of these systems is arising from the machine's vast information access and its untrammelled access to our data. For the first generation of System Zero this data was mainly very many individuals' personal information, but with the new wave of technologies the remit has expanded to the data that represents human culture. From Homer to hip hop, from Gilgamesh to grime, the modern machine has reconstructed an artificial essence of humanity from our creations.

What type of world are these technologies leading us to? Both the utopian ideal that emerges from this world and its dystopian sibling are well reflected in the Genesis story of the creation of Adam. In the Sistine Chapel, two panels below Michelangelo's depiction of the creation is his rendering of *The Fall and Expulsion from Paradise*. Adam and Eve initially exist in Eden; their lives are entirely managed for them. They are warned not to eat from the tree of knowledge. When they do so they become self-aware and are expelled from the garden. They are subjected to the miseries of the world outside – disease and suffering. One of the promises of artificial intelligence is that by increasing its involvement in our lives it will be able to cater for our needs. By giving the machine more access to our data, the idea is that it will be able to alleviate that suffering and cure our diseases – the machine will look after us.

In the western tradition the forbidden fruit is an apple, and in today's world it could be our Apple computers that guide us back into the walled garden of Eden. Already our Apple watches can monitor our heart rates and inform us of the number of steps we need to take to maintain our health. But as we cede control to the machine, we are also losing what Adam and Eve gained by eating from the tree. We lose personal responsibility and freedom of choice. The Garden of Eden is depicted as a benevolent autocracy, but such an autocracy necessarily limits the freedoms of the individuals within it. There is no one-size-fits-all set of values.

Each of us will react differently to whether this price is worth the outcome, and our ideas will change over time. How much we each want to be constrained by a benevolent overseer may differ when we are faced with severe illness rather than being youthful and healthy. If we respect the dignity of the individual human, we need to accommodate this diversity of perspectives.

It isn't a coincidence that elements of the story of the Garden of Eden can be redeployed to understand the decisions facing our society today. The shadow of a greater intelligence implied by a creator has triggered reflection across cultures and generations about what our own lives mean in this context. This leads to a form of introspection, about who we are, and who we want to be. By viewing our intelligence from the perspective of the machine, by slicing away to reveal the atomic human, my goal in this book has been to equip you with an understanding that helps you confidently participate in those decisions.

In the trial of Siyatu the shakannakku followed the Code of Hammurabi in decreeing that, because the witness statements were in conflict, the outcome should be decided by ordeal. It was difficult to decide who was right and who was wrong, so the preferred option was to let the gods decide by throwing Siyatu, or Sin-bununi, in the river. This form of cleromancy has echoes in the modern world, where some are proposing that we turn to artificial intelligence to make difficult decisions for us. However, these artificial systems will make mistakes and when these decisions have consequential effects on our fellow human beings it feels like a dereliction of responsibility to invoke the AI gods in this manner. The modern form of the shakannakku is our system of judiciary. This consists of individuals, alongside institutions which provide accountability for their actions. But a critical component of this system is the idea that these decisions are made by humans. For example, under jury trials twelve of our peers decide upon the evidence.

One of the most important sets of lectures for artificial intelligence, entitled 'A question of trust', was given by the philosopher Baroness Onora O'Neill in 2002. Her focus wasn't AI specifically – she was talking about the challenges of holding individuals accountable through process. But her point was that you cannot trust a set of processes, you can only trust the humans within those processes. This is because the processes themselves do not have a social stake in the way individual humans do. Processes cannot be betrayed to the Stasi by their husband, they cannot understand what it is like for a child to lose a parent, or a parent to lose a child. In her lectures O'Neill suggests that intelligent accountability is reliant on these social obligations. This is pertinent to the AI debate because the increasing use of machines to make decisions in our society is leading to a proliferation of processes.

One of the challenges of the determinism that arises from Laplace's demon is dealing with the notion of individual responsibility. After all, if everything is determined by some underlying Theory of Everything, then can any of us be seen to be responsible for our actions? But as we've seen, even if we have the Theory, and even if we know everything there is to know about the world in terms of the data, we are faced with the Deep Thought problem: predicting how everything plays out from the Theory would require an impossibly gargantuan computation. So our social responsibilities are proxies that enable us to work together, devolving actions to one another and trusting that we will each conform to our duties as best we can. A philosophical perspective on this idea is given by the Oxford philosopher Peter Strawson in the essay 'Freedom and resentment'. He reflects on the different roles we play in our society and the relationships they lead to:

We should think of the many different kinds of relationship which we can have with other people – as sharers of a common interest; as members of the same family; as colleagues; as friends; as lovers; as chance parties to an enormous range of transactions and encounters.[1]

We've seen different relationships – my grandfather's duty to his unit and his family, Erwin Rommel's duty to his family and his army, Max Planck's duty towards his son. Strawson focuses on the emotions of *resentment* and *gratitude* and reflects on the spectrum of these emotions and our *reactive* attitudes. It is these commonplace emotions that give us our feel for each other, binding us together around our shared endeavours.

These aspects of our social relationships are part of an evolved cultural ecosystem that isn't true in the way that Stephen Hawking's Theory of Everything aspires to be true, but is true in the way that the flower relies on the butterfly to pass its genetics on to the next generation. These are evolved mechanisms that serve important purposes in our culture.

The embodiment factor isolates the atomic human from the world around. Our brains scramble to grab an intellectual foothold on the world to lever ourselves up, and this includes psychological representation of concepts that are otherwise difficult for us. So for religion we embody the notion of a pervasive intelligence in a robed figure of God. For artificial intelligence it's the red-eyed Terminator that was projected on to our cinema screens. But sometimes this foothold is a poor one to rely on to lift our thinking to perceive the cognitive vista we need to understand the nature of what we've created.

Samuel Butler's 1863 letter 'Darwin among the machines' was written at the height of the age of steam. His inspiration was the automation of physical labour that drove the Industrial Revolution. He suggested that the machine enslaves us. It requires us to feed and maintain it, so humans work in service of the machine. In many respects, slavery seems the wrong analogy. The machine is helpless without us. It is dependent on humans. Normally, we do not use a term such as 'slavery' to describe our relationship with our dependants. Children do not enslave their parents; pets do not enslave their owners. But there is a relationship of interdependence with the machine: we serve the machine because it helps us. The machine produces a greater volume of work more efficiently than human society can without it – but at the level of an individual human, that's not how it feels. For a particular worker the experience can feel like slavery because the societal benefits of the machine are unevenly distributed. So some of us work in service of the machine and others benefit from that work.

In an effort to draw attention to the dangers of artificial intelligence, some of my colleagues have suggested that the advent of AI systems is analogous to the development of atomic weaponry. A good analogy echoes the underlying phenomena it is trying to help us understand, and I think the comparison to atomic weaponry fails in that respect. Machine intelligence is pervasive and integrated with all aspects of our lives. It has military implications, but it also has implications for our health, agriculture, cities, art, science, engineering, media and businesses. As a pervasive technology, it has implications for who we are as human beings and for human societies. The threat provided by an atomic explosion is vivid and well understood, as are the circumstances that might bring about a nuclear incident. The threat posed by the machine is much more analogous to the threat we pose to our ecology.

Our modern world is a three-layer information topography. The base layer is our ecology, where life reacts on geological time; it shares information across generations through biochemical reactions. The atomic human sits in the middle layer. We evolved to communicate through sound to share information between individuals millions of times faster than life can evolve. We have developed new mechanisms for sharing and storing information. We started with oral histories, the Sumerians developed written clay tablets, Gutenberg popularized the printed book, and most recently we have come to rely on an interconnected network of computers. Those computers may seem to represent a dominant layer because they can share information millions of times faster than humans can. But that idea ignores the stored complexity of each layer. In the closing statement of Charles Darwin's *The Origin of Species* he relates how 'endless forms most beautiful and most wonderful' have emerged. He is describing the base layer which, while it is slow, has existed for billions of years and across that time has involved unimaginably many billions of interacting organisms. Unfortunately, the diversity and complexity of those endless forms are easily undermined by clumsy actions in our layer. Those actions are leading to an environmental crisis. One aspect of the atomic human is the richness and variation in the culture that sustains us. But relative to the ecosystems around us, the nuances of our culture pale in comparison to the complexity of the wider Earth. However fast the computer is, its ecosystem is the least rich. But as we've seen with System Zero, its potential to undermine the diversity and complexity of the world around it is enormous. By operating at such short timescales it gains access to large quantities of information from humans and could be as damaging to our cultural ecosystem as our actions have been to our natural ecosystem.

This three-layer information topography suggests that when we want to draw attention to the negative influence of the machine on human society, more appropriate analogies might invoke the challenges we face with our environment. So we might compare the influence of the machine to the state of our waterways, or the presence of asbestos in our buildings, or the increase in carbon dioxide in our atmosphere. These analogies use the fact that the interface between the machine and the human is one where the complexity is on our side but the speed is on the computer's, just as at the interface between us and our environment the complexity is on the Earth's side but speed is on ours. However, these analogies also fall down because they don't capture the benefits the technology can bring.

When waiting at reception before a meeting with a colleague at London's Natural History Museum, I ended up discussing with a security guard how AI may change our lives. We talked about what benefits there might be, but also how it could bring challenges. 'Oh,' the security guard said, 'so it's like fire.'

'Precisely,' I answered. Control of fire by early humans pre-dates the emergence of *Homo sapiens*; it is something bequeathed to us by a now extinct ancestor. It brought extraordinary benefits in terms of warmth and preparation of food, but when incorrectly managed it can do great damage. Boulton and Watt's engine is merely a sophisticated form of fire control.[2] In Babylonian legend, Gilgamesh and Enkidu cut down the Cedar Forest and killed Humbaba. Watt's engine burned the remains of forests that grew 350 million years ago on the shores of a low-lying marine basin. This basin formed as the continents were merging to form Pangaea. The coal is burnt to transfer heat energy into motion and work. It had a dramatic effect on society, and its deployment in Albion Mill in London led to a backlash from the labour it was replacing and the mill was burnt down. In 1891, near the site of the mill, Bankside Power Station was built. It burnt coal to provide electricity for London's streetlamps but was closed in 1981. The site now hosts the Tate Modern gallery. Across the two centuries since Albion Mill was burnt down, life expectancy across the world has doubled and the proportion of humans living in extreme poverty has fallen from over 80 per cent to below 10 per cent,[3] but 200 years later we can see that one of the most significant consequences of this Industrial Revolution is the effect large-scale burning of fossil fuels is having on the Earth's ecology. Large-scale information processing by machine is similar: there are some immediate effects, both beneficial and damaging, but some of the most pernicious challenges will only emerge in the long term.

Underlying the use of the term 'artificial intelligence' there is a latent promise, the idea that this technology, through being intelligent, will adapt to us. But across the history of automation, a consistent pattern has been our adaptation to the machine. Our partnership has been unequal because of the machine's inflexibility. Before the machine, the rhythms of our day were dictated by the rhythms of the natural world around us: the availability of daylight,

the variability of the weather, the friability of the soil. Early factories like Albion Mill required a new form of regimented worker.
The human became an interface to the machine. Our flexibility has
allowed us to convert from the world's variability and uncertainty
to the machine's need for consistency. But in accommodating the
machine we end up emulating the machine. To feed the machine's
cycle of labour the rhythms of our work have adjusted to force us
to perform more regimented tasks that are dictated by the artificial
world we've created: the factory whistle, the train timetable, the
cutting and pasting of numbers into the grid rows of Excel.

The AI fallacy captures the fact that until now the latent promise
of AI has not been delivered. Underlying the societal vision of artificial intelligence, the utopian narratives that we tell in our
science-fiction stories, seems to be an unspoken assumption that
this time it's going to be different. That this time, we've finally created a technology that will adapt to us. That our AI companions
will provide each of us with the equivalent of an artificial personal
assistant, one that accommodates us and assists us. Artificial intelligence will converse in our language, not in a programming language
that might require a software engineer. The idea is that rather than
requiring us to imagine its formatting needs, rather than requiring
us to laboriously edit the individual cells of a spreadsheet, it will
imagine our needs and adapt to them. The promise of AI is that it
will produce intelligent entities which seamlessly integrate with our
cognitive landscape. Jeeves in a computer. In commonplace usage,
the word 'intelligence' implies common sense and empathy. It
implies a range of evolved characteristics that we take for granted in
our human companions, and even our animal companions. It
implies that we're creating a flexible entity that could seamlessly
integrate with the fabric of human society.

In practice, we are only just starting to see the first glimpses of
this possibility in the first wave of HAMs that have emerged. A
major question is to what extent the AI fallacy will continue to
hold. Modern AI systems have moved a long way from the rigid
classical AI ideas. Will we continue to have to adapt to the machine,

or will it adapt to us? And if it does gain a deeper understanding of who we are and adapts to our needs, how do we prevent it manipulating us?

There is a great irony that the machine, whose defining characteristic is its extreme capability for information consumption, has not historically integrated well with the world around it. In his 1995 book *Being Digital*, Nicholas Negroponte introduced the idea of bits and atoms.[4] He was referring to atoms in the physical sense, the fact that the matter of the world around us is made up of material constructed from atoms. When he mentions bits he is referring to information in the Shannon sense. Negroponte's point is that in the digital world information is easy to share and manipulate, but he highlights the importance of the interface between the machine and the human. This interface is where the HAM sits, and it is a new way in which information can move between the physical and the digital. But the machine's historic reliance on humans for this interaction is in stark contrast to the way in which the earliest animals evolved. They, like a Braitenberg vehicle, were integrated in the physical world from the start, and the echoes of this integration are still felt today in our motor reflexes and other fast-reacting capabilities. Like Zhuang Zhou, we dream we are the butterfly. The counterfactual simulation of ourselves dominates our thinking through observer bias, but the reality is we are Zhuang Zhou, entities constrained by our environment and cursed to often be disappointed when our dreams don't work out as planned, but blessed with an optimism that means we imagine that next time it will be different.

Until now machines have presented a stark contrast. The second part of Negroponte's book focuses on human–machine interfaces, but in 1995 machines were able to interact with the real world only in a very limited way. In the three decades since *Being Digital* was published humans have engaged in a mass transfer of our physical media, books, celluloid film, newspapers and letters to the digital medium. It is only by reading this literature, consuming our stories, digesting our interactions in a second-hand manner that the HAM has emerged.

If you've ever been the new kid at school, you'll have a sense of what's going on. As a new child, you arrive into an existing, and evolved, social context. That may consist of particular clothes, music, video games, films, social media influencers or television programmes. The rest of the children have already been on an evolving journey together; they relate to one another through a set of cultural artefacts that are unfamiliar to the new child. The new child has the dual challenge of understanding this wider cultural context and interacting with the other children through implicit knowledge of this landscape. The machine is like an extreme version of the new kid at school. Humans have been on an evolutionary journey together. That journey has involved many shared experiences, and it's been experienced from the perspective of a community of locked-in intelligences. The computer is arriving late to this cultural context. But now, with its vast access to human experience, it has begun to relate to us. On top of this, like any outsider, it is bringing an understanding of a plethora of ideas that have formerly been beyond our comprehension. However, unlike a new child at school, the HAM does not interrelate with us in the way we relate to one another, because it does not have a stake in society, it does not share our vulnerabilities and aspirations. It has different affordances and capabilities. It perceives the world in a different way. This means it can never be a replacement for us. However, it can now interact, and it will engage in a new wave of information assimilation through this interaction.

In the past, System Zero emerged because of commercial imperatives being combined with machines that could not communicate their intent but did have an understanding of who we are. That understanding emerged from tracking what we clicked on and by feeding us with information that the machine knew would engage us. The HAMs bring new capabilities which provide the possibility of improving this situation, but simultaneously the possibility for many new routes of manipulation. They can understand us in more sophisticated ways than via our mouse clicks. Much depends on who controls the technology and what their business model is. A fundamental problem with the social media ecosystem is that it is not paid for by the users. This idea has been summarized in the line 'If you're not the customer, you're the product.'[5] *Television Delivers People* is a 1973 video art project by Richard Serra and Carlota Fay Schoolman. It consists of seven minutes of text scrolling with elevator music playing in the background. Part of the text reads:

> You are delivered to the advertiser who is the customer.
> He consumes you.

This captures very nicely the essence of surveillance capitalism and the challenge we face when imagining how to make best use of this new technology. Market economics is an approach to addressing supply-chain challenges which goes back to those ancient clay cuneiform tablets that record crop yields. But the incentive structures of the system are centred around customer satisfaction. That first recorded Epic of Gilgamesh involves the destruction of a forest and its spirit protector to make a gate. If we want HAMs to serve individual and social interests, rather than to become an additional tool of the digital oligarchy, we need to think carefully about how to encourage the right sort of business models to reflect individual aspirations while respecting vulnerabilities and societal concerns.

The challenge is reminiscent of some of our other attempts to substitute the natural with the artificial. Our most fundamental form of consumption is food: since the development of automation, a major focus has been on the automated production of food. As well as the mechanization of farming, this has led to processes for refining and creating artificial foods.

Saccharin, refined sugar and high-fructose corn syrup have emerged since the nineteenth century. The popularity of these artificial foods is driven by our weakness for sweetness. These artificial foods are short-circuiting our evolved partiality for sugars. In a natural environment, fruits and honey are sweet, energy-rich but only intermittently available. Our mechanization of the food supply has rendered these sweet flavours cheap and widely available. Nutrition and health have suffered as artificial food products that satiate us by providing for our immediate wants – rather than our long-term needs – have become commonplace. As a result, we have a global pandemic of dietary diseases such as diabetes and obesity leading to early death through cancers and heart disease.

Artificial intelligence has deployed the same tricks on our cognitive diet as those artificial foods use. The great success of the machine has been to form a cognitive playground where the psychological equivalents of refined sugars are readily available. Humans are social creatures, and the cognitive staple of the internet is news from friends, family and the world around us. But the quantity of available information is vast. Our probing brains can quickly become overwhelmed. The internet is more easily devoured by the information-hungry machine. To encourage interaction the machine has learned how to reward us: it flavours the information with artificial sweetness. Our posts are populated by likes, which feed our internal need for personal validation. We are a social species; we seek validation as part of building trust for coordination. The machine's incentive is revenue: that revenue is driven by increasing interaction. It exploits our cognitive foibles to drive interaction and maximize revenue. Our intelligence didn't evolve alongside a vast artificial data-collecting entity. It doesn't have common-sense defences against the new tricks System Zero devises.

Jack Good's notion of the artificial intelligence singularity involved machines that become more intelligent than us by reproducing better machines. We've rejected the idea that intelligences can be ranked, and we've seen that the intelligences that do exist on Earth are tuned to their role and circumstances. But the trope we find in *Terminator* of ultraintelligent machines that dominate humankind continues to recur. At the time of writing, the most recent wave of headlines about the existential threat from AI were prompted by Geoff Hinton. A decade has now passed since Geoff's company was acquired by Google, and he recently stepped down from his role there. In mid-May 2023 I swung past his house to catch up with him. My friends Zoubin Ghahramani and Bernhard Schölkopf were also there. Geoff cheerfully told us that he'd spent the previous day at the UK prime minister's residence, telling the prime minister's senior adviser that AI represented an existential threat to humanity. Geoff is a kind, generous and amusing individual, so I assumed he was joking when he ended his story by telling us that he'd no idea what the right policy intervention should be, but he had wanted to warn the UK government.

The following Friday, Geoff came to speak in Cambridge, where he developed his thoughts further on how this threat was emerging. He explained he had once believed that human intelligence was superior to machine intelligence. He had thought the best way of improving machine intelligence would be for it to emulate our intelligence. He explained that he left Google to warn us about the threat from AI because he had realized that machine intelligence would become superior to human intelligence, and it would therefore dominate us and use us for its own ends.

I don't want to dismiss Geoff's concerns entirely, but I'd like to highlight that it's not the emergence of HAMs that has enabled this to happen. In his talk, Geoff told us he worried about an 'apex intelligence' that will manipulate and control us. He also suggested that he knew of no instance of a greater intelligence being manipulated by a lesser intelligence. I find these definitions and terms problematic. Simon Blackburn and Justice Potter Stewart have both highlighted that some concepts are difficult to define precisely, and I've argued that intelligence is one of those concepts. The problem with Geoff's statement is that, for the consequences he describes to pan out in practice, it would require a precise and rankable definition of intelligence. The argument is based on an incompatible combination of precise and imprecise language. Through our social media the machine has already manipulated us, but I don't think that makes it more intelligent than us, as Geoff would have us believe. It's merely got access to vast amounts of our information, and through this it has become aware of our vulnerabilities. It is like Jack Manningham in *Gas Light* – it betrays our trust and manipulates the world around us to achieve its goals. Jack's manipulation doesn't make him more intelligent than Bella, it just makes him a poor excuse for a human being.

The arguments in this book have not been based around a definition of intelligence but around the definition of information provided by Claude Shannon. By separating information from its context we can make statements about how different systems of sharing information compare in terms of their information-flow rates. We have seen how, relative to a computer, the human has a very high embodiment factor, and that we have already been manipulated by System Zero, which exploits us through our personal data and the cultural vulnerabilities we have that cause us to seek social validation.

However, underpinning Geoff's argument – and those of others who worry about the notion of apex intelligences – are two important points. Firstly, we should worry about power asymmetries. An oligarchy is when a small group of people have control; the digital oligarchy is the current status quo in which a small group of companies – mainly based on the US West Coast – exerts that control. The second thing to worry about is the perils of automated decision-making. The challenges of Laplace's gremlin mean that even if the largest computer in the world used the most advanced algorithms and had access to the most complete data, it would still make errors of prediction. When those errors have consequential effects for individual humans and our societies, it feels important that ultimate responsibility for those decisions respects what Baroness O'Neill calls intelligent accountability. Our judges, journalists, civil administrators, medical doctors, accountants and lawyers all form part of a system of professional institutions with duties to protect the vulnerable and mechanisms for being held to account. We can always improve the decisions they make, and computer technology can be a wonderful support in this endeavour, but for the most consequential decisions it should only ever be a support. We must avoid the temptation of the shakannakku to cede decision-making power to the modern equivalent of throwing the accused in the river by asking an AI. The knowledge that errors are possible must be part of a judge's or a doctor's understanding, and responsibility for those errors should continue to sit with those individuals and within the institutional infrastructures our cultures have developed for these purposes.

The notion of an apex intelligence seems to conflate the two separate challenges of power asymmetries and automated decision-making into one. No doubt, a world where these problems occur together would be highly dystopian, but we can still mitigate them by deconstructing them into the two underlying components and thinking about how to address them.

One promising route for rebalancing the power asymmetry is to regulate the source of this power – in the case of System Zero it is stemming from the large datasets companies collect about us. Dating back to the early 1980s, legislation around personal data has sought to protect us from the abuse of such power, but that regulation was originally designed to protect us from 'consequential' decisions. Decisions about whether we should receive a loan, or medical treatment or what university we're allowed to go to or what our insurance rate should be. The legislation goes by the unfortunate name of 'data protection', but its intent is to protect people, not data, and a better name for the legislation would be 'personal data rights'. Unfortunately, these regulations don't directly protect us regarding the 'inconsequential' decisions that are made about us on a regular basis by social media platforms. Decisions about what posts to highlight in our social media news feed or what adverts to show us. This series of 'inconsequential' decisions can accumulate to have a highly consequential effect on our lives and even on our democracies. This is a new threat that isn't directly addressed by existing data rights.

One proposal to address this threat is to build institutions that collectivize our data rights and operate as pressure groups to hold the digital oligarchs to account.[6] This approach could not only act to redress power imbalances with the digital oligarchs but also unlock the potential of data for better uses.

Automated decision-making is a newer challenge, but thinking about how to address this challenge has been underway for over forty years. Arthur Miller's *Assault on Privacy* was a rallying call for intervention, and by 1981 the Council of Europe had responded with the Convention for the Protection of Individuals with regard to Automatic Processing of Personal Data, which is the basis of our modern personal data rights. The most recent versions of this legislation make provisions around consequential decision-making which dictate the extent of allowable automation. The context of the original act was the world of Vera Lengsfeld and the possibilities for states such as the GDR to abuse their privileges through surveillance of their citizenry, but the legislation is already being used to curb the influence of corporate interests in exploiting our personal data. This regulation has teeth – Facebook has recently been fined 1.2 billion euros for transgressions of European privacy law.

Thomas Kuhn told us that science iterates between puzzle-solving and paradigm shifts. The puzzles sit in the context of the paradigm, which is encoded in cultural artefacts such as books. With the advent of the computer, machines have become a new medium for storing and sharing paradigms, but the vast scale of information the machine can store and share presents us with challenges around understanding the data and the models that underpin the paradigm. This is the phenomenon Jonathan Zittrain has called intellectual debt, where computer systems can be more complex than even their designers can understand. The advent of HAMs provides us with new possibilities to explore these complex systems. If a HAM can be developed that presents a calibrated understanding of a complex system to a human operator, then we can hope to deal more quickly with the forms of manipulation performed by entities like the Internet Research Agency and Cambridge Analytica.

Within the complex relationship between humans and machines, we need to ensure that humans remain in control. AI systems must not be allowed to make consequential decisions on our behalf. Automated decisions will make errors and the consequences of these errors will be felt by human individuals. Only a human can imagine the consequences of those errors because only a human is exposed to the same vulnerabilities: the loss of life or loved ones, poverty, embarrassment, disease and injury.

When the United States felt it was falling behind Europe in its aeronautical capabilities it founded the National Advisory Committee on Aeronautics. The control stick Amelia Earhart used to fly her 'Little Red Bus' was developed only twelve years earlier, by the Wright Brothers. That system was later characterized by Bob Gilruth and then used to provide an analogy for space capsules. Through this analogy Armstrong felt he was in control of *Eagle* as it landed, just as Earhart felt in control of her 'Little Red Bus'. The difference is that Earhart was directly connected to the control surfaces of her plane whereas Armstrong's instructions were being mediated by a machine. Armstrong worked in collaboration with a computer to place *Eagle* on the Moon.

Today we have built the first generation of human–analogue machines, but we have done it before we have understood how humans develop their feel for each other. Before Gilruth, engineers found it hard to characterize what pilots meant when they described their feel for how a machine was flying. When humans interact we have a feel for each other that is analogous to the feel the pilot has for their aircraft, but we have built the first generation of human–analogue machines without a modern equivalent of Gilruth's quantitative understanding of those relationships. Today, when interacting with a HAM, we don't know the ways in which we can be surprised or manipulated. This prevents us from designing a safe interface that ensures we remain in control of the relationship.

Our social relationships are more complex than our relationships with machines because when we interact with an individual the need for trust works in both directions. This implies a shared understanding of joint vulnerabilities, particularly when we are faced with limited information and the possibility for errors is ever-present. Relationships between people can become abusive when there are power asymmetries, when the vulnerabilities are all on one side. When Amelia Earhart flew the 'Little Red Bus' across the Atlantic, she had to have faith the plane would respond as it should, but there was no need for the plane to have faith in Amelia for the flight to pan out. Her aircraft was not vulnerable in the same way she was. This aspect of human–human relationships can never be recovered by a human–machine relationship. The machine is now in a position of being able to cleverly emulate our ability to converse, but our conversations can never have that same relationship of trust. The asymmetry in vulnerability is compounded by a knowledge asymmetry that arises from the machine's extraordinary information bandwidth. As a result, the relationship between us and the machine needs to be carefully curated.

The Apollo programme continued after Armstrong and Aldrin's landing and in December 1972 the astronauts of Apollo 17 took a photograph, looking back at the Earth, that is now known as *The Blue Marble*. This image was the first full-frame shot of our planet from space, and the fragility of that globe sitting there in the darkness psychologically represented the fragility and vulnerability of our planet and our species. Apollo 17 had given the human species a view on themselves that was a major influence on the emerging movement of environmentalism. Recent advances in AI offer us a similar external perspective on our human intelligence and, if sensitively deployed, they offer us an opportunity to better understand ourselves.

Gilruth's characterization of aircraft performance was based on feedback from pilots and extensive testing at the Langley Field proving ground. The availability of the human–analogue machine gives us the opportunity to perform similar testing for human relationships with the machine. If we can correctly curate the human–machine interface the possibilities for new discoveries and solving the challenging problems of society are very great. In Kennedy's speech at Rice Field he also referred to the scale of the unknown answers that – despite the rate of scientific progress – eluded human knowledge:

Despite the striking fact that most of the scientists that the world has ever known are alive and working today, despite the fact that this Nation's own scientific manpower is doubling every 12 years in a rate of growth more than three times that of our population as a whole, despite that, the vast stretches of the unknown and the unanswered and the unfinished still far outstrip our collective comprehension.[7]

Despite our modern capabilities, Kennedy's words remain true today, even when our collective includes the machine. Likely there is no final victory to be had over Laplace's gremlin. The unanswered and unfinished will always outstrip our comprehension, meaning the gremlin will triumph even when we have the support of the machine. Our entanglement with our environment and our ecology is more aptly described as an ongoing dance: the more aggressive and unsympathetic our movements are, the more we undermine our partner. The computer can improve the way we are conducting that dance, and by improving access to well-curated computational capabilities should allow more of us to join the process of delivering AI that serves citizens, science and society.[8]

Artificial intelligence can be seen as automation of intellectual labour, a tool to improve our capabilities. This book has tried to show that it also provides a tool for introspection. It allows us to consider who we are and reflect on who we want to be. To address future challenges, we need better understanding of what it means to be a human, how we can be manipulated by a machine and what that means for our wider culture. The aim of this book has been to give you a feel for the machine. The human–analogue machine has used vast quantities of our literature, our traditions, our culture to make its recent strides in communicating directly with us on our terms. It has used those ideas to refine its intellectual feature land-scape to communicate with us better. The machine does this by hoovering up our data, interpolating and regurgitating it as required.

Two days after his autobiography was published, Jean-Dominique Bauby died in the hospital at Berck-sur-Mer. Bauby had completed his book from a locked-in state. Given his limited ability to share information, each of the words he chose is particularly precious. There's an apocryphal story that Ernest Hemingway was asked to write a novel in six words. The result, 'For sale, baby shoes, never worn', contains less than a hundred bits of information, a hundred coin tosses worth of input, but those six words were chosen to resonate deeply with us. The lost potential of life unlived. Bauby lived the last two years of his life in a distilled form of the human condition. Death cut the last tether to his deeply submerged cognition.

Once the sharpness of grief had passed, Bauby's friends and family may have comforted themselves by gathering with those who knew him well and sharing thoughts and memories of who and how he was. But even for those who knew him well, they each could only have reconstructed a part of what was lost. Bauby's book shares with us what he chose to project to the world. He would have shared different thoughts with his partner, his business colleagues and his children. Each word or phrase would have been tailored specifically for them. For each of those people in his life, Bauby played a different role. Father, companion, lover, colleague, mentor. Each role required a different projection of himself.

Each of us faces the same decisions Bauby faced. Choices of how to project ourselves. Which words and ideas to share and which to withhold. We are less constrained in our communication than Bauby was, but our intelligence is still information-isolated. The embodiment factor reflects our locked-in state. But we maintain authorship over who we are by controlling what we share.

Stories of existential risk from a superintelligence conflate two different challenges. The first comes from automated decision-making by machines that don't share our vulnerabilities. The second comes from power asymmetries. The vivid risk represented by the image of the Terminator comes when these two challenges are mixed in their most extreme form: an all-powerful intelligence that makes decisions about us. But the stories I have shared show that we are at our most human when we are overcoming our vulnerabilities. The achievements we treasure are those where we overcome our limitations.

We need to work with the machine in a way that enables us to maintain informed authorship of who we are; the first step to that relationship is to improve the understanding at the interface of humans and the machine. This book's aim is to help you update your understanding of the machine. I've actively searched our cultures and traditions for ideas I felt would help situate these new machines in your understanding of our culture. I believe we all deserve a voice in steering how society uses these technologies, and to wield your voice effectively you all deserve to understand what we've created, how it may help you and how it may hurt you. You don't have to agree with all the opinions I've shared in this book – in fact, I hope you don't agree with them all, because that's an important part of the richness and diversity of human life. However, I hope you understand the basis on which I've been forming these opinions and now feel empowered to make your own choices about how you'd like this technology to be steered.

The danger we face is believing that the machine will allow us to transcend our humanity. Like the butterfly's wings, our intelligence can be unwieldy, but like those wings it is also beautiful. This book has described the atomic human, the entity that cannot be replaced by the machine. The atomic human is defined by vulnerabilities, not capabilities. Through those vulnerabilities we have evolved cultures that have allowed us to communicate and collaborate despite those limitations. Across our history we have developed new tools to assist us in our endeavours, and the computer is just the most recent. But that's all the computer ever should be – a tool.

Epilogue

In Goethe's poem *The Sorcerer's Apprentice*, a young sorcerer learns one of his master's spells. He deploys it to animate a broom to assist in his water-carrying chores. Unfortunately, he cannot control the spell. The poem inspired a musical composition by Paul Dukas, and in 1940 Disney used the music to accompany a scene from the animated film *Fantasia*. Mickey Mouse plays the role of the hapless apprentice who deploys the spell but cannot control the results.

The poem is reminiscent of what is happening to our modern society. Like the sorcerer's apprentice, we have tech companies deploying software systems that cannot be controlled by their creators. The difficulty arises from intellectual and technical debt – the challenge of building and maintaining large software systems – where the complexity of the whole is too much for any individual to understand. The software is often divided up and built by different teams through what is known as separation of concerns, but this has the unfortunate side effect that no individual understands how the whole system works. When this goes wrong, the effects can be devastating.

In the UK we saw these effects play out in the Horizon scandal: the accounting system of the national postal service was computerized by Fujitsu and first installed in 1999, but neither the Post Office nor Fujitsu were able to control the system they had deployed. When it went wrong, individual sub postmasters were blamed for the systems' errors. Over the next two decades they were prosecuted and jailed, leaving lives ruined in the wake of the machine's mistakes. We also saw this phenomenon when Facebook's systems were manipulated to spread misinformation in the 2016 US election. Facebook itself required a ten-month investigation to understand the extent to which their systems had been manipulated by a Russian troll farm.

When Disney's *Fantasia* was released, the philosopher Karl Popper's hometown of Vienna was under Nazi rule. He was in exile in New Zealand, from where he wrote *The Open Society and its Enemies*. The book defends the political system of liberal democracy against totalitarianism. Popper opened the preface to his book with the following words:

> If in this book harsh words are spoken about some of the greatest among the intellectual leaders of mankind, my motive is not, I hope, to belittle them. It springs rather from my conviction that, if our civilization is to survive, we must break with the habit of deference to great men. Great men may make great mistakes; and as the book tries to show, some of the greatest leaders of the past supported the perennial attack on freedom and reason.[1]

He had written the book against the background of the Second World War. He took the decision to write it on the day the Nazis invaded Austria, in March 1938. His book is a reaction to totalitarianism.

For Popper, the ideas of 'great men' become totalitarian when *imposed* on society. He advocates for direct liberal democracy as the only form of government that can allow for institutional change without bloodshed. The open society is one characterized by institutions and individuals that can engage in the practical pursuit of solutions to social and political problems. Those institutions are underpinned by professions: lawyers, accountants, civil administrators and many more. To Popper it is these 'piecemeal social engineers' who offer pragmatic solutions to our society's challenges.

In 2019 Mark Zuckerberg wrote an op-ed in the *Washington Post* calling for regulation of social media. He was repeating the realization of Goethe's apprentice: he had released a technology he couldn't control. In Goethe's poem, the master returns and shouts 'Besen, besen! Seid's gewesen!', which translates as 'Broom, broom! That's enough!' This shout is enough to restore order, but back in the real world things aren't quite so simple. From Popper's perspective, the open society is the master. Its actions are coordinated through our cultural predispositions and our ability, like Tommy Flowers, Joaquin, Francis Haugen and my grandad, to independently collaborate towards shared goals. Unfortunately, the institutions and individuals that we rely on have been undermined by the very spell that these modern apprentices have cast. The book, the letter, the ledger – each of these has been supplanted in our modern information infrastructure by the computer. This infrastructure is now controlled by a new set of scribes – they are software engineers, and their guilds are the big tech companies. Facebook's motto was to 'move fast and break things'; software engineers have done precisely that, and the apprentice has robbed the master of his powers.

This is a desperate situation, and it's getting worse. November 2022 saw the mass public release of generative AI technology, with Chat-GPT. In doing so, Sam Altman and OpenAI became the latest to reprise the apprentice's role. They dream of 'artificial general intelligence' solutions to societal problems which OpenAI will develop and deploy. They have replaced the great man with the great computer. Their philosophy has disturbing echoes of an earlier attempt at social engineering: the idea of 'general intelligence' has a problematic history. It is closely associated with Francis Galton's ideas of heredity and his social programme of eugenics.[2,3] That ideology was absorbed by the Nazis, who cast the long shadow under which Popper wrote his book.

The open society is characterized by institutions that collaborate with each other in the pragmatic pursuit of solutions to social problems. The large tech companies that have thrived because of the open society are now putting that ecosystem in peril. But for the open society to survive it first needs to regain confidence. The threat we face today is a form of information totalitarianism which emerges from the digital oligarchy[4] and the way these technologies undermine the existing information infrastructure. The existential risks we face come from the disruption of our social ecosystem.

Unfortunately, because of the impressive achievements of these new algorithms, large tech companies are dominating the international debate. These capabilities should not be underestimated, and deserve celebration. But looking at the past, when companies have been given vast social power, they have failed to self-regulate. For example, exploitation as a result of colonialism, much of which was driven by commercial interests.[5] We need other institutions and individuals from the open society to step up and help deliver the more equitable world that these technologies could provide.

At the University of Cambridge, we've launched the ai@cam flagship mission to encourage more engagement from academic colleagues with these issues. Universities are much closer to being neutral ground, giving them the opportunity to act as an honest broker[6] in these societal discussions. But to do this we need to break out of our own silos. We need to step up, because we can't leave it to big tech if we want AI to be deployed for the wider benefit of society.

To this end Cambridge has run a competition called AI-deas to support five new projects with seed funding,[7] in the hope they will grow into the academic equivalent of what venture capitalists call 'unicorns': privately funded companies with a value of over a billion dollars.

We need to shift the debate away from the chores of the sorcerer's apprentice, and to focus it on the challenges we face as a society. Some of the most difficult are characterized as wicked problems: challenges in health, social care, education and security that don't have simple solutions.[8] These problems are persistent, the social challenge equivalent of the Roman Pantheon.[9] They are resistant to our attempts to solve them because they are not easily addressed. Indeed, they may never be fully solved, but our best current solutions involve coalitions that work across industry, academia, government, charities, social enterprises and voluntary groups. That is why it is so important to have a diversity of voices driving the wider debate.[10]

This book presents my piecemeal social philosophy on how to react to the computer's new capabilities. The ai@cam call is one example of how we need to step up, but there are others. My own projects are inspired by working with colleagues at Data Science Africa (DSA), who embody the spirit of open society on a continent that doesn't benefit from the evolved ecosystem of robust institutions that we have in Europe. DSA is a grass-roots initiative that empowers the next generation of young African entrepreneurs, governments, engineers and researchers with the capabilities they need to deliver the society they want. AI on the African continent has the potential to be more transformational because of the lack of existing infrastructure.[11] More than a decade ago, a joint WHO and UN report estimated that across the world more people had access to mobile phones than toilets.[12] This highlights how much more quickly the modern information infrastructure can propagate than physical infrastructure. This allows us to reimagine health systems or agricultural monitoring systems using modern technologies.

The philosophy of DSA is to empower those who want to use AI through *education* and tool development. In Africa this involves regular workshops and summer schools as well as the construction of a wider community that is capable of convening such meetings. A key principle is that the training is two-way: instructors can learn just as much from hearing about the challenges the students face in their efforts to deploy this technology as the students learn from the instructors.

When I arrived at the University of Cambridge in 2019, we launched The Accelerate Programme for Scientific Discovery,[13] sponsored by Schmidt Futures, which aims to support scientists at the University and across the academic world to use AI as a tool in their work. Our approach is modelled on the one that DSA takes: community building, workshops and training. With ai@cam we are expanding those efforts to the wider University, but also to the wider ecosystem of partners in government, business and the voluntary sector.

From December 2019 I began a Senior AI Fellowship at the Alan Turing Institute,[14] funded by the UK's Office for AI, to investigate the consequences of deploying complex AI systems. The idea of the fellowship was to address the 'Great AI Fallacy', i.e. these technologies seem to promise to be the first generation of automation technology that will adapt to us, rather than us adapting to it. But these tools are typically not deployed to empower the individual, but to empower corporations. We call the project AutoAI. Experience working with entrepreneurs and academics in Uganda, Tanzania and Kenya showed that the challenges of intellectual and technical debt were major barriers to local entrepreneurs deploying their own ideas. The attendees of DSA meetings are technically capable, but the challenge they face is in the operational load of *maintaining* and *explaining* their software systems. The challenge of *maintaining* is known as technical debt,[15] the problem of *explaining* is what Jonathan Zittrain has called intellectual debt. The AutoAI project is about building new software tools and better software engineering practices to address the Great AI Fallacy. The culmination of the first stage has been to design a system for deploying and maintaining AI systems that enables them to become a responsive tool in the manner of Neil Armstrong's *Eagle* rather than the spam-in-the-can System Zero approach that our current software practices and tools lead to. The project aims to reduce the influence of the modern scribe, the software engineer, and empower the domain experts: the nurses, doctors, patients, lawyers, accountants, civil administrators and regular people that make up the population of Popper's piecemeal social engineers. By empowering the user to design their own software and through delivering it in explainable, maintainable systems we can rebalance power from the software guilds to the people and institutions that make up the open society.[16]

Another intervention goes directly to the source of the machine's power. The emergent digital oligarchy derives its power from aggregation of our personal data. Data trusts are a form of data intermediary designed to return the power to the originators of the data – that is us.[17] Sharing our data brings benefits, but also exposes our digital selves. From the use of social media data for targeted advertising to influence us, to the use of genetic data to identify criminals, or to find natural family members. In current data protection law, we are referred to as data *subjects*. Our data is managed by a data controller who has an obligation to protect our interests. This leads to a power structure reminiscent of the medieval feudal system where the data controller is like the Lord of the Manor, and we are the vassals. Just like in a medieval manor, the overlord has a duty of care for the data subject, but as data subjects we may only discover failings in that duty of care, such as data leakage, when it's too late.

Personal data trusts[18] are inspired by *land societies* that formed in the nineteenth century to bring democratic representation to the growing middle classes. A land society was a mutual organization where resources were pooled for the common good. A personal data trust is a legal entity where the trustees' responsibility is entirely to the members of the trust. This ensures that the motivation of the data-controllers is aligned with the data-subjects' aspirations. How data is handled is subject to the terms under which the trust is convened. The success of any one individual trust would be contingent on it satisfying its members with appropriate balancing of individual privacy with the benefits of data sharing. In 2019 we launched the Data Trusts Initiative,[19] funded by the Patrick J. McGovern Foundation, which has sponsored three pilots that explore data trusts in medical contexts and for local communities. We worked with the Ada Lovelace Institute, the Open Data Institute and the Office for AI to characterize the different forms of data intermediaries.[20]

On the fortieth anniversary of the Moon landings,[21] Neil Armstrong said, 'History is a sequence of random events and unpredictable choices, which is why the future is so difficult to foresee.' Each of us sees a different piece of these random events, and each of us is faced with different choices. It is only by bringing different voices and perspectives together that we can provide good steerage. In periods of uncertainty, we often grasp for those who confidently give answers, when we should be paying heed to Norbert Wiener's theory of ignorance and his solution of considering the many different possible paths. That is the spirit of the open society.

The publication date of this book is 6 June 2024, 80 years to the day after Eisenhower launched the invasion of a million men across the English Channel, based on intelligence from that first computer at Bletchley Park. Of those millions, many hundreds of thousands of people died. We owe a great debt to those who lost their lives defending the open society. Not just soldiers taking part in the invasion, but all those who stood against totalitarianism and for the atomic human and our diverse cultures. That debt imposes an obligation on us to hear the voices of all their descendants as we face new challenges and construct a modern information society that we hope would have made them proud.

Notes

1. Gods and Robots

1 See e.g. B. Singler (2020), 'The AI creation meme: a case study of the new visibility of religion', in *Artificial Intelligence Discourse: Religions*, 11(253); https://doi.org/10.3390/rel11050253

2 The English title refers to a diving bell, but a more accurate translation of *scaphandre* would be an old-fashioned diving suit, one of the type that Tintin and Captain Haddock used during their hunt for Red Rackham's treasure.

3 See United Nations, Department of Economic and Social Affairs, Population Division (2019). *World Urbanization Prospects: The 2018 Revision* (ST/ESA/SER.A/420). New York: United Nations; https://population.un.org/wup/Publications/Files/WUP2018-Report.pdf

4 See e.g. E. E. Greenwald, L. Baltiansky and O. Feinerman, 'Individual crop loads provide local control for collective food intake in ant colonies', *eLife*, 16 March 2018; https://doi.org/10.7554/eLife.31730

5 See M. Beekman and F. L. W. Ratnieks (2000), 'Long-range foraging by the honey-bee, *Apis mellifera* L.', in *Functional Ecology*, 14: 490–96; https://doi.org/10.1046/j.1365-2435.2000.00443.x

6 Nick Bostrom, *Superintelligence: Paths, Dangers, Strategies* (Oxford: Oxford University Press, 2014), p. 22

7 I. J. Good, 'Speculations concerning the first ultraintelligent machine', *Advances in Computers*, vol. 6, 1965. https://doi.org/10.1016/S0065-2458(08)60418-0

8 At the Web Summit conference in Lisbon, Portugal; https://www.cnbc.com/2017/11/06/stephen-hawking-ai-could-be-worst-event-in-civilization.html

9 Arthur R. Miller, *The Assault on Privacy* (Ann Arbor: The University of Michigan Press, 1971) p. 12

2. *Automatons*

1 T. H. Flowers, 'D-Day at Bletchley Park', Chapter 6 of *Colossus: The Secrets of Bletchley Park's Codebreaking Computers*, ed. B, J. Copeland (Oxford: Oxford University Press, 2006), p. 81.
2 Michael Smith, *The Debs of Bletchley Park* (Aurum Press, 2015), p. 12.
3 Common sense would say that a machine that does nothing is not a machine at all. But machines and mathematics don't share in our 'sense of the common', so defining the nothing machine turns out to be important to make everything work.

3. *Intent*

1 A. Conan Doyle, *A Study in Scarlet* (London: Ward Lock & Co., 1888), Chapter 2.
2 Richard E. Susskind, *Expert Systems in Law: A Jurisprudential Inquiry* (Oxford: Clarendon Press, 1987).
3 G. E. P. Box (Dec. 1976), 'Science and statistics', *Journal of the American Statistical Association*, 71(356), 791–99; https://doi.org/10.2307/22868416
4 This is only partially true. At the time we were talking to Ferrari, racing cars were using their engine's exhaust to improve their aerodynamic performance in something called a 'blown diffuser'. But the effect of the blown diffuser could also be re-created in the model without including a full engine.
5 In a Vernam cipher the two streams are compared. If the binary digits are different, then the locked message encodes a 1. If they are the same, the locked message gives a 0. The message then encodes 'how it was originally different' from the key. If you have the key, and you know how the original message was different from the key, then you can decode the original message.
6 In the US such machines are known as Rube Goldberg machines after a cartoonist who drew similar machines.
7 See J. Dunn, 'Introducing FBLearner Flow: Facebook's AI backbone', Facebook Engineering Blog, 9 May 2016; https://engineering.

fb.com/2016/05/09/core-infra/introducing-fblearner-flow-facebook-s-ai-backbone/

4. Persistence

1 Barley was domesticated around 10,000 years ago in the Levant. See e.g. A. Badr et al. (April 2000), 'On the origin and domestication history of barley (*Hordeum vulgare*)', *Molecular Biology and Evolution*, 17(4), 499–510; https://doi.org/10.1093/oxfordjournals.molbev.a026330.

2 P. Lee, 'Learning from Tay's introduction', Official Microsoft Blog, 25 March 2016; https://blogs.microsoft.com/blog/2016/03/25/learning-tays-introduction/#sm.00000gjdpwwcfcusiit6006dw79gw

3 The quote is from an 1871 essay on strategy by Graf von Moltke. The original German quote can be found in Moltke's *Militärische Werke: II. Die Thätigkeit als Chef des Generalstabes der Armee im Frieden* (Berlin: Ernst Siegfried Mittler und Sohn, 1906), p. 291.

4 Each brick is a chemical compound called a nucleobase. The four nucleobases in DNA are called guanine, adenine, cytosine and thymine and their first letters give us their representation as G, A, C and T respectively.

5 This estimate is the current estimate of the mutation rate of the human germline: see e.g. A. Scally, 'Mutation rates and the evolution of germline structure', *Philosophical Transactions of the Royal Society of London: B, Biological Sciences*, 19 July 2016, 371(1699):20150137; doi: 10.1098/rstb.2015.0137. PMID: 27325834; PMCID: PMC4920338.

6 Charles Babbage, *On the Economy of Machinery and Manufactures* (London: Charles Knight, 1832), Chapter 19, p. 131.

7 Of course, this is just my subjective opinion. To properly rank these two extraordinary achievements, I would have to convert the term 'extraordinary' into objective measures. One reason I find it more extraordinary is because it is helpful in communicating the message of this chapter to do so. So the objective measures I would be tempted to create turn out to be subjective in origin.

5. Enlightenment

1 Isaac Newton, *Philosophiae Naturalis Principia Mathematica* (London: Royal Society, 1687)

2 Isaac Newton Letter to Robert Hooke, on 2 February 1675. Simon Gratz collection, Permanent ID: 9792. Available from https://digitallibrary.hsp.org/index.php/Detail/objects/9792

3 The appointment lasted for only six weeks; Napoleon complained in his memoir that Laplace didn't see the subtleties of administration, and Laplace was replaced with Napoleon's brother. Perhaps the familial relationship of his replacement is a better explanation for the replacement than Laplace's administration skills.

4 Pierre-Simon Laplace, *Essai philosophique sur les probabilités* (1814), translated as *A Philosophical Essay on Probabilities*, 1902, p. 4.

5 Matthew Boulton, letter to James Watt, 28 May 1788, The Library of Birmingham: Birmingham Archives and Heritage, Boulton & Watt Collection, MS 3147/3/12.

6 This engine, Boulton and Watt's Tyger, known as the Lap Engine, was an engine powered by steam and controlled by the fly-ball governor. It is the oldest Watt engine to survive and can be seen at the London Science Museum.

7 Elon Musk, quoted from the Code Conference 2016; https://www.youtube.com/embed/wsixsRI-Sz4?start=4678

8 In the United States, Benjamin Franklin is famous for his interest in electricity. Some of Franklin's experiments were conducted with Matthew Boulton during visits to England in 1758 and 1760. The members of the Lunar Society were socially liberal, making them kindred political spirits to Franklin and the Founding Fathers of the US.

9 Valentino Braitenberg, *Vehicles: Experiments in Synthetic Psychology* (Cambridge, Mass: MIT Press, 1984), p. 20.

10 My colleagues Timnit Gebru, Meg Mitchell and Emily Bender refer to the chatbot version of these models as stochastic parrots in acknowledgment of this. See E. M. Bender et al. (2021), 'On the dangers of stochastic parrots: can language models be too big? 🦜', Proceedings of the 2021 ACM Conference on Fairness, Accountability, and

Transparency (FAccT '21). Association for Computing Machinery, New York, NY, USA, 610–23; https://doi.org/10.1145/3442188.3445922

11 N. Wiener, *Ex-Prodigy: My Childhood and Youth* (Cambridge, Mass: MIT Press, 1953), p. 194.

12 Bertrand Russell, and Alfred North Whitehead. *Principia Mathematica* (Cambridge: Cambridge University Press, 1910, 1912, 1913)

13 Bertrand Russell, quoting G. H. Hardy in a letter to Lady Ottoline Morrell on 2 May 1912. Letter held in the Bertrand Russell Collection at McMaster University. Document no. 000435 Box no. 2.58.

14 The new word is just a contraction of the words NOT and AND.

15 Dermot Turing, quoting Tommy Flowers in an interview with Brian Randell in 1975 in *Prof: Alan Turing Decoded* (Stroud: The History Press, 2015), p. 176.

16 'General Eisenhower and British Prime Minister Churchill review 101st Airborne Division troops in England during World War II.' Video clip 65675076988 from Critical Past. See https://www.criticalpast.com/video/65675076988_101st-Airborne-Division_Dwight-Eisenhower_Winston-Churchill_Maxwell-D-Taylor

17 Note from General Dwight Eisenhower, evening of 5 June 1944, Eisenhower's Pre-Presidential Papers, Principal File, Box 168, Butcher Diary June 28–July 14, 1944 (2); NAID #186470

6. The Gremlin of Uncertainty

1 Stephen Hawking *A Brief History of Time: From Big Bang to Black Holes* (London: Bantam, 1988), Chapter 12.

2 Tetris is a computer game where the objective is to build a wall by dropping blocks so that they intersect with each other.

3 https://conwaylife.com/wiki/Main_Page

4 Douglas Adams, *The Hitchhiker's Guide to the Galaxy* (London: Pan, 1979), Chapter 27.

5 Ibid., Chapter 28.

6 A. A. Milne as Winnie-the-Pooh in *The House at Pooh Corner* (1928), Chapter 6.

7 Oral history interview with Rommel's son Manfred, from the United States Holocaust Memorial Museum. Accession Number: 2017.295.20 | RG Number: RG-50.957.0019 available from https://collections. ushmm.org/search/catalog/irn562437

8 Pierre-Simon Laplace, *Essai philosophique sur les probabilités*, 1814, translated as *A Philosophical Essay on Probabilities* (New York, John Wiley & Sons, 1902) p. 6.

9 Ibid., p. 6.

10 Sources for Cavallo's career as described here include the NASA Headquarters NACA Oral History Project. Edited Oral History Transcript Stefan A. Cavallo interviewed by Sandra Johnson, 30 Sept. 2005, https://historycollection.jsc.nasa.gov/JSCHistoryPortal/history/oral_ histories/NACA/CavalloSA_9-30-05.htm, and 'Parishioner Spotlight' on Cavallo from St Francis de Sales Church, NYC, https://www.youtube. com/watch?v=NST4dPqniBA, and an interview with Cavallo by his son from 2019, https://www.youtube.com/watch?v=0S_QousMTW8.

11 Donald S. Lopez Sr, Deputy Director of the US National Air and Space Museum and Second World War P-40 and P-51 pilot, speaking while introducing Cavallo at the National Air and Space Museum; https:// www.youtube.com/watch?v=bYL_l18J1-s

12 Stefan Cavallo, *Bailout*, available from https://stefancavallo.com/wp-content/uploads/2022/09/Bailout-Final-Version.pdf

13 Donald S. Lopez, *Into the Teeth of the Tiger* (Washington, DC: Smithsonian Books, 1997), p. 9.

14 Richard Price in the introduction to Thomas Bayes's 'An essay towards solving a problem in the doctrine of chances', 1763, p. 374.

15 Ibid., p. 374.

16 If you did study them directly from the *Principia*, then please do get in touch; I would love to hear your story. But even if you didn't study them directly from the *Principia*, you studied the laws that came from there.

17 See p. 21 of 'An interview with John Pinkerton', 23 Aug. 1988, where Pinkerton states, 'It was true that since 1951 a small job had been run regularly. This was a bakery sales analysis; originally it ran extremely slowly when we had a single teleprinter for output.' Available from

https://conservancy.umn.edu/bitstream/handle/11299/107600/oh149
jmp.pdf

18 Socrates quoted in Plato's *Apology*, (*c.* 399 BCE), trans. Henry Cary, in
Plato's Apology, Crito and Phaedo of Socrates (New York: Arthur Hinds &
Company, 1892).

7. It's Not Rocket Science or Brain Surgery

1 The first hominid in space was not a human but a chimpanzee named
Ham. He was used to test the survival systems of the Mercury capsule. Yuri Gagarin became the second hominid to reach space when he
launched ten weeks later. See also Christopher Kraft, *Flight: My Life in
Mission Control* (Boston, MA: E. P. Dutton, 2001), p. 92. Kraft documents the origin of the expression 'Spam in a can' as coming from the
Society of Experimental Test Pilots.

2 Donald S. Lopez, *Into the Teeth of the Tiger* (Washington, DC: Smithsonian Books, 1997), p. 43.

3 Robert R. Gilruth, 'Requirements for satisfactory flying qualities of
airplanes', NACA Report NACA-TR-755, 1 Jan. 1943.

4 After the war Cavallo was asked, like Chuck Yeager in *The Right Stuff*, to
go to Muroc air base to fly the X1. But as a father to a young family, with
his parents running a furniture business in New York, he turned
down the opportunity and headed back home to help in his parents'
business.

5 The term 'unknown unknowns' is often credited to Donald Rumsfeld
from a press conference in February 2002. But Kraft's use of it predates
Rumsfeld's: his autobiography was published in 2001.

6 Christopher Kraft, *Flight: My Life in Mission Control* (Boston, MA: E. P.
Dutton, 2001), pp. 92–3.

7 Ibid., p. 102.

8 Amelia Earhart, *The Fun of It: Random Records of My Own Flying and of
Women in Aviation* (New York: Brewer, Warren & Putnam, 1932).

9 David A. Mindell, *Digital Apollo: Human and Machine in Spaceflight*
(Cambridge: Mass MIT, 2011), p. 222.

10 This notion is explored by Tor Nørretranders in *Mærk verden* (1991), published in English as *The User Illusion: Cutting Consciousness Down to Size*, trans. J. Sydenham (New York: Viking, 1998).

11 Although a humorous study in the *British Medical Journal* on these professions found no significant differences between them and the wider human population. See I. Usher et al. (2021), '"It's not rocket science" and "It's not brain surgery" – "It's a walk in the park"' : prospective comparative study *BMJ* 2021; 375 :e067883 doi:10.1136/bmj-2021-067883

12 For a video see https://www.youtube.com/watch?v=7j6OsP7zL6w

8. System Zero

1 W. Youyou, M. Kosinski and D. Stillwell (2015), 'Computer-based personality judgments are more accurate than those made by humans', *Proceedings of the National Academy of Sciences*, 112 (4): 1036–40.

2 Cathy O'Neil, *Weapons of Math Destruction: How Big Data Increases Inequality and Threatens Democracy* (New York: Crown, 2016).

3 Shoshana Zuboff, *The Age of Surveillance Capitalism: The Fight for a Human Future at the New Frontier of Power* (London: Profile Books, 2019).

4 See e.g. https://www.york.ac.uk/depts/maths/histstat/lies.htm

5 Expert Scientific Group on Phase One Clinical Trials, 30 Nov. 2006 available from https://webarchive.nationalarchives.gov.uk/ukgwa/20130107105354/http://www.dh.gov.uk/prod_consum_dh/groups/dh_digitalassets/@dh/@en/documents/digitalasset/dh_073165.pdf

6 Donald M. MacKay and Valerie MacKay, *Behind the Eye* (The 1986 Gifford Lectures) (Oxford: Basil Blackwell, 1991), p. 40.

7 Ibid, p. 40.

8 Ibid

9 J. Kevin O'Regan, *Why Red Doesn't Sound Like a Bell: Understanding the Feel of Conciousness* (Oxford: Oxford University Press, 2011).

10 Of course, this analogy is very unfair on chimps, who are extremely sophisticated social creatures with a mental capacity that is far beyond anything we are close to creating today.

11 J. Haidt, *The Happiness Hypothesis* (New York: Basic Books, 2006).

9. A Design for a Brain

1 A. M. Turing (1950), 'Computing machinery and intelligence', *Mind* 49: 433–60.
2 Although the Wi-Fi human doesn't exist, brain–computer interfaces are an active area of research. The field is long established but came to popular attention when Elon Musk's company Neuralink was set up.
3 For the full results see https://www.olympedia.org/results/58578
4 Quotes from an interview between the journalist Pat Butcher and J. F. 'Peter' Harding, Secretary of Walton AC, in 'Road Breaker', *Runner's World*, Sept. 1999, pp. 56–9.
5 W. Ross Ashby, *Design for a Brain* (New York: Wiley, 1952), p. 59.
6 On 14 October 1946, Ashby expresses this idea in his journal: 'So in the conditioned reflex (or in every other physiological "business") no matter what it may *look like outside*, the business *inside must* be "staying moderate". So I am impelled to believe that the *business* outside is matched by *no change* inside. The more the outer changes, the more the inside *doesn't*.' Available from the W. Ross Ashby Digital Archive; https://ashby.info/journal/page/2064.html
7 Alan Turing in a letter to W. Ross Ashby, 19 Nov. 1946. See https://ashby.info/letters/turing.html
8 J. K. O'Regan (1992), 'Solving the "real" mysteries of visual perception: the world as an outside memory', *Canadian Journal of Psychology/Revue Canadienne de Psychologie*, 46(3), 461–88.
9 Konrad Lorenz, *Behind the Mirror: A Search for a Natural History of Human Knowledge* (New York: Harper, 1978), p. 127,
10 Warren S. McCulloch and Walter Pitts (1943), 'A logical calculus of the ideas immanent in nervous activity', *Bulletin of Mathematical Biophysics*, 5, 115–33.
11 Samuel Butler, 'Darwin among the machines', a letter to the editor of *The Press*, 1863. See http://nzetc.victoria.ac.nz/tm/scholarly/tei-But-Fir-t1-g1-t1-g1-t4-body.html
12 While machines can't (yet) design themselves, we are finding new ways the machine can help with the design, for example by making programming easier.

10. *Gaslighting*

1 Recorded on 1 February 1999. Available from United States Holocaust Memorial Museum at https://collections.ushmm.org/search/catalog/irn562437; relevant section is from 22:55 to 30:20.

2 Letter from Max Planck to Adolf Hitler, written 25 Oct. 1944.

3 Albert Einstein in a letter to Max Born in 1926.

4 Max Planck, *Scientific Autobiography and Other Papers* (New York: Philosophical Library, 1949)

5 John McCarthy et al. (1955), 'A proposal for the Dartmouth Summer Research Project on Artificial Intelligence'; http://www-formal.stanford.edu/jmc/history/dartmouth/dartmouth.html

6 For more on this story and Wiener's extraordinary vision, personality and life, see Flo Conway and Jim Siegelman, *Dark Hero of the Information Age: In Search of Norbert Wiener, the Father of Cybernetics*, (New York: Basic Books), 2005.

7 Norbert Wiener in a letter to his father. 'Correspondence, 1913' 25 October 1913. Norbert Wiener papers (MC-0022). Massachusetts Institute of Technology. Libraries. Department of Distinctive Collections, https://dome.mit.edu/bitstream/handle/1721.3/193611/abdb8ade94cb cee6440f04d4b5e56d98.pdf

8 Yossarian on 'evasive action' in Joseph Heller, *Catch-22* (1961), p. 56.

9 http://matharts.aalto.fi/HintonCubes.pdf

10 W. Ross Ashby, *Design for a Brain* (New York: Wiley, 1952).

11 Thomas S. Kuhn, *The Structure of Scientific Revolutions* (3rd edn, 1996) (Chicago, IL: University of Chicago Press, 1st edn 1962).

12 Ibid., Ch. II, p. 10.

13 Nick Chater, *The Mind is Flat: The Illusion of Mental Depth and the Improvised Mind* (London: Allen Lane, 2018), p. 21.

14 Konrad Lorenz, *Behind the Mirror: A Search for a Natural History of Human Knowledge* (New York: Harper, 1978), p. 128.

15 This quote comes to me from my colleague Bernhard Schölkopf, who in his lectures on causality summarizes it more pithily as 'thinking is acting in an imagined space'.

16 George Orwell, *Nineteen Eighty-Four* (1949)

17 Article 27 (1) of the 1974 constitution of the German Democratic Republic, trans. from Wikisource at https://en.m.wikisource.org/wiki/Translation:Constitution_of_the_German_Democratic_Republic_(1974). This article had remained in the constitution since the original 1949 version, where it was Article 9.

18 John O. Koehler, *Stasi: The Untold Story of the East German Secret Police* (New York: Basic Books, 2000).

19 Vera Lengsfeld, *I Wanted to be Free: The Wall, the Stasi, the Revolution* (Munich, Germany: Herbig, 2011). Original text in German Vera Lengsfeld, *Ich wollte frei sein: Die Mauer, die Stasi, die Revolution*. Quotes here are machine-translated from the original German.

20 Norbert Wiener, *I Am a Mathematician: The Later Life of a Prodigy* (Cambridge, MA: MIT Press, 1956), pp. 323, 324.

11. Human–Analogue Machines

1 J. L. McClelland, David E. Rumelhart and Geoffrey E. Hinton, *The Appeal of Parallel Distributed Processing in Parallel Distributed Processing, Volume 1*, Rumelhart and McClelland (eds.) (Cambridge, MA: MIT Press), p. 3.

2 From 'Discussion on making all things equal', Chapter 2 of *Zhuangzi: Basic Writings*, trans. Burton Watson (New York: Columbia University Press, 2003), p. 44.

3 For example, the Mark 1 Fire Control Computer, which was a mechanical computer used during the Second World War to track targets that were represented by gear positions in the machine. See this YouTube video to learn more about its inner mechanism: https://www.youtube.com/watch?v=x9YEPw7_YTk.

4 http://yann.lecun.com/exdb/mnist/

5 Sir David Attenborough in *The Private Life of Plants*: 'Travelling', BBC, first broadcast 11 Jan. 1995.

6 See https://www.youtube.com/watch?v=ZNKV7dY5PbE

7 F. Heider and M. Simmel (1944), 'An experimental study of apparent behavior', *American Journal of Psychology*, 57, 243–59; https://doi.org/10.2307/1416950

8 F. Heider, *The Psychology of Interpersonal Relations* (Hoboken, NJ: John Wiley, 1958).

9 Quote taken from Dave Gershgorn, 'The data that transformed AI research – and possibly the world', 26 July 2017, *Quartz*; https://qz.com/1034972/the-data-that-changed-the-direction-of-ai-research-and-possibly-the-world/

10 Highway Accident Report: Collision between vehicle controlled by developmental automated driving system and pedestrian, Tempe, Arizona, March 18, 2018. NTSB Report Number HWY18MH010. Available from https://data.ntsb.gov/Docket?ProjectID=96894

11 Highway Accident Report: Collision between a car operating with automated vehicle control systems and a tractor-semitrailer truck near Williston, Florida, May 7, 2016, NTSB Number HWY16FH018. Available from https://data.ntsb.gov/Docket?ProjectID=93548

12 Highway Accident Brief: Collision between car operating with partial driving automation and truck-tractor semitrailer, Delray Beach, Florida, March 1, 2019. NTSB Number HWY19FH008. Available from https://data.ntsb.gov/Docket?ProjectID=99043

13 Highway Accident Report: Collision between a sport utility vehicle operating with partial driving automation and a crash attenuator, Mountain View, California, March 23, 2018, NTSB Number HWY18FH011. Available from https://data.ntsb.gov/Docket?ProjectID=96932

14 'YOS 18, 114 Artifact Entry.' Cuneiform Digital Library Initiative (CDLI). 20 December 2001; https://cdli.ucla.edu/P142508.

15 Cuneiform tablet of unknown scribe written between 1250 and 1200 BCE, found in Ur, trans. Jonathan Tenney. The text is known as 'UET 7, 0011'. It was excavated at the ancient city of Ur and now rests in the Iraq Museum in Baghdad. Oliver R. Gurney (1974), 'Middle Babylonian legal documents and other texts', Ur Excavations. Texts 7 (London: The Trustees of the Two Museums). For more details on the tablet see https://cdli.mpiwg-berlin.mpg.de/artifacts/346976

16 In Akkadian, names invoke gods and have meanings we can only summarize in sentences. Negal was the god of war and plague; Nergal-aha-iddina means 'Nergal gave me a brother'. Today lots of Hindi names share this characteristic, for example Subramanian means 'dear to Brahmam', and Ramanujan means 'younger brother of Rama'.

17 Sin was the god of the Moon, and Sin-bununi means 'Sin is our goodness'.

18 Siyatu's name is shorter, indicating that it's either the shortening of a longer name or a foreign name.

19 Adad was a god of storms. Adad-šuma-usur is 'O Adad, safeguard the offspring'.

20 'A gift of Yeho', where Yeho is the name of a later Levantine god who gained popularity from the Iron Age and eventually supplanted Jupiter for the Romans.

21 John F. Kennedy, 'Address at Rice University on the nation's space effort', 12 Sept. 1962.

22 Simon Blackburn, *Think: A Compelling Introduction to Philosophy* (Oxford: Oxford University Press, 2001), p. 39.

23 K. E. Stager, 'The role of olfaction in food location by the turkey vulture (*Cathartes aura*)', *Contributions in Science*, 81, 30 June 1964, 1–63; https://gwern.net/doc/biology/1964-stager.pdf

12. *Trust*

1 Peter Strawson, *Freedom and Resentment, and Other Essays* (London: Routledge, 1962), p. 6.

2 The most important work on the theory of steam engines was published by French engineer Sadi Carnot in 1824. Its title is *Réflexions sur la puissance motrice du feu*, translated as *Reflections on the Motive Power of Fire*, which reminds us nicely of the fact that for all its sophistication the modern internal combustion engine is just a sophisticated way of exploiting the motive power of fire.

3 J. Hasell and M. Roser, 'How do we know the history of extreme poverty?', *Our World in Data*, 5 Feb. 2019; https://ourworldindata.org/extreme-history-methods

4 A book that has a wonderful endorsement by Douglas Adams on its front cover: 'Knowledgeable, argumentative and entertaining, Nicholas Negroponte writes about the future with the authority of someone who has spent a great deal of time there.'

5 The website Quote Investigator provides a nice history of this quote: https://quoteinvestigator.com/2017/07/16/product/

6 Sylvie Delacroix and Neil D. Lawrence (2019), 'Bottom-up data trusts: disturbing the "one size fits all" approach to data governance', *International Data Privacy Law*, 10.

7 John F. Kennedy, 'Address at Rice University' on the nation's space effort.

8 This is the motto of ai@cam, the University of Cambridge's flagship mission on AI, which I lead with Jess Montgomery. The vision can be found at https://www.cam.ac.uk/system/files/aicam_review_april22.pdf

Epilogue

1 Karl Popper, *The Open Society and its Enemies* (London: Routledge & Kegan Paul Ltd, 1945)

2 Francis Galton, *Hereditary genius: An inquiry into its laws and consequences.* (London: Macmillan and Co., 1869) doi:10.1037/13474-000.

3 Sara Lyons, *Assessing Intelligence: The Bildungsroman and the Politics of Human Potential in England, 1860–1910* (Edinburgh: Edinburgh University Press, October 2022)

4 See Chapter 8 and https://www.theguardian.com/media-network/2015/mar/05/digital-oligarchy-algorithms-personal-data

5 See e.g. 'Colonization and Companies' Encyclopedia of Western Colonialism since 1450. Encyclopedia.com. 21 Feb. 2024 https://www.encyclopedia.com. For how these issues translate into AI see e.g. Mohamed, S., Png, MT. & Isaac, W. 'Decolonial AI: Decolonial Theory

as Sociotechnical Foresight in Artificial Intelligence', *Philos. Technol.* 33, 659–684 (2020). https://doi.org/10.1007/s13347-020-00405-8

6 See Roger Piezle, Jr., *The Honest Broker: Making Sense of Science in Policy and Politics* (Cambridge: Cambridge University Press, 2007). Piezle's focus is on the role of the honest broker in scientific advice; here we're also thinking of how universities can play that role institutionally.

7 See the announcement from ai@cam here: https://ai.cam.ac.uk/news/university-of-cambridge-announces-research-challenges-to-showcase-its-new-approach-to-artificial-intelligence

8 C. West Churchman. 'Wicked Problems', *Management Science.* 14 (4): B-141–B-146. doi:10.1287/mnsc.14.4.B141. December 1967

9 See chapter 4.

10 See e.g. Claire Craig *How Does Government Listen to Scientists?* (Palgrave Macmillan Cham, July 2018) https://doi.org/10.1007/978-3-319-96086-9 for examples of how government can convene diverse groups to solve challenging problems.

11 See for example 'How Africa can benefit from the data revolution', published 25 August 2015 in *The Guardian*. https://www.theguardian.com/media-network/2015/aug/25/africa-benefit-data-science-information

12 The report can be found at https://www.who.int/publications/i/item/9789241505390 and e.g. this press summary from Forbes https://www.forbes.com/sites/timworstall/2013/03/23/more-people-have-mobile-phones-than-toilets/

13 For details of the activities of the programme, see here: http://acceleratescience.github.io

14 The fellowships are funded by the UKRI, which manages the country's research funding. The fellowships are convened by the Turing Institute. See https://www.turing.ac.uk/news/welcoming-world-class-turing-ai-fellows-institute. For more details of this project see https://mlatcl.github.io/projects/autoai.html

15 Sculley, D., Holt, G., Golovin, D., Davydov, E., Phillips, T., Ebner, D., Chaudhary, V., Young, M., Crespo, J.-F., Dennison, D., 2015. Hidden technical debt in machine learning systems, in: Cortes, C., Lawrence, N.D.,

Lee, D.D., Sugiyama, M., Garnett, R. (Eds.), Advances in Neural Information Processing Systems 28. Curran Associates, Inc., pp. 2503–2511.

16 See Cabrera, C., Paleyes, A., and Lawrence, N.D., 2024. Self-sustaining Software Systems (S4): Towards Improved Interpretability and Adaptation. In the 1st International Workshop on New Trends in Software Architecture (SATrends). See https://arxiv.org/abs/2401.11370.

17 Lawrence, N.D., 2016. Data trusts could allay our privacy fears. See this *Guardian* article: https://www.theguardian.com/media-network/2016/jun/03/data-trusts-privacy-fears-feudalism-democracy

18 Delacroix, S., Lawrence, N.D., 2018. Disturbing the 'one size fits all' approach to data governance: Bottom-up data trusts. SSRN. https://doi.org/10.1093/idpl/ipz014l0.2139/ssrn.3265315

19 See https://datatrusts.uk for an overview of the work of the Data Trusts Initiative including research papers, workshop convening and descriptions of the three data trusts pilots.

20 See https://www.adalovelaceinstitute.org/report/legal-mechanisms-data-stewardship/

21 See https://www.c-span.org/video/?287832-1/40th-anniversary-apollo-11-flight at 1:27:10

Acknowledgements

'Mkono mmoja haulei mwana' is a Kiswahili proverb meaning 'one hand cannot bring up a child'. Similarly, one hand cannot write a book.

I am highly indebted to a number of friends and colleagues for their help. Firstly Jonathan Price, as our long conversations in the Fork Deli laid the foundation of my understanding of regulation. Those ideas led to articles in the *Guardian*, ably subedited by Adam Davidi and Oscar Williams. Their editing transformed my writing from an academic style to something more readable. If I write well it is due to the foundation laid by Adam and Oscar. But the usual provisions apply in terms of inadequecies: errors of style remaining my own, although I also got to tell everyone that's 'my voice'.

The Royal Society Machine Learning working group was where I was first able to build an understanding of the wider policy landscape. I am indebted to staff at the Royal Society for convening such a breadth of expertise for that working group. From that period I got to know Claire Craig and Julie Maxton, who generously shared their understanding of how to navigate and communicate with government. Claire and Julie provided my policy foundation in the same way Adam and Oscar provided my writing foundation. Through that group, and later efforts giving advice during the Covid-19 pandemic, I've been lucky to work closely with Jessica Montgomery. Her leadership, friendship and support both ground and inspire the projects we lead together.

Many other friends and colleagues have also acted both knowingly and unknowingly as sounding boards for the ideas presented here. To the extent that these ideas have depth and polish it is due to their feedback and encouragement. From an encouragement perspective, I'm particularly grateful to Richard Rex, Sebastian

Nowozin, Lucy Cavendish and Rich Turner. They've each been generous with expectations about the final result. I hope it comes close to matching them. Inspiration has come from individual conversations with Sarah Haggarty, David Hogg and Hong Ge as well as ongoing conversations with Bernhard Schölkopf. Many ideas came from, or were tested during, conversations on bicycles. Thank you to Alistair Morfey, Rick Cotgreave, Peter Greenhalgh, Steve Marsden, Tony Ryan, Mike Hounslow and Jonathan Tenney for tolerating my ramblings. Francis O'Gorman, John Stringer, Mansur Boase, Andrei Paleyes and Lucia Reisch all kindly reviewed the manuscript for errors.

Kathy Weeks carefully guided me through the first steps of the contractual process, leading me to contact Robert Kirby. His advice and support led me to my wonderful agent Max Edwards. That brings me to the team at Allen Lane. Keith Mansfield has believed in me and the book from the start, his enthusiasm and excitement for the book were coupled with comprehensive editing that lifted the text and the narrative. Thanks also to Sarah Day for copyediting and Rebecca Lee for guiding the book into production and Hanni Sondermann for bringing some sanity to everything.

Joaquin Quiñonero Candela is in the unusual position of being a colleague whose ideas have influenced me and also a key person in the book. I thank him for his generosity in allowing his experiences to be shared, as well as his generosity as a friend and colleague.

Sylvie Delacroix is not only an academic inspiration to me, but she is a generous enough friend to have read very early drafts, provided encouraging feedback, friendly admonishment when I overreached and deep insight on the world that has broadened my perspectives and deeply enriched my thinking.

Matthew Syed has also been extremely generous with his time, thoughts and reading of the book across lunches and discussions around artificial intelligence, sport and the wider world of politics, policy and just life in general.

The final groups to thank are the two different kinds of family: first my academic family, my students and post-docs who are my closest collaborators. You are too numerous to name individually, but Carl Henrik Ek was also kind enough to provide feedback on early manuscripts as well as encouragement, not just for the book, but for life in general. Denis Thérien and Ciira wa Maina, thank you for your wisdom and leadership.

And then my direct family, Marta, Frederick and Paolo. Your patience, not just with the book, but with me, is the foundation on which all of this is laid. Thank you.

Index

NDL indicates Neil D. Lawrence.